WHO SHOULD WE TREAT?

Who Should We Treat?

Rights, Rationing, and Resources in the NHS

Second Edition

CHRISTOPHER NEWDICK
Reader in Health Law at the University of Reading

OXFORD
UNIVERSITY PRESS

OXFORD

UNIVERSITY PRESS

Great Clarendon Street, Oxford OX2 6DP

Oxford University Press is a department of the University of Oxford.
It furthers the University's objective of excellence in research, scholarship,
and education by publishing worldwide in

Oxford New York

Auckland Cape Town Dar es Salaam Hong Kong Karachi Kuala Lumpur
Madrid Melbourne Mexico City Nairobi New Delhi Taipei Toronto
Shanghai

With offices in

Argentina Austria Brazil Chile Czech Republic France Greece
Guatemala Hungary Italy Japan South Korea Poland Portugal
Singapore Switzerland Thailand Turkey Ukraine Vietnam

Oxford is a registered trade mark of Oxford University Press
in the UK and in certain other countries

Published in the United States
by Oxford University Press Inc., New York

British Library Cataloguing in Publication Data

Data available

Library of Congress Cataloging in Publication Data

Newdick Christopher.
Who should we treat? : rights, rationing, and resources in the NHS / Christopher
Newdick.—2nd ed.
p. cm.
Includes bibliographical references and index.
ISBN 0-19-926417-1 (hard cover : alk. paper) — ISBN 0-19-926418-X (pbk). : alk.
paper) 1. National health services—Great Britain. 2. National health insurance—
Law and legislation—Great Britain. 3. Medical care—Law and legislation—Great
Britain. 4. Medical care—Great Britain. I. Title.
KD3210.N49 2005
344.4102—dc22 2004021962

3 5 7 9 10 8 6 4 2

ISBN 0-19-926417-1 (cased)
ISBN 0-19-926418-X (Pbk)

Typeset by Newgen Imaging Systems (P) Ltd., Chennai, India
Printed in Great Britain
on acid-free paper by
Biddles Ltd., King's Lynn

Preface

Health care plays an increasingly important role in national debate. At a time when medical science can do more to cure our ills, ease our pains, and prolong our lives, we are more anxious about doctors, hospitals, and the NHS as a whole. This book poses a difficult question: who should we treat, and, by implication, who not? It considers the forces that shape our health care system and the rights and duties of patients, clinicians, NHS managers, and government. The most visible force is clinical, or "Hippocratic" led by doctors. Equally significant, however, is the economic element, dominated by the funds allocated to the NHS by the Treasury. There are also political pressures on the system, often driven by popular concerns and electoral anxieties. And, most recently, law and patient rights have come to prominence. Each plays a crucial role in deciding *who should we treat* in the NHS, none is complete by itself. We examine each context, analysing the clinical, economic, political, and legal landscape of the NHS to show where problems arise and how they may be tackled.

Since the first edition of this book in 1995, the landscape of the NHS has changed dramatically. Market forces and incentive schemes are now an accepted way of driving efficiency and devolving power to local agents. Both create the need for regulators and this, together with the conviction of Harold Shipman and the *Bristol Report* in 2001, has prompted rafts of new bodies to monitor and supervise the NHS. Patient and public involvement in health care is vastly more significant. And both UK and European courts have enhanced patients' rights of access to health care. The net result has been to raise the profile of the NHS and to elevate expectations that patients will receive proper treatment, as and when they need it. Yet hard choices remain. There are electoral restrictions on the extent to which government can increase investment in health care. The problem is not whether choices should be made, but how and by whom?

The question forces us to consider how to balance individual rights with public interests. Should one always prevail over the other, or only sometimes? Who should decide; government, doctors, local people, patients? Should some treatments be excluded altogether and, if so, on what basis? These are the questions we address in this book. Chapters 1, 2, and 3 consider the problems of resource allocation; how and why they arise and some of the solutions (often inconsistent) that have been proposed to deal with them. Chapters 4 and 5 deal with NHS responses to these tensions, as reflected in its structure and evolution. Chapters 6, 7, and 8 discusses patients' rights to NHS resources, negligence and the new "NHS governance". Lastly, Chapter 9 considers how non-NHS providers are being encouraged to contribute to the NHS enterprise, including providers abroad. How are they permitted to do so, do patients have rights to care abroad, and what if things go wrong there?

Given the breadth of the subject, many people have helped and advised during the writing of the book. I should start by acknowledging the unfailing assistance I have received on the telephone from innumerable members of the Department of Health. I thank also my colleagues in Reading University, Dr Chris Hilson, Professor Helen King, and Mrs Jane Mills; Mike Sobanja (NHS Alliance), Sarah Derrett (University of Keele), Peter Yuen and Jon Sussex (Office of Health Economics), Tim Jost (Washington and Lee University, USA), and my colleagues on the Thames Valley Priorities Committee, especially Claire Cheong-Leen, Linda Morris (Reading PCT), Don Sinclair (Slough PCT), and Dr Isabel Mower (GP). My deepest thanks go to Lyn Newdick for reading every word and making it more logical and digestible and to my son, Harry, for his patience and for putting the whole thing in proper perspective. The challenge of a book of this sort is to see both the woods of policy debate and the trees of patients' rights in the system. I hope to have put both in their contexts and to have explained the tensions and pressures that drive the NHS from time to time.

Christopher Newdick
2004

Contents

Table of Cases

UNITED STATES

Table of Legislation

List of Abbreviations

AHA	area health authority
All ER	All England Law Reports
APMS	alternative providers of medical services
BAP	British Paediatric Association
BMA	British Medical Association
CHAI	Commission for Healthcare Audit and Inspection
CHC	community health council
CRHCP	Council for the Regulation of Health Care Professionals
CSAG	Clinical Standards Advisory Group
CSM	Committee on the Safety of Medicines
DGM	district general manager
DHA	district health authority
DLR	Dominion Law Reports
DNR	'do not resuscitate' orders
DRGs	diagnosis related groups
ECR	extra contractual referral
FCE	finished consultant episode
FHSA	Family Health Service Authority
GMC	General Medical Council
GMS	general medical services
HRGs	health related groups
HSGs	Health Service Guidelines
ICER	incremental cost effectiveness ratio
LQR	Law Quarterly Review
Med LR	Medical Law Reports
NCAA	National Clinical Assessment Authority
NHS	National Health Service
NHSE	National Health Service Executive
NICE	National Institute for Clinical Excellence
NLJ	New Law Journal
NPSA	National Patient Safety Agency
OECD	Organization for Economic Co-operation and Development
OSCs	overview and scrutiny committee, of local authorities
PALS	Patient Advocacy Liaison Services
PCT	primary care trust
PCTMS	primary care trust medical services
PFI	private finance initiative
PMS	personal medical services
PTSD	post-traumatic stress disorder
QALY	quality adjusted life year

RHA	regional health authority
SARS	sudden acute respiratory syndrome
SHA	special health authority
StHA	strategic health authority
UGM	unit general manager

1

Introduction—Problems of Resource Allocation

Health care resource allocation troubles patients, the public, doctors, NHS managers, and government yet we have no stable principle on which to respond to it. Should it depend simply on the needs of each individual? If so, should there be an upper limit on the funds devoted to single patients? And if limits are inevitable, should they be the same for us all, or is the quality and quantity of life that remains a relevant factor? If hard choices have to be made, should we focus more on acute care to make people better, chronic care to make them more comfortable, or preventive care to stop people becoming sick in the first place. Do we need more clinicians, more medicines or hospitals? Should children have greater priority than adults? If hard choices are unavoidable, who should make them, clinicians, local NHS managers, the community, or government?

This chapter explains why these questions present such difficulty. We discuss (I) the economics of health care and the problem of supply and demand and (II) the meaning of "health" and the problem of defining rights to health care. To anticipate our conclusion, we observe that there is no simple solution to the question of how health care should be allocated fairly between patients; no formula against which these difficult issues can be measured. As a result, judgment, discretion, and differences of opinion are endemic to the area.

I. The Economics of Health Care

It is trite to say that demand for health care exceeds the supply of resources made available to the NHS. The Organization for Economic Co-operation and Development reports that "spending in health care is outpacing economic growth in most OECD countries, forcing governments to find new funds or pass a larger share of the costs onto individuals".[1] But why is this so?

A. The Supply of Health Care

Bare statistics suggest that the NHS has received much generosity from government. Since its creation, the NHS has received an increased level of funding almost every

---

[1] *Health at a Glance 2003* (OECD, 2003), 1.

year. Each of us invests considerable sums of money in the NHS. Even when allowing for inflation, as adjusted by the GDP deflator:

... the NHS in 2002 ... cost more than seven times as much as in 1949, and the average cost per person [rose] to nearly six times the 1949 per capita cost ... The rate of rise in NHS expenditure has increased significantly compared to the five years between 1991 and 1996. Outlay in the NHS rose from 3.5 per cent of GDP in 1949 to 6.4 per cent in 2001.[2]

This represents expenditure of £883 per person in England, £995 per person in Wales and £1,102 per person in Scotland. There were more than 111,000 whole time equivalent doctors working in the NHS in 2000, equivalent to 186 doctors for 100,000 population. This is three times as many doctors as in 1951, despite an increase in UK population of less than 20 per cent over that period.[3] For hospital services, in 1951, there were 29 medical and dental staff per 100,000 of population. Now there are 122 per 100,000. There are twice as many nurses and midwives. In addition, the Service has become increasingly efficient. Today, modern nursing practice and technology treat more patients, more effectively, more quickly, and at less cost per patient than ever before. It is true that the number of hospital beds per thousand population has dropped from eleven in the 1950s to four in 2000–01. But in 1951 there were 3.8 million "finished consultant episodes", or FCEs (the number of in-patient cases treated, as measured by the numbers of discharges and deaths). By 2000–01 that figure had risen to 14.3 millions in the UK. One of the main factors for the increase has been the reduction in average length of stay in hospital which has fallen from forty-five days in 1951 to five days today.[4]

A similar trend is found in the supply of GP services. In 1991, there were 34,498 GPs practising in the UK. That number has increased almost every year to 37,885 in 2002. Average list sizes have also fallen, though only slightly, from 1,892 in 1991 to 1,779 in 2000.[5] The UK medicines bill in 2002 (at manufacturers' prices) is estimated at £7.8 billion, representing 12.3 per cent of total NHS spending or £129 per head of population. On average an estimated 11.6 prescriptions were dispensed per person in 2000–01 compared to 8.6 in 1991–92.[6] There were about 268 million consultations in 2000, an increase of 37 per cent since 1975, each taking an average of 8.8 minutes.[7] Recent NHS policy has benefited primary care because GPs have a proportionately larger share of resources. The share of NHS resources given to hospital services fell from 70 per cent in 1972 to 50 per cent in 1999.[8]

With this additional investment and increased productivity, why is there so much concern with NHS funding? One factor is inflation. For a number of reasons, inflation in the NHS has exceeded that in the general economy. Consequently, the service has needed consistently larger contributions from the Treasury simply to stand still. Salaries and wages have contributed to this problem

---

[2] P. Yuen, *Compendium of Health Statistics* (Office of Health Economics, 2002), para. 2.17.
[3] ibid., para. 4.11.   [4] ibid., para. 3.3.   [5] ibid., Table 4.10(a).
[6] ibid., para. 4.1.   [7] ibid., para. 4.12.   [8] ibid., para. 3.1.

because they account for around 60 per cent of the costs of health authorities.[9] In particular, nurses' salaries account for a substantial proportion of that sum and they have, with unanimous applause, slowly improved their conditions of service by achieving wage settlements in excess of inflation. But these increases have not always been matched by additional funding from the Treasury. In addition, until now, the UK has spent less on its health care system than relatively affluent nations elsewhere. The sums spent on health care as a percentage of GDP are represented in Figure 1.1 which demonstrates the differing levels of spending on health in other countries, distinguishing government and private expenditure.

If the UK has spent less on health care, has this relative parsimony with respect to health spending resulted in a less healthy population of people? Direct comparisons are notoriously difficult. At one level, average life-expectancy across much of Western Europe is comparable, as is infant mortality and morbidity. Equally, these may be the result of investment in public health measures such as sewerage and health and safety at work which are beyond the responsibility of state health care systems. But in respect of specific disease conditions, there is some evidence that the UK performs less well. The OECD has found that cerebrovascular disease (stroke) has a significant impact (estimated to be between 2 and 4 per cent of total expenditure) on modern health care budgets. It reports that the UK and Hungary have the lowest number of neurologists (0.4 per 100,000 population) and relatively high fatality rates. Although in general the OECD finds only a loose connection between the level of investment in stroke and mortality rates, "the UK is the very prominent exception, having much higher fatality rates given the level of expenditure . . . Thus, in most cases increasing costs were associated with better health outcomes. The main exception . . . was again in the UK."[10] The UK also compared unfavourably in respect of survival rates for breast cancer, where mortality rates were higher than would have been expected.[11] These findings were confirmed by Derek Wanless's report for the Treasury which noted that if the NHS could achieve standards of treatment for cancer equivalent to the average in Europe, a further 10,000 lives per year could be saved.[12] Cancer generates particular fear and sympathy and the government has directed that diagnostic tests should be

---

[9] ibid., para. 2.18.

[10] *Summary of Stroke Disease Study* (OECD, 2002) paras 73–74. Ischaemic heart disease has also been identified as a cause for concern in the UK. It is the world's leading cause of mortality and comprises "about 10% of total health expenditure in OECD countries". However, in common with Spain and Denmark, the UK was reported to be performing significantly lower numbers of revascularisations of patients who have suffered acute myocardial infarction (the death of part of the heart muscle which has been deprived of an adequate supply of blood arising from coronary artery blockage). *Summary of Ischaemic Heart Disease Study* (OECD, 2002) para. 1.

[11] "It would seem . . . that, given the restrictions in terms of availability of qualified medical staff, screening and radiation treatment equipment, financial constraints in terms if treatment may have had an impact on outcomes." *Summary of Breast Cancer Disease Study* (OECD, 2002) para. 41.

[12] Derek Wanless, *Securing Our Future—Taking a Long-term View* (HM Treasury, 2001) para. 5.41.

4

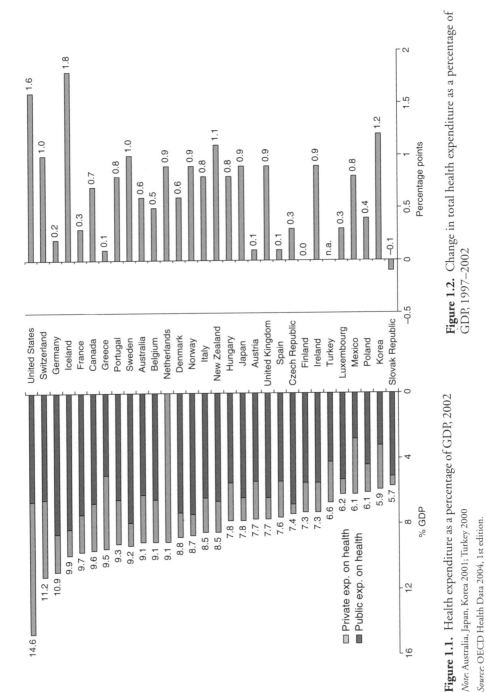

Figure 1.1. Health expenditure as a percentage of GDP, 2002

Note: Australia, Japan, Korea 2001; Turkey 2000

Source: OECD Health Data 2004, 1st edition.

Figure 1.2. Change in total health expenditure as a percentage of GDP, 1997–2002

performed within two weeks of referral and one would expect, therefore, that the OECD's statistics will soon be shown to be out-dated.[13]

Many of these differences are explicable in terms of the numbers of staff available to treat patients. In any event, the Wanless Report[14] helped to persuade the government of the need for much greater investment in the NHS. In his 2002 Budget the Chancellor announced further increases of NHS expenditure, representing an annual increase of 7.4 per cent per year in real terms between 2002–03 and 2007–08. Thus, NHS expenditure is planned to rise by 44 per cent by 2007–08 from £55.8 billion to over £90 billion,[15] by which time the NHS will account for 9.4 per cent of GDP, or almost £1,800 per person per year. In the meantime, the government has promised to utilise any spare clinical capacity that exists in the private sector, to send patients abroad for their treatment, or import clinical teams from abroad to ease long waiting lists at home.[16] One would expect that the differences in respect of specific treatments will begin to decline.

B. Demand for Care

Will additional health care resources ever catch up with the demands made of the NHS? We may once have believed that improved health care would increase levels of health in society and reduce demand for health care. Consider our ideas of "illness" and "health" in 1948 when the health service was created. There were six times as many infant deaths as today, many fewer lived into retirement, and average life expectancy was about 66, whereas it is now over 78.[17] With good reason, we had more limited expectations of medicine. At the same time, pharmaceuticals underwent rapid development. The treatment of sexual disease became possible with the discovery of sulphonamides during the 1930s. And in the 1940s, penicillin was put to astonishingly effective use during the Second World War. Supported by the creation of a national health service, this may have generated huge confidence in medicine, largely based on our successes with opportunistic infections and acute illnesses.[18] Government soon understood, however, that such optimism in the power of medicine was misplaced. As the first committee of enquiry into health service costs observed in 1956:

The growth of medical knowledge adds continually to the number and expense of treatments and, by prolonging life, also increases the incidence of slow-killing diseases. No-one can

---

[13] The National Audit Office has found that despite increased incidence of cancer, mortality rates have fallen: *Tackling Cancer in England—Saving More Lives* (HC 364, Session 2003–04).

[14] *Our Future—Taking a Long-term View* (HM Treasury, 2002) para. 5.46.

[15] *Expenditure Plans 2002–03 to 2003–04* (Cm. 5403, Department of Health, 2002) 31.

[16] As we discuss in Ch. 9. As one Secretary of State said, in commenting on these developments, "these reforms are about redefining what we mean by the National Health Service." Mr Alan Milburn, *Empowering front-line staff*, speech to British Association of Medical Managers Conference, 12 June 2002, www.doh.gov.uk/speeches/june 2002.   [17] P. Yuen, note 2 above, ch. 1.

[18] Our faith in medicine and the medical profession is severely criticised in I. Illich, *Limits to Medicine* (Pelican, reprinted 1988).

predict whether the speeding of therapy and the improvement of health will ultimately offset this expense; there is at present no evidence that it will; indeed, current trends seem to be all the other way . . . there is no reason at present to suppose that demands on the service as a whole will be reduced thereby so as to stabilise (still less reduce) its total cost in terms of finance and the absorption of real resources.[19]

These observations are confirmed by developments in the pharmaceutical industry which, despite some catastrophic set-backs (most infamous of which was the protracted dispute surrounding the drug Thalidomide), has provided an increasing range of medicines capable of saving patients from expensive and dangerous surgery, or enabling them to lead more active, productive, or peaceful lives. Also, medicine no longer focuses on opportunistic and acute illness. It routinely deals with chronic conditions such as the diseases of the cardio-vascular system, the respiratory system, the gastrointestinal system, and the central nervous system. Between 1972 and 1996, there was a marked increase in the numbers of patients reporting such chronic ill health (especially children).[20] Treatments for these conditions are long-term and last many years. These are the diseases of affluence and old-age which will put increasing pressure on resources.[21]

We are also developing our understanding of genetics in a way that may revolutionise our ideas about sickness and health.[22] Today, the Human Genome Project presents the possibility of developing treatment to attack the *genetic* causes of chronic illness. Cystic fibrosis, for example, is already being treated in this way.[23] And the pace of pharmaceutical development is likely to increase many times over.[24] Such techniques offer the potential for savings on conventional treatment of conditions such as heart and liver disease, diabetes, and cancer, but they are likely to be long-term, hugely expensive and their cost will threaten the availability of other treatments. They raise fundamental questions about the meaning of the words, "health" and "illness". As curative treatments become available for conditions which some explain in societal, or personal terms, rather than as illnesses, we will ask how best to respond to, for example, obesity, alcoholism, cigarette smoking, hyper-activity, and drug addiction. Should they qualify for care in the same way as other conditions?

As our notion of illness expands, so will our calls upon the health service. One Secretary of State remarked: "Every advance in medical science creates new needs that

---

[19] *Report of the Committee of Enquiry into the Costs of the National Health Service* (Cmnd. 9663, 1956) para. 95.

[20] *Living in Britain: Results from the 1996 General Household Survey* (Office for National Statistics, 1998) discussed by J. Sussex and P. Yuen, "McKeown Updated" in J. Sussex (ed.) *Improving Population Health in Industrialised Nations* (Office of Health Economics, 2000).

[21] See R. Porter, *Blood and Guts—A Short History of Medicine* (Penguin, Allen Lane, 2002) chs 1 and 5.

[22] J. Leneghan, *Brave New NHS?—The Impact of the New Genetics on the Health Service* (Institute for Public Policy Research, 1998).

[23] See *Report of the Committee on the Ethics of Gene Therapy* (Cm. 1788, 1992).

[24] G. Lister, "Linking the UK and International Contexts" in K. Barnard (ed.) *The Future of Health—Health of the Future* (Nuffield Trust, 2003) 158.

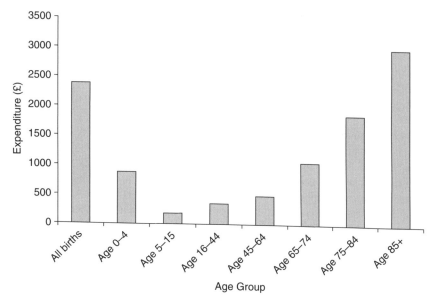

Figure 1.3. Hospital and Community Health Services: gross current expenditure per head of population, 2001–02

Source: Department of Health Annual Report 2004, p88.

did not exist until the means of getting them came into existence."[25] Indeed, precisely when we have greater medical benefit available, when we live longer and healthier lives than ever before, we are most anxious about our health. Today, medicine enables increasing numbers of us to survive well into retirement. But it also seems to provoke greater unease about morbidity and mortality, and greater need for medicine.

It is endemic to a system in which an expanding medical establishment faced with a healthier population, is driven to medicalizing normal events like menopause, converting risks into diseases, and treating trivial complaints with fancy procedures. Doctors and "consumers" are becoming locked within a fantasy that everyone has something wrong with them, everyone and everything can be cured.[26]

Medicine's success in preserving life enables the proportion of the population depend-ent on the service to expand relative to those whose taxable income supports it (a phe-nomenon common throughout the western world). Unsurprisingly, many of us need more frequent access to medical care towards the end of our lives. "In the next 30 years the UK will see a large rise in the dependency ratio (i.e. children under 15 and older people over 65 per 100 of working age) from the current level of 52 to 63 by

---

[25] Enoch Powell, *A New Look at Medicine* (Pitman Medical Publishing, 1966) 26.
[26] R. Porter, *The Greatest Benefit to Mankind—A Medical History of Humanity from Antiquity to the Present* (Fontana Press, 1997) 718.

2003."[27] The numbers of us aged 65 and over grew by nearly 4 million between 1950 and 2000, from 10.7 per cent of the population to 15.6 per cent. And those of us aged 85 and over are projected to grow from 1.2 million to nearly 2 million by 2031, rising from 1.9 per cent of the population to 3.5 per cent, see Figure 1.3.[28]

Before youthful brows furrow at the cost of treating increasing numbers of elderly citizens, note that age alone is not the cause of this additional expenditure. Each of us is likely to need more medical care at the end of our lives *whatever our age*. Of course most of us live into old age but the crucial consideration is not age, but the intensity of care we receive in the period before dying. In a large sample of patients who died in hospital, there was no increase in median days spent in a hospital bed, or of admissions, after the age of 45.[29] Thus, it seems, "the costs of acute health care in the last year of life do not increase sharply with age [indeed] it appears that the older a patient is, the lower their acute health costs in the period immediately before death".[30]

This strongly suggests that supply and demand in health care will never reach equilibrium; on the contrary, demand will continue to exceed supply and the debate as to rights to health care entitlements will become more intense.

II. Defining Health Care Rights

If we accept that an *unrestricted* guarantee of access to health care is impossible, what more limited rights to health care should we recognise? We need to understand what we mean by a *right* to health care. Yet both "health" and the notion of "rights" to health are difficult concepts.

A. "Health" and "Health care"

What is "health"? The word may be described in different ways as a scientific, or sociological phenomenon. Doctors are trained to focus on medical, or *biological* characteristics, on the presence or absence of observable disease. Examination will focus on matters of physiology, anatomy, and biochemistry and so detect deviations from *normal* physical and chemical functioning, perceptions of which will evolve over time. Western medicine since Hippocrates and Galen has put less emphasis on mystical and magical explanations of illness. Instead, reason and observation have played the dominant role. For many centuries, doctors sought to balance bodily "humours"— a theory which justified bleeding patients of their "excess" blood.[31] Today's medicine,

---

[27] P. Yuen, *Compendium of Health Statistics* (14th edn, Office of Health Economics, 2002) para. 1.1.   [28] *Department of Health Annual Report* (Department of Health, 2004) Fig. 6.3.
[29] T. Dixon, M. Shaw, S. Frankel *et al.*, "Hospital Admissions, age and death: retrospective cohort study" (2004) *British Medical Journal* doi:10.1136/bmj.38072.481933.EE.
[30] *Securing our Future Health: Taking a Long-Term View—Interim Report* (HM Treasury, 2001) para. 9.17.
[31] R. Porter, note 26 above, at ch. 3. The "humours" were bile, black bile, phlegm and blood.

assisted by the microscope, X-rays, anaesthetics, and the study of anatomy requires a new "biology".[32] Our major concerns are with biological mechanics, viruses, germs, and the auto-immune system. Tomorrow, perhaps the science of genetics (or nano-robotics) will become more dominant models of analysis.

Although this scientific conception tends to dominate our Western understanding of health, it is not the only measure because there are other dimensions to the notion of health which may be described as social, or cultural.[33] Health may be considered in broader, *functional* terms, as departures from "normal" social functioning which will depend on the nature of our perceptions. On this view, "what is considered normal health and what constitutes sickness or impairment are negotiable and the conventions vary from community to community".[34] Social and sexual stereotypes play a part. Nymphomania,[35] homosexuality,[36] and masturbation[37] are no longer widely perceived as illnesses. Society's attitude toward the responsibility of the individual is important. Take obesity, depression, and drug addiction. Are they the product of weak individuals who need to buck-up their ideas, or a symptom of illness which merits medical treatment? So too with hyperactivity, attention deficit, dyspraxia, and myalgic encephalomelitis (ME). Whether we consider these to be illnesses is not based solely on biological considerations, but social attitudes too. Until the twentieth century, hysteria was a condition largely confined to female patients. But could it also describe the "shell-shock" suffered by soldiers fighting on the front during the First World War?[38] More recently, perhaps, sympathising with those who suffer psychiatric damage from catastrophic events, we would describe similar symptoms as post-traumatic stress disorder (PTSD). And illnesses may be discarded and apparently re-emerge some time in the future. "English sweat" was recognised in the sixteenth century as a fatal illness but cases apparently dwindled and the illness disappeared from the books.[39] Today, sudden acute respiratory syndrome (SARS) seems to possess many of the symptoms described in English sweat.

A similar problem of definition arises in connection with *predispositions* to illness. What if I am entirely strong and healthy, but my family have a history of breast cancer. Should I be regarded as ill? Should the *risk* that I might become ill be sufficient to merit treatment? The question becomes more pressing as we develop ways of identifying genetic predisposition to diseases. Perhaps some such patients might be considered to be ill if the consequence of the disease, *if it occurs* would be

---

[32] See K. Wailoo, *Drawing Blood—Technology and Disease Identity in Twentieth-Century America* (John Hopkins University Press, 1999).

[33] See D. Mechanic, *Medical Sociology* (2nd edn, Free Press, 1978) ch. 1; and A. Radley, *Making Sense of Illness—the Social Psychology of Health and Disease* (Sage, 1995).

[34] R. Porter, note 26 above, at 36.

[35] C. Groneman, *Nymphomania—a history* (Fusion Press, London, 2001).

[36] B. Hansen, "American Physicians' 'Discovery' of Homosexuals, 1880–1990: A New Diagnosis in a Changing Society" in C. Rosenberg and J. Golden (eds) *Framing Disease—Studies in Cultural History* (Rutegers University Press, 1997).

[37] T. Szasz, *The Manufacture of Madness* (Paladin Books, 1977) ch. 11.

[38] I. Palmer, "War-based hysteria—the Military Perspective", in P. Halligan, C. Bass and J. Marshall (eds) *Contemporary Approaches to the Study of Hysteria—clinical and theoretical perspectives* (Oxford University Press, 2001). [39] R. Porter, note 26 above, at 168.

catastrophic, or if the disease, *if it occurs* would be very difficult to treat. On the other hand, if the disease in question is not catastrophic and is amenable to treatment, a different response might be appropriate. Thus (assuming effective treatment is available), a risk of cancer might be treated more sympathetically than a risk of appendicitis (or arthritis?).[40] Bear in mind that, in health systems which operate within finite resources (whether from taxation or health insurance), spending on those who do not manifest the signs and symptoms of illness inevitably diverts resources from those in undoubted need of care.

These problems of meaning might be eased if we could develop a clear definition of the word health. Unfortunately, there is no objective, or certain measure of the word on which to develop rights of entitlement. The World Health Organization has described health as "a state of complete physical, mental and social well-being and not merely the absence of disease or infirmity". By contrast, a Dutch committee has defined it as "the ability to function normally."[41] Clearly, these different definitions create very different expectations. As medical and pharmaceutical technologies advance, we will discover ways of treating many of the afflictions previously considered normal in ageing bodies. We already replace failing joints and permit otherwise strong and healthy people to regain mobility. We will probably develop ways of restoring failing sight, hearing, physical and mental agility. Indeed, the very process of "ageing" may come to be considered to be an "illness" for which treatment is available to prolong life for a further ten, or more years. In the absence of a clear idea of the meaning of words like "health" and "illness", it will always be difficult to draw lines around the treatment patients may legitimately expect within a health care system.

We should also understand that a right to *health* is not the same is a right to *health care*.[42] A broad conception of health will include claims to care which go beyond the responsibility of doctors and a health service. Many of the conditions which affect our health and well-being are based on our personal, economic circumstances and, particularly with disadvantaged communities, the extent to which governments support other public services, such as education, housing, welfare support, and a decent environment. These factors have a significantly greater impact on levels of public health than could ever be achieved by Departments of Health alone.[43] Many of the most significant improvements in public health have come about, not by

---

[40] The issue was considered in *Katskee v Blue Cross/Blue Shield* 515 NW 2d 645 (Nebraska Supreme Court, 1994) in relation to a family history of breast and ovarian cancer. Although the patient presented no physical evidence of the disease, her surgeons recommended hysterectomy and mastectomy. The court held that in these particular circumstances, the patient had a "disease" and was entitled to treatment under her policy of health insurance.

[41] See *Choices in Health Care* (Government Committee on Choices in Health Care, 1992) 49.

[42] But see K. Hessler and A. Buchanan, "Specifying the Content of the Human Right to Health Care" in R. Rhodes, M. Battin and A. Silvers (eds) *Medicine and Social Justice—Essays on the Distribution of Health Care* (Oxford University Press, New York, 2002) ch. 7.

[43] "The best estimates are that health services affect about 10% of the usual indeces for measuring health . . . the remaining 90% are determined by factors over which doctors have little or no control: individual life-style, social conditions and physical environment." D. Hunter, *Desperately Seeking Solutions—Rationing Health Care* (Longman, 1997) 18.

virtue of doctors or the NHS, but from advances in standards of public hygiene, the environment, and an affordable diet.[44] For example:

> The combined death rate from scarlet fever, diptheria, whooping cough and measles among children up to fifteen shows that nearly 90% of the total decline in mortality between 1860 and 1965 had occurred before the introduction of antibiotics and immunization . . . by far the most important factor was a higher host-resistance and better nutrition.[45]

But this is the stuff of politics; the level of investment we are prepared to divert into under-privileged sections of society, education, rates of income tax, and macro-economic policy. It is not the primary concern of the medical profession. In a democracy, it would be strange to give doctors a disproportionate influence in determining matters of this nature. They are the responsibility of politicians and the electorate.[46] Thus, "it is important to keep clear and distinct the roles of different professions with a clearly circumscribed role for medicine limited to those domains of life where the contribution of medicine is appropriate. Medicine can save lives; it cannot save society."[47] The debate about the responsibility of a national health service should be sensitive to the distinction between rights to *health care* which are the responsibility of government and doctors; and the general health and *well-being of the community* which is dependant on much broader, political concerns.

B. Rights to Health Care—Absolute, or Relative?

Having distinguished *health* from *health care*, should there be a right to health care capable of being enforced by patients? A right to something usually imposes a duty on someone else. Without the corresponding duty, the right has no substance.[48] When health is provided under a private contract, rights and duties arise between two parties, say under a contract of health insurance. The rights are express (though often unspecific) and enforceable. However, in a *public* health system supported by taxation, the right is more diffuse. Rights may be claimed against the public authority responsible for providing care, but the duty in this case is not owed solely to an individual patient. It is owed to a population of people. Duties

---

[44] T. McKeown, *The Modern Rise of Population and the Role of Medicine: Dream, Mirage, or Nemesis?* (Nuffield Provincial Hospital Trust, 1976).

[45] I. Illich, *Limits to Medicine* (Pelican, reprinted 1988) 24. The attribution of cause and effect in this area is notoriously difficult. See J. Mohan, *A National Health Service* (MacMillan, 1995) 22. However, as infectious diseases have come under control, the impact of medicine on contemporary standards of health is probably more significant. See J. Mackenbach, "How Important have Medical Advances Been?" in J. Sussex (ed) *Improving Population Health in Industrialised Nations* (Office of Health Economics, 2000).

[46] Indeed, many would distrust doctors in such a role. See, e.g., T. Szasz, note 37 above, for a persuasive, if slightly over-stated case, in relation to mental illness.

[47] D. Callahan, "The WHO Definition of Health" in T. Beauchamp and L. Walters (eds) *Contemporary Issues in Bioethics* (Wadsworth, 1982) 80.

[48] J. Leneghan (ed) *Hard Choices in Health Care* (British Medical Journal Publishing Group, 1997) ch. 1.

arising within such a system are not contained in a contract, but in a statute committed to the public interest and expressed in general and imprecise terms. Obviously, resources allocated to some patients will reduce the sum available for others. In such a public health system, what is the meaning of a "right" to health care? This requires a distinction between *absolute* rights, which exist irrespective of the rights and needs of other patients, and *relative* rights which are dependent on considering and balancing the rights of the community as a whole. Patients' rights of access to treatment within public health care systems are normally relative in the sense that they have to be assessed in the light of the rights of others. This makes claims by individuals more difficult to sustain.[49]

In the domain of *relative* rights, we quickly encounter the perennial debates familiar to politics. For example, should the NHS promote *equality* between NHS patients in the sense of providing equal access to equal standards of care, or *liberty* of choice as to where and when patients will be treated? Clearly, the ideas of equality and liberty are both laudable, but they are not always compatible. Equality can be understood in a number of ways. It might refer simply to equal distribution of resources to local health authorities throughout the NHS, i.e. equality of inputs. This might entail giving each region equal sums of money on a *per capita* basis. Alternatively, equality might include some mechanism for increasing the allocations to regions with additional health needs as reflected by local morbidity and mortality. Of course, much difficulty arises in devising a formula which accurately reflects these characteristics, never the less, the reference point is equality of investment according to the health needs of the community. Yet another criterion by which to assess equality is to compare the *outputs* of the investment. In other words, assuming the local health care system is operating effectively, regions which have poorer levels of health ought to be entitled to larger sums of investment in order to promote broadly equal standards of morbidity and mortality between local communities. Although, as we have seen, Scotland receives a larger *per capita* investment in health care than England, arguably it receives an insufficient allocation by reference to health outputs as reflected by the poor levels of health suffered by many of its citizens. Obviously, this argument is complicated because (as we have noted) many aspects of community health are the product of poor education, long-term unemployment, or poverty which are not the responsibility of the Department of Health. If equality of health *output* is a central concern of government, the NHS is entitled to considerably more support from central funds.

Alongside equality, however, successive governments have put special emphasis on the *freedom* of patients to choose in the NHS.[50] The idea of "fund-holding" practices introduced by the Conservatives in 1990 was to increase the freedom of GPs to use their own funds to respond to the needs and wishes of their patients. This

---

[49] But not impossible, as we discuss in Ch. 5 below.

[50] See, e.g., *The Expert Patient* (Department of Health, 1999); and *Shifting the Balance of Power— Securing Delivery* (Department of Health, 2001).

carried the advantage of enabling fund-holders' patients to get accelerated access to hospital care. It was abandoned by Labour, however, on the ground that it created a two-tier NHS which was divisive for putting the patients of non-fund-holders at an unfair disadvantage.[51] Yet, Labour has introduced new rights of patients to choose alternative hospitals with shorter waiting times, or to go abroad for treatment. It has also established "foundation hospitals" with additional freedom to manage their own resources, including the right to sell land and to engage staff on preferential salary scales. Their purpose is to forge new ways of improving services and to act as examples of good practice in the NHS. They too will seek to attract both staff and patients by providing enhanced services. These policies emphasise freedom, rather than equality and may be subject to criticisms similar to those leveled at fund-holding practices. What is the proper balance between the two?

The notion of *relative* rights to health care further compounds the problem of defining access to health care.

C. A Defined Package of Health Care?

As the Royal Commission on the National Health Service said in 1979: "demand for health care is always likely to outstrip supply . . . the capacity of health services to absorb resources is almost unlimited. Choices have therefore to be made about the use of available funds and priorities have to be set. The more pressure there is on resources, the more important it is to get the priorities clear."[52] What steps could be taken to make NHS priorities clearer? Would it be feasible to develop a fixed list of treatments which would generally be available within the health service?[53]

Clearly, such a proposal requires a mechanism for identifying health care priorities, but here again, we encounter the difficulty of definition. On what principle could such priorities be based? Some start with the proposition that priority should be given to those in most *need*, but what does this mean? Government may be concerned with the adverse political impact of waiting lists and wish maximum effort to be devoted to getting numbers down. By contrast, a health authority responsible for large numbers of elderly patients might wish to concentrate on the treatment of arthritis, or providing hip replacements. But a parent whose baby needs an urgent operation to repair a hole in the heart will say that there can be no greater need than to save a child's life. For the moment at least, we are very far from having any consistent principles on which "need" can be assessed. Discussions within the Department of Health have observed

---

[51] See C. Newdick, *Who Should we Treat?* (Oxford University Press, 1995) 48–59.

[52] *Royal Commission on the National Health Service* (Cmnd. 7615, 1979) para. 6.1. See also A. Maynard and K. Bloor, *Our Certain Fate: Rationing in Health Care* (Office of Health Economics, 1998).

[53] L. Doyal, "Rationing within the NHS should be Explicit—the Case For" (1997) 314 *British Medical Journal* 1114.

that: "Despite the frequent use of the term 'needs' there is little agreement even on what is meant by the term. Furthermore, there is very little work which explicitly assesses population needs in a way that is useful to health service managers, purchasers and planners."[54]

"Need" is particularly pertinent with respect to the assessment of highly sophisticated, hugely expensive, medical equipment, capable of achieving the most dramatic results for a relatively small number of patients. When there is a choice between achieving huge improvements in the conditions of those in very poor health (say cancer, or transplant patients), or more modest preventive measures designed to encourage the preservation of good health amongst larger numbers of people (say a general policy to reduce blood-cholesterol level) how ought choices to be made? The question is complicated by the need of hospitals, particularly special-ist hospitals, to be conscious of their public image in order to be attractive to doc-tors and patients. As US commentators have said, "we are doing more and more for fewer and fewer people, at higher and higher cost, for less and less benefit . . . it is a fact that we have yet to develop an effective method to assess technology and have no methods for determining whether or not new or existing technologies are useful and appropriate for inclusion in any reasonable health insurance scheme".[55] This points to the danger of misdirecting scarce resources and suggests we should be clearer as to the manner in which health care should be allocated.

Although serious attempts have been made to devise a framework within which specific entitlements could be identified,[56] the exercise is fraught with danger. If the object is certainty of expectation, there is a danger that any such list will be so tightly framed that it overrides clinical freedom and excludes many deserving cases. Alternatively, if the decision is left to individual clinicians to judge on the merits of each case, it will be so vague and imprecise as to be meaningless. As Klein observes, in practice, the issue has been approached the other way round. Rather than defining what will be included with the NHS, health authorities have excluded, for example, tattoo removal, varicose veins, and buttock lifts. But this has little impact on the financial problems facing health authorities, it is no more than "nibbling at the edges".[57] In addition, if these exclusions amount to "blanket bans" they are unlikely to satisfy the law of judicial review for being irrational; they exclude the possibility of exceptional cases being considered for treatment.[58] Thus, even a finite list would in law be required to be flexible to this extent. In any event, the difficulty in controlling costs is not the relatively infrequent intervention with a new and expensive procedure.

---

[54] *Assessing Health Care Needs—A DHA project discussion paper* (NHSME, 1991) 3. See also A. Stevens and J. Gabbay, "Needs Assessment needs assessment" (1991) 23 *Health Trends* 20.

[55] G. Annas, S. Law, R. Rosenblatt and K. Wing, *American Health Law* (Little Brown & Co, 1990) 293.

[56] B. New and J. Le Grand, *Rationing in the NHS: Principles and Pragmatism* (King's Fund, 1996).

[57] R. Klein, "Defining a Package of Health Care Services the NHS is Responsible for—the Case Against" (1997) 314 *British Medical Journal* 505.   [58] As we discuss in Ch. 5.

The real issue is not whether to perform appendectomy; it is whether to fund countless marginal interventions that are potentially part of the procedure—marginal blood tests and repeat tests; precautionary preventive antibiotic therapy before surgery; the number of nurses in the operating room; and the backup support on call in the hospital. Even more decisions about marginal elements will arise during the recovery phase; exactly how many days of hospital stay are permitted, how often the physician should make rounds, how many follow up tests there should be, and so on. Many of these are predicted to offer more benefits than harm, but with margins so small that one could argue that resources should be used elsewhere.[59]

A fixed, finite list of NHS treatments is doomed to fail both in practice and under judicial review. Does that mean there is no clearer way of describing the resource allocation process and that each decision will be left to the discretion of the individual doctor, or health authority who happens to be responsible for the patient from time to time? This too is unacceptable. If the process of resource allocation is inevitable, it should treat patients equally, fairly and within a consistent framework of principles. By themselves, ethical principles do not indicate which patients should receive priority. However, they provide a broad basis on which difficult decisions should be taken. In Chapter 5 we discuss the use of such frameworks by health authorities. They will become an indispensible component of decision-making in this area. Over time, their work could generate a common stock of experience within which hard decisions could be explained and defended on the basis of a fair and consistent response. This permits reasonable variations between health authorities and provides a framework within which such decisions should be made openly and consistently.

III. Conclusion

We are often in two minds about the costs of health service expenditure. As has been said: "we have one mind when we are well sitting in our living rooms, paying taxes, or writing out a cheque for health insurance. We have another mind when we have a health problem and are sitting in a physician's office."[60] There are problems of economics and entitlements in the way of describing rights to health care. But there is also people's reluctance to commit disproportionate sums to health care rather than (say) our housing needs, our food, or a university education. We should not assume, therefore, that rationing is always bad. Taxes devoted to paying for the NHS are comparable to a "premium" for health insurance. If we had a

[59] R. Veatch, "The Oregon Experiment: Needless and Real Worries", in M. Strosberg, J. Weiner *et al.* (eds) *Rationing America's Medical Care: The Oregon Plan and Beyond* (Brookings Institution, 1992), cited in R. Klein, note 57 (above).

[60] D. Eddy, "Connecting Value and Costs: Whom Do We Ask, and What Do We Ask Them?" (1990) 264 *Journal of the American Medical Association* 1737.

choice, we might exclude some care within such a policy so as to reduce the premium and put the savings to other uses. We might decline cardio-pulmonary resuscitation after we have reached a certain age, or forego the best possible, but most expensive, treatment if the "second best" is substantially less expensive but only marginally less effective. Some might prefer to balance the additional costs of the premium for such care with the alternative benefits the same money would purchase. Inescapably, whether the question is determined by us individuals, or for us by government, the issue of how health care resources should be allocated involves judgment. In the next chapter we discuss ways in which that judgment should be exercised.

2

Principles of Resource Allocation

Chapter 1 dealt with some of the conceptual and practical problems concerning health care resource allocation. Here, we consider a number of ideas and principles under which those matters might be managed and resolved. We consider the role of (I) clinical freedom and the Hippocratic Oath, (II) health economics and the theory of quality adjusted life years (QALYs), (III) government, and (IV) democracy in resource allocation. In the next chapter, we consider how the NHS in particular has responded to these challenges since its creation in 1946.

I. Clinical Freedom and the Hippocratic Oath

One of the most pressing problems in medical ethics concerns the current status and value of the Hippocratic Oath and the many international codes which have followed it. Under the Oath doctors promise that: "I will follow that system of regimen which, according to my ability and judgment, I consider for the benefit of my patients . . . Into whatever house I enter, I will go into them for the benefit of the sick." The modern statement of the principle is contained in the Declaration of Geneva, published by the World Health Organization. It says, *inter alia*, that the "health of my patient will be my first consideration". Similarly, the International Code of Medical Ethics provides that "a physician shall act only in the patient's best interests when providing medical care which might have the effect of weakening the physical and mental condition of the patient".[1] This principle has been at the heart of the NHS since its inception and one of its founding principles was to preserve the doctor's clinical freedom from outside interference.[2]

The nature of this commitment has been described (rather grandly) as follows:

In the course of treatment, the physician is obligated to the patient and no one else. He is not the agent of society, nor of the interests of medical science, nor of the patient's family, nor of his co-sufferers or future sufferers from the same disease. The patient alone counts when he is under the physician's care. By the simple law of bilateral contract . . . the physician is

---

[1] See these and other declarations in the appendices to *Medical Ethics Today* (British Medical Association, 1993). Note, however, that even Hippocrates himself seems to have refused to save Persians since they were enemies of the Greeks! See H. King, "The Power of Paternity: the Father of Medicine meets the Prince of Physicians" in D. Cantor (ed.) *Reinventing Hippocrates* (Ashgate, 2001).
[2] *A National Health Service* (Cmd. 6502, 1944) 47.

bound to not let any other interest interfere with that of the patient in being cured. But manifestly more sublime norms than contractual ones are involved. We may speak of a sacred trust; strictly by its terms, the doctor is, as it were, alone with his patient and God.[3]

This noble principle says, in effect, that the only constraint to patient care is the doctor's reasonable clinical opinion. But is it sustainable? Professional associations are unhelpfully ambiguous about tension between Hippocratic and economic principles. The General Medical Council says doctors should "make the care of your patient your first concern" but at the same time "make efficient use of the resources available to you".[4] Similarly, the American Medical Association considers that "while [the] responsibility to guard society's resources is an important one, physicians must remain primarily dedicated to the health care needs of their individual patients."[5] Neither, it seems, has resolved the difficulty between clinical ideals on the one hand and finite resources on the other.

In practice, doctors understand that they are responsible for groups of patients. The use of a bed, or operating theatre for one patient may delay, or deny treatment to someone else, and even an extended consultation with a GP may cause others to wait longer in the waiting room. For this reason elderly people have found it more difficult to be referred for surgery,[6] infertility treatment is restricted, those suffering mental illness have not always obtained care in hospital, and kidney dialysis has been available to relatively few. In reality, therefore, the idea of *absolute* clinical freedom may long have been an unaffordable myth[7] and there has been growing interest in encouraging doctors to justify their clinical actions from documented experience, or persuasive literature. Some would go further by saying that clinical freedom has been used as a cloak to hide doctors from justifying rationing decisions.

Rationing in the NHS has never been explicitly organised but has hidden behind each doctor's clinical freedom to act solely in the interests of his individual patient. Any conflict of interest between patients competing for scarce resources has been implicitly resolved by doctors judgments as to their relative needs for care and attention. The clinical freedom to differ widely as to their conception of need has led to inconsistencies of treatment between patients and to the allocation, without challenge, of scarce resources to medical practices

---

[3] Hans Jonas, "Philosophical Reflections on Experimenting with Human Subjects", in T. Beauchamp and L. Walters (eds) *Contemporary Issues in Bioethics* (Wadsworth Publishing Co, California 1978) 417. Quoted in T. Brennan, *Just Doctoring* (California University Press, 1991), 35. See also C. Newdick, "Public Health Ethics and Clinical Freedom" (1998) 14 *Journal of Contemporary Health Law and Policy* 355.

[4] *Good Medical Practice* (General Medical Council, 2001), para. 3. Previously, it said "a doctor should always seek to give priority to the investigation and treatment of patients solely on the basis of clinical need." *Contractual Arrangements in Health Care: Professional Responsibilities in Relation to Clinical Needs* (General Medical Council, 1992) para. 8

[5] Council on Ethical and Judicial Affairs, American Medical Association, "Ethical Issues in Managed Care" (1995) 273 *Journal of the American Medical Association* 330, 332.

[6] See the steep age-related decline in access to cancer care documented in *Tackling Cancer in England—Saving More Lives* (The National Audit Office, HC 364, Session 2003–04). See also *The Health of the U.K.'s Elderly People* (Medical Research Council, 1994).

[7] See J. Hampton, "The End of Clinical Freedom" (1983) 287 *British Medical Journal* 1237.

of no proven value. It is by no means clear that it is the patient who gains from clinical freedom.[8]

There are, however, pressures being exerted upon clinical freedom by (A) evidence-based medicine and (B) the notion of "waste" of NHS resources. We consider each in turn.

A. Evidence-based Medicine

In the past, when there was less clinical evidence of the treatments that worked (and those that did not), doctors were necessarily obliged to make decisions largely on the basis of clinical instinct. Here, clinical responses are driven by personal experience, rather than adherence to accepted standards of practice, and clinical freedom will generate wide variations of practice from one doctor to another. Today, however, large quantities of clinical research are available to guide doctors on many aspects of medical practice. Accordingly, medicine has moved away from a model of the Hippocratic Oath based largely on personal clinical "instinct" and now requires doctors to adjust their practice according to reliable clinical evidence. On the other hand, clinical guidelines have not put a strait-jacket around clinical freedom. Medical science is always developing. There will be areas in which the evidence is ambiguous, incomplete, or inconsistent and there will often be scope for differences of opinion in matters of diagnosis, prognosis, or clinical management. Doctors may also have been taught differently. Their own personal experience may be that some things work better than others; and, of course, a doctor who provides treatment that goes badly wrong will be less willing to resort to it in future.[9] This is part of the way in which medical science evolves.

Increasingly, however, government has become unsympathetic to the professional latitude enjoyed by doctors and is less likely to accept without question the fact of medical practice variations. It says:

There are unacceptable variations in performance and practice. The inequalities go beyond the provision of medicines and other treatments. There are inequalities in the way that some proven treatments get introduced to the NHS too slowly while other unproven treatment can be introduced too quickly. There are inequalities in waiting times for operations . . . There are inequalities in clinical practice—and in clinical outcomes . . . Such widely differing performance saps the confidence of the public in the very idea of a *National* Health Service.[10]

---

[8] M. Cooper, *Rationing Health Care* (Croom Helm, 1975) 59.

[9] T. Folmer Anderson and G. Mooney (eds), *The Challenge of Medical Practice Variations* (MacMillan, 1990) 21. See also *Factors Influencing Clinical Decisions in General Practice* (Office of Health Economics, 1990).

[10] *A First Class Service—Quality in the New NHS* (Department of Health, 1998) paras 1.6 and 1.8. See also *Variations in Health—What can the NHS do?* (Department of Health, 1995) and K. McPherson, "Why do Variations Occur" in T. Folmer Anderson and G. Mooney (eds) *The Challenge of Medical Practice Variations* (Macmillan, 1990) 17:

Medicine is widely held to be a science, but many medical decisions do not rely on a strong scientific foundation, simply because a strong scientific foundation has yet to be explored. Hence, what often happens in the decision-making process is a complicated interaction of scientific evidence, patient desire, doctor preferences and all sorts of exogenous influences, some of which may be quite irrelevant.

Medical evidence suggests that wide differences of practice exist without compelling scientific support. For example: "Between 1920 and 1950, hundreds of thousands of tonsilectomies were performed, almost all quite needless, while hysterectomies enjoyed a similar fad. Compare the vogue for caesarians nowadays."[11] A range of influences may be responsible. Medical "fashion" plays a role[12] so that views may become accepted without basic scientific evidence to support them. Fear of litigation may affect medical clinical practice.[13] Diagnoses may be made more for the patient's peace of mind than for clinical need.[14] Antibiotics are often prescribed for colds, flu, and sore throats caused by viral infections against which they are virtually ineffective.[15] Indeed, the method by which doctors are paid may also influence their willingness to treat. Systems which remunerate doctors according to the numbers of patients treated (the "fee for service" system, adopted in France and Germany) may encourage more medical interventions than those which pay doctors on the basis of the numbers of patients on their list, regardless of whether or not they receive treatment (the capitation fee, used in the UK).[16]

Consider the following examples. In an age-standardised sample of hysterectomy operations, 700 hysterectomies were performed per 100,000 American women, 600 per 100,000 in Canada, 450 in Australia, 250 in the UK and 110 in Norway.[17] Rates of caesarian sections have shown similar variations between countries.[18] The number of cardiac operations in the UK is lower than in other developed countries,[19] as has been the numbers treated for kidney failure.[20] Patterns of prescribing amongst European doctors show similar differences between countries;

[11] R. Porter, *Blood and Guts—A Short History of Medicine* (Penguin, Allen Lane, 2002) 129.

[12] J. Burnham, "Medical Practice a la mode: How Medical Fashion Determines Medical Care" (1987) 317 *New England Journal of Medicine* 1220.

[13] M. Ennis, A. Clark and J. Grudzinskas, "Change in Obstetric Practice in response to fear of litigation in the British Isles" (1991) 338 *British Medical Journal* 616. Estimates of the huge sums of money wasted in this way in America are discussed in T. Brennan, "Practice Guidelines and Malpractice Litigation: Collision or Cohesion" (1991) 16 *Journal of Health Politics, Policy and Law* 67 at 72.

[14] See C. Bradley, "Uncomfortable Prescribing Decisions: a Critical Incident Study", (1992) 304 *British Medical Journal* 294 and A. Speight *et al.*, "Underdiagnosis and Undertreatment of Asthma in Childhood" (1983) 286 *British Medical Journal* 1253.

[15] See *A Prescription for Improvement: Towards More Rational Prescribing in General Practice* (Audit Commission, 1994) para. 22.

[16] S. Sandier, "Health Service Utilisation Rates and Physician Income Trends" in *Health Care Systems In Transition: the Search for Efficiency* (OECD, 1990), who considers this influence on costs to be relatively weak.

[17] K. McPherson, *Variations in Hospitalization Rates: Why and How to Study Them* (King's Fund Institute, 1988).

[18] J. Lomas, "Holding Back the Tide of Caesarians" (1988) 297 *British Medical Journal* 569.

[19] *Summary of Ischaemic Heart Disease Study* (OECD, 2002). See also T. English and A. Bailey, "The U.K. cardiac surgical register, 1977–82" (1984) 298 *British Medical Journal* 1205; R. Brooks, J. Koesecoff *et al.*, "Diagnosis and Treatment of Coronary Disease: Comparison of Doctors' Attitudes in the USA and the UK" (1988) i *The Lancet* 750.

[20] A. Wing, "Why Don't the British Treat More Patients with Kidney Failure" (1983) 287 *British Medical Journal* 1157.

the Germans are most concerned about their hearts, the French—their digestive systems, and the English—the state of their minds.[21] Variations on this scale cry out for justifications. If we wish to maximise the overall benefits of the health service, "it is difficult to justify marginal operations when there are genuine unmet needs elsewhere . . .".[22] Equally, irrational treatment carries the risks of positively harming patients because medicine almost always presents an element of danger. The Audit Commission estimates that between 3 per cent and 5 per cent of all hospital beds in the UK may be occupied by people suffering wholly or largely from adverse drug reactions.[23] Clearly, therefore, there is legitimate interest in reappraising the value of clinical freedom with a view to harmonising practice and reducing waste. For this reason, pressure is being exerted on doctors to comply with clinical practice guidelines, to undertake medical audit of their procedures, and to be prepared to justify substantial differences between them.

Will the differing clinical instincts of doctors continue to be supportable? Some have individual patients uppermost in their minds and have always prescribed the best available treatment. Others with an eye on reducing expenditure, may try a "second-best" treatment first, and use the best only if that fails, or is inappropriate.[24] Modern medical ethics demand that doctors understand the economic impact of their decisions, of (what economists call) "opportunity costs", i.e. the range of treatments, the opportunities that will be forgone if the money to pay for them is diverted elsewhere. Evidence-based practice is an essential component of modern medicine. But can it *dictate* how the doctor should respond to the needs of individual patients? Doctors should preserve the ultimate discretion to determine whether a generic clinical guideline is appropriate to the needs of a particular treatment. This limitation on the extent of interference is illustrated by one of the recommendations of the Bristol Inquiry. It recommended that hospital doctors should all be required to observe the standards of care recommended by the National Institute for Clinical Excellence (NICE) and that "failure to comply with the standards, without reasonable justification, would entitle the employer to take whatever action was deemed appropriate [for example] retraining".[25] This explicit threat of sanctions for failing to adhere to NICE guidance was immediately rejected by NICE itself, on the ground that clinical guidelines are created to cater

---

[21] B. O'Brien, *Patterns of European Diagnoses and Prescribing* (Office of Health Economics, 1984).
[22] K. McPherson, "International Differences in Medical Care Practices" in *Health Care Systems in Transition: The Search for Efficiency* (OECD, 1990) 25.
[23] *A Prescription for Improvement: Towards More Rational Prescribing in General Practice* (Audit Commission, 1994) para. 3; citing T. Emerson, "Drug Related Hospital Admissions" (1993) 27 *Annals of Pharmacotherapy* 832; and C. Medawar, *Power and Dependence: Social Audit on the Safety of Medicines* (Social Audit, 1992). For this reason, the practise of "defensive medicine" is unwise.
[24] This is the recommendation of the Audit Commission in *A Prescription for Improvement: Towards more Rational Prescribing in General Practice* (1994) para. 44: "Practices should agree a policy that sets out their choice of first, second and third line drugs for key areas of prescribing, particularly where there are major safety considerations."
[25] *Learning from Bristol* (Cm. 5207, 2001) 389, para. 30.

for aggregates of populations not individuals. NICE's observations illuminate the limitations of generic guidelines. It said:

NICE has always indicated that health professionals, when exercising their clinical judgement, should take its guidance fully into account; but that it does not override their responsibility for making appropriate decisions in the circumstances of the individual patient. This principle is important because even the best clinical guideline is unlikely to be able to accommodate more than around 80% of patients for whom it has been developed.[26]

This suggests that whilst doctors who rely wholly on clinical "instinct" are unlikely to achieve a satisfactory standard of practice, as NICE suggests, nor will it be sufficient to be too rigidly bound by clinical guidelines. Responsible treatment requires doctors to keep well in mind the needs and wishes of individual patients; indeed, to follow guidelines as if they were a recipe in a cookery book, without regard to the patient's individual circumstances, would itself be a serious cause for concern. Guidelines should remain *guidelines* (although sometimes very persuasive ones), but not tramlines, and doctors should retain discretion to decide whether a patient falls within the framework of the recommendation, or not. On the other hand, it is perfectly reasonable to expect a competent clinician to be familiar with an authoritative and respected guideline and to accommodate its recommendations in his, or her decision. Modern medicine requires a reasoned analysis of their applicability to each patient. In other words, the decision to apply a guideline in individual cases is a matter for clinician and patient, but the decision not to follow it must be explicable by good reason and logic. Increasingly, the need for an explanation will not simply be to account to professional peers. When the effective use of resources is so important to the welfare of patients as a whole, NHS institutions will be entitled to an explanation too.

B. "Waste" of NHS Resources

Doctors should make optimum use of NHS resources. As the British Medical Association says: "Wastage of resources is unethical because it diminishes society's capacity to relieve suffering through the other uses that could be made of the wasted resources. Doctors working within the NHS need to be aware of cost-effectiveness as well as clinical effectiveness in the care provided for the patient."[27] What, however, is "waste" in the context of health care resources and to what extent does the question provoke issues of morality?

---

[26] NICE's Response to *Learning from Bristol* (NICE, 2002).

[27] *Medical Ethics Today: Its Practice and Philosophy* (BMA, 1993) 300. See also T. Brennan, *Just Doctoring: Medical Ethics in the Liberal State* (California University Press, 1991) at 183:

I believe physicians should put the beneficence model behind them. Medical ethics as just doctoring requires that physicians consider the political context in which care occurs. This includes consideration by physicians of the need to moderate health care costs . . . One must openly recognize it as rationing, and must help to ensure that the rationing is fair.

1. *Waste*

"Waste" is not a neutral word. Governments, health service managers, doctors, patients, and citizens may each have differing ideas about how resources should be spent. Used as a way of insisting that individual patients receive only the best treatment, it does not undermine the Hippocratic duty to do the best for patients. Many say that doctors should never compromise their clinical commitment to the individual.[28] But this notion may positively increase the costs of treatment by highlighting the many excellent, but expensive, new treatments that become available. By contrast, as we discuss below, health economists stress the need to distribute national resources efficiently and give "waste" a different meaning. This approach emphasises the clinical benefits to whole communities, rather than to individuals, and could modify the relationship between doctors and patients. One set of guidelines, for example, has recommended that the distribution of resources by hospitals and doctors should always be consistent with the policies established by governments at national level so that: "Health care professionals at the clinical level ought not to make any treatment decision that undermines legitimate attempts at a higher level to establish just and efficient use of resources."[29] The Bristol Inquiry sympathised with this view. It said: "Against a background of constrained resources, it may not always be right for the individual doctor treating a particular patient to insist on having his, or her way, if the price to be paid is to limit or impair the care available for other patients."[30]

Clearly, this idea seeks to change the clinical commitment each clinician has to his, or her patient in the interests of patients as a whole. This changes the traditional Hippocratic ideal and its implications are crucial to the health service we can expect in the future. Were such an approach to be adopted, doctors would become more openly involved in shaping and implementing social and economic policies and their clinical freedom with respect to individuals would have to be modified as a result. On the other hand, in this most delicate and fundamental area of practice, doctors have little training in the principles (whatever they may be) which might assist them:

Unfortunately, physicians have little experience with the task of bringing moral and social norms to bear on particular disputes and situations. [And] ethicists and jurists are not familiar with the medical and emotional nuances associated with the care of acutely ill and dying patients.[31]

---

[28] See R. Veatch, *The Patient-Physician Relation: The Patient as Partner, Part 2* (Indiana University Press, 1991) ch. 19; and A. Relman, "Dealing With Conflicts of Interest" (1985) 313 *New England Journal of Medicine* 749.

[29] *Developing Guidelines for Decisions to Forgo Life-Prolonging Medical Treatment* (The Appleton International Conference, reproduced in the supplement to (1992) 18 *Journal of Medical Ethics* Part IV, para. 16.   [30] *Learning From Bristol* (Cm. 5207, 2001) 387, para. 27.

[31] T. Brennan, "Do-Not-Resuscitate Orders for the Incompetent Patient in the Absence of Family Consent" (1986) 14 *Law, Medicine and Health Care* 13.

Given the trust and candour that must underpin the clinical relationship, and that doctors are experts in matters clinical, not economic, their major commitment should remain Hippocratic unless they are directed otherwise by clear, coherent and transparent managerial policies to the contrary. We return to the ways in which such policies might operate in Chapter 5.

2. Waste, or Morality?

There may also be a moral dimension to the notion of waste. What if a patient is the author of his own misfortune? He is obese,[32] or a heavy smoker, or drinker. Ought he to be considered for cardiac by-pass surgery when his life-style has contributed to his condition?[33] There is nothing in the Hippocratic Oath about the reciprocal obligations of patients to look after themselves and some doctors have taken a forthright approach to those who refuse to co-operate with the pre-conditions that have been set for surgery. Consider the following:

> I have had patients in the past who were intravenous drug users who injected filthy materials into their veins. These materials tend to lodge on the heart valves and cause infections, destroying the valves. For one patient, we replaced his own valve with an artificial one. Later the same month, the patient was readmitted with the same problem, having infected the artificial valve . . . What does medical ethics demand of me in such a case?[34]

Also, the extent to which patients fail to take the medicines in the manner prescribed by their doctors is well documented (but not well understood). This is the case even in respect of patients suffering from chronic and life-threatening conditions so that full therapeutic benefit is not achieved.[35] Is this a breach of the trust that should exist between doctor and patient? Should treatment be withdrawn as a result? In principle, so long as the decision to refuse treatment can be confined to *clinical* grounds, i.e. the risk inherent in the procedure is not justified by the patient's condition, or clinical benefit cannot be achieved because of the patient's failure to co-operate, it may be justifiable not to offer further treatment for that condition. But there are at least two difficulties with this approach.

First, how can we isolate the clinical reasons for the refusal, from the judgmental or the social? Many of us deliberately expose ourselves to risk by driving fast cars, or playing football. Should doctors be able to refuse treatment to accountants and lawyers in the City who choose to work under conditions of great stress and so expose themselves to risk of cardiac disorder? Many of us have no real choice in

---

[32] Obesity costs the NHS £200 million per year on treatment and related illnesses according to *Obesity* (Office of Health Economics, 1994).

[33] See M. Underwood and J. Bailey, "Coronary bypass surgery should not be offered to smokers" (1993) 306 *British Medical Journal* 1047.

[34] T. Brennan, *Just Doctoring: Medical Ethics in the Liberal State* (University of California Press, 1991) 176. The author also discusses an AIDS patient who threatened and spat at nurses. See pp. 147–52.

[35] See M. Marinker, *From Compliance to Concordance* (Department of Health, 1997).

exposing ourselves to danger. Those in the emergency services regularly face danger in the service of others and to earn a living. In addition, environmental, genetic, and psychological factors may have an effect which is difficult to quantify.[36] Indeed, there is a close correlation between social class and poor health. Socio-economic circumstances play the major part in differences in health between individuals. For example, the problems associated with smoking, drinking, and diet are more prevalent in lower social groups. "Factors, such as housing and income can effect health. Most importantly, several studies have shown how adverse social conditions can limit the choice of life-style and . . . living and working conditions appear to impose severe restrictions on an individual's ability to choose a healthy life-style."[37]

The second problem concerns the interests of third parties. Obviously, a refusal to treat a promiscuous patient with a contagious sexual disease would expose others to risk of infection. This could not be justified on moral or economic grounds. More subtle are the interests of children and other dependants who may suffer if parents are not treated. Who, in these cases, would really suffer? Ultimately, therefore, except, perhaps in a very narrow band of cases in which the patient is unlikely to derive clinical benefit from treatment, the problems involved in making distinctions on these grounds are so difficult that doctors ought not to make them.[38] As the General Medical Council says:

The investigations or treatments you provide or arrange must be based on your clinical judgment of the patient's needs and the likely effectiveness of treatment. You must not allow your views about patients' lifestyle, culture, beliefs, race, colour, gender, sexuality, disability, age, or social or economic status to prejudice the treatment you provide . . . You must not refuse or delay treatment because you believe that patients' actions have contributed to their condition.[39]

Of course, there will be occasions on which hard decisions have to be made without time for reflection. Take the hypothetical example of a road traffic accident in which a young woman has been run down by a drunken driver. Both are critically hurt. Who should receive treatment in the only intensive care unit available (assuming their injuries are equal), the young woman, or the drunk driver? What if the driver is the only breadwinner for his wife and children? Obviously, one's instinct is torn. The merits of the individual patients lean in favour of the young woman. The interests of third parties, however, incline us in the opposite direction. Doctors have no special expertise in making distinctions of this nature but the merits of the judgment are so delicate that law and morality should interfere with their judgment with great deference and caution.

---

[36] See the discussion in *Choices in Health Care* (Ministry of Welfare, Health and Cultural Affairs, The Netherlands, 1992) 62.

[37] M. Whitehead, "The Health Divide" in *Inequalities in Health* (Pelican, 1988) 305.

[38] See R. Veatch, note 28 above, at ch. 21.

[39] *Good Medical Practice* (General Medical Council, 2001) para. 5.

This suggests that matters of this nature are likely to remain at the discretion of doctors and the Hippocratic ideal will be durable and quite rightly resistant to change. Of course, as evidence-based research illuminates the treatments most likely to work best, NHS managers will increasingly be able to present doctors with persuasive evidence of the need to change ineffective practices. On the other hand, this may equally point to new drugs and procedures that are better and more expensive. Evidence-based medicine is not necessarily a solution to the need to manage scarce NHS resources.

II. Health Economics and the QALY

An alternative and more explicit principle of resource allocation would limit clinical freedom by focusing on the needs of whole communities, rather than individual patients. The principle of the quality adjusted life year (QALY) promotes an economic response to the problem associated with health resource allocation. Health economists have made a significant contribution to the way in which we consider these matters. Economics has been described as "the study of how men and society end up choosing, with or without the use of money, to employ scarce productive resources that could have alternative uses, to produce various commodities and distribute them for consumption among various people and groups in society. It analyses the costs and benefits of improving patterns of production".[40] The question is entirely pertinent to the health service. Health economics starts with the proposition that health service resources are scarce and that hard decisions between patients are unavoidable. It encourages us to consider an uncomfortable truth.

It is all too easy in considering "need" to assume that if a treatable condition exists, therefore (1) it should be treated and (2) it should be treated in the "best" possible way . . . If this were accepted, this would mean that all need should be treated and only the most effective treatments should be used. Both of these ignore the facts that resources are scarce and an overall better use of resources may be obtained from employing less effective but cheaper policies.[41]

Applied to scarce health service resources, economists ask, for example, how much of society's resources should be devoted to health and health care and how should they spent to maximum affect? Should priority be given to the elderly, rather than the mentally ill, and what criteria should be used in deciding? Should more surgical patients be treated as day patients? Should a new hospital be built? Is prevention "better" than cure, always, or just sometimes? How have economists influenced the

---

[40] P.A. Samuelson, *Economics* (McGraw-Hill, 1976) 5, quoted in G. Mooney, *Economics, Medicine and Health Care* (2nd edn, Harvester Wheatsheaf, 1992) 5.
[41] G. Mooney, note 40 above, at 70.

debate? We discuss (A) opportunity costs and scarce resources, and (B) consider whether QALYs can have a practical impact on health.

A. Opportunity Costs and Scarce Resources

Economics analyses the cost-benefit implications of our decisions about treatment. How can we generate best value from limited resources? The question forces us to consider the *relative* benefits of some treatments by comparison to others. Take the following example of a senior manager of a London hospital concerning:

> ... a lady who had a bowel disorder requiring total parenteral nutrition at a cost of £25,000 per annum. She was not from my district so we were cross-charging another district for it, otherwise we would not have allowed her to start treatment. She was in her early thirties, decided she wished to get pregnant so was sent to our IVF unit which made her pregnant with twins. She was admitted for the whole of her pregnancy to ensure the foetus had optimal growth, went into labour and her twins each spent six months in the neonatal intensive care unit before discharge. One died shortly after. We costed the complete episode and it totalled almost £300,000. That meant, in effect, that one of the wards we had closed last year, which would have treated a thousand patients, could have remained open if that had not taken place. I . . . am certain that many cases like this arise with the various new technologies available.[42]

In a case such as this, is it sufficient that the treatment produces *some* benefit, even if resources devoted to this patient could produce greater benefit elsewhere? Decisions to treat one patient, or one category of patients, may mean that others are denied care. Should we refine a principle on which different treatment, and patients, can be distinguished? Health economists have assisted this process by applying the notion of "opportunity cost" to health service spending, i.e. the benefits foregone as a result of using finite resources for one purpose rather than another:

> As resources are limited, not all that is desirable can be done. If resources are used in one way (for example, providing more physiotherapy for handicapped people) they cannot be used in other ways (such as screening for Down's syndrome or providing more hip replacements). Thus, in this example, providing benefit for handicapped people means giving up the chance to give benefits to pregnant women or elderly people. Whatever the best alternative use is judged to be, it is the benefits given up in that use that represent the "opportunity cost".[43]

In other words, in allocating priorities amongst patients, who do we decide not to treat? When should our natural compassion give way to the cold logic of economic analysis?

---

[42] K. Grant, "The balance of care provision in the National Health Service" in H. L'Etang (ed.) *Health Care Provision Under Financial Constraint: A Decade of Change* (Royal Society of Medicine, 1990) 138.

[43] G. Mooney, K. Gerard and C. Donaldson, *Priority Setting in Purchasing—Some Practical Guidelines* (National Association of Health Authorities and Trusts, 1992) 7.

Many would agree that if large quantities of resources are being used without knowledge of opportunity costs, then an element of planning is missing; and if it is unplanned it may be arbitrary and devoid of social policy. This is where health economists have made an important contribution to the debate. Prominent amongst a number of economic approaches to creating priorities is the quality adjusted life year (QALY).[44] This approach attempts to evaluate healthcare outcomes according to a generic scale. It asks (1) how much, and for how long, a treatment will improve the quality of a patient's life and (2) how much the treatment costs. In this way it seeks to compare the costs of generating QALYs, regardless of the particular treatment in question. The theory of the QALY counts each year of full health as one and, correspondingly, each year of declining health, as less than one on a sliding scale. Death scores 0. If the improvement in health after treatment is both significant and capable of being enjoyed over a long period of time, the patient accumulates units and scores high on the quality of life measure. If the treatment is relatively inexpensive, then the cost per unit of quality is low. The theory favours treatments which achieve the greatest increase in the quality of life, over the longest period, for the least cost. Conversely, if the cost of medical intervention is high, and the relative improvement in the condition of the patient is small, or capable of being enjoyed over a short period of time only, then the cost per QALY will be relatively high. On this basis, the adoption of health policies which produce the largest number of QALYs will be those which spend money most efficiently.

B. Can QALYs Make a Practical Impact?

QALYs are not alone in attempting to evaluate health outcomes on the basis of economics, but they cannot provide a complete answer to the question of health care entitlements. How, in practical terms, can one measure in numbers the degree of improvement in a patient's health after treatment? Is this susceptible to objective analysis? The matter could be handed over to democratic opinion, but illness manifests itself with infinite degrees of severity and, in the same patient, in many combinations of diseases. How could the scale be sufficiently sensitive to distinguish intensive care units for premature babies, hip replacements for those aged over fifty-five, and patients with diabetes complicated by liver disease and blindness? And how could it accommodate the subtle shifts over time in social attitudes to the concepts of "health" and "illness"?[45] Consider a patient who is confined to a wheelchair and who now needs treatment in hospital for an unrelated condition.

---

[44] See, e.g., A. Williams, "The Economics of Coronary Artery Bypass Grafting" (1985) 291 *British Medical Journal* 326; A. Maynard, "Logic in Medicine" (1987) 295 *British Medical Journal* 1537. Other measures have also been developed. See, e.g., L. Fallowfield, *The Quality of Life: The Missing Measurement in Health Care* (Souvenir Press, London, 1990) and R. Rosser, M. Cottee *et al.*, *Measures of the Quality of Life* (Royal College of Physicians, 1992).

[45] See R. Carr-Hill, "Assumptions of the QALY Procedure" (1989) 29 *Social Science and Medicine* 469.

Compared to a patient without disability, would he be put at a disadvantage by virtue of the QALY system which attaches value to the degree of improvement after treatment? If the disabled patient could never expect the same mobility as the able-bodied one, and would score lower on the scale, does the system not discriminate against those who are already ill or disabled? Many strong and healthy people dependent on wheelchairs would say that such a system was unfair because they derive just as much benefit from treatment as the able-bodied.[46] Indeed, they might say that such a judgment could only be made by those in a similar position, not by able-bodied administrators with no understanding of life in a wheelchair.

Much the same may be said with respect to elderly patients. Naturally, their expectation of life after treatment is shorter than in younger patients. Should they, as a category, be disfavoured on the "outcome" scale, on the basis that they have fewer years ahead of them in which QALYs could accumulate?[47] Clinical decisions may be influenced by the patient's age rather than his or her clinical prognosis, indeed strong and vigorous elderly patients may be disfavoured, even by comparison with less healthy younger patients whose outlook is less good.[48] Many elderly patients will derive terrific benefit from medical treatment and lead full and independent lives thereafter. A fit elderly person with a life expectancy of ten years might score (say) $10 \times 0.8 = 8$ QALYs. Compare this to a younger person with a serious illness and a life expectancy of thirty years, for whom medical intervention will have limited value. Say such a patient might score $30 \times 0.5 = 15$ QALYs. Should treatment automatically favour the younger patient irrespective of clinical merits? A more sensitive measure must be found.

Also, quite apart from the practical concerns, to what extent is the theory itself ethically acceptable?[49] It is true that, in one sense, it is entirely egalitarian as between patients; it favours none since it seeks only to maximise the number of QALYs and makes no attempt to say which categories of patient, or types of illness, ought to be given priority. As between a large number of patients with minor ailments and a smaller number with more serious complaints, it does not judge which should be given treatment, so long the total number of outcome units produced from each group is the same. It also focuses minds on the fact that decisions of one sort or another are already being made and that it is unethical to waste money and so deprive deserving patients of access to care. When a decision to treat one patient

---

[46] This point was made most persuasively by a post-graduate student of mine who was confined to a wheelchair and who became a successful solicitor in the City and would provoke issues under the Disability Discrimination Act 1995.

[47] J. Avron, "Benefit and Cost Analysis in Geriatric Care: Turning Age Discrimination into Health Policy" (1984) 310 *New England Journal of Medicine* 1294. Forthright support for such "ageist" discrimination is provided by D. Callahan, *What Kind of Life: the Limits of Medical Progress* (Simon and Schuster, New York, 1990).

[48] See I. Fentiman, U. Tirelli, S. Monfandi *et al.*, "Cancer in the Elderly: Why so Badly Treated?" (1990) 335 *The Lancet* 1020 and the discussion in *The Health of the U.K.'s Elderly People* (Medical Research Council, 1994).

[49] See A. Williams, "Cost-effectiveness analysis: is it ethical?" (1992) 18 *Journal of Medical Ethics* 18.

may deny treatment to others with similar need, consideration of opportunity-costs is an appropriate ethical concern.[50]

No-one will argue that considerations of cost and efficiency are irrelevant. But if they become the dominant or only concern, can they be described as ethical? The theory would erode the traditional view of the relationship between doctor and patient. The idea of the doctor promoting the best interests of the patient would have to be replaced. Instead, the interests of the individual would be secondary to those of the group. The notion of clinical freedom would be eroded because doctors would have no primary duty to the individual. Rather, the duty would be to efficiency and the maximisation of the greatest good for the greatest number. The matter is starkly put as follows:

Those [doctors] who advise on equity and efficiency ought to do so from a standpoint which is much wider than either the individual patient or indeed the individual practitioner and his patients. There has to be a strong case for those who proffer such advice being separated from the demands and prejudices of patient care . . . Hence emerges the role of the community physician . . . It can be argued that [issues of equity and efficiency] are not the province of the medical profession, outside community medicine, *except* as doers of society's will. In terms of equity and efficiency, clinicians need to be advised not the advisers.[51]

The weakness of this view as an ethical theory lies in its diluted concern for the individual. No-one could know what rights to care he or she would be entitled to receive until a calculation had been undertaken on the scale. Some for whom we might have great sympathy and compassion might score rather badly on such a calculation. For example, pure economic logic does not see a return in the treatment of pain, say in a patient suffering cancer, particularly if he has little chance of recovering his or her health.[52] Where does a consideration of the individual needs of such a patient fit into the priorities identified by QALYs?

More broadly, outcome measurements equate the idea of health "need" with the ability to benefit from treatment,[53] or health "gain". But it is equally plausible to consider need more broadly. One might ask as an alternative where is suffering most severe or which illnesses are the major causes of death and disease? Take the example of a young child with cerebral palsy. Inevitably, the child requires more expensive treatment than most children of his age, and both the quality and quantity of his life may be more limited. Measured by means of a QALY, the returns on the money invested in him may be smaller than equivalent sums spent on other

---

[50] "Decisions to forgo life-sustaining treatment under conditions of scarcity" from *The Appleton International Conference—Developing Guidelines for Decisions to Forgo Life-Prolonging Medical Treatment*, reproduced in (1992) 18 *Journal of Medical Ethics* 16.

[51] G. Mooney, note 40 above, at 118. At p. 150 he says: "Given their involvement with individual patients, members of the caring professions might have to be excluded from acting as society's agents in these matters." One doubts, however, whether there is such a thing as "society's will," particularly with respect to the new and relatively unexplored field of health service priorities.

[52] See F. Stoll, "Choosing Between Cancer Patients" (1990) 6 *Journal of Medical Ethics* 71.

[53] G. Mooney, K. Gerard and C. Donaldson, note 43 above, at 10.

groups of children in need of care. Many, however, would say that to deny him the care which enables him to realise his potential would be wrong. No doubt, the allocation of priorities on this basis would not produce the most QALYs and, to this extent, would not be most efficient, but it might correspond more closely to the sorts of values and goals with which most people would identify.[54] Indeed, some would say that our health service as a whole would be impoverished for attempting such a judgment:

Quality of life decisions made on behalf of those who are sick or disabled have no place in rigorous ethical thought . . . any grading of human beings according to value or worth is both repugnant and highly dangerous, since once one human life is judged worthless or expendable, all are inevitably reduced from an infinite to a relative value.[55]

Economists, of course will say that judgments of this nature are made every day; that the decision is inescapable and that the only difference is that QALYs attempt to perform the task on a rational and open basis. It may be, however, that the cold logic of efficiency will be insufficient proof that it is the only criterion on which decisions should be made. In the end, the concept of the outcome measurement is strongest when it is considered alongside the range of clinical, moral and compassionate considerations that motivate medical care. It informs, but it does not decide how money ought to be spent. As one economist has put it: "Cost and QALY values should be viewed as a way of asking questions about the resource consequences of interventions and their contribution to length and quality of life, not as the sole basis of decision-making."[56] Economic measurements are statements of the general goals that might be pursued by health service planners dealing with issues of "macro-allocation". Economic principles may well provide guidance to planners at central, regional, or district level, but they are often too blunt to guide those who have to distinguish between different patients awaiting treatment.

III. Resource Allocation and Government

To what extent should government play an active role in the rationing debate? A number of jurisdictions have taken a lead in influencing the allocation of health resources, most notably in Oregon, the Netherlands, Sweden, and New Zealand.

---

[54] One survey suggests that people do not sympathise with the logic of the QALY. Rather they adopt a view which favours treatment for the "needy", and give less emphasis to the question of cost. See E. Nord, "The Relevance of Health State After Treatment in Prioritising Between Patients" (1993) 19 *Journal of Medical Ethics* 37.

[55] Evidence from the Handicap Division of the Society for the Protection of the Unborn Child, quoted in the House of Lords *Report of the Select Committee on Medical Ethics* (HL 21–I, 1994) para. 167.

[56] M. Drummond, "Output Measurement for Resource Allocation Decisions in Health Care" in A. McGuire, P. Fenn and K. Mayhew (eds) *Providing Health Care: the Economics of Alternative Systems of Finance and Delivery* (Oxford University Press, 1991) 118.

Many others, however, have refused to venture into such a contentious and sensitive area of social policy. One reason for their reluctance is the uncertainty that shrouds the notion of "need" for health care. We discuss some of the models on which attempts have been made by the state to influence health resource allocation. We consider (A) top-down policies in which the state seeks to develop a list of treatments which will (and will not) be treated within the system and (B) bottom-up policies in which clinicians play the dominant role in allocating resources within available resources.

A. Top-down Policies

Many European systems of health care endeavour to embrace a notion of "social solidarity" in the provision of health care which, for convenience, are described as corresponding to the "Beveridge" or the "Bismarck" models.[57] Under the first, countries such as the UK, Sweden, Norway, Italy, and Spain commit themselves to a system under which health care is financed by the Treasury from general taxation. Under the second, in countries like Germany, the Netherlands, France, and Belgium, health care is financed through compulsory social insurance in which entitlements to care are based on standards and criteria agreed between the insurance providers and government. All commit themselves to a notion of social solidarity which emphasises the commitment of the entire community to social welfare. In the Netherlands, for example, a government report designed to assist the priorities debate in health care described the basis of this public "ethic" as follows:

Solidarity is the awareness of a unity and a willingness to bear the consequences of it. Unity indicates the presence of a group of people with a common history and common convictions and ideals. Group solidarity has played a prominent role in the history of health insurance. Solidarity can be voluntary, as when people behave out of humanistic motives, or compulsory, as when the government taxes the population to provide services to all . . . Compulsory solidarity is a central theme in social insurance.[58]

Within this environment, the report recommended that some types of care should not be provided within the Dutch system of social insurance. Instead, access to health care should be filtered through a number of tests, namely that the treatment is *necessary* from the community point of view, it has been demonstrated to be *effective*, it makes *efficient* use of resources, and cannot reasonably be left to the responsibility of the individual. Similarly, the final report of the Swedish Priorities Commission identifies the notions of human dignity, need, and solidarity as

---

[57] See C. Ham and A. Coulter (eds) *The Global Challenge of Health Care Rationing* (Open University Press, 2000), C. Ham (ed.) *Health Care Reform—Learning from International Experience* (Open University Press, 1997), ch. 1; J. Leneghan (ed.) *Hard Choices in Health Care: Rights and Rationing in Europe* (BMJ Publishing Group, 1997); and Brian Abel-Smith and Elias Mossialos, "Cost Containment and Health Care Reform: A Study of the European Union" (1994) 28 *Health Policy* 89.

[58] *Choices in Health Care* (Government Committee on Choices in Health Care, Zoetermeer, The Netherlands, 1992) 15.

principles on which questions of allocation should be founded.[59] Both commit themselves to excluding categories of care in order to provide a minimum guarantee to everyone.[60] This reappraisal of the idea of rights and the recommendation that they should be modified according to "communitarian" ethics is also gaining favour amongst social scientists elsewhere.[61] The serious difficulty faced by these proposals, however, is their absence of precision as to entitlements. Neither the Dutch, nor the Swedish report could offer a list of the types of care which should be excluded from a comprehensive package of benefits. The Dutch report suggested that in vitro fertilisation, homeopathic medicine, and dental care for adults could be excluded; but that sports injuries and homes for elderly people should be included.[62] By contrast, the Swedish report recommended inclusion of in vitro fertilisation, but excluded growth hormone deficiency (shortness of stature).[63] Never the less, the value of these reports is the candid engagement of government in an open and transparent debate. On the other hand, the categories proposed for exclusion are based on intuition and subject to change from time to time. And, given their limited reach, they would be most unlikely to release large savings in the health care budget. What further action could be taken by the state to control health care spending?

More extensive state involvement has been adopted in the state of Oregon, in the US. For those who are poor and unable to obtain private health insurance, Oregon depends on funding from central government, under the Medicaid system (like almost every other state in the nation). However, the Medicaid grant is insufficient to cover the health care requirements of all those who fall below the relevant level of income (the federal poverty level). Rather than axe entire categories of treatment, such as dentistry and prescription medicines, a policy was devised which attempted to compile "a list of health services ranked by priority, from the most important to the least important, representing the comparative benefits of each service to the population to be served".[64] A Health Service Commission was established to undertake the task which listed services by reference to specific treatments and specific conditions (for example, appendicitis and appendectomy). The list comprised 709 condition-treatments[65] which were grouped into one of seventeen general service

---

[59] *Priorities in Health Care* (Final Report of the Swedish Parliamentary Priorities Commission, 1995) 20.

[60] See the discussion of both the Dutch and Swedish reports in F. Honigsbaum, S. Holmstrom and J. Calltorp, *Making Choices in Health Care* (Radcliffe Medical Press, 1997).

[61] See, e.g., A. Etzioni, *The New Golden Rule—Community and Morality in a Democratic Society* (1997). Similar ideas have also been expressed in the health care context in M. Grodin (ed.), *Meta Medical Ethics: the Philosophical Foundation of Bioethics* (Kluwer, 1995).

[62] See *Choices in Health Care*, note 58 above, at 87–92.

[63] See *Priorities in Health Care*, note 59 above, at 121–30.

[64] *Evaluation of the Oregon Medicaid Proposal* (Congress of the US, Office of Technology Assessment, 1992) 4.

[65] The list was complied by reference to the World Health Organization, *International Classification of Diseases* (9th revision, Ann Arbor, MI, Edwards Bros Inc, 1980), which contains over 10,000 diagnoses. The list originally ran to 1,680 treatment-conditions and was reduced by a process of exclusion and consolidation.

Table 2.1. Rank of treatments

Condition and effects	Examples
1 Acute fatal, prevents death, full recovery	appendectomy, medical therapy for myocarditis
2 Maternity care, including disorders of the newborn	obstetric care of pregnancy; medical therapy for low birth-weight babies
3 Acute fatal, prevents death, without full recovery	medical therapy for bacterial meningitis; reduction of open fracture of joint
4 Preventive care for children	immunisations; screening for vision or hearing problems
5 Chronic fatal, improves life span and patient's well-being	medical therapy for diabetes mellitus and asthma; all transplants
6 Reproductive services	contraceptive management, vasectomy
7 Comfort Care	palliative therapy for conditions in which death is imminent
8 Preventive dental care	cleaning and fluoride
9 Proven effective preventive care for adults	mammograms; blood pressure screening
10 Acute non-fatal, treatment causes return to previous health state	Medical therapy for vaginitis; restorative dental service for dental caries
11 Chronic non-fatal, one-time treatment improves quality of life	hip replacement; medical therapy for rheumatic fever
12 Acute non-fatal, treatment without return to previous health state	relocation of dislocated elbow; repair of corneal laceration
13 Chronic non-fatal, repetitive treatment improves quality of life	medical therapy for migraine and asthma
14 Acute non-fatal, treatment expedites recovery of self-limiting conditions	Medical therapy for diaper rash and acute conjunctivitis
15 Infertility services	in vitro fertilisation, micro-surgery for tubular disease
16 Less effective preventive care for adults	dipstick urinalysis for haematuria in adults under age 60; sigmoidoscopy for persons under age 40
17 Fatal or non-fatal, treatment causes minimal or no improvement in quality of life	medical therapy for end state HIV disease; life support for extremely low birthweight babies (under 500 gm)

categories which distinguished acute and chronic illness, illnesses from which complete, or only partial recovery would be expected, illnesses which cause death or disability, effective and ineffective treatment, preventive and comfort care.[66]

The following categories, shown in Table 2.1, were developed in which numbers 1–9 were considered "essential" and 10–13 were designated "very important".[67]

[66] See generally, F. Honnigsbaum, S. Holmsrom, and J. Calltorp, *Making Choices in Health Care* (Radcliffe Medical Press, 1997).

[67] Taken from F. Honnigsbaum, *Who Shall Live? Who Shall Die?—Oregon's Health Financing Proposals* (King's Fund College, 1993) 25.

A separate ranking process took place within each category according to the "net benefit" gained from specific treatment which produced a final list of over 700 procedures. The net benefit was assessed by reference to treatment outcomes and, in a very general way, public opinion as to the value of different attributes of health care. The Health Service Commission also added its own preference for priority treatments after it found that the results of the first list seemed perverse (for example, obstetrical care was ranked low on the list and infertility treatment high.) The treatment-conditions were given a score from 1 to 0, representing the difference between perfect health and death on the basis of the equation in Table 2.2 below.[68]

Given the Medicaid funds made available to provide for those without health insurance, only the first 587 treatment-conditions could be provided under the scheme, and the location of the line may change from time to time. The remainder may not be made available under Medicaid. Priority was assigned according to the list of treatments shown in Table 2.3 below.[69]

The Oregon scheme presents a number of problems which are difficult to resolve. First, despite the list of 709 treatment-conditions and a spectacular equation, the system is often too insentive to differentiate sensibly between individuals.

Table 2.2. The Oregonian formula of the QALY

$$Y * \left[\sum_{i=1}^{5} (P_{i1} * QWB_{i1}) - \sum_{i=1}^{5} (P_{i2} * QWB_{i2}) \right]$$

[With treatment]   [Without Treatment]

with $QWB_{ik} = 1 + \sum_{i=1} d_{ijk} W_j$

where

B_n = the new benefit value ratio for the nth condition/treatment pair to be ranked. This value will be used in determining the actual rankings of health services from highest (0) to lowest ($-\infty$).

c = cost *with* treatment, including all medications and ancillary services as well as the cost of the primary procedure.

Y = the years for which the treatment can be expected to benefit the patient with this condition. This may be the remainder of the patient's lifetime or some shorter amount of time.

P_{i1} = the probability that the ith outcome will occur five years hence *with* treatment.

d_{ij1} = an indicator variable denoting the presence (= 1) or absence (= 0) of the jth health limitation (MOB, PAC or SAC) or chief compliant for the ith outcome *with* treatment.

w_j = the weight given by Oregonians to the jth health limitation or chief compliant ranging from 0 = no significant effect to -1 = death.

P_{i2} = the probability that the ith outcome will occur five years hence *without* treatment.

d_{ij2} = an indicator variable denoting the presence or absence of the jth health limitation or chief complaint for the ith outcome *without* treatment.

---

[68] ibid., at 44.   [69] ibid., at 30.

Table 2.3. Ranking of Selected Condition-Treatment Pairs

Condition	Treatment	Category	Rank
pneumonia	medical	1	1
appendicitis	appendectomy	1	5
ischaemic heart disease	cardiac by-pass op	3	149
HIV disease	medical	5	158
imminent death	comfort care	7	164
cancer of uterus	medical and surgical	5	186
end-stage renal disease	medical including dialysis	5	319
cataract	extraction	11	337
osteoarthritis	hip replacement	11	399
wisdom teeth	surgery	11	480
tonsils and adenoid disease	tonsillectomy and adenoidectomy	11	494
hernia without obstruction	repair	11	504
back pain (spondylosis)	medical and surgical	13	586
	all below 587 may not be funded		
varicose veins	stripping/sclerotherapy	11	616
bronchitis	medical	13	643
cancer where treatment will not result in 10% of patients surviving 5 years	medical and surgical	17	688
tubal disfunction	in vitro fertilisaion GIFT	15	696
haemmorrhoids, uncomplicated	haemmorrhoidectomy	17	698
AIDS, end-stage HIV disease	medical	17	702
extemely low birthweight (under 500 gm)	life support	17	708

Many conditions are not included in the list and patients often present themselves with more than one condition. Presumably a patient with two conditions, one of which was not funded under the scheme, could not sensibly be treated for only one of his complaints, particularly if the untreated disease was the more serious. In such a case, either both, or neither, ought to be dealt with. Equally, given the various forms in which illness may manifest itself, it seems absurd to preclude categorically treatment which will afford certain benefit to a patient. Conversely, for a condition above the line, it would be silly to introduce a presumption that treatment will be provided if the responsible doctor believes it will be futile. In both cases, clinical discretion must still play a part. As one of the framers of the plan said, "intuition is as important as mathematical formulas".[70]

Secondly, there is doubt as to the extent to which the public can be expected to make a serious contribution to the debate about health service priorities.

---

[70] Quoted in F. Honnigsbaum, note 67 above, at 45.

In Oregon, around 1,000 people were canvassed for their views but the community meetings were attended in the main by those employed in the health care system. Very few of those whom the scheme was intended to benefit participated in the debate. In any case, the issues often involve very sensitive and delicate ethical questions in which conflicting demands may best be considered over a period of time with a particular strategy in mind. They may be ill-suited to ranking on the basis of single questionnaires or discussions with random groups. The truth may be that lay people cannot be expected to contribute constructively to the question unless they also understand what has been achieved, whether further savings are possible, where medical services are least effective, how resources might be used more effectively, who would gain and by how much, and so on. For the cynically minded, there is a concern that those championing public involvement are not truly seeking to empower people to participate effectively but rather creating a veneer of legitimacy for management decisions about priorities.[71]

As the experiment in Oregon discovered, it is difficult to involve a representative cross-section of people in the exercise. Categories and classes of groups will be involved and some will effectively lobby for funds, but who will speak for the less articulate groups such as the mentally handicapped, the elderly, and those with "unpopular" diseases. Of course, if sufficient numbers of people could be involved the highest common denominator, or lowest common factor, of opinions could guide health care policy-making. But people have widely differing and inconsistent views about the concepts of health, illness, and disease[72] which will vary over time and amongst, for example, the young, the old, the disabled. This means that it would be impossible to define the overall objectives of the system, or to distinguish problems of health from those concerning the broader issues of life and society generally. And long-term planning would become very difficult.[73]

Thirdly, the whole process of putting patients into categories disguises the fact that doctors would retain a considerable measure of discretion in deciding how to treat a patient. Is the condition acute or chronic; is the patient likely to make a full, or partial recovery; if the condition is terminal, is it in its end-stages (for palliative care, rather than active treatment)?

All these are matters for individual clinical discretion which is flexible enough to include more patients than funds were designed to support. In this case, if doctors were to react in a compassionate way and tend to include, rather than exclude patients, the numbers of patients would increase. Given the same quantity of resources, the number of eligible treatment-conditions might have to be reduced and the difficult question presents itself all over again.

---

[71] D. Hunter, *Rationing Dilemmas in Health Care* (National Association of Health Authorities and Trusts, 1993) 27.

[72] See E. Campbell, J. Scadding and R. Roberts, "The Concept of Disease" [1979] 2 *British Medical Journal* 757.

[73] Thus, this approach was rejected as an general solution by a committee of enquiry in the Netherlands in *Choices in Health Care* (Ministry of Welfare, Health and Cultural Affairs, 1992) 51.

B. Bottom-up Policies

An alternative mechanism for explaining how resources are allocated is being considered in New Zealand which gives greater discretion to doctors in the process. But the system is also capable of exposing the responsibility of government (and by extension, the community) for the hard decisions that have to be made. Prior to this system, the National Advisory Committee on Core and Disability Services noted inconsistencies in access to services. Patients were often treated on the basis of the period of time spent waiting for treatment rather than on the basis of need, and some waited on lists indefinitely. It also noted the lack of communication with patients as to the availability of care.[74] Under the new arrangements, the clinical decision to admit patients to hospital for *elective* treatment (i.e. care which is not immediately necessary) may be assessed by reference to clinical priority assessment criteria (CPAC). For example, patients may be allocated points out of 100 according to the patient's degree of disability, level of pain, potential for harm through delay, social circumstances such as family/community impact and ability to work.[75] The system intends to concentrate limited resources on those in most "need" of care. Unlike the system used in Oregon, CPAC does not seek to list treatments that will be included, or excluded from care. Instead, the scoring system requires clinicians to make individual assessments of need. Under this approach, depending on the points accumulated, patients can be given a clear booking for admission to hospital immediately, or within six months, or admission may be denied and the patient returned to primary care supervision with the prospect of being reconsidered in the future.

The point on the scale of 1 to 100 at which treatment will be denied is directly related to resources made available to the service. Thus, each patient's assessment will be based on a common measure appropriate to the condition in question. Each component of the CPAC may be given a weight in the scoring system to reflect its persuasive value. For example, the degree of disability may carry greater weight than social considerations. The score required for a patient to be admitted for treatment will depend on the nature of the condition and the size and capacity of the hospital unit concerned, which may differ from unit to unit and from time to time. For example, in respect of cataract surgery, under the CPAC booking system, staff discovered that their funding for surgery was sufficient to treat only patients with a priority score of about 35 points and over. All had moderate to severe eyesight deficits which could no longer be helped by glasses. They could not drive, needed a magnifying glass to read, and found glare a major problem. These results persuaded the hospital to increase its funding. In turn, this permitted the unit to lower

---

[74] See R. Gauld and S. Derrett, "Solving the Surgical Waiting List Problem? New Zealand's Booking System" (2000) 15 *International Journal of Health Planning and Management* 259.

[75] See D. Hadorn and A. Holmes, "The New Zealand Priority Criteria Project" (1997) 314 *British Medical Journal* 131, 135. The system is comprehensively explained at www.nzgg-careplans.org.nz/library.

its eligibility threshold to approximately 28 points in order to include patients with less severe cataract problems.[76] In this way, the system displays the impact of funding decisions in a way that permits constructive comparisons to be made between them and generates greater certainty, transparency, and consistency.

Clearly, the weight accorded to different considerations involves judgment and the "objectivity" of this scale should not be over done.[77] A number of different CPAC scales may be used which produce different results. Some scales, such as that for coronary artery by-pass grafts, may be more generally accepted by doctors, than others. The exact numerical weight chosen to represent the patient's condition is at least partly a matter for subjective judgment for each individual doctor and it is difficult to compare patients' scores in one disease category with another. Doctors that lose confidence in the system may be more prepared to manipulate patients' scores to secure care, particularly those who regard themselves as patient advocates. Treatment for cancer might not be scored at all in order to give patients priority access. Some doctors give greater weight to social factors lying behind the patient's condition than others, such as conditions which affect children. Accordingly, a recent evaluation of the system recommended clarification both of the discretionary, or mandatory status of CPAC, the criteria on which patients will be prioritised for surgery, and the measurement of patient's needs and ability to benefit from care.[78]

At present, CPAC cannot provide a comprehensive response to the problem of health care allocation and it has yet to resolve the tension between the principle of "objective" health equality and legitimate clinical freedom.[79] The system will be criticised if it generates counter-intuitive conclusions which contradict clinicians' views of patients needs,[80] yet doctors often have varied and inconsistent perceptions of patient need which do not contribute to equity and fairness throughout the system. Never the less, the New Zealand Ministry of Health provides a mechanism which strives to address the problem in a transparent manner and which openly acknowledges that some patients who could benefit from treatment will not necessarily be admitted to hospital. From the perspective of the UK, in which

---

[76] B. Hefford and A. Holmes, "Booking Systems for Elective Services: The New Zealand Experience" (1999) 22 *Australian Health Review* 61.

[77] See S. Derrett, N. Devlin, P. Hansen and P. Herbison, "Prioritising Patients for Elective Surgery— A Prospective Study of Priority Assessment Criteria in New Zealand" (2003) 19 *International Journal of Technology Assessment in Health Care* 91; and S. Derrett, C. Paul, P. Herbison and H. Williams, "Evaluation of Explicit Prioritisation for Elective Surgery: a Prospective Study" (2002) 7 *Journal of Health Services Research and Policy* (Supplement 1) 14, noting that CPAC scores for surgery were weakly related to patients' ability to benefit from treatment.

[78] See *CPAC Evaluation Project—Descriptive Study* (Ministry of Health, New Zealand, 2002) ch. 12 and generally.

[79] S. Derrett, "Surgical Prioritisation and Rationing: Some Recent Changes" (2001) *New Zealand Bioethics* 3; S. Derrett, N. Devlin and A. Harrison, "Waiting in the NHS, Part 2: a Change of Prescription" (2002) 95 *Journal of the Royal Society of Medicine* 280.

[80] See W. Edgar, "Rationing Care in New Zealand—How the Public has a Say" in A. Coulter and C. Ham (eds) *The Global Challenge of Health Care Rationing* (Open University Press, 2000).

national politics pretends that NHS care will be available to all patients on the basis of need alone, this candour is both striking and refreshing.

IV. Resource Allocation by Democracy

An alternative approach to the resource allocation problem is to empower local people to decide issues of health resource allocation by means of local representation and consultation. In such a sensitive area, many sympathise with the idea that the system should respond to the wishes of those it serves. What mechanisms exist for conferring greater power on local people and what advantages and disadvantages do they present? What is the proper role of democracy in health resource allocation? "Democracy" has been described as a chameleon concept, a rhetorical flag which everyone seeks to capture.[81] In one sense, democracy is alive and well in the NHS. The Secretary of State for Health is an elected member of a government responsible for planning and organising the service. In addition, a wide range of forces influence his, or her decision-making, from local MPs and House of Commons Committees to demonstrations about the closure of local hospitals and national pressure groups. His, or her, failure to impress the public may well be reflected in future choices made by the electorate. On the other hand, this concept of democracy is restrictive; it fails to assess issues of concern in health care in particular, and general elections are too infrequent to be sensitive to local sentiment. Thus, it is said, democracy should become health-specific and more local.

Local democracy, however, presents its own problems. The British Medical Association has doubted whether such a system could work effectively.[82] Electoral turn-out at local elections is notoriously small and the real increase in democratic control might be very limited, especially if the electorate is historically committed to one political party only. In addition, the BMA is concerned that in a *national* health service, it is axiomatic that certain fundamental principles be preserved. To delegate responsibility for health services to local electors could undermine those principles by exposing the process to local political interests. Indeed, whole categories of treatment may be at risk if NHS priorities policy is dominated by democratic principles:

The public's priorities are not value free—they are most likely to prioritise treatments specifically for younger rather than older people and particularly life-saving treatments; [the research] also shows some public support (42%) for people with self-inflicted conditions receiving lower priority for care which raises ethical issues.[83]

---

[81] R. Klein and B. New, *Two Cheers?—Reflections on the Health of NHS Democracy* (King's Fund, 1998) 2.   [82] *Accountability in the N.H.S.* (BMA, 1994).
[83] A. Bowling, "Health Care Rationing: the public's debate" (1996) 312 *British Medical Journal* 674, cited in D. Hunter, *Desperately Seeking Solutions—Rationing Health Care* (Longman, 1997) 83.

In a service which promotes the virtues of equality and uniformity throughout the country, how much power should properly be devolved away from the centre when the consequences of doing so will, over time, promote divergence within the system?[84] When hard choices have to be made amongst competing demands, what mechanisms exist for increasing public involvement in the NHS?

A. Direct Involvement in NHS Resource Allocation

Could citizens have more direct impact on NHS investment be voting on specific issues of health policy? The difficulties of doing so are formidable. Assume that our need for medical treatment is unknown and unpredictable, that it may be extremely expensive, and that the only reasonable way to accommodate one's need for care over a period of time is through some form of insurance. In this case, we would have to decide the balance between the costs and benefits of insurance behind a veil of ignorance.[85] How much health insurance cover should we purchase and at what cost? The process would require some understanding of government policy, local needs and demands, knowledge of existing patterns of investment, and the relative costs of spending finite resources in one way rather than another. Is this issue best resolved by periodic appeals to local electorates? Much more would be required by way of education in order to enable electors to make well-informed decisions about the allocation of scarce resources. To generate an informed response, much information would have to be distributed, both about the costs, risks, and benefits to individuals personally and the community as a whole. The information would be dense, complicated, incomplete, uncertain, and misunderstood. The manner in which it was presented would provoke fierce argument over its objectivity and bias. Relatively few people might be expected to participate in the exercise. And, of course, the result would be far from unanimous.

Would society always choose the best possible treatment? What if the "best" cost twice as much as the "second-best" but it was only marginally more effective? Would we choose insurance that preserved our lives in a persistent vegetative state, or expensive medical intervention that extended our lives for an additional year, in vitro fertilisation (if so for one cycle, or three?), transsexual surgery, and treatment for impotence? How would we accommodate "the public interest" and how often would voting take place? Would we include insurance for expensive chemotherapy to treat cancer if there was a only 1:5,000 chance a single individual would contract the disease? How would long-term NHS strategy be possible? Would men vote on the affordability of treatment intended solely for women (such

---

[84] See L. Doyal, "The Moral Boundaries of Public and Patient Involvement" in B. New (ed.) *Rationing, Talk and Action in Health Care* (King's Fund, 1997) and J. Butler, *The Ethics of Health Care Rationing—Principles and Practices* (Cassell, 1999) ch. 4.

[85] See J. Rawls, *A Theory of Justice* (Harvard University Press, 1971) and the discussion in J. Butler, note 84 above, ch. 3.

as obstetrics, or cervical screening)? And what sympathy might one expect for less popular groups such as patients with mental illness and asylum seekers? How public-spirited is it reasonable to expect people to be when they are directly responsible for bearing the costs of their altruism? Indeed, if personal choice is the predominant concern of democracy why not introduce health insurance policies in which the extent of health coverage is selected and paid for by individuals? Yet, as experience in the US demonstrates, this is likely to create higher administration costs and leave a significant minority of people with little, or no insurance at all.[86] (And, of course, since most Americans are insured under their contracts of employment by means of block contracts agreed between employers and health insurers, their free choice is heavily restricted in any case.)

Too much democracy, then, could create erratic and inconsistent policy objectives that make long-term strategy difficult, or alternatively ossify the need for tough decisions because local decision-makers fail to address important tensions in the system. Some might decide that greater resources should be devoted to the "preventive" medicine rather than care for elderly patients. Others might invest in cancer care rather than the treatment of sexually transmitted diseases, or drug rehabilitation. Yet others may find consensus between differing opinions so difficult that the system cannot react to changing circumstances. If some categories of patient or treatment were excluded from the NHS so that the system no longer had "comprehensive" aspirations, the Secretary of State would be under a duty to promote a national service and to over-rule the expression of local opinion. To this extent, there are policy and legal limitations to the logic of direct democracy.

B. Local Democracy by Consultation

A more limited response is to engage the public in consultation which gives interested groups the opportunity to influence and persuade, but stops short of handing decision-making power to local representatives. As we discuss in Chapter 9, this is the model preferred by government, perhaps because it is a compromise which permits the Secretary of State to safeguard his statutory responsibilities to the NHS and to increase the influence of local voices.[87] A number of systems for consulting local opinion have been suggested, for example, citizen's juries, advisory health panels, opinion polls, "round-tables", and health authority priorities committees.[88] None have executive power, never the less, they often command respect and are likely to influence the nature and shape of NHS services. Health authorities would be expected to say how recommendations have been incorporated into

---

[86] C. Schoen, K. Davis, C. DesRoches *et al.*, "Health Insurance Markets and Income Inequality: Findings from an International Health Policy Survey" (2000) 51 *Health Policy* 67, suggesting that health care systems based on private insurance cover fewer patients than social insurance-based systems.

[87] The process is not new, see *Local Voices* (NHS Management Executive, 1992).

[88] See A. Coote and J. Lenaghan, *Citizen's Juries: Theory into Practice* (Institute of Public Policy Research, 1997).

local policy and explain why certain views have been rejected. They will have to be careful to include the views of less articulate or popular groups. As the Scottish Executive comments, great care must be taken to assess the validity and quality of the product of consultation:

Consultation can produce results that do not represent the views of local people as a whole . . . It is important to consider the make up of the local community and to avoid the risk of token consultation or involvement. It would be a mistake, for example to expect one person to be able to represent an area's black and ethnic community unless they can tap into the whole spectrum of cultures, interests and needs concerned . . . In addition, special efforts should be made to reach excluded groups such as young and old people, gypsy travellers etc.[89]

Despite its difficulties, consultation may be preferable to handing executive power to local representatives. First, since the product of consultation only has to be considered and taken into account, policy objectives are more likely to remain stable over longer periods of time and basic ethical and minimum standards preserved. Of course, consultation with advisory groups lacks the authority of elected representatives. They have no democratic mandate to represent their local community and, perhaps, no expertise to do so. Say a difficult decision has to be made on the closure of a local hospital in order to concentrate resources and clinical expertise on another hospital site elsewhere. Many with close connections to the hospital threatened with closure will simply reject the view of "unelected strangers" that their local hospital should be closed. This warns us that neither democracy, nor consultation make hard choices disappear; rather they may simply transfer responsibility for unenviable decisions to different people. Processes of democracy and consultation, therefore, offer almost as many problems as solutions in the NHS. Klein and New offer them two "perhaps rather grudging" cheers but urge "more sparing use of the ambiguous, contestable and contentious notion of 'democracy' as a hurrah word in debates about the NHS".[90]

V. Conclusion

Clearly, none of these approaches to health care resource allocation provides a complete answer to the problem. Whether the solution is dominated by doctors, economists, politicians, or "citizens": "The debate about priorities will never finally be resolved. Nor should we expect any final resolution. As medical technology, the economic and demographic environment, and social attitudes change, so almost certainly will our priorities."[91] In these circumstances of uncertainty, in which reasonable people will often differ, what matters most is how the debate

---

[89] *Consultation and Public Involvement in Service Change—draft interim guidance* (HDL(2002)42, Scottish Executive, 2002), Annex C, para. 9.   [90] R. Klein and B. New, note 81 above, at 27.
[91] R. Klein, "Dimensions of Rationing: Who Should do What?" in *Rationing in Action* (BMA, 1994) 103.

takes place, who is included in it, and the processes by which decisions are made. The essential question is not *what* we can have, but *who* decides the matter and *how*?[92] This focuses attention not on over-arching rights of access, but on processes which illuminate how decisions are made and highlight the needs for consistency between patients. With this in mind, we now turn to the way in which the NHS has responded to these challenges since its creation in 1946.

[92] See generally, N. Daniels and J. Sabin, *Setting Limits Fairly—Can we Learn to Share Medical Resources* (Oxford University Press, New York, 2002).

3

Managing Resources in the NHS

We saw in Chapter 1 how demand for health care is always likely to exceed the supply of resources we make available for it. In Chapter 2 we examined principles on which the issue of resource allocation could be resolved and saw that none provided a comprehensive solution. This brings us to a third question—how has the NHS in particular responded to the tensions provoked by scarce resources? The structure of the NHS has to grapple with one, major tension. It must recognise the need for central government to plan for and invest in the NHS, and to be held accountable for its successes and failures. But it also needs *local* incentives to encourage individuals and institutions to work efficiently in patients' interests. In an environment of scarce resources, how can the balance be struck between central and local control? In this chapter, we consider (I) rationing in the NHS and (II) the the evolution of policy on NHS management and organisation.

I. Rationing in the NHS

Government avoids use of the word "rationing," preferring "priority-setting" as a euphemism.[1] There is a "stoical refusal" on the part of government to lead public debate on the subject.[2] "Priorities are what ministers boast of; rationing is what opposition politicians accuse them of."[3] Indeed, government encourages precisely the opposite belief that, as the Prime Minister said shortly after his election 1997, "if you are ill or injured there will be a national health service there to help; and access to it will be based on need and need alone".[4] To what extent are claims of this

---

[1] Surprisingly, given the history of resource shortages in the NHS, the first report on "priority setting" did not appear until 1976, see *Priorities for Health and Personal Social Services in England: a consultative document* (Department of Health and Social Security, 1976).

[2] D. Hunter, *Desperately Seeking Solutions—Rationing Health Care* (Longmans, 1997) 97.

[3] R. Klein, P. Day and S. Redmayne, *Priority Setting and Rationing in the National Health Service* (Open University Press, 1996) 66.

[4] *The New NHS—Modern, Dependable* (1997, Cm. 3807), para. 1.5. By contrast, in 1999 the UK government told the European Commission under Council Directive 89/105/EEC (the Transparency Directive) that: "A medicinal product . . . may be excluded [from the NHS] where the forecast aggregate cost to the NHS of allowing the product . . . to be supplied on NHS prescription . . . could not be justified having regard to . . . in particular: the Secretary of State's duties pursuant to the NHS Act 1977 and the priorities for expenditure of NHS resources." See *R (Pfizer Ltd) v Secretary of State for Health* [2002] EWCA Civ 1566, [2003] 1 CMLR 19, para. 4.

nature credible? The Bristol Inquiry was very critical of successive governments for their portrayal of patients' rights in the NHS. It observed that:

> Governments of the day have made claims for the NHS which were not capable of being met on the resources available. The public has been led to believe that the NHS could meet their legitimate needs, whereas it is patently clear that it could not. Healthcare professionals, doctors, nurses, managers, and others, have been caught between the growing disillusion of the public on the one hand and the tendency of governments to point to them as scapegoats for a failing service of the other . . . The NHS was represented as a comprehensive service which met all the needs of the public. Patently it did not do so . . . [5]

> . . . What governments cannot do is to renew its commitment to a comprehensive, accessible healthcare service for all and then fail to fund it to the level of the demand government makes of it. Governments have got away with this in the past, but not now. Expectations have been raised and the public is watching.[6]

Government rhetoric notwithstanding, how does rationing occur in the NHS? We consider (A) rationing by government, (B) rationing by health authorities, and (C) rationing by doctors.

A. Rationing by Government

Decisions at the *macro*-level of government are made by the Treasury, which allocates resources between government departments including the Department of Health. Within those constraints, the Department of Health allocates resources to health authorities (currently known as primary care trusts (PCTs)). It may promote the care of particular groups, such as elderly patients within a National Service Framework.[7] Or it may insist that treatments recommended by the National Institute for Clinical Excellence (NICE) are funded as a matter of priority by local health authorities,[8] issue guidelines requiring health authorities to treat cancer within shorter periods of time, guarantee access to expensive treatment for a particular category of patient,[9] or insist that health authorities reduce patient waiting times across all areas of care. Government rarely quantifies the extent of the expenditure it requires from health authorities, yet each new policy requires PCTs to divert money from existing uses to those preferred by government. PCTs are subject to a statutory duty to remain within their financial allocations[10] and their budgets are already stretched. Any re-diversion of funds requires a local decision to *disinvest* from existing treatments and patients in order to support the new costs.

---

[5] *Learning from Bristol* (Cm. 5207, 2001) 57, para. 31. The report urges we should "make explicit that which has been implicit", 261, para. 27.   [6] ibid., 308, para. 17.

[7] See *National Service Framework for Older People* (Department of Health, 2001).

[8] See Secretary of State's Directions on NICE, Department of Health, 11 December 2001. We discuss NICE in Ch. 8 below.

[9] *Cost Effective Provision of Disease Modifying Therapies for People with Multiple Sclerosis* HSC 2002/004 (Department of Health, 2002).

[10] National Health Service Act 1977, s. 97D as amended. The duty is discussed in Ch. 5 below.

Inevitably, therefore, government is indirectly involved in rationing. Never the less, it refuses to involve itself in the rationing debate. The Health Committee of the House of Commons has urged government to develop a framework of guidance for local decision-makers to guide the way in which scarce resources are allocated. For example, in 1995, it expressed concern at the variations in practice between health authorities and "the absence of any firm lead from the Department of Health". The Health Committee recommended that the Department "set out the framework within which purchasers should be expected to define the local package of services, and set out the criteria by which those decisions may be scrutinised, debated and, if needs be, challenged by individuals".[11] The reply of the then Conservative government was a polite refusal, which precisely missed the point of the original request. It said:

To draw up a national list of treatments which will and will not be provided would be an exercise fraught with danger. No one list could ever hope to accommodate the range and complexity of the different cases which clinicians face all the time. There would be a real risk of taking decisions out of the hands of doctors.[12]

Note, that the original request was *not* for a "list of treatments which will and will not be provided". It was for a "framework within which" decisions should be made. In 2002 the Health Committee again pressed the government for greater guidance on matters of NHS resource allocation. It said:

. . . it is not sufficient to have implicit healthcare prioritisation . . . the Government must work to achieve a comprehensive framework for healthcare prioritisation, underpinned by an explicit set of ethical and rational values to allow the relative costs and benefits of different areas of NHS spending to be comparatively assessed in an informed way.[13]

Again, however, the government balked at the request, at least for the present. It said that its policy guidance in National Service Frameworks and NICE established some areas of priority and that "a comprehensive, empirically-based framework could . . . only be achieved in the long-term", although it continued: "The establishment of NICE could . . . be seen as an important first step in that direction."[14]

So government offers no comprehensive framework of guidance within which investment in health care should take place. Instead, it requires over 300 PCTs in England, local health boards in Wales, and health boards in Scotland to develop

---

[11] *Priority Setting in the NHS: Purchasing* (Session 1994–95, House of Commons Paper 134–I) para. 113.

[12] *Government Response to the First Report from the Health Committee* (1995, Cmnd. 2826) para. 4. On the other hand, note the view of one Secretary of State in 1992, "the first step in a strategic approach must be the establishment of clear priorities so that action and resources can be directed to best effect. This is necessary because if everything is regarded as a 'priority' then there is, in effect, no priority at all." Mrs Virginia Bottomley in *The Health of the Nation* (Department of Health, 1992).

[13] *National Institute for Clinical Excellence* (House of Commons Paper 515–I, Session 2001–02) 50, para. (ee).

[14] *Government Response to the Health Committee's Second Report of Session 2001–02 on the National Institute for Clinical Excellence* (2002, Cm. 5611) 16.

their own processes for doing so. This leads to a colossal waste of time and resources. This reticence of UK governments to formulate a priorities framework is not shared by governments abroad. Sweden, the Netherlands, and New Zealand have all acknowledged the tension between demand and supply in health care and contributed to the resource allocation debate,[15] as has the state of Oregon in the US. Of course, each such system exposes government to the political charge of rationing health to its citizens. But as the pressures upon resources become more intense, the pretence that rationing is someone else's fault is no longer sustainable. If rationing is a fact of life, it should take place within the framework of equality, fairness, and consistency between patients.

The NHS should be encouraged to emphasise its national dimension and be honest and transparent with citizens about the services it can afford to support. Early drafts of such a framework could properly be limited to *procedural* mechanisms for making hard choices with resources which health authorities should respect. The identification of the *substantive* care each patient is entitled to receive will always present an immense challenge. Never the less, even at this more limited level of involvement, government would be discouraged from making the wholly unsustainable claims of the NHS which were so criticised by the Bristol Inquiry; and citizens would not be misled as to the constraints imposed by the system upon the health care that government chooses to afford.

B. Health Authority Rationing

Once the cost of the government's requirements has been set aside, and within the resources remaining within their discretion, PCTs allocate funds to hospitals and doctors according to local policies and strategies. We have already noted that the statutory duty on health authorities and PCTs to remain within their financial allocations requires priorities to be identified. Should resources be spent on a smaller number of treatments that save lives, such as transplant surgery, or a larger number of less expensive treatments that enable people to live more fulfilled lives, such as care at home for elderly patients? Should we focus on *acute* care, such as reducing long waiting lists for orthopaedic care, especially if it enables otherwise strong and healthy elderly patients to return to full mobility with prosthetic hips, or knees? Or is long-term, *chronic* care such as that required for mental illness, or HIV/AIDS more important? Should money be invested in preventive medicine, for example the long-term reduction of blood pressure so that fewer patients suffer from strokes and coronary heart disease over the next 20 years? Should children have greater access to care than adults and should elderly patients have equal access to treatment? Should some treatments be excluded altogether other than in highly exceptional circumstances, such as cosmetic and transsexual surgery and in vitro fertilisation,

[15] See C. Ham, *Health Care Reform—Learning from International Experience* (Open University Press, 1997) and D. Hunter, note 2 above, ch. 5.

or because the condition is self-inflicted, such as tattoo removal? These are the routine concerns of health authorities and PCTs and require sensitive, well-informed and consistent decision-making.

Prior to the "internal market" reforms of 1990, NHS rationing at the *meso*-level was a largely covert business. As the Bristol Inquiry remarked, until the late 1980s the Department of Health did not audit clinical performance in the NHS.[16] These matters were for the discretion of doctors and local NHS managers. After 1991, however, the internal market required health authorities to be more explicit about resource allocation decisions by entering "NHS contracts" (also called service level agreements) with local hospitals so that, today, arrangements between PCTs and hospitals are necessarily more transparent.[17] Of course, given the tensions involved in resource allocation, hard choices are unavoidable. And when the discretion is delegated to PCTs, there are likely to be wide variations in practice throughout the NHS. Although there is concern about "post-code rationing", the structure of the NHS dictates that, unless directed otherwise by the Secretary of State, local health authorities are responsible for deciding where and how their resources should be allocated. National service frameworks and NICE guidance impose some uniformity, but in the absence of a framework of guidance from the centre of the sort recommended by the House of Commons Health Committee, post-code differentials are inevitable. As the strain on scarce resources becomes more intense, so the incidence of variations between different localities is likely to increase. The question is not whether there are variations in the NHS, but how local decision-makers have arrived at their decisions.

In principle, as we discuss in Chapter 5, the law requires minimum standards of fairness and consistency in the decision-making process. This means that such decisions should not be taken at random, or by single individuals such as a director of public health. It is the business of a properly constituted standing committee, well informed by a cross-section of expertise. Many authorities, however, do not have such committees and, of course, governments which deny the existence of rationing hardly encourage their creation. Those that do not are at risk of judicial review. However, some such committees exist and have developed and refined their approaches to rationing within "ethical frameworks" which seek to provide a mechanism by which the interests of individuals can be balanced against those of the community. To generate robust, reliable, and consistent decisions, priorities committees ought to have regular discussions with neighbouring authorities so that inconsistencies can be identified, modified, or justified. Of course, they must arrive at their own decisions in the light of local conditions. On the other hand, co-operation promotes uniformity, consistency, and equality in the NHS. Indeed, there is much to recommend a *national* forum for debate and discussion within

---

[16] *Learning from Bristol*, note 5 above, 303, para. 2
[17] See C. Ham and B. Coulter, "Explicit and Implicit Rationing—Taking Responsibility and Avoiding Blame for Health Care Choices" (2001) 6 *Journal of Health Services Research and Policy* 163.

which local purchasers might establish precisely the framework for resource allocation which the government refuses to promote.

C. Rationing by Clinicians

In their turn, clinicians may have to ration the care available to patients. Of course, it is at this micro-level that rationing causes most anguish. It is likely to affect both our access to care in the first place, and the level and quality of care we receive once access is achieved. Typically, rationing is said to occur through "deterrence, delay, deflection denial, and dilution" of care.[18] However, "the availability of evidence does not match the importance of the subject . . . there is remarkably little direct evidence about how funding constraints influence medical decisions or about the criteria used when allocating scarce resources to individual patients . . . the thorny thickets of clinical autonomy have effectively deterred researchers".[19] Patients may have to wait to visit their GP. Once an appointment has been made, there is a decision as to whether treatment is appropriate or not, and if so with what medication? Should the patient be admitted to hospital? If so, how many diagnostic tests will be considered necessary? How will the patient be treated, and how quickly will they be discharged? Will doctors give elderly patients the same access to care as younger patients?[20] To whom will limited treatment by kidney dialysis be offered?[21] Will smokers be given access to coronary by-pass surgery?[22]

Each of these decisions may be influenced to a significant extent by the availability of resources. In particular, doctors may be offered incentives under which they receive money for achieving targets and objectives.[23] Incentives which encourage doctors to reflect more carefully about their practice are justifiable because doctors may make decisions for reasons that have nothing to do with the illness of the patient.[24] In respect of treatments with no significant therapeutic

---

[18] See generally S. Harrison and D. Hunter, *Rationing Health Care* (Institute for Public Policy Research, 1994); D. Green and L. Casper, *Delay, Denial and Dilution—The Impact of Rationing on Heart Disease and Cancer* (Institute for Economic Affairs, 2000); J. Spiers, *The Realities of Rationing* (Institute for Economic Affairs, 1999).

[19] R. Klein, P. Day and S. Redmayne, *Managing Scarcity Priority Setting and Rationing in the NHS* (Open University Press, 1996) 83.

[20] J. Grimly Evans, "Health care rationing and elderly people" in M. Tunbridge (ed.) *Rationing of Health Care in Medicine* (Royal College of Physicians, 1993).

[21] T. Halper, *The Misfortunes of Others—End-Stage Renal Dialysis in the UK* (Cambridge University Press, 1989).

[22] M. Underwood and J. Bailey, "Coronary Bypass Surgery should not be Offered to Smokers", (1993) 306 *British Medical Journal* 1047.

[23] See D. Orentlicher, "Paying Physicians More to do Less: Financial Incentives to Limit Care" (1996) 30 *University of Richmond Law Review* 155.

[24] *Non*-clinical factors are said to exercise a significant influence on clinical decision-making. "It is, on occasion, simply a matter of fashion; the fact that new methods become available does not make the continued use of the old negligent unless and until they are shown to be wrong or to carry an unacceptably higher risk to the patient than the new." *Newbury v Bath HA* (1999) 47 BMLR 139, 162.

value, incentives may play a useful role. Equally, there is also a danger that they may obstruct the care patients need.[25] Indeed, cost constraints, rather than being "extraneous" to the doctor-patient relationship, may become so absorbed into professional practice that they become an integral part of the clinical decision-making process.[26] Little is known about the impact of incentives on practice, or whether they damage patient care. In 2000–01, incentive payments averaged over £1,200 per GP and sums of this size could certainly have a significant impact on prescribing activity.[27] Further work is needed to determine whether they compromise the quality of care given to patients.

In any event, NHS regulations on incentive payments do not permit GPs to save money at their patients' expense. Treatment should continue to be provided on the basis of clinical need.[28] Subject to this caveat, payments may be invested in extra practice nurses, or equipment "including diagnostic equipment, ECG machines, blood testing equipment, sterilisers, nebulisers, fetal heart detectors, cryothermic probes and defibrilators . . . which will enhance the comfort or convenience of patients".[29] NHS regulators should wish to be reassured that incentives are not undermining the doctor's duty to his, or her patient. During the 1980s it was suggested that "most patients appear willing to accept their doctor's word if he says that no further treatment of a particular disease is warranted".[30] Today, however, encouraged by government, patients may be less willing to take such a passive approach to their care. As we discuss below, if incentives become widespread, patients will need to be reassured that the doctor's advice has not been motivated by financial considerations of which the patient was unaware.

Clinical guidelines may also play a role in resource allocation by focusing treatment on those most in need of care. For example, guidelines may recommend treatment be limited to certain categories of patient only. Say guidelines for cardiovascular disease recommend treatment for those at serious risk of having a heart attack within ten years. They target patients with a risk of *at least* 20 per cent over

[25] T. Hope, D. Sprigings and R. Crisp, " 'Not Clinically Indicated': Patients' Interest or Resource Allocation?" (1993) 306 *British Medical Journal* 379.

[26] See A. Williams, "Health Economics: The End of Clinical Freedom?" (1988) 297 *British Medical Journal* 1183.

[27] See M. Ashworth, R. Lea, H. Gray *et al.*, "How are Primary Care Organisations using Financial Incentives to Influence Prescribing?" (2004) 26 *Journal of Public Health* 48. The new National Health Service (General Medical Services Contracts) Regulations 2004 (SI 2004 No. 291) introduce further extensive incentive payments, and are discussed at pp. 109–14 below.

[28] As required by the National Health Service (General Medical Services Contracts) Regulations 2004 (SI 2004 No. 291), Sched. 6, para. 39, discussed at pp. 109–14 below.

[29] See National Health Service (Functions of Health Authorities) (Prescribing Incentive Scheme) Regulations 1998 (SI 1998 No. 632), as amended by SI 2000 No. 661 and the National Health Service (Health Authorities in England)(Prescribing Incentive Scheme) Directions (Department of Health 1998), in the Schedule. (Unlike the scheme previously available to GP fund-holders, GPs may not use incentive monies for "the purchase of land or premises", e.g. a building extension to a practice which increases the equity in the property in which the partners have a financial interest.)

[30] H.J. Aaron and W.B. Scwartz, *The Painful Prescription: rationing hospital care* (The Brookings Institution, 1984) 101.

a ten-year period.[31] Treatment is not recommended, therefore, for those at lower risk of a heart attack.[32] "Acceptable" risk is driven by balancing patient need with the cost of providing treatment. So too, the number of diagnostic tests to be performed may be limited because, as the tests are repeated, the likelihood of discovering disease becomes increasingly more remote and the cost of each test relative to the number of patients detected to have the illness becomes more expensive. When is the likelihood of discovering disease so small that further tests should be discouraged? No doubt many such guidelines are entirely sensible. In one famous example of repeat tests for bowel cancer, the likelihood of the sixth test detecting the disease was so remote that the cost per case detected was US$47 million![33] In this way, to varying degrees, clinical guidelines may also serve to encourage doctors to be prudent with health care resources.

II. Evolution of NHS Management

In the light of this discussion, we now turn to the evolution of managerial responses to the tensions in the NHS since 1948.

A. Central Command and Control?

Before 1948, health care had been provided to many working people on a charitable and voluntary basis over which central government had no direct control.[34] This system had serious disadvantages. It led to variable and inconsistent standards in which planning for a *national* system of care was difficult. In addition, because doctors were self-employed, they tended to work in areas of relative affluence amongst relatively healthy patients who could afford to pay medical fees. As Nye Bevan, the architect of the NHS, remarked, the "best hospital facilities were available where they were least needed".[35] It was recognised by 1948, especially after the experience of the Second World War,[36] that the systematic planning of health care, the estimates of need for new investment in the NHS and the creation of long-term strategy, all require some central direction and control. With this need to create a well-organised and effective health care system, it is sometimes suggested that the

---

[31] e.g., see "Joint Recommendations on Prevention of Coronary Heart Disease in Clinical Practice" (2000) 320 *British Medical Journal* 705.

[32] See Ole Frithjof Norheim, "Clinical Guidelines: Healthcare Rationing and Accountability for Reasonableness" in J. Tingle and C. Foster (eds) *Clinical Guidelines: Law Policy and Practice* (Cavendish, 2002).

[33] D. Neuhauser and A. Lewicki, "What do we Gain from the Sixth Stool Guaiac?" (1975) 293 *New England Journal of Medicine* 226, discussed by R. Gillon, "Ethics, Economics and General Practice" in G. Mooney and A. McGuire (eds) *Medical Ethics and Economics in Health Care* (Oxford University Press, 1988) 127.

[34] See D. Green (ed.) *Before Beveridge—Welfare Before the Welfare State* (Institute of Economic Affairs, 1999).   [35] See HC Deb., vol. 422, col. 44–7, 30 April 1946.

[36] See, e.g., Consultative Council on Medical and Allied Services (The Dawson Report) (Cmnd. 692, 1920) and J. Mohan, *Planning, Markets and Hospitals* (Routledge, 2002) chs 3 and 4.

NHS was set up as a "command and control" model of management. For example, in launching its own reforms in 2000, the Labour government said: "The 1948 settlement assumed central accountability for the NHS. The sound of every bedpan was to reverberate around Whitehall, in Nye Bevan's immortal phrase [but] the NHS cannot be run from Whitehall."[37] To what extent, however, was the NHS ever run by Whitehall?

Despite the need for central authority over the NHS, a coherent "top-down" organisational model did not emerge from the nationalisation of health care in 1948 for a number of reasons. One was the laudable commitment of government to preserve clinical freedom. Thus, the White Paper of 1944 on which the system was based declared that "every man and woman and child can rely on getting all the advice and treatment and care which they need in matters of personal health"[38] and promoted the "[f]reedom for the doctor to pursue his professional methods in his own individual way, and not to be subject to outside clinical interference".[39] This was more than a rhetorical flourish. The undertaking was subsequently incorporated into the GP "contract" with health authorities and has become the basic ideology on which the NHS is based. The promise was repeated in 1991 in Prime Minister John Major's *Patient's Charter* which stated: "The [Conservative] Government believes that there must be no change to the fundamental principles on which the [NHS] was founded and on which it has continued ever since, namely that services should be available to every citizen on the basis of clinical need, regardless of ability to pay." And, as we have seen, following Labour's re-election for the first time since 1979, Tony Blair re-affirmed that the health service will be "based on need and need alone".[40] This culture of "professional perfectionism"[41] confers massive autonomy on individual clinicians and puts a severe obstacle before those who wish to influence clinical behaviour. Unsurprisingly, it also exerts considerable upward pressure on resources which politicians and managers find difficult to disturb.

Pressure on resources was compounded by another factor. The NHS gave rise to an institution of immense size, and brought together a vast range of skills and experience—clinical, managerial, and at various levels, political. Obviously, their interests were not always compatible; a decision to invest in one aspect of the NHS (say a hospital re-building programme, or neonatal care) inevitably diverts resources from others uses. Yet, other than the ideological commitment to providing care on the basis of need, the NHS had no central agenda, or system of prioritising its resources. In its absence this function tended to remain most heavily influenced by the medical profession whose major concerns were clinical, not financial.[42]

[37] *The NHS Plan* (Cm. 4818, vol. 1, 2000) para. 6.2.
[38] *A National Health Service* (Cmd. 6502, 1944) 5.   [39] ibid., 47.
[40] *The New NHS—Modern, Dependable*, 1997 (Cm. 3807, 1997) para. 1.5.
[41] R. Klein, *The New Politics of the NHS* (4th edn, 2002, Prentice Hall, Harlow) 28.
[42] ibid., 35–6. S. Harrison, *et al.*, *Just Managing: Power and Culture in the National Health Service* (1992); Bill New and Julian le Grand, *Rationing in the N.H.S.—Principles and Pragmatism* (1996).

A third reason for the relative lack of central authority may have been the surprisingly modest investment committed to health care by successive governments after 1946. In 1954, the Secretary of State for Health, Iain MacLeod, showed that "while capital expenditure on housing and education had increased dramatically (by 100 per cent and 43 per cent respectively between 1949–50 and 1952–3), expenditure on hospitals had actually fallen, by 2.3 per cent".[43] Capital expenditure on health "[was] viewed by the Treasury essentially as consumption, and not in any wider sense as an investment" upon which greater public wealth might be generated (such as education).[44] Until the 1990s, this parsimony reduced the opportunity to invest in the reform upon which central authority could be founded. It created a climate in which tight central control of costs was inevitable. "The paradox of the financial stringency was that [while] it led to tighter control over the total budgets available to health authorities, it also weakened the centre's ability to use incentives to persuade the periphery to follow national policies: the Ministry could neither command nor bribe."[45]

Although expenditure on the NHS increased during the 1960s and 1970s,[46] resources were never so plentiful, and systems never so sophisticated, as to change the balance of power between the centre and the periphery. Successive Secretaries of State wearied of the problems involved with NHS funding. Enoch Powell said in 1966: "One of the most striking features of the National Health Service is the continual, deafening chorus of complaint which rises day and night from every part of it, a chorus only interrupted when someone suggests that a different system altogether might be preferable, which would involve the money coming from some less (literally) palpable source."[47] Similarly, in 1969, Richard Crossman noted the capacity of the NHS to devour infinite resources.[48] Accordingly, the relationship between the centre and periphery has been described as a truce, based on mutual frustration:

> Implicit in the structure of the NHS was a bargain between the State and the medical profession. While central government controlled the budget, the doctors controlled what happened within the budget. Financial power was concentrated at the centre; clinical power was concentrated at the periphery. Politicians in the Cabinet made decisions about how much to spend; doctors made decisions about which patient should get what kind of treatment.[49]

Needless to say, as pressure on resources increased, the "truce" was not entirely satisfactory for any of the parties. For clinicians the price of non-interference was insufficient facilities to practice in the way they thought proper. Yet managers had

---

[43] Confidential memorandum to the Treasury, cited in J. Mohan, *Planning, Markets and Hospitals* (Routledge, 2002) 90.   [44] J. Mohan, note 43 above, at 94, citing Treasury papers.

[45] R. Klein, note 41 above, at 40.   [46] J. Mohan, note 43 above, at chs 6 and 7.

[47] J. Enoch Powell, *A New Look at Medicine and Politics* (Pitman Medical, 1966) 16.

[48] R. Crossman, *Paying for Social Services* (Fabian Society, 1969), discussed in R. Klein, above.

[49] R. Klein, note 41 above, at 64.

limited power to influence the allocation of resources between specialties. At the same time, money is wasted if there are insufficient managerial incentives to keep doctors up-to-date with clinical developments and to adopt a reasonably cost-effective practice. As the events surrounding the Bristol Royal Infirmary demonstrate, government is ultimately held responsible if undue deference for clinical autonomy robs the system of the capacity to monitor and compare clinical performance. Unsurprisingly, with these tensions institutionalised into the NHS, the 1970s saw a decade of "disillusionment" in the NHS, characterised by strike action by junior doctors, unfavourable comparisons with care provided elsewhere in Europe, the reorganisation of the system and the report of a Royal Commission on the NHS in 1979.[50]

The government's commitment to the preservation of clinical freedom, the failure to develop overriding clinical, managerial, or political objectives, and the absence of the financial means by which change might be rewarded, all impeded the "top-down" model of management. Indeed, the Department of Health never intended that it should exercise such an autocratic style of management. It did not have superior knowledge of local needs and, as we have seen, was committed in any case to the Hippocratic ethic of care on the basis of need. It had the power to award capped global budgets to health authorities and to issue numerous circulars to advise, encourage, and exhort. But the manner in which the resources were spent, and the response to advisory circulars remained largely within the discretion of senior doctors and local health authorities.

B. The Rise of "Managerialism" in the NHS

Almost as soon as it was elected in 1979, the new Conservative government announced its intention to overhaul the NHS. It was concerned first, with the relatively weak role played by management, and secondly, the failure to favour the most efficient hospitals by enabling them to treat larger numbers of patients. Before the 1980s, the role of managers was compared to that of "diplomats". Their function tended to be passive, to reconcile conflicts between competing demands (from doctors, nurses, patients, and managers themselves) and "to react to problems rather than to pursue objectives".[51] Managers exercised limited control because most of the activities of hospitals were determined centrally, or by senior clinicians acting in isolation. In addition, the absence of precise information on how and where money was spent in the service made the process of effecting change difficult. In place of the general manager was a system of "consensus management" of the NHS, in which the disparate interests—doctors, nurses, and managers—were

---

[50] ibid., ch. 4.

[51] See generally S. Harrison, D. Hunter, G. Marnoch and C. Pollitt, *Just Managing: Power and Culture in the National Health Service* (Macmillan, 1992) 26. This usefully considers much of the research conducted on the changing nature of the manager's role in the NHS.

expected to produce generally acceptable local policies.[52] During this time managers engaged in "problem-solving, organisation and maintenance and the facilitation of processes. [Managers accepted] the notion of 'clinical freedom', that . . . restrictions on the doctor-patient relationship should be minimal, or at most confined to control over aggregate resources".[53]

Such a system, even during the 1970s, was not without its critics. In 1979, the Royal Commission remarked that "there is a risk that consensus management may sap individual responsibility by allowing it to be shared: it is important that managers should not be prevented from managing the services for which they are responsible".[54] And there is always the danger that the agenda of consensus management is really driven by sectional interests—clinical, managerial, trade union, or pressure group—which could lose sight of patient need. Also, there was concern that there were too many decisions from central government which had too little local influence.[55] Pressure to reform the entire system developed during the 1980s and, at the invitation of the Prime Minister, Mrs Margaret Thatcher, a small group with a record of success in commerce was appointed to advise as to ways in which the NHS should be managed. Its recommendations were contained in the Griffiths Report which commented: "One of our most immediate observations from a business background is the lack of a clearly-defined management function throughout the NHS. By general management we mean the responsibility drawn together in one person, at different levels of the organisation, for planning, implementation and control of performance."[56] Accordingly, it recommended that specific targets should be set and regularly assessed against performance. It said:

The NHS does not have the profit motive, but it is, of course, enormously concerned with control of expenditure. Surprisingly, however, it still lacks any real continuous evaluation of its performance against criteria . . . Rarely are precise management objectives set; there is little measurement of health output; clinical evaluation of particular practices is by no means common and economic evaluation of those practices is extremely rare . . . Businessmen have a keen sense of how well they are looking after their customers. Whether the NHS is meeting the needs of the patient, and the community, and can prove that it is doing so, is open to question.[57]

---

[52] The idea of consensus management is described in P. Strong and J. Robinson, *The NHS Under New Management* (Open University Press, 1990) ch. 1.

[53] S. Harrison *et al.*, note 51 above, at 37. The same point is made by the Audit Commission in *Trusting in the Future: Towards an Audit Agenda for NHS Providers* (HMSO, 1994) para. 4.

[54] *Royal Commission on the National Health Service* (Cmnd. 7615, 1979) para. 20.15.

[55] ibid., para. 6.9.

[56] *NHS Management Inquiry* (The Griffiths Report, Department of Health and Social Security, 1983) 11. The contrary view is that "a system which substitutes line management for consensus is no way to run a multi-disciplinary service, which depends on cooperation at all levels, and whose problems call for analysis . . . rather than rules promulgated from general managers ignorant alike of economics and of health". See D. Black, *A Doctor Looks at Health Economics* (Office of Health Economics, 1994) 21.   [57] *NHS Management Inquiry*, note 56 above, at 10.

It also recommended a management structure for the NHS in which the creation of policy at national level would clearly be distinguished from the responsibility for its implementation and operation; and that, at each level of operation, managers should be set specific responsibilities and targets and be held accountable for them. The reform was described as follows:

> . . . the key division between general practice and the hospital sector was left untouched . . . What did change was their management. In each tier [was] installed a single leader, a general manager. The NHS as a whole was given a management board with a chief executive, every region now had a regional general manager, every district a DGM [district general manager], every unit a UGM [unit general manager]. There was, for the first time, a single line of command from the top to the bottom of the service.

> The general managers, as their titles suggested, managed everyone. Whereas the old district administrators simply chaired the meetings of the management team, each general manager was a real boss, in charge of the treasurers, the cleaners, the nurses, the doctors, the personnel department—the lot. Here, then, was a revolution . . . In short, it was general managers, not the clinical trades, who were now to decide . . . [58]

At an organisational level, the Griffiths Report had significant impact on NHS structures and is now reflected at every level of the NHS.[59] Inevitably, the result of this change of emphasis was to move organisational power toward managers. Many doctors resisted such a trespass into their clinical autonomy for being subversive of the Hippocratic ethic. At the same time, managers were unaccustomed to exercising authority in the manner recommended by Griffiths. At a *practical* level, therefore, the report did not have a significant effect on the balance of power in the NHS; "it lacked an engine to drive it".[60] As we shall see in Chapter 8, however, the engine was created by the events surrounding the Bristol Inquiry, which thoroughly destabilised the medical profession and gave government the opportunity to erect a new structure of governance around both clinicians and managers themselves.

C. Devolution and Markets in Health Care

Alongside the rise in the influence of managerial power in the NHS, has been the commitment to devolve power to local decision-makers, especially by means of markets in health care. The NHS has tried two experiments with markets. The "internal market" was introduced in 1991 and abandoned in 1998 by the Labour government when it created a second form of market under the policy of "shifting the balance of power" to local decision-makers and patients. Both depend on the devolution of power to local communities. We discuss each in turn.

---

[58] P. Strong and J. Robinson, note 52 above, at 23.
[59] The new structure was introduced without the need for legislation, within the broad framework established by the National Health Service Act 1977. See also, *Implementation of the NHS Management Enquiry Report*, HC(84)13 (Department of Health, 1984).
[60] R. Klein, note 41 above, at 129.

1. The NHS "Internal Market": 1990–97

In 1990 the government was concerned with a system of distributing financial resources according to the perceived "needs" of a resident population (according to its mortality and morbidity), without considering the efficiency of the hospitals responsible for providing treatment. This became known as the "efficiency trap". Those which reduced their unit costs and became most efficient were unable to admit more patients because they would exceed their financial allocation. Hospitals funded simply according to the requirements of their population's needs would not feel an incentive to manage their funds as effectively as those whose funding is performance related. Indeed, when there is no relationship between the amount of money allocated and the numbers of patients treated, the more efficient hospital appears to suffer a penalty. By treating more patients it spends its allocation more quickly and exhausts its funds before the end of the financial year. Alain Enthoven, whose writing influenced the eventual shape of the health service reforms, wrote of the NHS in 1984:

> The NHS runs on the ability and dedication of the many people who work in it . . . But other than the satisfaction of a job well done—which I do not wish to minimise—the system contains no serious incentives to guide the NHS in the direction of better quality care and service at reduced cost . . . In the non-competitive NHS, the manager who attempts to implement efficiency-improving changes is more likely to be seen as a cause of problems.

> In fact, the structure of the NHS contains perverse incentives. For example, a District that develops an excellent service in some specialty that attracts more referrals is likely to get more work without getting more resources to do it. A District that does a poor job will "export" patients and have less work, but not correspondingly less resources, for its reward . . . management and consultants in a District risk weakening the case for a new hospital wing they have been campaigning for by solving their waiting list problem by referring patients to other districts with excess capacity [and] GPs have weak or no incentives to reduce referrals. They have neither the incentives nor the resources to make extra efforts to keep people out of hospital.[61]

One solution to the efficiency trap was to enable efficient hospitals with spare capacity to offer their services to larger numbers of patients. Obviously, an incentive was required to enable such a hospital to fund the additional work undertaken and "the market" suggests that the money ought to come from those hospitals which, relatively speaking, work below full capacity. Those hospitals which can do most, at least cost and at highest quality, ought to receive larger sums of funding than those that cannot. This was the logic on which the "internal market" was based. It sought to enable purchasers of health care the freedom to choose between providers (the hospitals) who would, thus, be forced to compete with one another

---

[61] A. Enthoven, *Reflections on the Management of the National Health Service—An American looks at incentives to efficiency in health services management in the UK* (Nuffield Provincial Hospitals Trust, 1985) 13–15.

for price and quality and value for money. In the light of this report, during a television interview in 1987, the Prime Minister announced her intention to chair a working party to reconsider the funding of the NHS. The announcement coincided with the adverse publicity which surrounded a child with a heart defect who was refused intensive care facilities because of shortages of staff and other resources.[62] It came as a surprise because less than a week beforehand the Secretary of State for Social Services, John Moore, had delivered a major speech in the House of Commons on the future of the NHS which made no reference to such a review.[63]

Under the National Health Service and Community Care Act 1990 competition was introduced by separating purchasers (or commissioners), from providers of care. In England and Wales, health authorities, and GP fund-holders were primarily responsible for commissioning health care which was provided by NHS Trust hospitals. Momentum in the market was supplied by enabling GP fund-holders to compete for quality by having the discretion to use their funds in the ways they considered most appropriate for their patients. Similarly, NHS Trust hospitals were obliged to attract custom by providing a high quality, low cost service to patients. Contracts between commissioners and providers were negotiated at local level and, subject to national policy constraints, the assessment of health needs was to be dominated by local influences.

In the early days of the reforms, the commitment to open competition between providers of health care was largely unqualified.[64] The internal market for health was promoted by the slogan "money follows the patient", as if to imply that patients and their doctors would be able to choose when and where treatment would be given. But this was never an accurate description of the policy. "In fact, the new system was not internal, nor was it a market in more than a restricted sense . . . It was not so much a matter of the patient dictating where the money went, but the patient following whatever channel the professionals dictated."[65] Before long, therefore, there was a recognition that market principles had limitations. It was more accurate to think of the internal market for health as a "mixed economy", in which the tendencies of unrestricted competition will often be inappropriate and occasionally unlawful. Subsequently, therefore, the government conceded that regulation of the market was necessary to promote the aspirations of the NHS: "Without a regulatory framework the internal market in health services, like markets in other sectors, is likely to develop anti-competitive features, such as

---

[62] The case is that of *R v Central Birmingham Health Authority, ex parte Collier* (unreported, reproduced in part in I. Kennedy and A. Grubb, *Medical Law* (Butterworths, 2000) 340). The case is discussed in Ch. 5.

[63] See J. Butler, "Origins and Early Development" in R. Robinson and J. Le Grand (eds) *Evaluating the NHS Reforms* (King's Fund Institute, 1994) 16.

[64] See J. Butler, *Patients, Policies and Politics* (Open University Press, 1992).

[65] C. Webster, *The National Health Service—A Political History* (2nd edn, Oxford University Press, 2002) 202.

monopolies (of purchasers as well as providers), barriers to entry, poor information, inappropriate pricing, and collusion."[66]

The introduction of the internal market did not introduce dramatic changes to patterns of health authority purchasing from hospitals. One reason for this inertia is the absence of an equation which enables particular categories of health care, or patient, to be given priority. Rather, there is a "multiplicity of policy objectives in the NHS . . . there is no master formula or methodology which allows purchasers to prioritise between the many competing priorities—national, regional and local—which are crowding in on them".[67] A further reason for the failure of this version of the market is illustrated with the hindsight of the Bristol Inquiry. It was more concerned with quantity, or patient "throughput" and the cost of treatment, than with the quality of care provided and systems of governance. Although the government sought to enable purchasers to become more sensitive to issues of quality by means of NHS Comparative Performance Guides, the statistics were too crude to provide reliable evidence of quality. As one commentator said "there remains one basic blind spot . . . there is little or no information on the impact of health care services on the health of individual patients or the community at large. Indeed such is the design of hospital information systems that no real distinction is made between patients who leave hospital alive and those who die there".[68] Thus, there was insufficient information on which responsible purchasers could make informed decisions.

2. Shifting the Balance of Power: *Labour's market for health care*

The Labour government of 1997 promised a fresh overhaul of the system, stressing its commitment to a national health service, based on partnership, local responsibility, and public confidence. It said that although it would rid the system of "the divisive internal market system of the 1990s . . . not everything about the old system was bad".[69] Through the rhetoric of white papers and party politics, what balance was struck in the reforms that followed? First, the government retained the "purchaser-provider" split which had been the cornerstone of the 1990 reforms, but the language of the NHS changed, with emphasis on co-operation, rather than competition (a process which started with the previous Conservative government). NHS contracts became "service level agreements" and "purchasers" became "commissioners" of care with a duty to promote local health care objectives. To what

---

[66] *Managing the New NHS: Functions and Responsibilities in the New NHS* (NHS Executive, 1994) para. 10.3. See also *Changing the Internal Market* EL(97)33 (NHS Executive, 1997).

[67] S. Redmayne and R. Klein, *Sharing Out Resources: Purchasing and Priority Setting in the NHS* (National Association of Health Services and Trusts, 1993) 30.

[68] P. Kind, *Hospital Deaths—The Missing Link: Measuring Outcome in Hospital Activity Data* (Office of Health Economics, 1988) 1. See also J. Appleby and S. Boyle, "Finding the Facts" *Health Service Journal*, 3 February 1994, 24.

[69] *The NHS—Modern, Dependable* (Cm. 3807, 1997) paras 2.1 and 2.5. Influential on Labour's thinking was C. Ham, *Public, Private or Community—What Next for the NHS* (Demos, 1996).

extent, therefore, has the new, "middle" (or "third") way adjusted the balance of power as between central and local decision-makers?

Labour's promise to abandon the "divisive" internal market system is over-stated for a number of reasons. First, as Alain Enthoven himself said when he re-examined the effects of the NHS internal market in 1999, the market had never really been given a chance.[70] He argued that insufficient resources had been left to the discretion of health authorities, there was insufficient information on which to invest their funds, and government continued to apply too much pressure for a proper market to operate. The Labour government also took a wholly pragmatic view of the difficulties involved in raising capital to fund new hospitals. As a result, like its Conservative predecessor, it has abandoned the view that NHS services should be provided solely by *publicly* funded providers. "What counts is what works."[71] Accordingly, it has embraced the contribution available from the private sector in the form of the private finance initiative (PFI) (in which hospitals may be financed, designed, owned, and operated by private interests for NHS use), and the public-private concordat in which private staff and facilities are to be routinely accessible to NHS commissioners on the basis of value for money.[72] Thus, competition between hospitals will be as intense as before.

Secondly, patients will have the right to choose where they will be treated. A scheme that started for some treatments in 2003 will be extended to all patients from December 2005. All patients who have waited more than six months for elective surgery will be offered the choice of between four and five alternative providers. The referral will be made by the GP and may be to another hospital, treatment centre, GP with a specialist interest, private, or overseas hospital. Responsibility for entering into arrangements with alternative providers will fall to PCTs which will appoint "patient care advisors" to advise and assist patients in making a choice.[73] Clearly, provided hospitals earn revenue according to the numbers of patients they treat, they will need to be attractive to patients in order to stay in business. Note too that Foundation Trust hospitals have been created specifically to enhance competition of this nature between providers as an incentive to improve standards. To a much greater extent than before, money *will* follow the patient because patients will be encouraged to compare, for example, waiting times, the physical condition of the hospital, and clinical performance statistics in deciding where to go for treatment.

Thirdly, the system for remunerating hospitals is to be transformed so that hospitals are paid in a way that more accurately reflects the work they actually perform. Under the old system of NHS contracts, contract prices between hospitals varied and popular hospitals could inflate prices to reflect the demand for their

---

[70] Alain C. Enthoven, *In Pursuit of an Improved National Health Service* (The Nuffield Trusts, 1999).   [71] *The New NHS—Modern, Dependable* (Cm. 3807, 1997) ch. 2.
[72] Discussed in Ch. 9 below.
[73] *Patient Choice—Guidance for PCTs, NHS Trusts and SHAs on offering patients choice of where they are treated* (Department of Health, 2003).

service. Now, the system of bargaining over fees has been modified. In place of the system in which individual health authorities negotiated separate prices with each hospital (with its administrative and "transaction" costs), most hospital activity is to be sold to PCTs at a standardised rate, no matter where it is provided. This uniform pricing structure has been introduced follows the model of diagnostic related groups (DRGs) in the US.[74] In the NHS, the practice is referred to as health related groups (HRGs) in which diseases are categorised according to a standard price tariff based on the aggregate cost of treating a mix of patients in that category. The fundamental incentive in HRGs is that all hospitals will be paid for acute hospital care on a flat-rate, per-case basis, regardless of the length of time the patient spends in hospital.[75] The system will need to be very sensitive and complex. It will have to accommodate many disease-conditions (or health related groups) to make sufficient allowance for variations in patient circumstances and regional costs. In principle, however, efficient hospitals will generate savings from their efficiency and improve their facilities. Inefficient hospitals will have the incentive to become more efficient. "PCTs will have better information on the activity that providers are delivering for them and their patients. Providers should be more responsive to PCTs and patients as they will gain funding by being able to do more planned activity and risk losing funding if they do not deliver the services agreed."[76]

The uniform pricing system will extend to contracts agreed with private hospitals.[77] Of course, there is a danger that a "one-tariff fits all" will be insensitive to local conditions and put some hospitals at an unfair disadvantage by comparison to others.[78] Around 500 HRGs are planned. Given the huge variety of treatments patients may receive, this is likely to be insufficient to capture the real costs of treating individuals and the system will need to become more sensitive. There is also concern that this approach will put improper pressure on hospitals to discharge some patients prematurely because the hospital's revenue is fixed[79] (although PCT-purchasers will monitor the quality of care, for example, by recording re-admission

---

[74] See D. Frankford, "The Medicare DRGs: Efficiency and Organizational Rationality" (1993) 10 *Yale Journal on Regulation* 273.

[75] HRGs are concerned with acute care. The system will not apply to longer-term care such as psychiatric services where costs will continue to be agreed on a block, or case-by-case basis. For the same reason, allowance has to be made for "cost-outliers" whose poor condition justifies a stay in hospital far in excess of that contemplated by the tariff.

[76] *Reforming NHS Financial Flows—Introducing Payment by Results* (Department of Health, 2002) para. 3.2.

[77] See *The Government's Response to the House of Commons Health Committee's First Report on the Role of the Private Sector in the NHS* (Cm. 5567, 2002) 13.

[78] See K. Walshe, "Suspended Sentence" *Health Service Journal*, 11 March 2004, 16. Doubt as to the sensitivity of "national" rates to local conditions in the US is expressed by J. Lave, "Hospital Reimbursement Under Medicare" (1984) 62 *Millbank Memorial Fund Quarterly* 251.

[79] US evidence suggests that DRGs did not damage the quality of care provided to patients, see W.H. Rogers *et al.*, "Quality of Care Before and After Implementation of the DRG-based Prospective Payment System" (1990) 264 *Journal of the American Medical Association* 1989. The US is familiar with "DRG creep", in which patients are routinely assigned to higher cost DRGs in order to increase hospital revenue.

rates). HRGs will require hospital managers to exert far greater control over doctors whose practices impose costs which exceed the remuneration available in the tariff. Increasingly, the traditional notion of clinical freedom will be replaced with institutionally imposed clinical guidelines, protocols, and "care-pathways" in which there will be less room for manoeuvre.

III. Conclusion

Where should the balance of power lie in the management of NHS resources? We have seen how policy in the NHS has evolved since its inception. The command-economy model of management was never systematically imposed on the service, as a result of which government tended to suffer the blame for a failing service over which it had relatively little direct control. The Conservative's solution to the problem by means of an "internal" market has now been replaced with another by Labour which embraces "external" providers more openly. Indeed, one commentator has said "Labour has emerged as an exemplary convert to the ideal of public-private partnership [and] has hardly departed from the path of the New Public Management charted by the Conservatives."[80] Are markets the best way of maximising efficiency in the NHS? Or, is it mistaken to assume that a model of behaviour that works in the private sphere will be equally effective in public life? By their emphasis on competition and consumerism in which the success of some is won at the cost of others, do markets corrode the public interest in public services? When hospitals are at risk of going out of business if they cannot compete successfully, do markets require them to put their own interests before the interests of those they serve and undermine the public conscience and the trust that the public should have in the institution as a whole?

This latter view, which would have been natural in the nineteenth century, has not been influential recently. But the pendulum may yet swing back in its favour if the market becomes too aggressive, or destructive.[81] Perhaps "the public" themselves can become more influential in shaping the service and responding to the pressures it generates. Government policy is now promoting this policy (as we discuss in Chapter 8), but its success will depend on greater candour about the balance between central and local power, as well as the hard choices that have to be made between deserving cases. Note too, however, that health markets are not easily governed by "consumers" because patients do not buy health services and do not have sufficient information on which to make informed decisions. Any devolution of power of this nature has to be understood in the context of the new systems of governance which have proliferated throughout the NHS. What this

---

[80] C. Webster, note 65 above, at 251.
[81] See the persuasive case in its favour by D. Marquand, *The Decline of the Public* (Polity Press, Cambridge, 2004).

may mean in practice is that top-down management by the centre will be replaced with horizontal control by regulatory bodies, leaving little room for autonomy.[82] Clearly, micro-regulation presents its own risks. Rather than encouraging local initiative and diversity, it may breed feeble, unimaginative responses, always conscious of the need to hit targets and objectives, but indifferent to the needs of local people. Clearly, the debate about the proper locus of power in the NHS is far from over.

[82] *Foundation Trusts* (House of Commons Health Committee, Session 2002–03, HC 395–I), 19.

4

Organisation of the NHS

We have considered the problems and possible solutions associated with health resource allocation. In addition, we traced the evolution of NHS policy since 1948. Now, we examine in more detail the structure and organisation of the NHS today by means of (I) a general overview of the NHS, (II) the NHS at the macro-level, i.e. the Secretary of State and special health authorities, (III) the NHS at the meso-level, i.e. strategic health authorities, primary care trusts and care trusts, and (IV) the micro-level of NHS trust hospitals, GPs, and other primary care providers.

I. Overview of the NHS Today

Given the complexity of the structure of the NHS, it is helpful to have an overview of the modern system as a whole before looking in more depth at the particular bodies that operate within it. The NHS is organised principally under the National Health Service Act 1977. In this overview, we examine the provision of primary and secondary care in the NHS and the system of NHS management.

A. Primary and Secondary Care

The 1977 Act provides separate regimes of NHS regulation for primary and secondary care. Primary care (the care provided at the first point of contact with the NHS) is supervised by primary care trusts, largely through general practitioners and other clinicians (especially dentists, nurses, and pharmacists). Regulations set down the rights and obligations between providers, PCTs and patients. This system is provided under "Part 2" of the 1977 Act. Significantly, as explained below, the duty to prescribe in primary care is not cash-limited because it is based on whether care is "needed".

By contrast, secondary care and NHS community care ("hospital and community health services") are governed by Part 1 of the 1977 Act. These services are usually provided by NHS trust hospitals and Foundation trust hospitals. This distinction between Part 1 and Part 2 is important. On the one hand, it makes it difficult for PCTs to exercise resource-constraint over the prescribing decisions of responsible GPs. On the other, because the PCT is awarded a fixed annual budget, any unplanned expansion of GP expenditure under Part 2 of the Act will necessarily be at the expense of hospital expenditure under Part 1. The purchase of additional hospital facilities may have to be deferred, or the appointment of new clinical staff postponed. For this reason, primary care occupies a sensitive position in the structure of the NHS. As a response to this pressure PCTs (like doctors) are subject to incentives to control primary care expenditure. PCTs may be set targets and objectives including the trusts' Part 2 expenditure.[1] In this way, overall allocations to PCTs will be increased if they meet their targets. Similar incentives to improve performance in NHS trust hospitals have been created by use of the "star-rating" system, in which additional funds and freedoms are accorded to hospitals with three star ratings (discussed below).

One further comment about the primary/secondary care distinction is needed. Since 1997 both the previous Conservative governments and the Labour governments have been committed themselves to enhancing the power and influence of primary care. To some extent this policy of "shifting the balance of power"[2] into primary care is achieved by giving primary care trusts greater control over the allocation of local resources. Equally significant, however, is the policy of encouraging primary care clinicians—GPs, pharmacists, nurses, and allied professionals—to become "special interest practitioners". In this way, some of the specialist care previously undertaken in hospital can be performed by GPs.[3] And correspondingly, care previously restricted to GPs, may now be provided by other clinicians. For example, nurses and pharmacists may qualify as "supplementary prescribers" with discretion to prescribe and manage patients' medicines on the basis of a "clinical management plan" agreed by the patient.[4] Of course, these new rights also carry new legal responsibilities and many of the complaints in medical negligence previously directed at doctors (discussed in Chapter 6) will inevitably be made against other clinicians too. Never the less, with the skills available to other clinicians, together with the need to provide a fast and efficient health service, it is natural to encourage other professionals to play a less subservient role in the provision of patient care. With these changes, the traditional role of clinicians in primary and secondary care will become more flexible and the old distinction between the two, more difficult to draw.

B. Management of the NHS

The NHS has been in a state of "continuous revolution"[5] since 1980. Fund-holding GPs have come and gone. The internal market has come, gone and returned again under a different cloak. Personal Medical Services and the Private Finance

---

[1]   Under National Health Service Act 1977, s. 97C, substituted by National Health Service Reform and Health Care Professions Act 2002, s. 8.

[2]   *Shifting the Balance of Power within the NHS—Securing Delivery* (Department of Health, 2002).

[3]   *Practitioners with Special Interests* (NHS Modernisation Agency, 2003).

[4]   *Supplementary Prescribing by Nurses and Pharmacists within the NHS in England* (Department of Health, 2003) and the Prescription Only (Human Use) Amendment Order 2003 (SI 2003 No. 696).

[5]   C. Webster, *The National Health Service—A Political History* (Oxford University Press, 2002) ch. 3.

Initiative are becoming established. District Health Authorities and Family Health Service Authorities were replaced by Health Authorities, which have themselves been replaced by Primary Care Trusts. Since 1982, there has been some form of organisational upheaval almost every year.[6] The House of Commons Health Committee is "seriously concerned that the perpetual flux to which the NHS is subject does not permit the climate of stability vitally needed in order to allow clinicians and managers to concentrate on improving care for patients".[7] Others suggest that this state of perpetual revolution is no more than a smoke-screen to divert attention from the real challenges facing the NHS. Contemporary rhetoric about public accountability and consumer involvement

is not matched by any real commitment to provide the missing evidence about cost-effectiveness on which any well-informed involvement would depend. But since something has to be seen to being done, what better responses could there be than institutional reform? It is dramatic, gets widely reported, [and] it distracts everyone from thinking about the fundamental problems . . . And since it takes some time to shake down again, it takes some time for people to realize that they still have to confront the problem of priority setting, for which they still do not have clarity of objectives, nor data on costs and outcomes, nor appropriate performance measures. But by then the politicians have changed and the new ones are dreaming up some new organizational reform to help keep the system in a permanent muddle.[8]

"Muddle" is exacerbated by another factor. The laws governing the NHS have not been consolidated since 1977. New and "amendment" NHS Acts have deleted, inserted, amended, and substituted chunks of the 1977 Act, and, indeed, almost every Act that has followed it. Statutes and regulations are often amended within months of coming into force. Yet successive governments have declined to introduce a consolidating act in which all the changes are contained in one piece of legislation. Consequently, those wishing to understand the various rights and obligations arising within the NHS must have access to dozens of subsequent acts of Parliament, a large pair of scissors, and a great deal of time to delete and replace parts of the 1977 Act with the subsequent changes. Indeed, by the time the enterprise was complete, further deletions and substitutions would be required by the passage of further reforms. For practical purposes, therefore, other than via on-line data retrieval services paid for by large subscriptions, the rights and duties which arise in connection with the NHS today are simply inaccessible. In an area of such sensitivity, which occupies such a high political profile, this is a very poor reflection on any government committed to an open and transparent system of regulation.

---

[6] K. Walshe, "Foundation Hospitals—a New Direction for NHS Reform?" (2003) 96 *Journal of the Royal Society of Medicine* 106.

[7] *Foundation Trusts, Second Report of Session 2002–03* (HC 395–I, 2003) para. 170.

[8] R. Klein and A. Williams, "Setting Priorities: what is holding us back—inadequate information, or inadequate institutions?" in A. Coulter and C. Ham (eds) *The Global Challenge of Health Care Rationing* (Open University Press, 2000) 20 (the view is that of Williams). See also M. Warner, *Re-designing health services; reducing the zone of delusion* (Nuffield Trusts, 1997).

Given the pace of change in this area, government should pass consolidating legislation every (say) five years to illuminate properly the rights and duties which arise within the NHS.

Within this unstable and impenetrable environment, various statutory duties are imposed upon the Secretary of State under the National Health Service Act 1977, notably, that he should "promote a comprehensive health service". These duties are not performed by him personally. His *national* responsibilities are delegated to "special health authorities" which may be created by the Secretary of State "for the purpose of exercising any functions which may be conferred on them by or under this Act".[9] A large number of such bodies have been created with national responsibilities, for example, the Mental Health Act Commission, the National Blood Authority, the National Clinical Assessment Authority, the National Institute for Clinical Excellence, the National Patient Safety Agency, the NHS Litigation Authority, the Retained Organs Commission, and UK Transplant.

By contrast, his *local* functions are performed by middle-tier health authorities (PCTs) by regulations or directions. The Secretary of State is under a duty to fund PCTs to enable them to perform the statutory duties on his behalf. Their most important function is to purchase or "commission" care for patients within their annual financial allocations. Management of these local functions is assisted by the National Health Service Executive and strategic health authorities (StHAs). StHAs are positioned between the Secretary of State and PCTs and act as performance managers of local PCTs. In addition, in the wake of the deaths of children at the Bristol Royal Infirmary, a raft of additional regulatory bodies have been created to monitor and supervise the performance of the NHS.

With this general overview in mind, we now consider the duties and responsibilities of the various institutions of the NHS, namely, at the macro-level (of the Secretary of State and special health authorities), the meso-level (of strategic health authorities, primary care trusts and care trusts) and at the micro-level (of NHS trust hospitals and GPs).

II. Macro-structure—Secretary of State

A number of general statutory duties are imposed on the Secretary of State, the most broad-ranging of which is contained in sections 1 and 3 of the National Health Service Act 1977 (which are amongst a few provisions to have remained largely unchanged since the National Health Service Act 1946). Section 1 provides:

> (1) It is the Secretary of State's duty to continue the promotion in England and Wales of a comprehensive health service designed to secure improvement (a) in the physical and mental health of the people of those countries, and (b) in the prevention, diagnosis and treatment of illness, and for that purpose to provide or secure the effective provision of services in accordance with this Act.

[9] National Health Service Act 1977, s. 11.

(2) The services so provided shall be free of charge except in so far as the making and recovery of charges is expressly provided for by or under any enactment, whenever passed.[10]

In addition, section 3 provides that "it is the Secretary of State's duty to provide . . . to such extent as he considers necessary to meet all reasonable requirements":

(a) hospital accommodation;

(b) other accommodation for the purpose of any service specified under this Act;

(c) medical, dental, nursing and ambulance services;

(d) such other facilities for the care of expectant and nursing mothers and young children as he considers are appropriate as part of the health service;

(e) such facilities for the prevention of illness, the care of persons suffering from illness and the after-care of persons who have suffered from illness as he considers appropriate as part of the health service; [and]

(f) such other services as are required for the diagnosis and treatment of illness.

How are these duties reflected in the structure of the NHS?

A. A Comprehensive Health Service

What is a "comprehensive health service"? Clearly, these duties confer considerable discretion upon the Secretary of State. This duty was included in the National Health Service Act 1946 and was discussed in the White Paper of 1944 entitled *A National Health Service*, on which it was based. Discussing the meaning and scope of a "comprehensive" service, it said:

The proposed service must be "comprehensive" in two senses—first, that it is available to all people and, second, that it covers all necessary forms of health care . . . The service designed to achieve it must cover the whole field of medical advice and attention, at home, in the consulting room, in the hospital or the sanatorium, or wherever else is appropriate—from the personal or family doctor to the specialists and consultants of all kinds, from the care of minor ailments to the care of major diseases and disabilities. It must include ancillary services of nursing, of midwifery and of the other things which ought to go with medical care. It must ensure that everyone can be sure of a general medical advisor to consult as and when the need arises, and then that everyone can get access—beyond the general medical advisor—to more specialised branches of medicine or surgery.[11]

---

[10] Prescription charges are subject to many exemptions; only 20% of those who need a prescription have to pay a charge. One Secretary of State said that the charge is levied, not to defray the cost of the medicine, but as "a contribution to the NHS". See the reply of Mr B. Mawhinney, the Minister for Health, to the House of Commons Health Committee, *Priority Setting in the NHS: The NHS Drug Budget* (HC 80-vii, Session 1993–94) para. 878. For some patients on long-term medication, the costs may be significant. A more equitable system is proposed in *A Fairer Prescription for Charges* (Social Market Foundation, 2003), suggesting that all medicines vital for life and for chronic conditions be provided free, but that others are subject to bands of charges depending on how essential, or non-essential the medicine is. However, where to "band" medicines would be very controversial.

[11] *A National Health Service* (Cmd. 6502, 1944) 9.

The NHS's original intention was "to bring the country's full resources to bear upon *reducing ill-health* and promoting good health in all its citizens"[12] so that investment in the NHS would stabilise as the level of public health improved. We soon recognised, however, that this ambition was unachievable because "demand for health care is always likely to outstrip supply . . . the capacity of health services to absorb resources is almost unlimited".[13] Accordingly, as we discuss in the next chapter, the duty has been interpreted by the courts in a way that gives the Secretary of State broad discretion as to the nature and quantity of the services provided within the NHS. As a result, procedures and mechanisms have been developed to regulate the demands that can be made of it.

The Secretary of State is also under a to duty to pay to each StHA "sums not exceeding the amount allotted [to it] by the Secretary of State",[14] and to pay to each PCT sums equivalent to their general "Part 2" expenditure, and sums not exceeding the amount allotted to it toward meeting its "main" (or Part 1) expenditure in that year.[15] Until recently, the distribution of NHS resources to health authorities was calculated with reference to a weighted capitation formula[16] which assessed health needs according to:

(1) the projected size of the population concerned;

(2) the numbers of elderly people in the population;

(3) the health needs of the population, distinguishing between general, acute and psychiatric care, and morbidity and mortality ratios; and

(4) an allowance for local market forces with respect to the cost of labour and the higher costs of the Thames regions.

Now, however, an element of "performance funding" has been included in the resource allocation mechanism so that additional sums may be allocated dependent on the completion of projects and objectives, some of which are tied to the achievement of targets. Thus:

Where the Secretary of State has made an initial determination of the amount ("the initial amount") to be allotted for any year to a Primary Care Trust . . . he may increase the initial amount by a further sum if it appears to him that over a period notified to the Trust (a) it satisfied any objectives notified to it as objectives to be met in performing its functions; or (b) it performed well against any criteria notified to it as criteria relevant to the satisfactory performance of its functions (whether or not the method of measuring its performance against those criteria was also notified to it).[17]

---

[12] *A National Health Service* (Cmd. 6502, 1944) at 5, author's emphasis.

[13] *Royal Commission on the National Health Service* (Cmnd. 7615, 1979) para. 2.9.

[14] National Health Service Act 1977, s. 97(A1), amended by National Health Service Reform and Health Care Professions Act 2002, s. 7.

[15] National Health Service Act 1977, s. 97C(1) substituted by National Health Service Reform and Health Care Professions Act 2002, s. 8.

[16] See *Hospital and Community Health Services Resource Allocation: Weighted Capitation Formula* (NHS Executive, 1994).

[17] National Health Service Act 1977, s. 97C(3) inserted by National Health Service Reform and Health Care Professions Act 2002, s. 8. And the sum may be reduced again subsequently by an amount not exceeding "the initial amount", see s. 97C(6).

In this way, hospitals and trusts may be awarded "star ratings" on which additional resources may depend. Over the past decade, NHS hospitals have been required to keep performance data. Present arrangements assess hospitals against a limited number of key targets and indicators, the most important of which include the number of patients waiting more than eighteen months for in-patient treatment, the number of patients waiting more than twenty-six weeks for outpatient treatment, the numbers waiting on trolleys for more than twelve hours, whether less than 1 per cent of operations have been cancelled, whether patients with suspected cancer have waited more than two weeks to be seen in hospital, hospital cleanliness and a satisfactory financial position.[18] "Where a Trust has a low rating based on poor performance on a number of key targets and indicators, this does not necessarily mean that a hospital is unsafe, does not contain some very good clinical services or that the staff are not working hard in often difficult circumstances. It does mean that performance must be improved in a number of key areas."[19] By contrast, three star trusts will be given greater autonomy, less regular monitoring and an additional capital allocation of up to £1 million to support service development. NHS bodies with zero rating will be required to develop immediate recovery plans.

Hospitals and health authorities complain that they have insufficient funds to achieve that which government requires of them—that many of the targets and objectives are unachievable within the resources available. Never the less, the circumstances in which the resource allocation formula could be successfully challenged are limited. An analogous issue arose concerning expenditure guidance issued by the Secretary of State for the Environment to local authorities, which was challenged for being so unreasonable that no reasonable person addressing himself to the issue in question could have come to such a decision (known as "*Wednesbury* unreasonableness"). Lord Scarman described the reluctance of the courts to become embroiled in the politics of resource allocation as follows:

We are in the field of public financial administration and we are being asked to review the exercise by the Secretary of State of an administrative discretion which inevitably requires political judgment on his part . . . I cannot accept that it is constitutionally appropriate, save in very exceptional circumstances, for the courts to intervene on the ground of "unreasonableness" to quash guidance framed by the Secretary of State and by necessary implication approved by the House of Commons, the guidance being concerned with the limits of public expenditure by local authorities and the incidence of the tax burden as between taxpayers and ratepayers . . . these are matters of political judgment for him and for the House of Commons. They are not matters for the judges . . . I refuse in this case to examine the detail of the guidance or its consequences.[20]

---

[18] See *NHS Performance Ratings—Acute Trusts, Specialists Trusts, Ambulance Trusts, Mental Health Trusts 2001/02.* www.doh.gov.uk/performanceratings/2002/national.html.   [19] ibid.
[20] *R v Secretary of State for the Environment, ex p Nottinghamshire CC* [1986] AC 240, at 247. And see the consideration of the case in *R v Secretary of State for the Environment, ex p Hammersmith and Fulham LBC* [1991] 1 AC 521.

On the other hand, the Audit Commission has suggested that the performance rating system is capable of distorting clinical data. Some three star trusts were judged by auditors to be performing poorly and as having management shortcomings, while others rated weak under the star system performed well.[21] As one pressure group observed "under the star rating system, the University Hospital Birmingham NHS Trust is one of the best performing acute trusts. It meets eight out of nine key Government targets . . . It also has some of the highest readmission rates and the worst record for MRSA [methicillinin-resistant *staphylococus aureus*] infections in the country."[22] There is also a concern that star-ratings may be over-sensitive to small fluctuations in performance so that the same hospital may have widely different assessments in successive years.[23] An incentive system which systematically rewarded trusts which were performing poorly and penalised success because it failed to measure meaningful criteria would be amenable to "exceptional" challenge by way of judicial review for unreasonableness.[24]

B. To Whom is the Duty Owed?

The duty to promote a comprehensive health service is owed to the people of England and Wales who are "ordinarily resident" in Great Britain, their spouse and children.[25] What is the position of overseas visitors to the UK? An overseas visitor is "a person not ordinarily resident in the United Kingdom".[26] Regulations provide that, subject to specified exemptions, when an authority provides an overseas visitor with NHS services "that Authority . . . shall make and recover from the person liable . . . charges for the provision of those services".[27] This responsibility to recover the costs of the care provided is expressed as a duty, rather than a discretion

---

[21] *Achieving the NHS Plan* (Audit Commission, 2003) para. 42.

[22] Quoted in *Foundation Trusts* (House of Commons Health Committee, Second Report of 2002–03, vol. I, HC 395–I), para. 86. The Committee also commented on the volatility of the system: "the majority of trusts had different star ratings in 2001–02 and 2002–03" (ibid., para. 87). For similar misgivings, see *Performance Indicators, The Good, The Bad, and the Ugly* (Royal Statistical Society, 2003), saying that the star rating system is often misleading, is treated with suspicion and tends to demoralise and antagonise NHS staff.

[23] See "Black Hole of Despair Swallows up the Stars that Fell to Earth" *Health Service Journal*, 5 August 2004, 10

[24] See K. Rowan, D. Harrison and N. Black, "Hospitals' Star Ratings and Clinical Outcomes" (2004) 328 *British Medical Journal* 924, 925: "star ratings do not reflect the quality of clinical care provided by hospitals. Patients do just as well in a trust with no stars as they do in one with three stars."

[25] National Health Service Act 1977, s. 121, as amended by the Health and Medicines Act 1988, s. 7.

[26] National Health Service (Charges to Overseas Visitors) Regulations 1989 (SI 1989 No. 306), as amended, reg. 1(2). The phrase ordinarily resident "refers to a man's abode in a particular place or country he has adopted voluntarily and for settled purposes as a part of the regular order of his life for the time being, whether of short or long duration". See *Shah v Barnet LBC* [1983] 1 All ER 226, 235 *per* Lord Scarman.

[27] National Health Service (Charges to Overseas Visitors) Regulations 1989 (SI 1989 No. 306), as amended, reg. 2(1) as amended by the National Health Service (Charges to Overseas Visitors) (Amendment) Regulations 2004 (SI 2004 No. 614).

and payment may be required before treatment is given, or continued. Thus, in a case involving an overseas visitor suffering renal failure who needed kidney dialysis, a hospital refused to continue with the treatment without firm guarantees that it would be paid for the costs it incurred. Upholding the hospital's *duty* to do so, the court said:

... services are made available to overseas visitors as a commercial operation, not as a humanitarian gesture . . . however acute the condition or deserving the patient, the trust has no discretion to waive the obligation to pay . . . when Parliament imposed on the trust the express obligation to recover charges, it must be taken to have given the trust the ordinary means to discharge that obligation, including the right to require payment in advance or an acceptable guarantee of payment . . .[28]

However, the duty is subject to exemptions. First, a number of specified *services* are exempted from charge, for example, accident and emergency care, treatment for notifiable diseases, sexually transmitted diseases, and treatment under the Mental Health Act 1983.[29] Also, categories of overseas visitors are exempted, for example, persons who are working here (for however short a period); persons who have been ordinarily resident in the UK for not less than one year before treatment (even if they originally arrived for the purpose of medical treatment); those applying for, or who have, refugee status; those detained in prison under the Prison Act 1952; or those whose services are provided under reciprocal arrangements between the UK and an overseas country. The exemptions also extend to the person's spouse and children.[30]

Patients treated as overseas visitors are not to be confused with private patients. The responsible doctor may not charge a fee for treatment unless the patient wishes to be treated under a private contract (say a contract of insurance). Those treated as overseas visitors may be asked to sign an undertaking to pay and should be treated with the same urgency and priority as NHS patients. Guidance suggests that if clinical attention is required without delay, then treatment must always take priority over enquiries into the patient's ability to pay NHS charges. The sum charged is subject to local discretion and should be assessed on a suitable commercial basis. Where prior payment is not possible, but the patient requires immediate treatment it is suggested that "the NHS hospital should provide such treatment as is clinically required to stabilise the patient sufficiently to allow them to return safely to their country of residence for continuing care".[31] However, a difficult question arises as to what is to become of those with life-threatening conditions who have no overseas insurance cover, or who come from countries with health care systems that cannot respond to their needs.

The matter was considered by the European Court of Human Rights in *D v United Kingdom*,[32] in which the applicant had obtained a visitor's visa but was

---

[28] *R v Hammersmith Hospitals NHS Trust, ex p Reffell* (2000) 55 BMLR 130, 135.
[29] National Health Service (Charges to Overseas Visitors) Regulations 1989, SI 1989 No. 306, as amended, reg. 3. [30] ibid., reg. 4.
[31] See *NHSiS Manual of Guidance: Overseas Visitors* (The Scottish Office) ch. 3, para. 8.
[32] (1998) 42 EHRR 149.

detained on arrival in England on suspicion of smuggling drugs. He was convicted to a term of imprisonment. During that time, he was discovered to be suffering from AIDS and was treated, in accordance with the regulations, as an NHS patient. On the completion of his sentence, the Secretary of State ordered his deportation from the UK, but the applicant resisted under the provisions of Article 3 of the Convention. His country of residence was St Kitts in the West Indies which could not continue to provide him with the care that he needed. In finding for the applicant, the Court confirmed that, as a general rule, nation states had no obligation to provide care for "aliens" who had no right to receive it under domestic law. Never the less, in the extreme circumstances of this case, in which care had commenced with the UK, it would have been inhuman and degrading to return a man in the terminal stages of an illness to a country which had no facilities to provide adequate medical and palliative care.[33] Was it crucial that treatment for the illness had commenced within the UK when the applicant was an NHS patient? If not, will it apply, for example, to applicants for asylum whose claims have been rejected and illegal immigrants pending their deportation? The full extent of its impact remains to be assessed.

In any event, the government intends to reform the regulations on overseas visitors who receive NHS care. It considers the system currently operates in a way that is inconsistent and, in any case, is being used in a way that was never contemplated when the original regulations were enacted in 1989.[34] Certainly, it is odd that UK residents who move to another country should immediately lose entitlements to NHS care because they are no longer "ordinarily resident",[35] whilst business visitors to the UK and their immediate family become fully entitled to it no matter how short their visit.

III. Meso-structure—Managing the NHS

Within this macro-structure, what are the mechanisms for distributing health service resources to doctors and patients? We consider: (A) the delegation of the Secretary of State's duties, (B) strategic health authorities, and (C) primary care trusts.

A. Delegation of Secretary of State's Duties

Performance of the duties imposed upon the Secretary of State under the National Health Service Act 1977 is delegated to special health authorities (SHAs),

---

[33] Reg. 6A of the 2004 (Amendment) Regulations (above) now confers discretion on the Secretary of State to provide NHS treatment without regard for "humanitarian reasons".

[34] Proposed *Amendment to the National Health Services (Charges to Overseas Visitors) Regulations 1989—A Consultation* (Department of Health, 2003).

[35] Although they retain their NHS rights if they live in the UK for at least six months of the year, see reg. 4A of the 2004 (Amendment) Regulations, above.

strategic health authorities (StHAs), and primary care trusts (PCTs) by statutory regulations[36] and directions.[37] This raises the question: how much real authority does the Secretary of State retain over the NHS? Internal regulation of the health service is commonly achieved by means of health service circulars, and various other statements of policy from the Department of Health. Regulations clearly have statutory effect,[38] but what is the distinction between "directions" and Departmental "circulars"?

Under section 17 of the National Health Service Act 1977 the Secretary of State may give directions to health authorities, SHAs, PCTs, and NHS Trusts, and "[a]ny person or body to whom directions are given in pursuance of any provision of this Act or Part 1 of the National Health Service and Community Care Act 1990 shall comply with the directions".[39] Directions relating to the allocation of monies have to be clear and precise but "they do not have to be given in any particular form. It must be made clear that funds have to be used in a particular manner. There is no magic form of words that is required and I do not think that the use of the word 'direct' is necessary in order to constitute a 'direction'".[40]

In appearance, directions may resemble a formal statutory regulation, set out in numbered paragraphs. Alternatively, an NHS circular may have the status of a direction. The distinction between directions and circulars was considered in *R v North Derbyshire HA, ex parte Fisher*[41] with respect to the circular *New Drugs for Multiple Sclerosis* EL(95)97 which recommended that the drug beta interferon be considered for sufferers of multiple sclerosis. The question arose as to whether the circular had the status of a direction and, therefore, placed a duty on the health authority to provide the treatment. The circular included the following statements:

7. Key aims . . . are to: target the drug appropriately at patients who are most likely to benefit from treatment . . .

9. Purchasing authorities and providers are asked . . . to develop and implement a prescribing approach for Beta Interferon through hospitals . . .

---

[36] National Health Service (Functions of Strategic Health Authorities and Primary Care Trusts and Administration Arrangements)(England) Regulations 2002 (SI 2002 No. 2375).

[37] National Health Service Act 1977, ss. 16D–18 (inserted by Health Act 1999, s. 12, as amended by National Health Service Reform and Health Care Professions Act, Sched. 1) and Primary Care Trusts (Functions) Directions 2000.

[38] Note that any such delegation must remain within the statutory framework which surrounds the NHS. In reviewing this matter, the court must "begin by examining the nature of the statutory power which the administrative authority . . . has purported to exercise and asking, in the light of that examination, what were, and were not, relevant considerations for the authority to take into account in deciding to exercise its power". *Per* Lord Bridge in *Gillick v West Norfolk and Wisbech AHA* [1985] 3 All ER 402, 426. The question may be far from straightforward, as the disagreement between the Court of Appeal and House of Lords in *Gillick* demonstrates.

[39] National Health Service Act 1977, s. 126(3C) (inserted by Health Act 1999 s. 65 and Sched. 4, para. 37(5)).

[40] *R v Secretary of State for Health, ex p Manchester LMC* 25 BMLR 77, 89, *per* Collins J.

[41] (1998) 8 BMLR 327. See also *R v Secretary of State for Health, ex p Manchester LMC* 25 BMLR 77, 89, *per* Collins J.

10. . . . providers are asked to give sympathetic consideration to such GP referrals, taking into account local priorities.[42]

Dyson J considered the distinction between directions and circulars as follows. He said:

The difference between a policy which provides mere guidance and one in which the health authority is obliged to implement is crucial. Policy which is in the form of guidance can be expressed in strong terms and yet fall short of amounting to direction. There is no reference in the circular to the word "directions" and read as a whole there is no indication that the circular is intended to trigger the statutory duty of compliance to be found in section [17] of the 1977 Act. The circular includes words such as "asks", "suggested", "taking into account", it does not include the word "shall" or any of the other badges of mandatory requirement . . . If the circular provided no more than guidance, albeit in strong terms, then the only duty placed upon the health authority was to take it into account in the discharge of their functions. That would be susceptible to challenge only on *Wednesbury* principles if they failed to consider the circular, or they misconstrued or misapplied it whether deliberately or negligently.[43]

Thus, his Lordship rejected the claim that the circular mandated any action on behalf of the health authority. On the other hand, different considerations arise if the Secretary of State "directs" NHS bodies that funds are to be used for *particular* purposes. In this case, if they are applied for different purposes, they will be used contrary to the directions and unlawfully. For example, funds paid to a health authority for the specific purpose of reimbursing GPs for the costs of staff, rent, and premises improvements could not be diverted to other general medical services uses. As the court put it:

. . . it has been made as clear as it could be that these funds which have been allocated for the purpose of reimbursement of the practice costs, the rents and the improvement grants are to be used for those and for no other purposes . . . there was here a direction and that money could not as a matter of law, be used in the way that it was used. Accordingly, as it seems to me, that use was unlawful.[44]

This makes an important legal distinction, but it may sometimes be imperceptible to NHS managers. Guidelines and circulars confer legal *discretion* on local decision-makers, but they may also be accompanied by political imperatives that effectively compel managers to adhere to them, irrespective of their local views. In practice, the telephone call from the senior official in the Department of Health makes them mandatory. We should note, however, that decisions made on the basis of such pressure are amenable to judicial review. As we discuss in the next chapter, decision-makers are required to understand the legal powers available to them and

[42] (1998) 8 BMLR 330 (col. 2)–331 (col. 2).
[43] ibid., 331 (col. 2). However, the applicant succeeded on an alternative ground, namely that the authority had failed to give proper consideration to the circular or government policy in relation to the circular. See the discussion in Ch. 5 below.
[44] *R v Secretary of State for Health, ex p Manchester LMC* (1995) 25 BMLR 77, 89, *per* Collins J.

to implement them properly. Were they to consider themselves bound by a policy that was merely discretionary, they could be said to have acted *illegally*, or *irrationally* for misconstruing their powers and failing to consider the whole range of options available to them. No such case has ever been brought, but as decision-making becomes more transparent, local managers should be aware of the distinction between NHS "guidance" and "directions".

Now we discuss the bodies to whom the Secretary of State's duties are delegated.

B. Strategic Health Authorities

In England, the NHS reorganisation of 2002 created about 30 strategic health authorities (StHAs) to replace around 100 "health authorities". (In Wales the functions are performed by local health boards. Equivalent functions are performed by health boards in Scotland.)[45] They are accountable to the Secretary of State, will agree performance targets with the Department of Health, and monitor and guide PCTs and NHS Trusts. In doing so, they should create a strategy for improving quality through clinical governance and support mechanisms for involving patients, the public, and other interested parties in developing and implementing plans. They will also monitor the extent to which PCTs and NHS Trusts comply with the recommendations and guidance of the Commission for Health Audit and Inspection, the National Clinical Assessment Authority, and other statutory authorities.[46] At the same time, however, following the deaths of children in the Bristol Royal Infirmary, government has been keen to establish a large number of other regulatory and supervisory bodies to set standards, monitor, supervise, and hold accountable local decision-makers in matters of clinical and corporate governance. In reality, therefore, the phrase "shifting the balance of power" is misleading. The balance of power has shifted to intermediate regulators. Some say there is a danger that so much regulation and control will generate passive, unimaginative, entirely reactive, and defensive management styles more concerned to achieve a handful of pre-selected targets than to improve standards generally in the local health community.[47]

C. Primary Care Trusts

The duty each PCT is "to the extent that it considers necessary to meet all reasonable requirements, exercise its powers so as to provide primary medical services within

[45] National Health Service Act 1977, s. 8, substituted by National Health Service Reform and Health Care Professions Act 2002, s. 8. For Scotland, see the National Health Service (Scotland) Act 1978, as amended.

[46] See generally, *Shifting the Balance of Power within the NHS—Securing Delivery* (Department of Health, 2002) para. 26–35 and Annex A.

[47] See D. Hunter, *Things Can Only Get Better—A Commentary on Implementing the NHS Plan* (Durham Business School, 2001).

its area, or secure their provision within its area".[48] Over 300 PCTs have been created to act as the "purchasers" or "commissioners" of medical, dental, pharmaceutical, and optical NHS care for their local communities. They must assess their local health needs and develop plans for improving standards whilst meeting national targets. In doing so, they will consult with clinical staff, patients, and local people. PCTs must co-operate with the responsible StHA and (with respect to long-term care) local authorities and are responsible to the Secretary of State through the StHA. PCTs manage and regulate the services provided by general practitioners (GPs), dentists, pharmacists, and opticians under their Terms of Service.[49] In particular: "It is the duty of every Primary Care Trust, in respect of each financial year, to perform its functions so as to secure that the expenditure of the trust which is attributable to the performance by the trust of its functions in that year do not exceed [its income]."[50]

A variety of pressures may be imposed upon chief executive officers of PCTs to encourage adherence to this duty. The ultimate sanction is for PCT officers to be suspended, or removed from their posts, or to be made subject to directions.[51] Given the increased role of the Department of Health and the National Institute for Clinical Excellence (NICE) in creating National Service Frameworks and other guidance, the business of achieving local and national objectives and remaining within a fixed financial allocation becomes increasingly challenging.

The benefits of delegating power to local decision-makers inevitably carry disadvantages. For example, the NHS is concerned with the incidence of "post-code rationing" in which access to health services throughout the country varies according to the policy and practice of particular health authorities.[52] If this was a matter of concern in respect of 100 health authorities, how much more pressing will it become with over 300 PCTs? In addition, the sub-division of management of the NHS into relatively small groups of patients (around 100,000 patients per PCT) creates difficulties in connection with the planning of specialist services. This problem was raised in relation to cystic fibrosis patients and neonatal intensive care in 1993.[53] These illnesses present the NHS with a demand for high-cost, low-volume specialist care. Unless it is already provided, many PCTs may decide not to make special arrangements in this area of care because significant investment in facilities is not justified given the unpredictable nature of the demand. Instead, PCTs will be expected to form consortia and to agree to specialist centres within a region of the country to which patients should be sent. With the increased number

---

[48] National Health Service Act 1977, s. 16CC, inserted by Health and Social Care (Community Health and Standards) Act 2003, s. 174.

[49] See generally, *Shifting the Balance of Power within the NHS—Securing Delivery* (Department of Health, 2002), para. 13–22 and Annex A.   [50] National Health Service Act 1977, s. 97(D).

[51] ibid., s. 84. New "intervention orders" were added to the powers by Health and Social Care Act 2001, s. 13.

[52] The National Institute for Clinical Excellence has been created to moderate these differences, and is discussed in Ch. 8.

[53] See *Cystic Fibrosis* and *Neonatal Intensive Care* (Clinical Standards Advisory Group, 1993).

of PCTs, the raft of additional systems of governance being imposed upon them, and the vast number of relatively uncommon illnesses for which consortia would need to be arranged, one would not be surprised to find some areas of care, in some parts of the country, for which adequate treatment was not provided.

IV. Micro-structure—Providing NHS Services

At the *micro*-level of the NHS, we consider (A) NHS Trust hospitals, (B) Foundation Trust hospitals, and (C) primary care services.

A. NHS Trust hospitals

NHS Trust hospitals obtain their income from capital allocations from the Department of Health and by entering into "NHS contracts" with PCTs as purchasers of health care. Section 5(1) of the National Health Service and Community Care Act 1990 provides that the Secretary of State may by order establish bodies, to be known as NHS Trusts:

(a) to assume responsibility, in accordance with this Act, for the ownership and management of hospitals or other establishments or facilities which were previously managed or provided by Health Authorities or Special Health Authorities, or

(b) to provide and manage hospitals or other establishments or facilities.

The order shall be made by statutory instrument and may be amended or revoked.[54] The NHS Trust shall carry out "effectively, efficiently and economically the functions for the time being conferred on it by [such] an order"[55] so that its annual revenue is sufficient to meet its outgoings.[56] NHS Trust hospitals are funded from the revenue generated by contracting with NHS purchasers and others. The nature and function of NHS Trust hospitals is set down in the regulations by which they have been created which generally provide as follows:

(1) The trust is established for the purposes specified in section 5(1)(a) of the [1990] Act.

(2) The trust's functions (which include the functions which the Secretary of State considers appropriate in relation to the provision of services by the trust for one or more health authorities) shall be—

    (a) to own and manage hospital accommodation and services provided at [name and address];

    (b) to manage community health services provided from [name and address].

---

[54] The requirements of such an order are specified in the National Health Service and Community Care Act 1990, Sched. 2, Part I, as amended by Health Authorities Act 1995, s. 2(1), Sched. 1, para. 69(a).   [55] 1990 Act, Sched. 2, para. 6(1).

[56] See 1990 Act, s. 10. See also the restrictions imposed in the powers to borrow money in Sched. 7B to the 1990 Act.

Subject to specific financial provisions:[57]

... an NHS Trust shall have power to do anything which appears to it to be necessary or expedient for the purposes of or in connection with the discharge of its functions, including in particular power—

(a) to acquire and dispose of land other property;

(b) to enter into such contracts as seem to the trust to be appropriate;

(c) to accept gifts of money, land or other property, including money, land or other property to be held on trust, either in general or any specific purposes of the NHS trust or for all or any purposes relating to the health service; and

(d) to employ staff on such terms as the trust think fit.[58]

Strikingly, this precision in relation to the financial position of NHS Trusts is not matched in respect to their duties to patients. In pursuit of its financial objectives, could a Trust simply cease admitting patients over a certain age, or close the units it considered too expensive, or offer care to private fee-paying patients only, as a means of fulfilling its financial objectives? Could it allow the hospital to be used entirely by a company specialising in the provision of private health care, which would tend to exclude those suffering from chronic illness and focus resources on acute care only?[59] Could it cease the business of health care altogether and lease its premises to a shopping complex?

The powers and responsibilities of NHS Trusts arise exclusively from the statute under which they are created. Their rights and obligations are confined within these statutory limits and any action taken beyond them will be *ultra vires* and unlawful. "What you have to do is find out what this statutory creature is and what it is meant to do; and to find out what this statutory creature is you must look at the statute only, because there and there alone, is found the definition of this new creature."[60] Not all of the functions and responsibilities of NHS Trusts can be specified expressly and it is perfectly proper for such statutory bodies to undertake activities which are "incidental to, or consequential upon those things which the Legislature has authorised".[61] The express powers of NHS Trusts have to be interpreted in their statutory context.

Thus, the responsibility to own and manage "hospital accommodation and services" defines the nature of the duty imposed and precludes any other activity.

---

[57] Detailed in the National Health Service and Community Care Act 1990, Sched. 3.

[58] ibid., Sched. 2, para. 16(1).

[59] See the National Health Service and Community Care Act 1990, Sched. 2, para. 13:

An NHS Trust may enter into arrangements for the carrying out, on such terms as seem to the trust appropriate, of any of its functions jointly with any Regional, District or Special Health Authority, with another NHS Trust or with any other body or individual.

[60] *Hazell v Hammersmith and Fulham LBC* [1990] 3 All ER 33, at 46 *per* Woolf LJ.

[61] *A-G v Great Eastern Railway Co* (1880) 5 App Cas 473, at 478 *per* Lord Selborne LC. See also *Baroness Wenlock v River Dee Co* (1885) 10 App Cas 354. For an example of *ultra vires* activity see, e.g., *A-G v London CC* [1990] 1 Ch 781.

The Secretary of State's power to confer rights and duties under these regulations is confined to the powers available to him under the National Health Service Acts themselves. The National Health Service Act 1977 imposes a specific duty to continue the promotion of a comprehensive health service.[62] By implication, therefore, NHS Trusts must be obliged to promote the same objectives as the Secretary of State.

B. NHS Foundation Trusts

NHS Foundation Trust hospitals have been created by the Health and Social Care (Community Health and Standards) Act 2003[63] for central control to be replaced by (in the Government's words) "proper accountability to the local community so that both public and staff have a direct say in how their local services are provided. They will offer a new form of social ownership by the public not by the state—not for private profit but in the public interest".[64] One of the reasons for introducing NHS Foundation Trusts is to encourage competition between hospitals as an incentive to improve services to patients. Will Foundation hospitals be able to promote their own interests at the expense of other NHS bodies? For example, what if successful "Hospital A" attracted patients from further afield, as a result of which reduced numbers of patients attended "Hospital B"? The fewer patients attending Hospital B lead to a decline in its income and the need to reduce its clinical capacity. For patients who cannot travel to Hospital A, this is a reduction in the standard of NHS service. Another example was suggested by the House of Commons Health Committee which said:

> . . . the possibility that a Foundation might decide to sell off a community hospital, bringing benefits to the Foundation Trust through increased access to capital, but disadvantaging the broader community it served . . . This serves as a useful illustration of the problems that could be caused by shifting resources to individual organisations which have a responsibility to their own members, without having, as PCTs do, a responsibility for strategic overview of the health needs of a whole community.[65]

Bear in mind that Foundation Trusts are being introduced precisely when patients are being given greater choice as to the hospital in which they will be treated. Hospitals will compete with one another for income, perhaps by "poaching" staff from other hospitals with more attractive salary packages. The BMA fears that "a system of winners and losers seems inevitable, in which funding flows away from unpopular providers, possibly trapping them in a cycle of decline in which they have a higher proportion of more complex and unprofitable cases but fewer

---

[62] See ss. 1 and 3.

[63] Part 1. It is a good example of an Act amending other Acts which have only recently come into force. For example, it amends the National Health Service Reform and Health Care Professionals Act 2002, the Health and Social Care Act 2001, the Care Standards Act 2000, and the Health Act 1999.

[64] *A Guide to Foundation Trusts* (Department of Health, 2002), para. 1.10.

[65] *House of Commons Inquiry into NHS Foundation Hospitals* (2003, HC 395–I), 112.

staff".[66] And the Health Committee predicts that if foundation trusts, by their increased access to resources, develop services in a way that lowers waiting times or improves quality, GPs and patients will obviously chose to use the foundation trust, rather than poorer-performing local hospitals.[67]

Responding to these pressures, the Department of Health says: "In line with its statutory duty of partnership an NHS Foundation Trust will be expected to use these new freedoms in a way that fits with key NHS principles and does not undermine the ability of other providers in the local health economy to meet their NHS obligations."[68] But it is relaxed about the prospect of competition for staff and patients between NHS hospitals: "With regard to inequity of staffing, significant movement of staff between organisations already exists within the NHS. There is nothing wrong with one member of staff leaving one trust and going to another, as long as the competition is fair . . . NHS Foundation Trusts will not be able to use unfair competition to attract staff."[69] Of course, each foundation trust has a duty to *consult* on the planning, development, and operation of it services,[70] but will this be sufficient to moderate an ambitious and acquisitive board of directors?

How will NHS foundation trusts be regulated? Like any other corporate body, foundation trusts require a constitution which provides (1) who owns it and what are its objectives and (2) how is it governed and to whom is it accountable. To this extent, the challenge of Foundation Trusts is similar to that of any corporate body. In the private sphere, corporate objectives are identified by the board of directors which is accountable to shareholders, and any director may be removed for poor performance. There are no shareholders of Foundation Trusts, so who governs them?

1. Ownership and Objectives

A Foundation Trust is a "public benefit corporation" constituted in accordance with the Health and Social Care (Community Health and Standards) Act 2003.[71] NHS Foundation Trust status is available to non-NHS providers, provided the application is supported by the Secretary of State.[72] Ownership is vested in "members"; i.e. people who *live in an area* specified in the constitution (the "public constituency"), who are *employed (or engaged)* by the corporation (the "staff constituency"), have *attended the corporation's hospital* (the "patient constituency"), or people who live in wider electoral areas.[73] The government considers:

This is a real and not a paper exercise in social ownership. As such the rights of membership will therefore confer some limited but real legal responsibility. The members will be the

---

[66] Quoted in *House of Commons Inquiry into NHS Foundation Hospitals* (2003, HC 395–I), 133.
[67] ibid.   [68] *Guide to Foundation Hospitals* (Department of Health, 2002), para. 1.37.
[69] *Government's Response to the Health Committee's Second Report of Session 2002–03 into Foundation Trusts* (hereafter, *Government's Response*) (Cm. 5876) para. 36.
[70] 2003 Act, s. 30, amending Health and Social Care Act 2001, s. 11.
[71] See s. 1 and Sched. 1.   [72] 2003 Act, s. 5.   [73] 2003 Act, Sched. 1, para. 3(1).

"guarantors" of a Foundation Trust hospital. This means that if the organisation became insolvent and had to be wound up its members would each be liable under the terms of the NHS Foundation Trust's constitution, to pay a nominal sum (£1) toward any outstanding liabilities.[74]

What number of local people would be considered representative of the community; 20, 200, 2,000, 20,000? And how should the various local interests (including minority interests) be represented? The statute does not define the precise nature and extent of the members' rights in respect of NHS Foundation hospitals because "each Foundation Trust will have considerable freedom as to how it implements arrangements for social ownership".[75] However, "each must take steps to secure that (taken as a whole) [the membership] will be representative of those eligible for such membership".[76] Will these arrangements create more democracy in the NHS? The Health Committee doubts it:

. . . the proposed shifts in governance for Foundation Trusts are replacing a distant, but established form of democracy (the Secretary of State) with a new one and untried one. If this policy is adopted, Boards of Governors will ultimately represent the only form of democracy overseeing the NHS, because . . . local people will not have the power to remove the independent regulator if they think it is acting against their interests, as they do with elected politicians . . . it is important that democratic accountability is maintained at a national level.[77]

The corporate objectives of NHS foundation trusts are specified by each trust's constitution, but their first duty is to promote the objectives of the NHS. "An NHS foundation trust is a public benefit corporation which is authorised . . . to provide goods and services for the purposes of the health service in England"[78] and may do anything it considers necessary or desirable to do so. "In particular, it may (a) acquire and dispose of property, (b) enter into contracts, (c) accept gifts of property . . . (d) employ staff"[79] and borrow money for these purposes.[80] Note, however, that local corporate objectives must remain consistent with the targets and objectives set down by, for example, the Commission for Healthcare Audit and Inspection (CHAI). As the government says:

. . . the primary purpose of an NHS Foundation Hospital will be to provide NHS services for NHS patients. National standards and national priorities for the NHS will be reflected in the national standards, the performance ratings and through commissioning requirements, all of which will place a requirement on NHS Foundation Trusts to provide services in line with national priorities and standards.[81]

[74] *Guide to Foundation Trusts, supra* note 64, at para. 2.15.
[75] *House of Commons Inquiry into NHS Foundation Hospitals* (2003, HC 395–I) 32–4.
[76] 2003 Act, s. 6(2)(b).
[77] *House of Commons Inquiry into NHS Foundation Hospitals* (2003, HC 395–I) para. 64.
[78] 2003 Act, s. 1(1)   [79] 2003 Act, s. 18.
[80] 2003 Act, s. 17(1), subject to a "prudential borrowing code", see s. 12.
[81] *Government's Response* (Cm. 5876) para. 10.

2. Governance and Accountability

Governance and accountability of NHS Foundation Trusts is exercised through a variety of channels. "Members" have statutory ownership, but they have little direct control of NHS Foundation Trusts and less influence than do shareholders over private companies. Operational power in NHS Foundation Trusts is exercised by the board of directors; indeed: "all the powers of the corporation [are] exercisable by the Board of Directors."[82] Members elect the board of governors according to the rights vested in their respective constituencies.[83] In turn, the board of governors appoints, or removes, the non-executive members of the board of directors; the executive directors are appointed, or removed, by the chairman, chief executive, and other non-executive members.[84] Of this division of power the government concedes:

The powers of an NHS Foundation Trust are exercisable by the Board of Directors . . . However, governors do have significant powers over appointment and removal of directors . . . Members of an NHS Foundation Trust will *not* have a right to veto action by the NHS Foundation Trust . . . [and] the Board of Governors will *not* have the power to veto actions taken by the Board of Directors.[85]

Discretion has been left to the local bodies to develop their own systems of governance,[86] but at least one member of the board of governors must be appointed by one of the PCTs and one from a local authority for whom the trust provides services.[87] Power, therefore, resides firmly with the board of directors, not with members, nor the public at large. Much apathy surrounded voting for the first round of NHS Foundation Trusts, both with respect to the "public" and "staff" constituencies. Members' involvement in the electoral process was described as "appalling," perhaps reflecting cynicism about the role of governing boards; "why bother if the boards are going to be window dressing, while the real power is concentrated in the hands of the executive team?"[88]

Authorisation to become an NHS Foundation hospital and general oversight is vested in the "independent regulator" which "must secure that the principal

---

[82] 2003 Act, Sched. 1, para. 15(2).   [83] 2003 Act, Sched. 1, para. 9.

[84] 2003 Act, Sched. 1, para. 17. More than half of the board of governors must be elected by the "members", see Sched. 1, para. 9.

[85] *Government's Response* (Cm. 5876, 2003) para. 10, emphasis added.

[86] "It will be up to applicants to develop proposals on the size and composition of its Board of Governors to suit its local circumstances" (para. 2.16). But: "The governors will be under a general duty to inform the Independent Regulator of any action by the Management Board that appears to be inconsistent with the terms of the licence" (para. 2.33), *Guide to Foundation Trusts*, note 64 above.

[87] 2003 Act, Sched. 1, para. 9. The duty is for one of each of all the relevant PCTs and local authorities to serve on the board because some hospitals serve so many PCTs. "The Secretary of State told us that approximately 50 PCTs commission specialist services from Moorfield's Eye Hospital in London, with no single PCT responsible for more than 2% of Moorfield's income. As he put it " 'clearly, it would be pretty difficult if they get to Foundation Trust status to have 50 PCTs on the board' ". *House of Commons Inquiry into NHS Foundation Hospitals* (HC, 395–I), para. 34.

[88] R. Klein, "The First Wave of NHS Foundation Trusts" (2004) 328 *British Medical Journal* 1332, 1333.

purpose of the trust is the provision of goods and services for the purpose of the health service in England".[89] Authorisation shall be given on such terms as the independent regulator thinks appropriate, taking into account such matters as the reports of CHAI and the applicant's financial position.[90] Many issues, however, are dealt with specifically in the statute. The independent regulator may require specific goods and services to be provided to the NHS, including those serving the needs of particular health bodies, the needs of particular persons, the place and the period during which they will be provided.[91] In addition, the income derived from providing private care shall be no greater than the proportion earned before the hospital became a NHS Foundation hospital.[92] Similarly, the regulator may forbid NHS Foundation hospitals from disposing of "protected" property, i.e. property designated as protected in the regulator's authorisation.[93] Foundation trusts must prepare an annual report for the independent regulator explaining their activities.[94] In everything it does, the independent regulator "must exercise its functions in a manner that is consistent with the performance by the Secretary of State of the duties under sections 1, 3, and 51 of the National Health Service Act 1977".[95]

Were an NHS foundation to abuse its dominance in the NHS, mechanisms exist to modify its behaviour. A counter-pressure is exerted by virtue of the duty to co-operate imposed on NHS bodies generally,[96] although this is very imprecise and untested obligation. In addition, as we have seen, the Board of Governors must include representatives of commissioning PCTs and local authorities. Also, some issues may require national action, for example, members may raise concerns with the Independent Regulator, or CHAI and the Secretary of State "will be able to instruct CHAI to investigate an NHS Foundation Trust if there is a major issue of concern connected with service provision".[97]

NHS Foundation Trust status is reserved for hospitals with three-star status. It is unclear what will happen to hospitals whose ratings fall. Ultimately, the independent regulator has power to remove directors and transfer property, or liabilities to another NHS body.[98] However, failure to maintain three-star status alone could not be a ground for such action because there is considerable volatility in the awarding of stars to NHS hospitals: "almost half (16 out of 35) of acute hospitals rated as 3-star in 2000–01 lost their 3-star rating in 2001–02".[99] Foundation status will presumably have greater stability than star-ratings.

---

[89] 2003 Act, s. 14(2).   [90] 2003 Act, s. 6(3) and (4).   [91] 2003 Act, s. 14(4) and (8).
[92] 2003 Act, s. 15. The government is "particularly keen to see NHS Foundation Trust applications that propose to convert existing NHS facilities currently wholly used for paying patients into facilities for the exclusive use of NHS patients." *Guide to Foundation Trusts* (Department of Health, 2002) para. 3.16.   [93] 2003 Act, s. 16.
[94] 2003 Act, Sched. 1, para. 26(2).
[95] 2003 Act, s. 3 (the sections concern the promotion of a comprehensive health service, the provision of specific services, and the provision of teaching services).
[96] By Health Act 1999, s. 26, as amended by the 2003 Act, s. 29.
[97] *Government's Response* (Cm. 5876) para. 13.   [98] 2003 Act, ss. 23 and 25.
[99] *House of Commons Inquiry into NHS Foundation Hospitals* (2003, HC 395–I) 93.

NHS Foundation Trusts will enter legal contracts with PCTs and therefore be regulated by law (rather than "NHS contracts" which are unenforceable in law). The need to agree contractual terms is necessary because NHS foundation trusts will not be subject to the Secretary of State's directions. As a result, outputs will need to be agreed with PCTs and formalised under legally binding contracts. Government believes that this "will introduce greater clarity and transparency in the relationship between PCT and NHS Foundation Trust and ensure that these organisations are properly accountable for their respective commitments".[100] It also carries disadvantages in legal costs and the Department of Health has produced a draft contract to guide the parties in their negotiations. The contract should specify the range of services that are to be provided by an NHS Foundation Trust, the volumes of services to be provided, the cost of services to be provided using health related group (HRG) prices, and include penalty and incentive clauses to encourage prompt and efficient performance.[101] The government prefers that contractual disputes should be governed by a system of compulsory arbitration,[102] but since the matter is governed by the law of contract, it is presumably for the discretion of the contracting parties.

C. Primary Care Services

Until recently, primary care was provided on the same basis throughout the country. It was provided only by GPs, acting as independent contractors, in agreement with their health authorities, under the same terms throughout the NHS. This had the benefit of uniformity, but it had a number of disadvantages. First, it remunerated GPs on the basis of the numbers of patients on their list, with very little financial incentive to improve the quality of services they provided. As a result, good, bad and indifferent GPs were paid according to the same scale. Secondly, because the contract was uniform throughout the country, it was unable to focus attention on the particular needs of specific areas or communities. As a result, the service found it difficult to encourage practices to locate where there were special health needs.

Two changes have been introduced since 1997 which encourage greater variety, both in the people that provide primary care and the way they do so. Under the new arrangements, as well as with GPs, PCTs may enter agreements with NHS employees, or private companies.[103] And the terms of the "contract" (and the rewards available from it) may vary from place to place depending on the nature and level of the service provided. Thus (as we have seen) each PCT must, to the extent to which it considers necessary to meet all reasonable requirements, provide or secure the provision of primary medical care within its area. It may do so itself, or "make contractual arrangements with any person" to do so.[104] Today,

---

[100] *Guide to Foundation Hospitals* (Department of Health, 2002) para. 4.5.

[101] ibid., para. 4.9.   [102] ibid., para. 11.

[103] National Health Service Act 1977, s. 16CC(2), inserted by, Health and Social Care (Community Health and Standards) Act 2003, s. 174.

[104] 1977 Act, s. 16CC(1) and (2) (inserted by the 2003 Act, s. 174).

therefore, these services may be provided either under (1) the General Medical Services (GMS) Regulations, (2) the personal medical services (PMS) Directions, (3) by the PCT itself, though primary care trust medical services (PCTMS), or (4) by alternative providers of medical services (APMS). We deal with each in turn.

1. General Medical Services (GMS)

PCTs may enter into contract with a "contractor" to provide GMS in accordance with statutory regulations. The contract may be with a doctor, a medical partnership, or a limited company provided at least one of the shares is owned by a doctor.[105] The contractor "shall carry out its obligations under the contract with reasonable care and skill"[106] but the nature and extent of the GMS provided depends on the agreement entered into. The GMS Regulations provide for three levels of service: essential, additional, and enhanced. "Essential" services are the minimum level of services that may be provided by a GMS contractor. They are:

. . . services required for the management of its registered patients and temporary residents who are (a) ill, or believe themselves to be ill, with conditions from which recovery is generally expected, (b) terminally ill, or (c) suffering from chronic disease, delivered in the manner determined by the practice in discussion with the patient [and] the provision of appropriate ongoing treatment and care to all registered patients and temporary residents taking account of their specific needs including the provision of advice . . . and the referral of the patient for other services under the Act.[107]

Essential services must be provided in "core hours" (i.e. 8 a.m. to 6.30 p.m. on any day from Monday to Friday except Good Friday, Christmas Day, and Boxing Day)[108] to such extent as is necessary to meet reasonable needs.[109] The contractor may also undertake more extensive *additional services* by agreeing to provide one or more of the following: cervical screening, contraceptive services, vaccinations and immunisations, childhood vaccinations and immunisations, child health services, maternity medical services, and minor surgery.[110] In addition, the contractor may provide *enhanced services* by responding to a particular need in the community as agreed with the PCT.[111] Each level of contract is subject to differing levels of remuneration which take account of compliance with standards of achievement and levels of performance.[112]

---

[105] National Health Service (General Medical Services Contracts) Regulations 2004 (SI 2004 No. 291), reg. 4   [106] ibid., Sched. 6, para. 65.

[107] ibid., reg. 15(3) and (5).   [108] ibid., reg. 2.

[109] Note, however, that if the PCT is unable to find an alternative provider, the contractor may be required to provide services out of hours (see Sched. 3, reg. 5(14). In addition the contractor must provide in core hours "the immediately necessary treatment of any person to whom the contractor has been requested to provide treatment owing to an accident or emergency at any place in its practice area", ibid., reg. 15(6).

[110] ibid., Sched. 2. The right to opt out of "additional services" may be refused if those services are not locally available elsewhere, see Sched. 2, para. 3(1).   [111] ibid., reg. 2.

[112] 1977 Act, s. 28T(3), inserted by the 2003 Act, s. 175.

Payment may be made by reference to a "quality and outcomes framework", a voluntary system of financial incentives which intends to reward contractors for good practice and participation in an annual quality improvement cycle. In this way, contractors may accumulate a maximum of 1,050 points from various aspects of their practice as follows:

(1) the clinical domain: 76 indicators in ten areas (coronary heart disease, stroke or transient ischaemic attack, cancer, hypothyroidism, diabetes, hypertension, mental health, asthma, chronic obstructive pulmonary disease, and epilepsy) worth up to 550 points;

(2) the organisational domain: 56 indicators in five areas (records and information, patient communication, education and training, practice management, and medicines management), worth up to 184 points;

(3) the practice experience domain: 4 indictors within two areas (patient survey and consultation length), worth up to 100 points;

(4) the additional service domain: 10 indicators within four areas (cervical screening, child health surveillance, maternity services, contraceptive services), worth up to 36 points.

A further 180 points is available from (1) holistic care payments (which measure overall clinical achievement) and (2) quality practice payments (which measure overall achievement in the organisational, patient experience, and additional services domain).[113] Each point is valued at around £75, although the sums will vary depending on the resources invested in the system. Some will question whether this framework will improve the quality of patient care, or whether it will focus doctors' attention on those aspects attached to financial rewards and deflect attention from others. For example, the treatment of pain attracts no credit under the quality and outcomes framework. Yet the NICE estimates that around two million people suffer serious pain from osteo- and rheumatoid arthritis in England and Wales.[114] Will these patients find prescribers' attention so distracted by targets that the treatment of pain becomes less significant?

Providers may choose whether they enter "NHS contracts" which are not enforceable in the courts, or ordinary contracts in which disputes may ultimately be settled by litigation.[115] Both forms of agreement, however, will be expected to seek to settle matters locally before moving to the national dispute resolution procedures administered by the Family Health Services Appeal Authority, or (for non-NHS contractors) a court. NHS contracts are more familiar and, perhaps, easier to work with, but the GMS Regulations also permit deductions from GPs'

---

[113] *Delivering Investment in General Practice—Implementing the new GMS contract* (Department of Health, 2004) para. 3.5.

[114] *Guidance on the use of Cyclo-oxyginase (Cox II) selective inhibitors for osteoarthritis and rheumatoid arthritis* (NICE, 2001), para. 2.1.

[115] NHS Contracts are discussed on pp. 381 *et seq* below.

remuneration for non-performance of terms in excess of the damage caused to the PCT. In *R v Secretary of State for Health, ex p Hickey*[116] a doctor was subject to a £2,000 deduction for failing to be on duty as required by his terms of service, although he had caused no serious financial damage to the health authority. The court reasoned that this was consistent with the regulatory nature of the (previous) GMS contract. However, under the private law of contract, awards of damages are limited to the loss actually inflicted by the breach on the innocent party. And penalty clauses in excess of reasonable compensation, intended simply to penalise the contract-breaker will not be enforced.[117] This rule would limit the deductions that could be made from "non-NHS contract" contractors for non-performance and, to this extent, makes them more attractive.

Unlike the previous system in which patients registered with a particular doctor, patients have the right only to "express a preference" as to the practitioner by whom they wish to be treated and the contractor shall endeavour to comply with any preference expressed "but need not do so if the performer (a) has reasonable grounds for refusing to provide services to the patient; or (b) does not routinely perform the service in question within the practice".[118] Some will see this as a dilution of the previous contract. Further, doctors have the right to refuse patients admission to, or remove them from, their lists for "reasonable grounds".[119] However, given the Secretary of State's duty to promote a comprehensive service, contractors cannot be entirely free to refuse patients access to care and the GMS contract reserves to PCTs the right to "assign" patients to contractors without their agreement. Of course, this is not a desirable solution to a problem since the forcing of one party on another is hardly conducive to a productive relationship. Never the less, especially in areas in which there are few contractors, a small number of practices may find that patients with whom they have a poor relationship are regularly assigned to their lists.[120]

A serious problem may arise, however, with violent patients. Speedier procedures are available to remove patients who have "committed an act of violence on the practice premises",[121] whether towards doctors, practice staff, or patients. But

---

[116] (1993) 10 BMLR 12.

[117] See *Ruxley Electronics v Forsyth* [1995] 3 All ER 268 and *Dunlop Pneumatic Tyre Co Ltd v New Garage and Motor Co Ltd* [1915] AC 79.   [118] See 2004 Regs, Sched. 6, para. 18(1).

[119] 2004 Regs, Sched. 6, para. 17(1). The reasons must not relate to "the applicant's race, gender, social class, age, religion, sexual orientation, appearance, disability or medical condition". The patient is entitled to a warning before removal and an explanation in writing within 14 days if they are refused admission to the list, see paras 20(3) and 17(3).

[120] Before making such a assignment the PCT must consider "(a) the wishes and circumstances of the patient . . . ; (b) the distance between the patient's place of residence and the contractor's practice premises; (c) whether, during the six months ending on the date on which the application for assignment is received by the PCT, the patient's name has been removed from the list of patients of any contractor in the areas of the PCT . . . (d) whether the patient's name has been removed . . . under para 21 [violent patients] (e) such other matters as the PCT considers to be relevant." 2004 Regs, Sched. 6, para. 34.

[121] ibid., see Sched. 6, para. 21. Presumably an "act" includes threatening behaviour amounting to assault.

what if the PCT expects that the patient may continue to present a danger wherever he, or she is assigned? Ultimately, although such a patient is unlikely to forfeit their right to care, their access to practice premises may have to be restricted and arrangements made to provide treatment elsewhere (for example at a police station) in order to protect the safety of others. Were someone to be injured in circumstances in which an attack ought to have been foreseen and guarded against, the matter could provoke an action in negligence.

2. Personal Medical Services (PMS)

PMS offers further flexibility as to the agreements that may be entered between PCTs and primary care providers. The rights and duties of PMS contractors are set down by regulations broadly comparable to the GMS Regulations.[122] However, there is no definition of the extent of services that have to be provided.[123] PMS providers may elect to provide practice-based, "essential" services on the model described in the GMS Regulations, or provide different services, for example, to particular patient groups such as those with a specific disease, a client group such as homeless people, or drug addicts, or a wider service in a drop-in centre. PMS is essentially a local contract designed to respond to local needs. Clearly, if a PMS provider agreed to supply a less than comprehensive range of services, the PCT would be required to arrange for the remaining services to be provided by other providers.

Rates of remuneration are to be agreed between the parties, as are the standards by which performance is to be assessed. The PMS contract may adapt the Quality and Outcomes Framework used by GMS contractors, for example, by having fewer indicators and a different evidence base. Accordingly, it is crucial for the contract to describe accurately the services to be provided, to whom, and how performance is to be assessed and remunerated (and it may do so by means of an "NHS contract", or a private contract enforceable in the courts).[124]

3. Provision by PCTs (PCTMS)

PCTs may provide the services themselves by employing their own staff, or engaging practitioners as independent contractors.[125] Staff may work full time, providing a full range of services, or on a part-time, or sessional basis for general, or particular

---

[122] The National Health Service (Personal Medical Services Agreements) Regulations 2004, SI 2004 No. 627.

[123] The National Health Service (Primary Care) Act 1997, s. 1(8) defined them as "services of a kind that may be provided" under the Terms of Service of the GMS Regulations, but this section is repealed by Health and Social Care (Community Health and Standards) Act 2003, s. 178.

[124] The other mandatory terms are set down in regs 10–18 and Sched. 5.

[125] National Health Service Act 1977, s. 16CA, inserted by Health and Social Care (Community Health and Standards) Act 2003, s. 170.

services. The services may be based on the "essential" services provided under the GMS model, or vary, or depart from it altogether depending on local needs and skills. PCTs are duty bound not to exceed their annual financial allocations. However, like the other mechanisms for providing care, the PCT "shall ensure" that their own providers supply the drugs and appliances that are needed by their patients.[126] PCTs may not, therefore, generate financial savings by imposing caps on the prescribing costs on PCTMS providers. This form of service provision enables PCTs to take the initiative in localities which are not able to attract other providers.

4. *Alternative Provider Medical Services (APMS)*

APMS extends the opportunity to provide primary care to a range of other organisations such as a private companies, not-for-profit organisations, NHS and Foundation Trusts, and PCTs (and includes GMS and PMS practices).[127] The logic of APMS is to encourage innovation in areas of historic under-provision where, for example, there has been difficulty recruiting and retaining GP practices. As in the case of PMS agreements, the nature and extent of the agreement will depend on local needs and interests. Again, some mandatory terms must be included in every APMS contract, for example, whether or not it is an NHS contract, the services to be provided, where and to whom, and how performance will be assessed and remunerated. Many of the mandatory terms included in the PMS regulations are also to be included in APMS contracts. In particular, the duty to prescribe is the same as in PMS (i.e. to prescribe the drugs and appliances which are needed), rights of entry and inspection of premises, the duty to co-operate with investigations (including by the National Clinical Assessments Authority), and provisions as to termination.

Given that APMS may be provided by commercial parties, special provision is made to exclude financial interests from the contract. In particular, the PCT shall ensure that APMS contracts prohibit the demanding of fees or other payments for treatment or prescriptions (other than as permitted by the PMS and GMS Regulations) and that decisions to refer patients for other services are made without regard to the party's own financial interests. Presumably, the PCT and other regulators will wish to be reassured that these terms are properly observed (and there is a mandatory duty to participate in an appropriate appraisal system).[128]

V. Conclusion

These developments illuminate the modern diffusion of power in the NHS. The bi-polar "truce" that existed between government and doctors until the 1980s no

---

[126] Direction 12, *Primary Care Trust Medical Services Direction 2004*, Department of Health, 21 April 2004.
[127] See the Alternative Provider Medical Services Directions 2004, Department of Health, 21 April 2004. [128] ibid., Directions 8, 9, and 7 respectively.

longer exists. Instead, government has recognised the difficulty of controlling the NHS from the centre. It has created market competition, targets, and incentives to drive change. Clearly, this is a very different environment. Will it place the emphasis on quantity at the expense of quality? Will competition and incentives enhance or erode trust between patients, doctors, and NHS managers? These are questions for the future. Equally, the new NHS does not make hard choices go away. Who makes the difficult decisions on resource allocation and how do they do so? These are the questions we address in the next chapter.

5

Priority Setting, Patients' Rights, and Judicial Review

Now we examine the practical responses of health authority decision-makers to the financial pressures imposed upon them and the way in which the courts have developed a legal framework within which their decisions should be made. As the process of resource allocation has become more visible, so the courts have become more willing to demand reasons from health authorities for the difficult decisions they have to make. In this, we shall see a marked change of attitude. During the 1980s and early 1990s, the courts were entirely deferential to health authority decision-making in this area. Today, however, there is much greater willingness to scrutinise resource allocation decisions and, if needs be, to overturn them and refer them back for reconsideration.

We have noted how helpful it would be for government to clarify the basic objectives of the NHS and explain the principles on which its resources should be allocated.[1] Despite the additional sums invested in the NHS under the Labour government, hard choices remain, provoked by the development of new treatments for chronic diseases, the increasing need to cater for our long-term care in old age, and the increase in gene therapy and "life-style drugs" which improve aspects of our lives which, until recently, might not have been connected with "health". Yet, other than through the guidance of the National Institute for Clinical Excellence (NICE) and National Service Frameworks, local resource allocators are given no assistance on how to allocate NHS resources. The task is performed in England, by over 300 primary care trusts (PCTs). In these circumstances, as we have seen, post-code differentials between differing authorities are inherent in the structure of the NHS.

With this in mind, the following discusses (I) access to hospital care, (II) access to GP care, (III) the boundary between NHS and social services care, and (IV) the impact of the Human Rights Act 1998.

---

[1] NHS managers now have a *Code of Conduct* which requires "NHS managers to be . . . given clear, achievable targets [and] judged consistently and fairly through appraisal." The Code has the status of Secretary of State's "Directions," see *Code of Conduct for NHS Managers* (Department of Health, 2002) para. 3.

I. Access to Hospital Care

To what extent are the rights and duties arising under the National Health Service Act 1977 capable of being enforced by judicial review? The purpose of judicial review is to examine public authority decisions to test whether they have been taken within the ambit of their legal authority, reasonably and properly. Bear in mind that, in judicial review, the court has no jurisdiction to take the decision on the authority's behalf. A successful application will result in the matter being referred back to the decision-maker for reconsideration in the light of the court's guidance. PCTs work under the dual duty to promote a comprehensive health service on behalf of the Secretary of State and not to exceed their annual financial allocations. This requires them to make hard choices. Recall that they are also duty-bound to adhere to any *directions* issued by the Secretary of State and to accommodate the costs associated with the recommendations of NICE. The manner in which this is done varies between PCTs, but the strong recommendation of the recent authorities is that the process should be robust, fair, and consistent and always admit the possibility of individual patients presenting exceptional circumstances which merit access to care notwithstanding a policy guideline to the contrary.

Claims for judicial review may be brought against statutory bodies under three broad heads, namely illegality, irrationality, and procedural impropriety. We will put the cases into each category. Note, however, that these are not water-tight compartments and the same claim may often be brought within more than one ground of judicial review.

A. Illegality

The claim in illegality alleges that the public authority has acted in a way which is inconsistent with its statutory powers. Public authorities derive all their authority from statute. Therefore, "it is axiomatic that a public authority which derives its existence and its powers from statute cannot validly act outside those powers. This is the familiar *ultra vires* doctrine . . .".[2] This means that the NHS decision-makers must understand correctly the law regulating their decision-making powers and give them proper effect.[3] The founding principles of the NHS are based on the Secretary of State's duties in sections 1 and 3 of the National Health Service Act 1977 to "promote a comprehensive health service", and to provide "to such extent as he considers necessary to meet all reasonable requirements" specified NHS services.[4] The inexact wording of these sections forewarns of the difficulties of

---

[2] Lord Woolf MR in *R v N and E Devon HA, ex p Coughlan* [1999] Lloyd's Rep Med 306, para. 64.
[3] *Council of Civil Service Unions v Minister for the Civil Service* [1985] AC 374, 410.
[4] Both of which we discussed in Ch. 4 above.

identifying precisely when NHS resource allocators move outside the ambit of their lawful statutory powers.

Surprisingly, perhaps, the first case on NHS resource allocation was heard only in 1980 in *R v Secretary of State for Social Services, ex p Hincks*.[5] Plans for a new orthopaedic unit in the city of Birmingham had been approved by the Secretary of State in 1971, postponed in 1973 and eventually abandoned in 1978. It was alleged that, since the Secretary of State had acknowledged the need for the new unit, he must have failed in his duty to promote a "comprehensive health service" under section 1 of the 1977 Act by failing to provide it. The Court of Appeal decided, however, that the Act cannot be interpreted to impose an absolute duty to provide services, irrespective of economic decisions taken at national level. The provision has to be read subject to the implied qualification that the Secretary of State's duty was "to meet all reasonable requirements such as can be provided within the resources available",[6] which "must be determined in the light of current Government economic policy".[7]

The Court of Appeal has confirmed its view that the duty imposed by section 3 is not absolute. In *R v N and E Devon Health Authority, ex p Coughlan*[8] it said the Secretary of State's duty:

. . . is limited to providing the services identified to the extent that he considers that they are *necessary* to meet *all reasonable requirements* . . . there is scope for the Secretary of State to exercise a degree of judgment as to the circumstances in which he will provide the services . . .

When exercising his judgment he has to bear mind the comprehensive service which he is under a duty to promote as set out in section 1. However as long as he pays due regard to that duty, the fact that the service will not be comprehensive does not mean that he is necessarily contravening either section 1 or section 3 . . . a comprehensive health service may never, for human, financial and other resource reasons, be achievable . . . In exercising his judgment the Secretary of State is entitled to take into account the resources available to him and the demands on those resources . . . The [NHS] Act does not impose an absolute duty to provide the specified services. The Secretary of State is entitled to have regard to the resources made available to him under current government economic policy.

Thus, difficult decisions may have to be made allocating NHS resources which will be difficult to attack on grounds of illegality. However, such a case is not impossible. The extent of the duty under the National Health Service Act arose in *Ex p Coughlan*. The health authority proposed to transfer the residents of a residential home out of NHS care and into the care of the local social services department (where they would be means tested for the care provided). However, the Court of Appeal considered the proposal illegal for two reasons. First, the statutory framework creating the respective duties of the NHS and social services departments restricted the freedom of the NHS to act in this way (we discuss the distinction

---

[5] 1 BMLR 93 (decided in 1980).   [6] ibid., at 95 *per* Lord Denning MR.
[7] ibid., at 97, *per* Bridge LJ.   [8] [1999] Lloyds Rep Med 306, paras 23–25.

between NHS and social services care below). The NHS had discretion as to the eligibility criteria it used for determining which long-term care "residents" should be entitled to NHS care. But it was not entitled to transfer to the social service department duties which the statute had imposed upon the NHS;[9] to attempt to do so was *ultra vires*. This warns NHS bodies that the discretion conferred upon them may be broad, but it is not infinite and it is *illegal* to seek to move out of NHS care groups that the National Health Service Act 1977 regards as NHS patients. This right of the NHS to manage its resources in its own discretion has not been considered in other contexts, but one wonders whether the shortage of NHS dentists in some parts of the country might form the basis of a similar complaint.[10]

Secondly, the *Coughlan* case considered the extent to which a public authority could restrict its own discretion by creating a "legitimate expectation" that certain benefits would be available. Miss Coughlan had been given a specific promise that, if she moved from her previous residential home, her new residence would be a home for life. She moved on the strength of that promise, but the health authority subsequently decided to close the new home. The reason for its change of heart was not fickle or irresponsible, It was that the new home was expensive to maintain and was imposing a disproportionate drain on local NHS resources. Was it entitled to go back on its promise?

Promises of this nature may have a number of legal consequences depending on their substance, the manner in which they are made, and the way in which the promissee responds to them. They may have no legal impact at all in the sense that they are general "political" promises made without a guarantee, for example, that NHS patients should not be on waiting lists longer than x months before being seen, or that they should have a choice as to where they will be treated. In these examples, the promise is not specific to individuals and will probably amount to no more than a "target", or aspiration at which the NHS should aim its sights. However, as the promise becomes more specific and the number of people to whom it is made is more limited, it may become enforceable. Again, depending on the terms of the promise, it may simply require the authority to take certain factors into account when making its decision, or to enter into consultation with those affected by it before coming to its decision. These are *procedural* rights to have one's interests considered, but no more.[11]

In the *Coughlan* case, however, the residents had been given a specific promise, and had moved from their previous home on the clear understanding that, if they did so, they would not have to move from the next. The resource-based reasons for closing the new home notwithstanding, the promise of "a home for life" created a *substantive* right to enforce the promise. The health authority's promise limited the discretion that would otherwise have been available to it. The rationale may

---

[9] [1999] Lloyds Rep Med 306, para. 48.
[10] See M. Boulos and G. Picton-Phillips, "Is NHS Dentistry in Crisis?" (2004) 3 *International Journal of Geographics* 19.   [11] *Ex parte Coughlan*, note 9 above, para. 57.

be based on the principle of promissory estoppel (which holds that some non-contractual promises are binding), that it is inequitable to permit A to induce B to do something on the strength of A's promise and then, after A has taken the benefit of B's action, permit him to renege on the promise.[12] In this way, therefore, "the decision to move Miss Coughlan against her will and in breach of the Health Authority's own promise was in the circumstances unfair. It was unfair because it frustrated her legitimate expectations of having a home for life . . ."[13] The court qualified the principle of *substantive* legitimate expectations by conceding that such a promise would not be enforceable if there was a sufficient overriding public interest to justify a departure from what had been promised. In this case, however, no such countervailing consideration existed and the residents were entitled to remain in their new home.

B. Irrationality

The courts have reserved for themselves the right to review the decisions of managers and administrators if they are *Wednesbury* unreasonable, i.e. so unreasonable that no reasonable person addressing himself to the issue in question could have come to such a decision.[14] Obviously, discretion must be exercised fairly, impartially, and in the light of all the relevant evidence. Lord Diplock has described the power of review as follows:

It applies to a decision which is so outrageous in its defiance of logic or of accepted moral standards that no sensible person who had applied his mind to the question to be decided could have arrived at it. Whether a decision falls within this category is a question that judges by their training and experience should be well equipped to answer, or else there would be something badly wrong with our system.[15]

This seems to impose a very high threshold on plaintiffs. More recently, however, the notion of "unreasonableness" has been explained by Lord Woolf MR. He said: "Rationality . . . has two faces: one is the barely known decision which simply defies comprehension; the other is a decision which can be seen to have proceeded by flawed logic."[16] It is the second of these two notions which has become more prominent recently. Clearly, it gives the courts power to question the internal logic of the decision. The changed attitude of the courts in this matter is striking and has led them to quash decisions which, previously, might have escaped scrutiny. Part of the reason for the change is explained by the recent interest of the courts in obtaining satisfactory *reasons* for the decision under review. There has been "a perceptible trend towards an insistence on greater openness, or . . . transparency in

---

[12] See *R v Devon CC, ex p Baker* [1995] 1 All ER 78, 89.
[13] [1999] Lloyds Rep Med 306, para. 89.
[14] *Associated Provincial Picture Houses Ltd v Wednesbury Corpn* [1948] 1 KB 223.
[15] In *Council of Civil Service Unions v Minister for the Civil Service* [1985] AC 374, 410.
[16] *R v N and E Devon HA, ex p Coughlan* [1999] Lloyd's Rep Med 306, 323 col. 2.

the making of administrative decisions".[17] As authoritative commentators have
said, there are many advantages to such a duty:

> To have to provide an explanation of the basis for their decision is a salutary discipline for
> those who have to decide anything that adversely affects others . . . it encourages a careful
> examination of the relevant issues, the elimination of extraneous issues, and consistency in
> decision-making. Moreover [it may] deter applications which would be unsuccessful. In
> addition, basic fairness and respect for the individual often requires that those in authority
> over others should tell them why they are subject to some liability or have been refused some
> benefit.[18]

Inevitably, there are also disadvantages, for example, that such a duty places further
burdens and expenses on decision-makers which may encourage "anodyne, unin-
formative and standard reasons". On balance, however, "the advantages of providing reasons so clearly outweigh the costs that fairness requires that the individual
be informed of the basis for the decision".[19]

The following traces this evolution of (1) judicial passivity and (2) the trend
after 1995 in which the courts have adopted a more critical, or "hard-look"
approach to cases of this nature.

1. Judicial Passivity

During the 1980s, two cases gave the impression that the courts would generally
defer to the decisions of local decision-makers in the resource allocation process
and that the prospects of success in action for judicial review were remote. Thus, in
R v Secretary of State, ex p Walker[20] a health authority were satisfied that a premature
baby required an operation to his heart. The health authority was unable to
perform the procedure as a result of a decision not to staff all the intensive care
units in its neonatal ward. The plaintiff alleged that her baby had been denied the
surgical care the hospital acknowledged he needed. Rejecting the application for
an order that the operation be performed, the Master of the Rolls, Sir John
Donaldson, said:

> It is not for this court, or indeed any court, to substitute its own judgment for the judgment
> of those who are responsible for the allocation of resources. This court could only intervene
> where it was satisfied that there was a prima facie case, not only of failing to allocate
> resources in the way in which others would think that resources should be allocated, but of
> a failure to allocate resources to an extent which was *Wednesbury* . . . unreasonable.[21]

In *Ex p Walker*, there was no immediate danger to the baby and, had an emergency
arisen, the operation would have been performed.[22] In *R v Central Birmingham*

---

[17] *Doody v Secretary of State for the Home Department* [1993] 3 All ER 92, 107.
[18] de Smith, Woolf and Jowell, *Judicial Review of Administrative Action* (Sweet and Maxwell, 1995),
para. 9–042.   [19] ibid., para. 9–045.
[20] (1987) 3 BMLR 32.
[21] *R v Secretary of State for Social Services, ex p Walker* 3 BMLR 32, 35 (decided in 1987).
[22] ibid., at 34.

Health Authority, ex p Collier,[23] however, a four-year-old boy was suffering from a hole in the heart. In September 1987, his consultant said that "he desperately needed open heart surgery" and placed the boy at the top of the waiting list, expecting that intensive care facilities would be made available by the hospital within a month. By January 1988, the operation had been arranged and then cancelled on a number of occasions because no intensive care bed could be made available. The Court of Appeal was invited to order that, given that the boy would probably die unless the operation were performed, the operation should be carried out. It said, however, that:

> . . . even assuming that [the evidence] does establish that there is immediate danger to health, it seems to me that the legal principles to be applied do not differ from the case of *Re Walker.* This court is in no position to judge the allocation of resources by this particular health authority . . . there is no suggestion here that the hospital authority have behaved in a way which is deserving of condemnation or criticism. What is suggested is that somehow more resources should be made available to enable the hospital authorities to ensure that the treatment is immediately given.

Understandably, the courts cannot tell hospital managers which cases should take priority over others. They have no expertise to do so. And, during litigation on behalf of an individual patient, who will speak for the large numbers of patients who are not party to the dispute but who may be affected by its outcome, and for those particular patients whose operations will have to be cancelled if someone else is treated first?[24] To some extent, as the Court of Appeal has said subsequently, "affordability, in the sense of choosing between competing priorities as to where funds should be allocated, must be regarded as a political decision to be taken by Government" (and NHS bodies).[25] On the other hand an inability to create *substantive* criteria on which resources should be allocated should not prevent the courts from scrutinising the *procedures* and reasons by which decisions are made. *Ex p Collier* concerned a child, as everyone agreed, in need of common, life-saving cardiac surgery who had been placed top of the waiting list by his responsible doctor, yet the hospital was unable to make facilities available. How could this have

---

[23] Unreported, 1988. Discussed in Christopher Newdick, *Who Should We Treat? Law, Patients and Resources in the N.H.S.* (Oxford University Press, 1995) 124–35.

[24] The point was made subsequently in the Court of Appeal, by Balcombe LJ, who said:

I would stress the absolute undesirability of the court making an order which may have the effect of compelling a doctor or health authority to make available scarce resources (both human and material) to a particular child, without knowing whether or not there are other patients to whom those resources might more advantageously be devoted.

Re J [1992] 4 All ER 614, 625. But Lord Mustill in *Airedale NHS Trust v Bland* [1993] 1 All ER 821, 879 has taken the opposite view: "it is not legitimate for a judge in reaching a view as to what is for the benefit of the one individual whose life is in issue to take into account the wider practical issues as to allocation of limited financial resources . . ." With respect, such an "individualistic" approach to rights is capable of undermining the public interest.

[25] *R (on the application of Pfizer Ltd) v Secretary of State for Health* [2002] EWCA Civ 1566 [2003] 1 CMLR 19, para. 17.

happened? On what system of priorities was such an apparently meritorious patient considered so much less urgent than the other cases demanding care and attention? Were the nursing staff attending to other patients in greater need of care? Could the operation not have been performed in another hospital? Had anyone taken proper responsibility for the case? The most troubling aspect of the matter is that no-one seemed to know exactly why intensive care facilities could not be made available to the patient. Counsel for the boy accepted that he simply did not know why the surgery had been cancelled; as he said, "it may be good reason or bad reason".

Applications of this gravity deserve proper consideration. Subsequent NHS guidelines issued by the Department of Health specified that, for patients with recognised clinical needs, "it is not acceptable for a purchaser to refuse authorization [for treatment] solely on the grounds of the proposed cost of the treatment in relation to the contracted services".[26] In another context, there has been discussion of a type of decision which "cries out for reasons"[27] and it is suggested that, in the light of the more recent cases, *Ex p Collier* should now be regarded as wrongly decided, not for failing to order that treatment take place, but for failing to scrutinise the reasons why treatment could not be provided.

2. The "Hard-Look"

Subsequent cases have suggested much greater willingness of the courts to examine two particular factors in claims that decisions to deny access to care are irrational, or disproportionate, namely: (a) matters relating to the *process* of priority setting and (b) decisions as to the *efficacy and necessity* of particular treatments.

(a) The Process of Priority Setting

R v NW Derbyshire Health Authority, ex p Fisher[28] was the first rationing case in which judicial review succeeded against a health authority. It arose following the refusal of the health authority to purchase beta interferon for patients suffering from multiple sclerosis. The case was complicated by a number of explanations for the refusal which the judge described as "disingenuous". One explanation was that £50,000 had notionally been allocated to fund its purchase, but it was insufficient to provide treatment to everyone who needed it. Therefore, some deserving cases referred at the end of the year would have to be denied treatment simply by virtue of the accident of the date of their referral. This, it was suggested, was so unfair

---

[26] *Guidance on Extra Contractual Referrals* (NHSME, 1993) para. 51.

[27] *R v Higher Education Funding Council, ex p Institute of Dental Surgery* [1994] 1 All ER 651, 661. And see generally on the emerging duty on decision-makers to give reasons for their decisions in some circumstances (none on access to health care), *R v Civil Service Appeal Board, ex p Cunningham* [1991] 4 All ER 310 and *Doody v Secretary of State for the Home Department* [1993] 3 All ER 92.

[28] (1997) 8 Med LR 327.

that it would be better to provide no such treatment at all. The court rejected this explanation for being wholly unreasonable. It said:

The reason given by [the Director of Public Health] is that the money could only be allocated on a first come, first served basis, which was unfair. I regard this as an irrational reason. If correct it would be a reason for refusing to make any expensive treatment available in almost all circumstances. When deciding whether to prescribe treatment to a patient a clinician has to have regard to many factors including the resources available for that treatment and the needs of and likely benefit to that patient as compared with other patients who are likely to be suitable . . .

It is absurd to suppose that before any patient is prescribed any expensive treatment a survey must be made of all patients who are, or might be, in need of the same treatment in the area. I do not accept that this was a rational justification for not releasing additional funds.[29]

The refusal was overturned by the court by an order of certiorari and referred back to the health authority for reconsideration in the light of the court's observations. Similarly, in *R v NW Lancashire Health Authority, ex p A, D and G*[30] the applicants suffered from "gender identity dysphoria". The health authority accepted that the condition was an illness, but it adopted a policy which allocated low priority to procedures it considered to be clinically ineffective. The applicants sought judicial review of the refusal to pay for transsexual surgery. A number of procedures were expressly identified as falling within the lowest 10 per cent in terms of priority and would not be provided "except in cases of overriding clinical need", for example, gender reassignment, cosmetic plastic surgery, reversal of sterilisation, correction of shortsightedness, and most alternative medicine and homeopathy. The policy was explained to the court by the authority's consultant in public health medicine. He said that the authority had limited financial resources and could not afford to fund all services of proven clinical effectiveness. In order to serve all those for whom the authority was responsible, it had to make difficult decisions. He said, however, that the case of each of the applicants was considered on its merits, although he conceded that, with respect to gender reassignment, it was difficult to imagine what an exceptional clinical need for such services might be other than substantial evidence of serious psychiatric pathology.

In principle, Auld LJ approved the principle of NHS priority setting. His Lordship said that health authorities will naturally give greater priority to life threatening and other grave illnesses than to those obviously less demanding of medical intervention. The precise allocation and weighting of priorities is clearly a matter of judgment for each authority, bearing in mind its statutory responsibilities to the community it serves. Treatment of transsexualism could normally be

---

[29] ibid., 337 (col. 1). Arguably, a "wait-and-see" approach to treatment might be appropriate if the condition was stable and not deteriorating and the wait was (say) three months. At the end of such a period, care could be offered to those most in need.

[30] [1999] Lloyd's Rep Med 399.

placed lower in its scale of priorities than, say, cancer, heart disease, or kidney failure and authorities could differ as to the criteria for determining the need for treatment. However, the court would not be entirely passive in its review of such a policy. In the first place, Auld LJ recommended that authorities introduce a fair and consistent policy as a means of undertaking this responsibility. As he put it: "It makes sense to have a policy for the purpose—indeed, it might well be irrational not to have one." Secondly, the policy must examine the circumstances relevant to such a decision. His Lordship continued:

. . . in establishing priorities—comparing the respective needs of patients suffering from different illnesses and determining the respective strengths of their claims to treatment—it is vital: for (1) an authority accurately to assess the nature and seriousness of each type of illness, (2) to determine the effectiveness of various forms of treatment for it and (3) to give proper effect to that assessment and that determination in the application of its policy.[31]

To these considerations, Buxton LJ added that "the authority can legitimately take into account a wide range of considerations, including the proven success or otherwise of the proposed treatment; the seriousness of the condition . . . and the cost of that treatment".[32] Both, however, emphasised the duty to incorporate into the decision the needs and circumstances of the individual applicant. Thus, such a policy must genuinely recognise the possibility of there being an overriding clinical need and require each request for treatment to be considered on its individual merits. As Buxton LJ said:

. . . the more important the interests of the citizen that the decision affects, the greater will be the degree of consideration that is required of the decision-maker. A decision that, as is the evidence in this case, seriously affects the citizen's health will require substantial consideration, and be subject to careful scrutiny by the court as to its rationality. That will particularly be the case in respect of decisions . . . which involve the refusing of any, or any significant, treatment . . .[33]

On the facts of the case, the Court of Appeal considered that, in reality, the Authority had closed its mind to the possibility of making transsexual surgery available in any circumstances. It had adopted a blanket ban. Buxton LJ said that although the health authority had a mechanism for reviewing "exceptional cases":

. . . it is important that the starting point against which exceptional circumstances have to be rated is properly evaluated and that each case is considered on its individual merits . . . The Authority's relegation of what was notionally regarded as an illness to something less, in respect of which an applicant for treatment had to demonstrate an overriding clinical need for treatment, confronted each [applicant] with a very high and uncertain threshold.[34]

When compared to *Ex p Collier*, these cases illustrate a dramatic increase in the willingness of the courts to scrutinise the reasonableness of rationing decisions.

[31] [1999] Lloyd's Rep Med, 399, 408.   [32] [1999] Lloyd's Rep Med, 399, 411.
[33] ibid., 412. Clinical evidence surrounding decisions of this nature will often be incomplete and leave room for differences of opinion.   [34] ibid., 408.

Exactly how demanding the courts will become is unclear, yet the balance between scrutiny and deference is crucial. A determined judge would almost always be able to find fault with the relevance of factors considered, or not considered, by a decision-maker, or the weight attached to them.[35] On the other hand, too great a willingness by the courts to overturn decisions of this nature will tend to "judicialise" the process by making health authorities over-sensitive and defensive. It would tend to divert resources from patients to internal administrative proced-ures, legal costs, and the need to manage judicial review. Clearly, there is often no "right" answer in these matters and the courts should recognise the "polycentric" nature of the competition for finite resources and that decisions may have to be made to "prioritise" the priorities themselves. Dealing with one urgent matter may serve to delay the management of another. A similar point has been made in a dif-ferent context in the Canadian Supreme Court in which it was stated:

> It is important to remember that a Legislature should not be obliged to deal with all aspects of a problem at once. It must surely be permitted to take incremental measures. It must be given reasonable leeway to deal with problems one step at a time, to balance possible inequalities under the law against other inequalities resulting from the adoption of a course of action, and to take account of the difficulties, whether social, economic, or budgetary, that would arise if it attempted to deal with social and economic problems in their entirety, assuming such problems can ever be perceived in their entirety.[36]

Piecemeal and sometimes urgent responses to pressures (financial and clinical) as they arise cannot be assessed against a precise measure. Decision-makers may give differing weight to similar factors, or choose a different principle on which to respond to the same problem. Provided they have considered the relevant factors (and excluded irrelevant ones), in particular by understanding why neighbouring authorities' assessments might differ, and responded reasonably to the matter, the courts should be sensitive to the risks of diverting resources from one deserving group to another before interfering with their decisions.

(b) Assessment of Clinical Efficacy and the Need for Treatment
The second area in which the courts have developed greater readiness to scrutinise resource allocation decisions is in respect of the assessment of clinical efficacy and the need for treatment. As a general rule, if there is good evidence of clinical effectiveness then the treatment should be given fair and equal consideration in the priorities process. Equally, good evidence that the treatment offers only marginal

---

[35] In *Marcic v Thames Water Utilities Ltd* [2002] 2 All ER 55 the CA criticised a private utility company's system for estimating the need of residents for flood protection. It adopted a scoring system to decide how resources for flood relief should be allocated which considered the nature of the pre-mises (e.g. school, hospital, or private dwelling), whether the water was foul or free standing, whether the customer had had to vacate the premises, its frequency, and the vulnerability of the customer. But it did not consider how long the flooding had occurred, the value of the property concerned, or whether the owner had spent money trying to deal with the problem. However, the judgment was reversed by the House of Lords: [2003] 1 All ER 135.

[36] *McKinney v University of Gulph* [1990] 3 SCR 229 (SCC) 317, *per* La Forest J.

benefits might justify a position low on the priorities list, especially if its costs are very high. Good evidence of ineffectiveness would generally lead to exclusion from NHS provision.

What, however, if there is *equivocal* evidence of effectiveness surrounding the treatment? Here, the relative cost of the treatment deserves greater attention. It would not be prudent to devote disproportionate funding to treatments that might not be effective. In *R v Cambridge District Health Authority, ex p B*[37] a ten-year-old girl with leukaemia was refused the resources required to provide her with remedial (as opposed to palliative) treatment that might have prolonged her life. An application to secure resources on her behalf was denied on the grounds that:

(1) the doctors responsible for treatment considered it to be so untested that it was "experimental";
(2) its prospects of success were very small, i.e. between 1 and 4 per cent overall;
(3) it would have debilitating side-effects which, given her prospects, were not in her best interests; and
(4) given her prospects, the total cost of the two stages of procedures (some £75,000) could not be justified.

The unanimous clinical view of the doctors was that the procedure should not be carried out and the health authority accepted that view, confirming at the same time that the decision had been taken in the light of "all the clinical and other relevant matters . . . and not on financial grounds".[38] The case was taken to the Court of Appeal. It said:

Health authorities of all kinds are constantly pressed to make ends meet. They cannot pay their nurses as much as they would like; they cannot provide all the treatment they would like; they cannot purchase all the extremely expensive equipment they would like; they cannot carry out the research they would like. Difficult and agonising judgments have to be made as to how a limited budget is best allocated to the maximum advantage of the maximum number of patients. That is not a judgment the court can make. In my judgment, it is not something that a health authority . . . can be fairly criticised for not advancing before the court.

. . . it would be totally unrealistic to require the authority to come to the court with its accounts and seek to demonstrate that if this treatment were provided for the benefit of B then there would be a patient C, who would have to go without treatment.[39]

Thus, the matter remained within the authority's discretion. Although there was the possibility of some benefit, it was insufficient to justify treatment; given her poor prospects, it was not in the patient's best interests and it would have been wasteful in the circumstances of the case.

[37] [1995] 2 All ER 129.
[38] See ibid., at 138. The patient died of her illness about a year later. In the US, see also *McLaughlin v Williams* 801 F. Supp 633 (S.D. Florida, 1992) for a comparable application concerning a liver/bowel transplant for a baby, but offering greater prospects of a successful outcome.
[39] [1995] 2 All ER 129, 137.

However, a more refined approach to the question of equivocal evidence arose in *Ex p A, D and G* as to the equivocal clinical evidence that transsexual surgery is an effective treatment for gender dysphoria. The Deputy Director of Public Health said that there was uncertainty about the medical evidence supporting surgery in the treatment of the illness. He said (1) that he would require good evidence of clinical effectiveness as a general rule in all cases and (2) that the evidence in this case had not been subjected to randomised controlled trials, and that, to the extent that some research had been conducted, it was likely to be biased, and did not indicate what the long-term results of surgery might be. Experts for the defendants, however, were convinced of its value and took the contrary view of clinical effectiveness. How should such a difference of professional opinion be resolved? Auld LJ said:

It may be that there is medical support for such scepticism . . . I say nothing about the scope for debate between doctors on the matter. I do not need to do so because the authority accepts in these proceedings that [transsexualism] is an illness. It follows that its policies should, but do not, properly reflect that medical judgment and accord the condition a place somewhere in the scale of its priorities for illnesses instead of relegating it to the outer regions of conditions which it plainly does not so regard.[40]

Similarly, Buxton LJ said that, given the existence of a respectable body of opinion in favour of surgery for transsexualism, "it is unreal to submit that body of opinion to research trials of the type envisaged in the health authority's paper" (i.e. randomised control trials).

I emphasise that the mere fact that a body of medical opinion supports the procedure does not put the health authority under any legal obligation to provide the procedure: the standard here is far removed from the *Bolam* approach in cases of medical negligence. However, where such a body of opinion exists, it is . . . not open to a rational health authority simply to determine that the procedure has no proven clinical benefit while giving no indication of why it considers that is so.[41]

This indicates that blanket bans will not generally be acceptable. Once responsible medical opinion supports a procedure, it should be assessed against a fair and consistent framework which admits the possibility of exceptional circumstances. Statistical evidence that a health authority has admitted such cases would be helpful in an action for judicial review. A policy which purports to allow for exceptional circumstances will be scrutinised to see that that it does so in fact. The mistaken logic in this case was the acceptance of the condition as an illness, but treating it in practice as if it was not an illness.

This approach applies to another situation. What if a patient demands access to the very best treatment available, but it is expensive and the PCT purchases a less expensive alternative? In *R v East Lancashire Health Authority, ex p B*[42] four children

---

[40] Lloyd's Rep Med 399, 408.   [41] Lloyd's Rep Med, 309, 412.
[42] LEXIS, unreported, Queen's Bench Division, 27 February 1997.

suffered haemophilia and required transfusions of the Factor VIII blood component. Their parents were concerned about the risk of infection by hepatitus A from *human* Factor VIII which, although subject to purification by the National Blood Authority, contained a very small risk of containing the virus. Instead, they wished to have *recombinant* Factor VIII, manufactured from genetically engineered animal tissue and which carried a still lower risk. Recombinant Factor VIII cost between £500,000 to £600,000 per year for the four children concerned. Yet the risk of infection by human Factor VIII was small, the condition not serious, not uncommon in children and a vaccination was available. In these circumstances, the health authorities refused to purchase recombinant Factor VIII. The court refused the parents leave to apply for judicial review. The health authorities were familiar with the clinical and economic arguments in the case. They were entitled to have a policy governing the matter. Provided they were open to persuasion of the need for exceptional cases, in the absence of reasons why the children had special need for the more expensive treatment, the court would not interfere with their decision.[43]

However, a blanket ban may be acceptable to restrict access to treatment which is accepted to be ineffective (although the meaning of the word "ineffective" will provoke disagreement). The question has arisen in relation to the availability of in vitro fertilisation treatment, which varies throughout the country; age limits differ, as do the criteria by which women may be eligible for consideration. Should the woman be in a stable married relationship, or may single, or lesbian women apply? Is childlessness essential, and does it matter that there are children from a *previous* relationship?[44] In *R v Sheffield Health Authority, ex p Seale* the authority restricted the availability of IVF treatment to women over 35. The reason for the "cut-off" was that female fertility declines with age and that after that time, the likelihood of achieving a pregnancy through IVF was small and that the limited resources available for the service were better directed towards younger women. The applicant was 37. She argued that the failure to give her any individual clinical assessment as to her fertility was irrational and that some doctors considered 35 to be too low a threshold. The application was rejected. Auld J considered that each case should be considered on its own merits "in cases of critical illness", but continued:

... it is reasonable ... for an authority to look at the matter in the context of the financial resources available to it to provide this and the many other services for which it is responsible under the National Health Service legislation. I cannot say that it is absurd for this authority, acting on advice that the efficacy of this treatment decreases with age and that it is generally less effective after the age of 35, to take this as an appropriate criterion when

---

[43] This was despite the fact that the childrens' doctor had already commenced recombinant Factor VIII and the treatment would have to be withdrawn.

[44] See A. Plomer, I. Smith and N. Martin-Clement, "Rationing Policies on Access to *In Vitro* Fertilisation in the National Health Service" (1999) 14 *Reproductive Health Matters* 60. IVF treatment is now subject to NICE (discretionary) guidelines: *Fertilty: Assessment and Treatment for People with Fertility Problems*, Clinical Guideline 11 (National Institute for Clinical Excellence, 2004).

balancing the need for such provision against its ability to provide it and all the other services imposed upon it in the legislation.[45]

This suggests that the legitimacy of a blanket ban may depend on the nature of the service in question and that some may command less intensive scrutiny than others. Contrast his Lordship's approach in *Ex p Seale* with that in *Ex p A, D, and G* (above). Recall that in the latter case, he said "it is important that . . . each case is considered on its individual merits . . .". Buxton LJ agreed saying "the more important the interests of the citizen that the decision affects, the greater will be the degree of consideration that is required of the decision-maker". Surely applicants for transsexual surgery do not demand greater scrutiny than those seeking IVF. More probably, the law has evolved and treatment should not be subject to blanket bans unless the clinical evidence of its inefficacy is overwhelming. Specific treatments may be placed low in the priorities framework. Never the less, provision should be made for a review panel to consider exceptional cases.

C. Procedural Impropriety

Say a health authority denies treatment because it is too low on its priorities list, or excludes it altogether, other than in *exceptional circumstances*. How should such exceptional circumstances be recognised? Often, exceptional circumstances will be identified in discussion with the patient and the GP. Although they may not be possible to identify precisely, the circumstances might cover, for example, the patient being exposed to a significant risk of an *additional* and *severe* illness. If such a process results in a denial of treatment, what procedures should be available to review the decision? We should distinguish three stages of procedure:

(1) the creation of the policy;
(2) the application of the policy to individual patients—both of which we have dealt with; and
(3) the review of that application in an "exceptional" case.

Such a review must comply with the rules of natural justice.

The rules of natural justice apply at stage (3). They stipulate that:

(a) the patient must know of the reasons for the adverse decision—he or she must know the reason upon which the adverse decision was based;

(b) patients must have the opportunity to explain why they believe the decision is mistaken (perhaps on a pro forma which shows which questions and issues are relevant); and

(c) the matter should be given independent consideration by a panel which is not connected with the original decision (for example, not part of the stage (2) application).

[45] *R v Sheffield HA, ex p Seale* (1995) 25 BMLR 1, 3.

Procedures in matters of this nature are not intended to be formal. In *R (on the application of F) v Oxfordshire Mental Healthcare NHS Trust*[46] the applicant wished to be discharged from mental hospital into accommodation in Manchester on an extra-contractual basis costing £100,000. Instead, the authority proposed to discharge her locally to a unit with which it had an existing contract. This was not ideal for the applicant, but it was adequate from a clinical perspective. She took the matter to her local Priorities Forum. It rejected her claim and she sought judicial review of its decision. The court considered the priorities committee hearing and whether more formal representation should have been available. Rejecting the application for judicial review, the court said:

The health authority had to act fairly, but such decisions involving the allocation of scarce resources, where granting one request will inevitably mean refusing others should not be judicialised . . . Fairness requires that the claimant should have the opportunity to tell the Forum in writing why it was contended that resources should be allocated to her . . . Fairness did not require that she should see the material that went before the Forum . . . since these documents raised no new point. A meeting of the Forum is essentially a discussion between medical experts. It is not to be equated with a contested hearing, and rules of disclosure which might be appropriate for such a hearing should not be imposed upon the Forum's deliberations . . . Decisions on funding affect lives, not just liberty. That is not a good reason to judicialise them. They are agonisingly difficult decisions, and they will not be made any easier or better if they are encumbered with legalistic procedures.[47]

These developments strongly suggest that health authorities and PCTs should develop transparent priorities frameworks which treat patients equally, fairly, and consistently, together with a mechanism for considering "exceptional" cases. Failure to do so exposes the authority to the risk of challenge on the grounds of irrationality and procedural impropriety.

We have noted that judicial review does not give the courts authority to *insist* that a particular treatment is provided. However, they may lean heavily on decision-makers to encourage them to do so. In the *Simms* case[48] the applicants were suffering severe neuro-degenerative disorders caused by new variant Creutzfeld-Jacob disease. The disease was fatal and there was no proven treatment available. The doctors wished to try a new treatment which was largely untested. However, the hospital ethics committee was concerned that such treatment should be used in this way. In the desperate circumstances of the case, the court considered that it would be lawful to use the treatment, notwithstanding its uncertain effects. Reflecting on the misgivings of the ethics committee, the court said "it would be an unbelievably cruel blow to have the High Court say Yes to the treatment and the two committees of the hospital to say No. The committees, of course, must exercise their own discretion as to the applications made to them . . . If the committees reject the applications . . . I would invite the Department of Health, in this unique

---

[46] [2001] EWHC 535.   [47] ibid., paras 77 and 80.   [48] [2003] 1 All ER 669.

case, to consider how best to help the families . . ."[49] Unsurprisingly, these observations were sufficient to secure treatment for the patients concerned. As a general rule, however, notwithstanding their natural sympathies, courts should not seek to direct how scarce resources should be spent on untested treatments. Were they to be inclined to do so on the basis that every last effort should be tried to save a patient's life, many patients who were amenable to effective care might find priority being diverted to treatment of uncertain value. Such a policy would not generate maximum public benefit.

II. Judicial Review—Primary Care

Unlike hospital doctors, GPs and other primary care providers are governed by their contracts with PCTs.[50] These are hugely detailed and cover a broad range of issues from practice premises and registering new patients to dispute resolution and rights of inspection. However, in this section we pay particular attention to prescribing rights. Is there such a right and, if so, what does it mean? In particular, does it permit the withholding of necessary care to an individual in the interests of other patients on grounds of cost? We consider the duty to prescribe and the "black" and "grey" lists.

A. The Duty to Prescribe

Regulations encourage prudence in spending on medicines. Practices are subject to indicative amounts, or "target budgets" in which: "The members of a practice shall seek to secure that, except with the consent of the PCT or for good cause, the orders for drugs, medicines and listed appliances given by them . . . in any financial year does not exceed the indicative amount notified for the practice . . ."[51] Notice that the target may be exceeded for a "good cause". The regulations, however, forbid "wasteful" prescribing where the cost or quantity of the drug or appliance is "in excess of that which was reasonably necessary for the proper treatment of the patient".[52] The PCT may withhold, or make deductions from, payments owed to the contractor for breach of this term.[53] What is "excessive" and how should prescribers react to patients with expensive needs? Guidance from the NHS Executive suggests that:

. . . there are several types of prescribing which may give rise to a perception . . . that there may have been excessive prescribing [for example] where it appears that far too much of a drug is prescribed for the condition under treatment . . . where two drugs with the same

---

[49] ibid., paras 70 and 72. [50] See Folio 157 *et seq* above.
[51] See National Health Service and Community Care Act 1991, s. 18 and National Health Service (Indicative Amounts) Regulations 1991, SI 1991 No. 556.
[52] National Health Service (General Medical Services Contracts) Regulations 2004 (SI 2004 No. 291). Sched. 6, para. 46. [53] See ibid., Sched. 6, para. 116(2).

apparent mode of action are prescribed when beneficial synergy is not expected . . . where too many drugs appear to have been prescribed for a single condition. This may be where treatment is begun or drugs are added without deletion of previous treatment [or] where additional drugs are routinely prescribed prophylactically to meet infrequent side effects.[54]

On the other hand, the terms of service also require that a prescriber "shall order any drugs, medicines or appliances which are needed for the treatment of any patient who is receiving treatment under the contract by issuing to that patient a prescription form or a repeatable prescription".[55] Do these words permit the prescriber to prescribe treatment irrespective of cost that he, or she reasonably believes the patient needs? Or could it be argued that the duty should be read in a "community-based" sense and permit the doctor to ration treatment in the interests of patients as a whole? Two analogous cases have considered the issue of needs and resources which point to different conclusions.

In *R v Gloucestershire County Council, ex p Barry*[56] the applicant had been assessed by the local authority as requiring specific services under the Chronically Sick and Disabled Persons Act 1970. Section 2(1) provides that: "Where . . . it is necessary in order to meet the needs of [a] person for [an] authority to make arrangements [for that person] it shall be the duty of that authority to make those arrangements." Owing to reductions in its block grant from central government, the authority proposed to reduce the services it provided, despite the fact that his needs remained unchanged. Notably, the needs in question did not relate to the health care, but the adaption of the person's home, meals on wheels and, *inter alia* access to radio, television, and library facilities, various leisure activities, and occasional holidays. Should these "needs" be interpreted by reference to the individual needs of the person concerned (the patient-led approach), or subject to the resources available to the authority (the resources-led approach)? The House of Lords considered that the word "needs" in the 1970 Act should be given a flexible, resource-based interpretation. It said:

> The words "necessary" and "needs" are both relative expressions, admitting in each case a considerable range of meaning. They are not defined in the 1970 Act . . . In deciding whether there is a necessity to meet the needs of the individual some criteria have to be provided . . . In the framing of the criteria to be applied . . . the severity of the condition may have to be matched against the availability of resources.

Thus, the authority was entitled to adjust the services it provided to take account of its resources because the applicant's *statutory* "needs" could diminish, even though his *actual* needs were the same.

---

[54] *Excessive prescribing by GPs: referral to a Professional Committee* EL(92)90 (NHSME, 1992), Annex B, para. 8.

[55] National Health Service (General Medical Services Contracts) Regulations 2004 (SI 2004 No. 292), Sched. 6, para. 39(1). "The prescriber" means (a) a doctor, (b) an independent nurse prescriber, and (c) a supplementary prescriber, see 2004 Regs, reg. 2.

[56] [1997] 2 All ER 1, 16. Note, however, that the Court of Appeal had taken the opposite view.

But a more demanding approach was taken in *R v East Sussex County Council, ex p Tandy*.[57] The case concerned analogous statutory duties imposed by the Education Act 1993 on a local education authority to provide sick children with "suitable education" at home. The applicant was a teenage girl suffering ME. She had previously received five hours' tuition a week at home. Owing to resource constraints, the authority proposed to reduce her home tuition to three hours. Was the education authority entitled to take its limited resources into account in determining what was a suitable education for the girl? In the context of this statute, the House Lords rejected the argument that this particular duty was resource-based. Lord Browne-Wilkinson said "there is nothing in the Act of 1993 to suggest that resource considerations are relevant to the question of what is suitable education . . . The duty is to make arrangements for what constitutes a suitable education for each child. That duty will not be fulfilled unless the arrangements do in fact provide suitable education for each child." Significantly, his Lordship warned against using the judiciary to reorganise the order of social priorities which had been identified by Parliament. He said:

Parliament has chosen to impose a statutory duty, as opposed to a power, requiring the local authority to do certain things. In my judgment, the courts should be slow to downgrade such duties into what are, in effect, discretions over which the courts would have very little control. If Parliament wishes to reduce public expenditure on meeting the needs of sick children, then it is up to Parliament so to provide. It is not for the courts to adjust the order of priorities as between statutory duties and statutory discretion.[58]

Accordingly, the local authority was obliged to divert resources away from those activities over which it had *discretion*, in order to comply with the *duties* imposed upon it. Which of these cases has most persuasive weight in the interpretation of prescribers' duties in the NHS? Certainly, the government considers that the GP's duty to prescribe is not constrained by resources. It has said in relation to the creation of PCTs:

The new system will continue to allow individual GPs to decide what is best for the patient, whether for example, to prescribe drugs or refer patients to hospital on the basis of their clinical judgement. The freedom to refer and prescribe remains unchanged. Patients will continue to be guaranteed the drugs, investigations and treatments they need.

There will be no question of anyone being denied the drugs they need because the GP or Primary Care Group have run out of cash. GPs' participation in a primary care group will not affect their ability to fulfil their terms of service obligation always to prescribe and refer in the best interest of their patients. Primary Care Groups will be expected to live within their budgets. Where a group is forecasting an overspend it must work with its host authority to manage the position in-year and adjust the group's future financial and service plans accordingly.[59]

The only NHS case to have considered the question was in relation to the previous GMS Regulations. The matter arose when a new medicine for erectile dysfunction (*sildenafil*, sold as "Viagra") received a licence. The Secretary of State, concerned at

---

[57] [1998] 2 All ER 769.   [58] ibid., 777.
[59] *Developing Primary Care Groups* (Department of Health, 1998) HSC 1998/139, paras 52–53.

the possibility that there might be considerable demand for the medicine, issued guidance urging that GPs "should not prescribe sildenafil. Health Authorities are also advised not to support the provision of sildenafil at NHS expense to patients requiring treatment for erectile dysfunction, other than in exceptional circumstances which they should require to be cleared in advance with them."[60] The manufacturer challenged the guidance for being unlawful in that it contradicted the GP's duties contained in the terms of service, which were amenable to change only through Parliament. Collins J considered two provisions of the previous terms of service; that (under paragraph 43) "a doctor shall order any drugs or appliances which are needed for the treatment of any patient to whom he is providing treatment under these terms of service by issuing to that patient a prescription form", and (under paragraph 12): "A doctor shall render to his patients all necessary and appropriate personal medical services of the type usually provided by general practitioners."[61] His Lordship held that the Secretary of State's letter was unlawful and declared it void for contradicting Parliament's will as expressed in the regulations governing the duties of GPs in the NHS. Curiously, he considered that duty was contained in paragraph 12, rather than 43. He said:

> . . . paragraph 43 in my judgment does not impose a duty to prescribe a drug . . . The doctor's duty is contained in paragraph 12(1) . . . The doctor must give such treatment as he, exercising the professional judgment to be expected from an average GP, considers necessary and appropriate . . . If a GP decides that a particular treatment is necessary, it must inevitably be appropriate . . .[62]

Exactly why the duty did not arise from the clear words of paragraph 43 is not explained. Never the less, whether contained in paragraph 12, or 43, its impact is the same. The duty to respond to patient need will not always be straightforward, especially if there is a difference of opinion between doctor and patient. Never the less, the doctor's duty is to consider all the clinical circumstances of the case including the patient's preferences, but to make a decision within his or her own reasonable discretion. Nor should doctors exceed their expertise by attempting treatment which should be undertaken by a specialist by means of a referral to hospital. With these caveats, however, the Secretary of State's guidance was declared unlawful for trespassing upon the proper statutory responsibilities imposed on GPs by the GMS Regulations. It would have been permissible for the Secretary of State to advise doctors to be cautious in using the drug, but such advice must make clear that "the GP's clinical judgment is supreme". One would expect a similar response to the duties contained in the 2004 Regulations.

Certainly, it is difficult to explain the logic in health policy for making rationing lawful and, indeed, routine (as we say above), in secondary care, whilst making it

[60] *Treatment for Impotence* (Department of Health, 1998), HSC 1998/158.
[61] Both were contained in the National Health Service (General Medical Services) Regulations 1992 (SI 1992 No. 635), Sched. 2.
[62] [1999] Lloyd's Med Rep 289, 296 (col. 2). Para. 12(1) is now contained in reg. 15(4)(b) of the 2004 Regs.

apparently unlawful in primary care in which the duty to prescribe is dictated by the patient's individual need. Perhaps the explanation is more political and historical; given that the duty originated with Nye Bevan, the architect of the NHS—it has a distinguished pedigree which may be difficult to disturb!

B. The "Black" and "Grey" Lists

The general duty to prescribe in primary care is subject to qualification by two lists, one which contains treatments which may *never* be prescribed within the NHS (the "black" list), the other which contains treatments which may be prescribed in specific circumstances only (the "grey" list).[63] These lists are necessary because the right to prescribe does not operate on the basis of a specific list of treatments available within the NHS—there is no white list. Instead, the matter is for GPs acting within their reasonable clinical discretion. With the exception of products to treat erectile dysfunction, which have now been added to the grey list, neither list deprives doctors of treatments which provide significant therapeutic benefit to patients. The black list contains thousands of items, some of which suggest that GPs must have taken a very flexible view of their patient's needs in the past. Excluded from the NHS, therefore, are cosmetic products, soaps, shampoos, sunscreens, mild analgesics, mild cough remedies, toothpastes, baby foods, cranberry juice, vitamin supplements, decaffeinated coffee, herbal tea, powdered milk, Ribena, Lucozade, "wines" and Flora margarine! By contrast, the grey list contains a very small number of restrictions mainly concerned with clinical safety.

These lists enable Parliament to restrict the treatments available to GPs under the Terms of Service. Although they may not be provided *within* the NHS, "black", or "grey" listed products may be prescribed outside the NHS under a private arrangement "in the course of [NHS] treatment".[64] In this way, patients who are prepared to pay may have a private prescription, but since NHS treatment is provided without charge, the prescriber may not charge for providing it. Note, however, that (other than with respect to erectile dysfunction) neither list has been used as a means of rationing NHS treatment. This supports the argument that the duty to prescribe is intended to enable doctors to respond to the needs of their individual patients. If Parliament wishes to restrict that freedom for reasons of cost it is at liberty to do so within the Regulations. However, in the absence of Parliamentary intervention, doctors should not presume any such duty falls upon them. This is significant because PCTs have new powers to remove doctors from the medical list if "the continued inclusion of the person concerned in the list

---

[63] See Health and Social Care (Community Health and Standards) Act 2004, s. 28U and the 2004 GMS Regs, Sched. 6, paras 42 and 43. The "black" and "grey" lists are contained in the National Health Service (General Medical Services Contracts) (Prescription Drugs) Regulations 2004 (SI 2004 No. 629).

[64] National Health Service (General Medical Services Contracts) Regulations 2004 (SI 2004 No. 291), Sched. 6, para. 42.

would be prejudicial to the efficiency of the services which those included in the list undertake to provide".[65] In the light of this discussion, such a right of removal presumably exists against GPs who prescribe irresponsibly in the sense that they prescribe treatments of no therapeutic value, perhaps because they simply do what patients *want*, or (as discussed above) prescribe irresponsible doses to patients, duplicate treatment, or routinely treat for very rare adverse reactions to medicines. Such cases deserve censure because they waste limited resources and are probably negligent in their approach to treatment. On the other hand, expensive but *responsible* prescribers ought not to be criticised under these Regulations.

III. Distinction Between NHS and Social Services Care

A particular difficulty which has long troubled the NHS is the point at which a person ceases to be a "patient" in the NHS and becomes a "resident" (or "client") within the responsibility of social services departments of local authorities. The roots of the distinction date from 1942, when the Beveridge Report recommended that our welfare system should separate responsibility for providing health care on the one hand, and social services on the other.[66] His proposal was given effect by distinguishing the functions of the NHS and social services in (respectively) the National Health Service Act 1946 (now the 1977 Act) and the National Assistance Act 1948. The former is the responsibility of the Secretary of State and is available to patients without charge (except as is provided in regulations), whereas the latter is the responsibility of local authority social services departments and is means tested. Included within the people's "means" are the houses they own.[67]

Clearly therefore, patients, NHS Trust hospitals and local authorities need to know upon whom falls the expense of funding care. The distinction becomes the more important as we grow older and more dependent on others, especially as people often have to sell their homes in order to meet costs of social services care. Oddly, however, the distinction between the two responsibilities has never been clear. As long ago as 1953, the Minister of State for Health, Mr Iain Macleod described it as "perhaps the most baffling . . . in the whole of the National Health Service".[68] Some clarification of this difficult question has been provided by the Health Service Ombudsman and the courts in judicial review.

---

[65] Health and Social Care Act 2001, s. 25.

[66] *Social Insurance and Allied Services* (Cmnd. 6404, 1942), paras 426 *et seq.*

[67] Thus, nursing home residents' assets must be assessed to test the level of contribution they should make, if any, towards the cost of their care. See the National Assistance (Assessment of Resources) Regulations 1992 (SI 1992 No. 2977) as amended, in particular, by the National Assistance (Assessment of Resources) (Amendment) (England) Regulations 2002 (SI 2002, No. 410) on capital limits. In Scotland, both nursing and "personal" care are provided without charge. See the Community Care and Health (Scotland) Act 2002.

[68] Parliamentary Debates, vol. 522, col. 167 (14 December 1953). See generally C. Newdick, "Patients, or Residents?: Long-Term Care in the Welfare State" (1996) 4 *Medical Law Review* 144.

A. Intervention of the Health Service Ombudsman

The matter was brought to prominence by the Health Service Ombudsman, Mr William Reid, in 1993 in connection with the refusal by a health authority to support the costs of providing chronic care. The applicant's 55-year-old husband had suffered a serious stroke, serious neurological damage and a heart attack which had left him totally dependent on nursing care. Leeds Health Authority provided acute care until satisfied that his condition had stabilised and that he was no longer likely to improve. At that stage, however, it described his condition as "chronic" and stated that it "did not provide for any long stay medical beds in hospital or have any contractual arrangements for such beds in private nursing homes".[69] Accordingly, the patient was discharged to a private nursing home which incurred costs to his family of £6,000 a year over two years before the case was heard by the Ombudsman. The application challenged the right of the Health Authority to refuse to provide NHS care to a patient in this condition. Sir William found in favour of the applicant. He said:

The patient was a highly dependent patient in hospital . . . and yet, when he no longer needed care in an acute ward but manifestly needed what the National Health Service is there to provide, they regarded themselves as having no scope for continuing to discharge their responsibilities to him because their policy was to make no provision for continuing care . . . In my opinion the failure to make available long-term care within the NHS for this patient was unreasonable and constitutes a failure in the service provided by the Health Authority.[70]

The Authority agreed to compensate the applicant for her expenses and to undertake the costs of her husband's future care. The difficult question remains, however, what is it that "the National Health Service is there to provide"? The question becomes the more important when hospitals are encouraged to discharge patients in order to maintain beds for new admissions, but local authorities may be reluctant to accept financial responsibility for additional "clients" within their social services departments.[71]

The Health Service Ombudsman's adjudication led to the introduction of new NHS guidance which provided a flexible "eligibility framework" within which health authorities and social service departments have discretion to distinguish between NHS and social services care. As a result, there is much diversity of practice throughout the NHS. Thus, health authorities retained responsibility for:

The needs of people who because of the nature, complexity or intensity of their health need will require continuing inpatient care arranged and funded by the NHS in hospital or in a

---

[69] *Failure to Provide Long term NHS Care for a Brain-damaged Patient* (Health Service Commissioner, HC 197, Session 1993–94) para. 18.

[70] ibid., para. 22. For a similar Health Service Ombudsman case, see *Health Service Commissioner's Report* (HC 11, Session 1995–96) 121.

[71] The Community Care (Delayed Discharges etc) Act 2003 has created a statutory duty on social services departments to pay NHS hospitals delayed discharge payments for the days that a person in need of community care is unable to leave hospital because social services accommodation has not been provided.

nursing home [including those] who require routinely the use of specialist health care equipment or treatments which require the supervision of specialist staff; have a rapidly degenerating or unstable condition which means that they will require specialist medical or nursing supervision.[72]

Given the delegation of responsibility to local decision-makers and the persistent difficulties of funding, the guidance was often applied in a restrictive manner. The following year, the Department of Health issued further guidance saying that local criteria had been introduced in ways that could exclude eligible patients from NHS care. Reminding health authorities of the previous guidance, it said: "Some eligibility criteria for continuing patient care seemed to place too much emphasis on the need for people to meet multiple criteria to qualify for NHS funded care" and to attach too much significance on the need for specialist care as a decisive criterion.[73]

B. Judicial Review

In the meantime, the matter was brought to the attention of the courts by way of judicial review in *R v North and East Devon Health Authority, ex p Coughlan*.[74] The applicant had been involved in a serious car accident and was seriously damaged. She became a resident in a nursing home and her condition was described as "tetraplegic, doubly incontinent requiring regular catheterisation, partially paralysed in the respiratory tract, with consequent difficulty in breathing, and subject not only to the attendant problems of immobility but to recurrent headaches caused by an associated neurological condition".[75] The guidance introduced after the first Health Service Ombudsman's case had suggested that "specialist or intensive medical or nursing support for people in nursing homes"[76] should be the responsibility of the NHS, but not other care of a more general nature. In the Divisional Court, Hidden J decided that any nursing care provided in a nursing home was the responsibility of, and should be paid for by, the health authority. The implications of the decision were profound and would have necessitated a very substantial diversion of additional funds to health authorities.

The matter was taken to the Court of Appeal which sought to distinguish the responsibilities arising within the NHS and social services departments by reference to section 21 of the National Assistance Act 1948 which provides, *inter alia*:

> (1) a local authority may with the approval of the Secretary of State, and to such extent as he may direct, shall, make arrangements for providing (a) residential accommodation for persons aged eighteen or over who by reason of age, illness, disability or any other circumstances are in need of care and attention which is not otherwise available to them . . .

---

[72] *NHS Responsibilities for Meeting Continuing Health Care Needs* HSG(95)8 (Department of Health, 1995) Annex A.
[73] *NHS Responsibilities for Meeting Continuing Health Care Needs—Current Progress and Future Priorities* EL(96)8 (Department of Health, 1996). [74] [1999] Lloyds Law Rep Med 306.
[75] ibid., 310, col. 1. [76] Health Service Guidance (95)45, para. 4.1.

. . .

(5) References in this Act to accommodation provided under this Part thereof shall be construed . . . as including references to board and other services, amenities and requisites provided in connection with the accommodation except where in the opinion of the authority managing the premises their provision is unnecessary . . .

. . .

(8) Nothing in this section shall authorise or require a local authority to make any provision authorised or required to be made . . . by or under any enactment not contained in this Part of this Act or authorised or required to be provided under the National Health Service Act 1977.

Lord Woolf MR reversed the decision of Hidden J that all nursing services are properly the responsibility of health authorities. Of section 21(1), he said "the express reference to age, illness and disability as being among the characteristics of the person who is seeking accommodation . . . indicate that in many cases there is likely to be a need for nursing services as part of the care provided". Similarly, in relation subsection (5), his Lordship said the words "board and other accommodation" also appear to include nursing services subject to the qualification that they are "provided in connection with the accommodation". Consistent with this view, he said of section 21(8) that the powers of the local authority "are not excluded *by* the existence of a power in the [National Health Service Act 1977] to provide some service, but they are excluded where the provision is authorised or required to be made *under* the [1977 Act]".[77] In other words:

The subsection's prohibitive effect is limited to those health services which, in fact, have been authorised or required to be provided under the [1977 Act]. Such services would not therefore include services which the Secretary of State legitimately decided under section 3(1) of the [1977 Act] it was not necessary for the NHS to provide . . . The Secretary can exclude some nursing services from the services provided by the NHS. Such services can then be provided as a social or care service rather than as a health service . . .

The distinction between those services which can and cannot be so provided is one of degree which in borderline cases will depend on a careful appraisal of the facts of the individual case. However, as a very general indication as to where the line is to be drawn, it can be said that if the nursing services are (i) merely incidental or ancillary to the provision of the accommodation which a local authority is under a duty to provide to the category of persons to whom section 21 refers and (ii) of a nature which it can be expected that an authority whose primary responsibility is to provide social services can be expected to provide, then they can be provided under section 21. It will be appreciated that the first part of the test is focusing on the overall quantity of the services and the second part on the quality of the services provided.[78]

On the facts, the Court of Appeal, considered that the applicant's disabilities were of a severity which were beyond the scope of local authority responsibility. The question of how the judgment applies to other nursing home residents suffering,

---

[77] ibid., 316, col. 2.   [78] ibid., 316, col. 2–317, col. 1.

for example, varying degrees of dementia is unresolved. The judgment makes clear that some nursing care provided in nursing homes is the responsibility of the NHS, provided it is sufficient in nature or duration. Accordingly, the Health and Social Care Act 2001 now defines "nursing care" as "any services provided by a registered nurse and involving (a) the provision of care, or (b) the planning, supervision or delegation of the provision of care, other than any services which, having regard to their nature and the circumstances in which they are provided, do not need to be provided by a registered nurse".[79] The duty to develop "eligibility criteria" by which to assess need, and to determine whether care should be provided within the NHS, is conferred on the NHS and social services departments[80] within a framework set down in revised Secretary of State's directions.[81] Of course, nursing home residents responsible for paying nursing home fees remain entitled to NHS care (such as the services of their GP, or admission to hospital) without charge.

Local eligibility criteria remain confusing and unsettled. They were reconsidered in 2003 by the Health Service Ombudsman, Ms Ann Abraham, in respect of individuals suffering from Alzheimer's disease, stroke, and vascular dementia which made them wholly dependent on others. In each case, health authorities had applied locally devised guidance upon which they denied responsibility for meeting the full costs of their care. Adjudicating in favour of these patients, the Ombudsman said:

Some of the local criteria I have seen appeared to be significantly more restrictive than the [Department of Health] guidance permitted. For instance: some explicitly say that only patients requiring continued consultant supervision, or on site medical expertise, are eligible for NHS-funded care: others seem to suggest that in explanatory text, or to imply that people requiring hospital care are eligible. Yet it is clear from the 1995 guidance, and reinforced by the additional [1996] guidance that some other patients should be eligible.[82]

The Ombudsman continued that, the *Coughlan* ruling notwithstanding, review of the eligibility criteria had been very limited and remained unchanged even when they appeared to conflict with the judgment. She said "I would have expected the Department of Health, when reviewing the performance of health authorities, to have picked this up. But I have seen some evidence to suggest that the Department provided little real encouragement to authorities to review their criteria [and] one letter . . . could justifiably have been read as a mandate to do the bare minimum."[83] Accordingly, the Ombudsman considered that all those who had wrongly been required to pay for medical care should receive compensation.[84] She also

---

[79] See s. 49.

[80] National Health Service and Community Care Act 1990, s. 47.

[81] See the directions in *Guidance on Free Nursing Care in Nursing Homes* (HSC 2001/17, LAC (2001)26, Department of Health, 2001). See also *Ex parte Coughlan: Follow Up Action* (HSC 1999/180, LAC(99)30, Department of Health, 1999).

[82] *NHS Funding for Long-term Care of Older and Disabled People* (HC 399, 2nd Report, Session 2002–03) para. 19.   [83] ibid., para. 21.

[84] ibid., para. 29. The problem has to some extent been eased since October 2001 by the requirement of the Health and Social Care Act 2001 that "nursing care" should be provided without charge.

urged government to provide improved national guidance to local NHS bodies as to the criteria to be adopted in drawing the distinction between NHS and social care. The area continues to baffle the NHS. As larger numbers of us require long-term care, and are so vulnerable and dependent on others, it is crucial to develop greater clarity and consistency as to the NHS care we are to expect at this time of our lives.

IV. Impact of the Human Rights Act 1998

Does the Human Rights Act 1998 change the way in which judicial review applies to matters of NHS resource allocation? Of course, it is likely to carry significant weight in matters affecting *private* rights such as the rights to information about treatment, minimum standards of treatment, sterilising mentally handicapped patients, confidentiality, rights to self-determination, and the status of living wills. To what extent, however, will the Human Rights Act become involved in applications to obtain access to public resources, for example, to treatment for a life-threatening condition, particularly if such a decision will tend to divert funds earmarked for other patients? The European Court of Human Rights has sounded a note of caution as to the extent to which it can become involved in allocating funds within the public services. In the context of a claim concerning policing levels in the community, it said:

Bearing in mind the difficulties involved in policing modern societies, the unpredictability of human conduct and operational choices which must be made in terms of priorities and resources, such an obligation must be interpreted in a way which does not impose an impossible or disproportionate burden on the authorities. Accordingly, not every claimed risk to life can entail for the authorities a Convention requirement to take operational measures to prevent that risk from materialising.[85]

Similar reservations were expressed in connection with an application for housing. The European Court of Human Rights said: "Whilst it is clearly desirable that every human being has a place where he or she can live . . . and which to call a home there are unfortunately in the Contracting States many persons who have no home. Whether the state provides funds to enable everyone to have a home is a matter for political, not judicial decision."[86] Human rights must create universal, minimum standards that cannot be dependent on the wealth available to individual countries. The standards imposed on relatively affluent countries in northern Europe must be equally achievable in countries with smaller gross domestic product. If this is correct, the European Court will be sensitive to the danger of insisting upon standards of public services which, within present resource constraints,

---

[85] *Osman v UK* [1998] 29 EHRR 245, para. 116.
[86] *Chapman v UK* [2001] 33 EHRR 399, para. 99.

could not be made available throughout the signatories of the European Convention.

Note too that the European Court preserves for the member states certain latitude with respect to many of the rights protected by the Convention under the "margin of appreciation" and the doctrine of proportionality. This margin of discretion is especially significant in relation to the competing claims that arise between private and public interests. The Court has considered the balance between the private rights of those living beneath flight paths approaching Heathrow airport and whose sleep is regularly disturbed (under the Article 8 right to "private and family life"), with the national and commercial interests of preserving a thriving international airport. Like the issue of public resource allocation, there is no "right" answer, nor any objective means of identifying which factors are relevant to the decision, or the weight to be accorded to them. In the Heathrow case, the government had adopted policies to reduce and discourage night-time noise, yet the weight of air traffic continued to increase. Never the less, a majority of the Strasbourg Court determined that although the state is required to give due consideration to the rights arising under Article 8, "it must in principle be left a choice between different ways and means of meeting the obligation. The Court's supervisory jurisdiction . . . is limited to reviewing whether or not the particular solution adopted can be regarded as striking a fair balance."[87] This too suggests that differing domestic responses to claims in the area of health care resource allocation would also be accorded a wide measure of discretion.

One mechanism for restricting the duty of the state to provide positive access to health resources is to say that mere *inactivity* exposes the authorities to no liability under the Convention. In the absence of some unwarranted action on their part, there is no wrong which can be the subject of challenge. In the transsexuals' case of *Ex p A, D and G*, Buxton LJ said, denying the relevance of Article 8 to the application, "in this case there has occurred no *interference* with either the applicants' private life or with their sexuality. The ECHR jurisprudence demonstrates that a state can be guilty of such interference simply by inaction [but] such an interference could hardly be founded on a refusal to fund medical treatment."[88] Clearly, this would provide a powerful defence to NHS bodies in respect of failure to provide the whole range of services. This, however, may be too narrow a view of the rights available under the Convention having regard to the development of the idea of "proportionality" and its special application to human rights cases.

---

[87] *Hatton and others v UK* (App. 36022/97), para. 123. However, under the Canadian Charter of Rights and Freedoms, Canadian courts are willing to direct that particular patients obtain access to specific health care. See, e.g., *Auton v British Columbia (A-G)* (2002) 220 DLR (4th) 411 (British Columbia Court of Appeal) (access to novel treatment for autism) and *Eldridge v British Columbia (A-G)* (1997) 151 DLR (4th) 577 (Supreme Court of Canada) (access of deaf patients to paid interpreters to assist their use of hospital services).

[88] *R v NW Lancashire HA, ex p A, D and G* (2000) 53 BMLR 148, 173.

A. Proportionality

If one takes the view that there are reciprocal rights and duties which flow between the state and its citizens,[89] the proper analysis of applications for access to health resources requires a number of steps. The introduction of the Convention requires a balance to be made between competing public and private rights. As Lord Steyn has said:

> . . . from time to time the fundamental right of one individual may conflict with the human right of another . . . a single minded concentration on the pursuit of fundamental rights of individuals to the exclusion of the interests of the wider public might be subversive of the ideal of tolerant liberal democracies. The fundamental rights of individuals are of supreme importance but those rights are not unlimited: we live in communities of individuals who also have rights . . . The European Convention requires that where difficult questions arise a balance must be struck.[90]

Such a balance is assisted by the notion of "proportionality". The origin of the concept in the European Convention stems from the qualifications placed on a number of rights that shall not be interfered with *except* as is "necessary in a democratic society". This concept of *necessity* implies a "pressing social need" in which "the interference is proportionate to the legitimate aim pursued . . .".[91] It has been persuasively suggested that this requires the court to have regard to specific considerations in balancing the competing interests, namely, that: (a) the measure contains a legitimate aim; (b) the interference must be a suitable response to a pressing social need; (c) it is necessary in a democratic society; and (d) it is proportionate to the legitimate aim pursued.[92] The Strasbourg Court recognises the need for a "fair balance between the demands of the general interests of the community and the requirements of the protection of the individual's human rights"[93] and that member states possess a margin of appreciation in the precise balancing of those interests.[94]

Until relatively recently, the English courts were very reluctant to embrace the notion of proportionality in English law. As Lord Lowry explained in *Ex p Brind*, given their lack of expertise and training, the courts should be slow to usurp the jurisdiction of public officers, many of whom are elected to their posts. A more interventionist approach would jeopardise stability in the law and "The losers in

---

[89] See the comment of the Supreme Court of India in *Paschim Banga Khet Maxdoor Samity v State of West Bengal* 1996 AIR 4226, 2429: "The Constutution envisages the establishment of a welfare state [in which] the primary duty of government is to secure the welfare of the people. Providing adequate medical facilities for the people is an essential part of the obligations undertaken by the Government in a welfare state." [90] *Brown v Stott* [2001] 2 All ER 97, 118.

[91] *Sunday Times v UK* (1979) 2 EHRR 245, para. 62. Indeed, under the right to life provisions of Article 2, the test is more emphatic: "no more than *absolutely* necessary."

[92] See M. Fordham and Thomas de la Mere, "Identifying the Principles of Proportionality" in J. Jowell and J. Cooper (eds) *Understanding Human Rights Principles* (Hart, 2001) 53 and generally.

[93] See *Soering v UK* (1989) 11 EHRR 439, para. 89.

[94] See *Handyside v UK* (1976) 1 EHRR 737, para. 48.

this respect will be members of the public . . ."[95] This represents a relatively passive view of the role of the court in assessing the propriety of public decision-making; it presumes that provided the decision-maker remains within the confines of his statutory powers, his discretion is immune from review. More recently, however, this approach has been modified. Laws J has explained how the court should seek to balance competing administrative and constitutional rights. His Lordship said, emphasising the evolution of the law:

> *Wednesbury* . . . is not, at least any longer, a monolithic standard of review. Where an administrative decision abrogates or diminishes a constitutional or fundamental right, *Wednesbury* requires that the decision-maker provide a substantial justification in the public interest for doing so . . . reasonableness itself requires in such cases that in ordering the priorities which will drive his decision, the decision-maker must give a high place to the right in question. He cannot treat it merely as something to be taken into account, akin to any other relevant consideration; he must recognise it as a value to be kept, unless in his judgment there is a greater value which justifies its loss.[96]

Similarly, in *R v Lord Saville, ex p A*, although the Court of Appeal confirmed that a court will not generally interfere with the exercise of an administrative discretion on substantive grounds it added "in judging whether the decision-maker has exceeded this margin of appreciation the human rights context is important. The more substantial the interference with human rights, the more the court will require by way of justification before it is satisfied that the decision is reasonable."[97] The matter is one of balance, but there can surely be no doubt that the old *Wednesbury* deference will be modified in cases of this nature. Lord Steyn in *Ex p Daly* has suggested a number of differences between the doctrine of proportionality and the traditional "unreasonableness" test. For example the doctrine of proportionality may require the reviewing court:

> . . . to assess the balance which the decision maker has struck, not merely whether it is within a range of reasonable decisions. Secondly, the proportionality test may go further than the traditional grounds of review in as much as it may require attention to be directed to the relative weight accorded to interests and considerations. Thirdly . . . the intensity of the review . . . is guaranteed by the twin requirements that the limitation of the right was necessary in a democratic society, in the sense of meeting a pressing social need, and the question whether the interference was really proportionate to the legitimate aim being pursued.[98]

---

[95] *Ex p Brind* [1991] 1 AC 696, 767. Never the less, a "total lack of proportionality" would offend the *Wednesbury* test, see ibid., 762.

[96] *Chesterfield Properties plc v Secretary of State for the Environment* [1998] JPL 568, 579.

[97] [1999] 4 All ER 860, 871, in which Lord Woolf MR agreed with the submissions of Mr David Pannick QC in *R v Minsitry of Defence, ex p Smith*, [1996] 1 All ER 257, 263.

[98] *R v Secretary of State for the Home Department, ex p Daly* [2001] 3 All ER 433, 446. Lord Cooke added: "I think the day will come when it will be more widely recognised that the *Wednesbury* case was an unfortunately retrogressive decision in English Administrative law, in so far as it is suggested that there are degrees of unreasonableness and that only a very extreme degree can bring an administrative decision within the legitimate scope of judicial review" at 447.

This difference with respect to the intensity of the court's scrutiny in human rights cases is illustrated in Jaymee Bowen's case of *Ex p B*, discussed above. Recall that the Court of Appeal refused to rule the merits of the case (although it certainly heard the relevant evidence). It appeared to adopt a passive and essentially deferential role to the difficulties faced by the health authority. Contrast, therefore, the approach of Laws J, who understood the case to give rise to a claim to the right to life. In the High Court, his Lordship subjected the refusal to approve access to treatment to the closest scrutiny. Having heard substantial evidence as to the clinical merits of the proposed treatment, he said:

> Funds for health care are not limitless . . . But merely to point to the fact that resources are finite tells one nothing about the wisdom or, what is relevant for my purpose, the legality of a decision to withhold funding in a particular case. I have no evidence as to what kinds of case, if any, might be prejudiced if the respondents were to fund B's treatment. I have no idea where in the order of things the respondents place a modest chance of saving the life of a 10 year-old girl. I have no evidence about the respondent's budget, either generally, or in relation to "extra contractual referrals". The [Director of Public Health's] evidence about money consists only in grave and well-rounded generalities . . . Where the question is whether the life of a 10 year-old child might be saved, by however slim a chance, the responsible Authority must . . . do more than toll the bell of tight resources. They must explain the priorities that have led them to decline to fund the treatment.[99]

Will this more demanding approach to individual cases gain favour in the light of the Human Rights Act?[100] Will every exercise of discretion to allocate resources to one patient, or group of patients, rather than another require detailed explanation? With respect to the larger macro-issues, the courts tend to defer to the exercise of lawful discretion, especially in connection with matters of "social policy, the allocation of finite financial resources between the different calls made upon them or (as in the *Dorset Yacht* case) the balance between pursuing desirable social aims as against the risk to the public inherent in so doing. It is established that the courts cannot enter upon the assessment of such 'policy' matters."[101] But what about decisions in respect of individual patients? For example, in *Ex p Mellor*, a prisoner sought judicial review of the refusal of the Home Office to permit him IVF facilities to artificially inseminate his wife. Although the Court of Appeal dismissed the application, it said: "It did not follow that it would always be justifiable

---

[99] *R v Cambridge DHA, ex p B* (1995) 25 BMLR 5, 16–17. His Lordship referred to the asylum case of *Bugdaycay v Secretary of State for the Home Department* [1987] 1 All ER 940, 952, *per* Lord Bridge: "The most fundamental right is the individual's right to life and, when an administrative decision . . . is said to . . . put the applicant's life at risk, the basis of the decision must surely call for the most anxious scrutiny."

[100] For a similar approach see *B v Minister of Correctional Services* 50 BMLR 206 (decided in 1997), in which prisoners suffering HIV detained in the Western Cape successfully applied for access to anti-viral medicines. Brand J accepted that "if a proper case were to be made by the respondents that, due to the constraints of its own budget, the Department of Correctional Services could not afford the medical treatment claimed by the applicants, I might have . . . have found that adequate medical treatment for the applicants is dictated by such budgetary constraints" at 221.

[101] *X v Bedfordshire CC* [1995] 3 All ER 353, 369–370, *per* Lord Browne-Wilkinson.

to prevent a prisoner from inseminating his wife artificially, or indeed naturally. The interference with fundamental human rights permitted by article 8.2 involved an exercise in proportionality. Exceptional circumstances could require the normal consequences of imprisonment to yield because its interference with a particular human right was disproportionate."[102]

Some indication of the courts' willingness to engage in a human rights review of each case of this nature is suggested by recent developments under the Mental Health Act 1983. For example, the right of patients to have the lawfulness of their detention reviewed at regular intervals under Articles 5 and 6 cannot be compromised by a failure to invest adequate resources in the Mental Health Review Tribunals. It is no defence for the state to say that there are more urgent demands for resources elsewhere in the system which prevents proper review taking place.[103] There has also been a suggestion that the court must play a more active role when considering the lawfulness of decisions to treat patients without their consent. In the *Wilkinson* case the question arose as to how such a decision should be scrutinised in judicial review. The appellant contended that a number of his human rights were raised by the case and that the court could not be satisfied of the need for him to be treated without his consent unless the doctors were available for cross-examination. The respondents argued that the court's responsibility was simply to review the lawfulness of the matter on the papers and not to require the doctors to present themselves in court. The Court of Appeal held that in a case of such gravity, it had to be satisfied of the precedent fact of the patient's need for treatment in these circumstances. A *Wednesbury* review would not be sufficient. Hale LJ said:

. . . the court has power to make an independent determination of what is the patient's best interests in the broadest sense, not limiting itself to applying the *Bolam/Bolitho* test of medical negligence[104] . . . The wishes and feelings of the incapacitated person will be an important element in determining what is, or is not, in his best interests. Where he is actively opposed to a course of action, the benefits which it holds for him will have to be carefully weighed against the disadvantages of going against his wishes, especially if force is required to do this.[105]

As to the manner in which the court should satisfy itself of this matter, her Ladyship said:

Whatever the position before the Human Rights Act, the decision to impose treatment without consent upon a protesting patient is a potential invasion of his rights under art 3 or art 8. Super-*Wednesbury* is not enough. The Appellant is entitled to a proper hearing, on the merits, of whether the statutory grounds for imposing this treatment upon him against his

---

[102] *R (on the application of Mellor) v Secretary of State for the Home Department* [2002] QB 13, 29.
[103] *R (KB) v Mental Health Review Tribunal and Secretary of State* [2002] EWHC 639, paras 45–47, *per* Stanley Burnton J.
[104] Discussed in Ch. 6, under which clinicians are not negligent if they have acted in a way which is consistent with a responsible body of medical opinion.
[105] *R (Wilkinson) v Broadmoor SHA* [2001] EWCA Civ 1545, [2002] 2 WLR 419, para. 64.

will are made out, ie whether it is treatment for the mental disorder from which he is suffering and whether it should be given to him without his consent.[106]

Clearly, such a requirement presents the risk of diverting personnel from hospitals by requiring their attendance in court which presents its own resource implications. On the other hand, the other members of the Court of Appeal did not go as far as this and in *R (on the application of N) v Doctor M*, the Court expressed a different view. While confirming that the court should be satisfied that all the relevant factors have been examined properly and proportionately, it said that the *Wilkinson* case was not be a charter requiring routine mental health cases to be cross-examined in court because "the court's role is essentially one of review".[107] Certainly, the need for treatment must be "convincingly shown to exist"[108] on more than a "mere" *Bolam* test so that the court must be reasonably satisfied in respect of, for example:

(a) how certain is it that the patient does suffer from a treatable mental disorder, (b) how serious a disorder is it, (c) how serious a risk is presented to others, (d) how likely is it that, if the patient does suffer from such a disorder, the proposed treatment will alleviate the condition, (e) how likely is it that the treatment will have adverse consequences for the patient and (f) how severe may they be.[109]

Never the less, matters of this nature would not routinely have to be adduced orally before the court:

If a patient obtains independent medical evidence to the effect that the treatment is not medically necessary . . . it may be clear to a court, even without oral evidence, that the case in favour of treatment has not been convincingly shown. Conversely, it may be clear to the court, simply on a reading of the written material, that the necessity for treatment has been convincingly shown, and that cross-examination will not lead to a different conclusion.[110]

Great care is needed to balance the rights of mental health patients to liberty with providing proper and sufficient medical attention for their own safety and that of others. The same applies to cases such as Jaymee Bowen's, where the right to life itself may be in issue. However, given the limitations of the court's expertise, both as to the clinical merits of individual cases and the "opportunity costs" of diverting funds to one particular case, there comes a point where it is bound to defer to the opinions of responsible doctors and managers. To this extent a "super-*Wednesbury*" review is appropriate, in which scrutiny will be sufficiently intense to ensure that the matter has been given proper attention, but it will not otherwise incline the court to take decisions on behalf of those empowered to do so.

B. Human Rights Act Damages

Damages are available against a public authority which otherwise acts in breach of the Human Rights Act if "the court is satisfied that the award is necessary to afford

---

[106] ibid., para. 83.   [107] (2002) 72 BMLR 81, para 39.   [108] ibid., para. 18.
[109] ibid., para. 19.   [110] ibid., para. 36.

just satisfaction to the person in whose favour it is made".[111] A small number of cases have considered the circumstances in which damages are appropriate. In *R (KB) v MHRT*[112] claimants had been detained under the Mental Health Act 1983 and succeeded in their claims that they had not been granted speedy access to a Mental Health Review Tribunal to determine if their continued detention was necessary. This action concerned their right to damages under the Human Rights Act 1998. The court commented that the Strasbourg cases established no clear principles on which damages should be quantified. Instead, it awarded global sums without detailing how they had been calculated. As a result, domestic courts had to develop their own principles. The court considered that there might be circumstances in which no award for a breach of the Act would be appropriate because the remedial action of the public authority following the judgment of the court would provide adequate remedy. Equally, an award would be appropriate if damages would have been available for the same tort in English law. Further, such an award might be higher than that usually awarded for similar infringements by the Strasbourg Court.[113] Of course, any such award will necessarily tend to diminish the resources available to the public authority to fulfil its statutory duties. However: "Parliament requires the court to make an award of damages . . . where that is required by the Convention. It must be taken to have provided the resources to meet such awards."[114]

On the facts of this case, in which patients lawfully detained under statute had not been granted proper access to an appropriate authority to have its continued lawfulness reviewed, there was no comparable tort in English law on which damages could be awarded. The court stressed that the infliction of distress and disappointment on others will not always merit compensation. Never the less, given the anxiety suffered by these particularly vulnerable patients, Human Rights Act damages were appropriate. Bear in mind that the delays caused to the applicants in this case were not caused by lazy, or insensitive tribunal members. They arose from the limited funding made available to Mental Health Review Tribunals. Limitations of this nature are bound to impose strain on a system. A slightly different approach, more sympathetic to the "institutional" and resource limitations imposed upon public authorities, was adopted in *Anufrijeva (rep of Kuzjeva) v Southwark LBC*,[115] in which claimants for asylum had not been provided with accommodation wholly suitable to their needs because one member of the family was elderly and unable to manage stairs. The local authority had genuinely sought to achieve the best it could for the family, given the pressures on its own resources. In these circumstances the court rejected the claim for damages under the Article 8 right to "respect for private and family life". It said:

It will be rare for an error of judgment, inefficiency or maladministration occurring in the purported performance of a statutory duty . . . to give rise to an infringement of art 8

---

111 Human Rights Act 1998, s. 8(3).   112 [2003] 2 All ER 209.
113 ibid., para. 47, *per* Stanley Burnton J.   114 ibid., para. 50.
115 [2002] All ER (D) 37.

and . . . it is likely that the acts of the public authority would have to have departed so far from the performance of the public authority's statutory duty so as to amount to a denial or contradiction of the duty to act. It is likely that the circumstances of the infringement would be confined to *flagrant and deliberate failures* to act in the face of obvious and gross circumstances affecting the art 8 rights of an individual.[116]

Similar sympathy for the resource limitations within which public authorities work was expressed in *R (Bernard) v London Borough of Enfield*,[117] another claim for damages against a local authority for failure to provide suitable housing to a disabled person. The court said that if a public authority is notified of a serious problem and takes prompt action to deal with it, then further monetary compensation to afford "just satisfaction" may not be required.[118] In this case, however, the failure appeared to the court to have been systematic, deliberate and had persisted for 20 months. Even at the date of the trial, the authority had not offered any satisfactory explanation or apology for its failure. In these more serious circumstances, the court said, awarding a total of £16,000 to the applicant and her husband:

The larger the award to the claimants . . . the less there will be for the London Borough of Enfield to spend on providing social service facilities for the many others in need of care within the borough . . . To set against this public disbenefit, it is very much in the interests of society as a whole that public authorites should be encouraged to respect individuals' rights under the Convention. A "restrained" or "moderate" approach to quantum will provide the necessary degree of encouragement whilst not unduly depleting the funds available to the defendant for the benefit of others in need of care.[119]

V. Conclusion

Let us now reflect on the case of *Collier v Birmingham Health Authority* (1988), discussed earlier, in which a boy of four was not given life-saving heart surgery despite being top of his consultant's list of patients. No satisfactory explanation was offered for the failure, but the court refused to intervene in the matter. Both the domestic law of judicial review and the Human Rights Act 1998 would now take a close interest in the case, both to ensure that the circumstances of the case were lawful, perhaps under the right to life provisions of Article 2, or respect for private and family life under Article 8. Recall *Ex p A, D and G*, in which applicants for transsexual surgery succeeded in the application because of the *manner* in which the authority had come to its decision. As a result, PCTs must think carefully about the procedures within which these difficult decisions are made. Rather than each authority inventing the same wheel over 300 times (assuming the continued refusal of government to offer guidance in this matter) PCTs should

---

[116] *per* Newman J, para. 105, emphasis added.   [117] [2002] EWHC 2282.
[118] ibid., para. 40.   [119] *per* Sullivan J, para. 58, emphasis added.

enter collaborative agreements, perhaps at regional level, to share each other's experience and expertise. In this way, reasonably robust, transparent, coherent, and consistent policies might develop throughout the NHS to the benefit both of patients and PCTs themselves.

Thus, aided by the Human Rights Act 1998, the courts have rightly become willing to subject decisions of this nature to more intense scrutiny to ensure that discretion has been exercised in a reasonable and proportionate manner. This approach reflects a more general movement in the balance of power between individuals and public authorities. It is also consistent with a similar more critical attitude to the law of medical negligence and it is to that subject that the next two chapters are devoted.

6

Standards of Care and Medical Negligence

For the vast majority of patients, their experience of the NHS is one of complete satisfaction, indeed, of profound gratitude to all those involved with their care and the system as a whole, which rightly remains one of our most cherished public institutions. It is not just that the NHS and its staff frequently restore our health and independence; by their respect for our dignity and autonomy, clinicians also enable us to make informed and independent decisions at the end of our lives. By its nature, however, medical negligence is like a pathology department; it is only called into action when something seems to be wrong. Here therefore, we look at the exceptional cases where something seems wrong between patients and clinicians. Remember, that few professions routinely face the risk of causing so much damage to those they serve, sometimes as a result of the smallest oversight made under pressure. Also, medicine offers limited guarantees and treatment that offers considerable benefit may also carry unavoidable risks, some of which may be catastrophic. Patients have to decide whether the small possibility of risk is justified by the larger probability of benefit. Doctors may cause damage to their patients, therefore, without in any way behaving carelessly.

With these caveats in mind, this chapter discusses (I) the impact of medical negligence in the NHS, (II) the liability of the clinician, and (III) patients' rights of informed consent to medical care.

I. Impact of Medical Negligence in the NHS

The existing system for compensating victims of medical accidents has a number of drawbacks.[1] Negligence may be said to focus on the clinician's carelessness, so that the finger of blame points to the right person and, to this extent, it may encourage others to be more careful in future. But the disadvantages of the system heavily outweigh its advantages. First, in a system that should promote trust and candour between the parties, negligence creates a defensive atmosphere around accidents. Instead of encouraging clinicians to bring mistakes into the open so that others can learn from them, they will naturally want to hide them from view for

---

[1] P. Cane (ed.) *Atiyah's Accidents, Compensation and the Law* (6th edn, Butterworths, 1999); D. Coneghan and W. Mansell, *The Wrongs of Tort* (2nd edn, Pluto, 1999).

fear of litigation. As a result, the patterns of accidents and "near-misses" that might reveal high-risk practices remain concealed, even from the clinicians themselves. As *Learning from Bristol* commented:

> Clinical negligence litigation does not represent a systematic approach to accountability, far less to the proper analysis of error. Rather it is an entirely haphazard process . . . Few cases actually see the light of day in court. Indeed in many of the more obvious cases of error . . . the claim is settled and no public airing of the issues ever takes place. What might be learned from such cases cannot thus be shared across the NHS . . . Paradoxically, those cases which are not settled, and thus become publicly known, tend to be those in which it is less certain that a hospital or a particular individual was at fault. Thus, at its extreme, we have the bizarre situation under the current system of clinical negligence litigation, in which the worst excesses rarely come into view, while the borderline cases attract the attention of the press and public.[2]

Litigation is also expensive. In claims valued at less than £35,000, the legal and administrative costs are generally higher than the award of damages itself.[3] Only in the higher value claims do costs form less than half of the award in damages. The total cost of medical negligence to the NHS is estimated to have increased (at 2002 prices) from £6.33 million in 1974–75 to £466 million in 2002.[4] Although this is only around 1 per cent of the annual expenditure of the NHS, the pace of growth suggests we should be cautious about the future. But there is another cost to the NHS. Litigation is often prolonged and acrimonious. It may destroy trust between doctor and patient, but it also demoralises and saps the confidence of those who have continuing duties to other patients. Far from inspiring others to greater standards of care, it may foster the practice of defensive medicine, in which needless (and sometimes dangerous) treatments are given, not in the patient's best interests, but to enable the clinician to demonstrate that he had taken every available precaution just in case things go wrong. In a sense, therefore, medical negligence litigation provokes further waste. Bear in mind too that solicitors, and perhaps counsel will have to be instructed. Except for those eligible to receive Legal Aid, or for whom the risk of a five-figure sum in costs is not prohibitive, litigation is often too uncertain and too expensive to justify the risk of losing. For practical purposes, therefore, very many people on "middle incomes" simply do not have access to the courts to resolve disputes of this kind in any event.

Although negligence is expensive, it is not necessarily reliable. Research suggests that many entirely meritorious claims never litigate. For one reason or another—personal, financial, moral—patients, or their relatives, do not pursue litigation. Other meritorious cases proceed, but have their actions dismissed owing to the uncertainties inherent in the law. In both cases negligence is unable to exert any

---

[2] Cm. 5207, 2001, 364–5, para. 28.

[3] See *Handling Clinical Negligence Claims in England* (National Audit Office, HC 403, Session 2000–01).

[4] *Making Amends—A consultation paper setting out proposals for reforming the approach to clinical negligence in the NHS* (Department of Health, 2003) para. 35.

legal pressure on the doctor or institution at fault. By contrast, many cases are taken without evidence that the patient's injuries have resulted from medical negligence, and while many such unmeritorious cases fail, a significant minority succeed (again, by virtue of the uncertainty of litigation) and doctors are held responsible in the absence of fault.[5] This may create the suspicion that the law of negligence is unreliable and sometimes unjust.

Government is contemplating reforming this system. It does not favour a "no-fault" system of compensation of the type used in New Zealand and Sweden. Although such systems have advantages in that they lead to the speedier resolution of disputes and foster greater co-operation between patients and clinicians, they also have disadvantages. For example, the issue of attributing cause and effect (causation) would remain in such a system and this is always difficult in medical cases because the patient is often suffering illness, or disability before visiting the doctor. Also, a no-fault system set up to compensate medical "accidents" would give rise to dispute as to whether the patient was damaged by an accident, or rather by an unavoidable and irreducible risk, adverse reaction, or side-effect inevitably attached to every such procedure. But the most serious reservation about such a system concerns its potential cost. As the Chief Medical Officer, Professor Sir Liam Donaldson, has said: "For a comprehensive no-fault system to be affordable, awards [of damages] would have to be significantly reduced from current levels. For more serious injuries and higher levels of awards this is unlikely to be acceptable." He estimates that "even with a 25% reduction in the current level of compensation the cost of a true no-fault compensation scheme would vary between £1.6 billion per year . . . to almost £28 billion . . . This compares with £400 million spent on clinical negligence in 2000/01."[6]

Instead, he recommends a pilot scheme in which a tribunal acting for an NHS Redress Scheme for claims up to £30,000 would investigate when things have gone wrong, offer remedial treatment and care if needed, an explanation and an apology, and financial compensation, if appropriate. The criteria on which redress would be based are that:

(1) there were serious shortcomings in the standard of care;
(2) the harm could have been avoided; and
(3) the adverse outcome was not the result of the natural progression of the disease.[7]

Assessment could be carried out by the Commission for Healthcare Audit and Inspection (CHAI), the Health Services Commissioner,[8] the NHS Litigation

---

[5] See J. Posner, "Trends in Malpractice Insurance 1970–85" (1986) 49 *Law and Contemporary Problems* 37. The research is from the US, but it seems likely that the trends would not be entirely different in the UK.

[6] *Making Amends*, note 4 above, at 112 and para. 59. There is also concern that if such a system were to remove the right to bring legal proceedings, there might be Human Rights Act 1998 implications.

[7] ibid., 120.

[8] The Health Service Ombudsman has been able to investigate clinical complaints since 1996, and they now dominate her work. This is a speedier and less expensive process than litigation.

Authority, or by local investigation. The precise standard against which "serious shortcomings" should be assessed will, for the present, be the *Bolam* standard discussed below. However, the consultation invites suggestions for alternative measures too. In this way, the National Patient Safety Authority (discussed in Chapter 8) could trace patterns of comparable incidents and recommend remedial action.

Such a scheme appears to have the advantage of a *systemic* approach to managing risk and compensating injuries which have been caused through fault. On the other hand, since there is no disincentive to bringing a claim, it may also tend to encourage the bringing of complaints within the NHS Redress Scheme. Then, if the prospects of an action in negligence are considered good, claims may be encouraged to re-commence in the courts leading to an increase in medical negligence litigation, which would contradict the underlying the purpose of the scheme.[9] Whatever the mechanism for resolving claims arising from medical accidents, the *principles* on which they will be assessed will continue, for the present, to be based on negligence; it will not compensate those whose injuries arise without fault. Also, the system would not extend to claims in excess of £30,000 (other than in respect of birth-related neurological impairment) which will continue to be governed solely by the law of medical negligence. We discuss medical negligence next.

II. Liability of the Clinician

We start with circumstances in which action is taken against the clinician alone. Every action in negligence requires the plaintiff to show that the defendant owed him a duty of care, that the defendant failed to achieve a standard of care demanded by law, and that it was this failure which caused the plaintiff's injuries. An award of damages depends on proof of fault; it has nothing at all to do with the mere fact that the plaintiff has suffered terrible injury and grief. Unless each one of these elements is satisfied, the plaintiff will fail to recover compensation. Under these principles, many who suffer the most tragic and catastrophic damage are left to cope alone on the contributions made by the social security system.[10] Our examination considers medical negligence and the court's role in assessing clinical logic.

However, the limitations of her office mean that the number of final adjudications is only around 200 per year. See generally, M. Seneviratne, *Ombudsmen—Public Services and Administrative Justice* (Butterworths, 2002) ch. 5.

[9] B. Capstick, "The Future of Clinical Negligence Litigation?" (2004) 328 *British Medical Journal* 457.

[10] Judges remark at the harshness of such a system which pays so little regard to the needs of patients who suffer injury in the absence of negligence. See, e.g., *Whitehouse v Jordan* [1981] 1 WLR 246.

A. Medical Negligence[11]

Once a clinician accepts responsibility for a patient, he or she will usually owe them a duty of care.[12] The duty is imposed because clinicians are able to foresee that carelessness could cause damage to the patient. In the majority of cases, therefore, the difficulty faced by the patient is not to establish the existence of a duty of care—rather, it is to prove that, in treating the patient, the clinician failed to achieve a satisfactory standard of care.

Cases which do not concern professional judgment are assessed according to the objective standards of the man on the street (or the Clapham omnibus). The question whether an employer is liable for exposing an employee to an unsafe system of work, or the driver of a car is responsible for the injuries caused to a pedestrian, can often be considered by the judge who applies his or her own common sense to the question of the standard of care that ought to have been achieved. This approach may also be appropriate to *clinical* activities which are matters of common sense. "Thus an accepted practice is open to censure . . . (no expert testimony required) . . . in matters not involving diagnostic or clinical skills, on which an ordinary person may presume to pass judgment sensibly, like failure to remove a sponge."[13] Poor handwriting on a prescription form is inexcusable,[14] as is the duty to ensure that doctors to whom patients are referred for treatment have sufficient information on which to proceed.[15] Doctors who fail to read patients' notes before prescribing drugs to which they are allergic will be dealt with by reference to the standards of the reasonable person.[16] So too with psychiatrists who form emotional relationships with vulnerable patients,[17] and doctors who perform untested cosmetic surgery on children which disfigures their faces.[18] And in complaints which first came to light in Alder Hey hospital, concerning the widespread practice

---

[11] See M. Jones, *Medical Negligence* (3rd edn, Sweet & Maxwell, 2003); and I. Kennedy and A. Grubb, *Medical Law* (3rd edn, Butterworths, 2000) ch. 5. In rare circumstances of "gross negligence," the doctor may be convicted of *criminal* negligence. The doctor's conduct must be especially egregious, see *R v Prentice, R v Adomoka, R v Holloway* [1993] 4 All ER 935 (the first of which concerned the unintentional but fatal misuse of *vincristine*) and, for a successful prosecution see *R v Adomoko* [1995] 1 AC 171. The number of prosecutions for gross negligence has risen sharply since 1990, see R. Ferner, "Medication errors that have led to manslaughter charges" (2000) 321 *British Medical Journal* 1212; and J. Holbrook, "The criminalisation of medical mistakes" (2003) 327 *British Medical Journal* 1118.

[12] In a small number of cases a more restricted duty arises, most notable amongst which concerns doctors who simply examine patients on behalf of others, e.g. insurers or prospective employers.

[13] *Hucks v Cole* [1993] 4 Med LR 393, 394 (decided in 1968), *per* Lord Denning MR. See *Mahon v Osborne* [1939] 2 KB 14 on a failure to remove swabs.

[14] See *Prendergast v Sam & Dee Ltd* [1989] 1 Med LR 36.

[15] *Chapman v Rix* [1994] 5 Med LR 239. Lord Goddard said "I hardly regard this as a medical question at all." at 245. [16] See *Chin Keow v Government of Malaysia* [1967] 1 WLR 813.

[17] See *Landau v Werner* (1961) 105 SJ 1008.

[18] See *Doughty v North Staffordshire HA* [1992] 3 Med LR 81.

of retaining organs of deceased children without parental consent, as a result of which parents suffered psychiatric illness, it was said:

The argument of the defendants, based on evidence of a practice universally adopted by clinicians over many years, is a strong one. Yet having carefully considered the evidence and examined the argument I find myself unable to accept it. Looked at objectively, from a common sense point of view, in my judgment, a significant number, if not all, bereaved mothers of recently deceased children would want to know if organs from their deceased child were to be retained following a post-mortem examination.[19]

On the other hand, professionals commonly exercise judgment which is not within the court's common sense. Solicitors,[20] surveyors,[21] architects,[22] and bankers[23] may be involved in matters which have to be assessed according to the standards expected of reasonable practitioners in the field. How does this more deferential approach operate in respect of the medical profession?[24]

Clearly, the signs and symptoms that ought to be considered, the exploratory tests that ought to be conducted, or the treatment that ought to have been offered are matters requiring professional judgment. The standard of care required is normally assessed by reference to a reasonable body of practitioners in that area. It is very broadly expressed because medicine is often as much an art as a science and permits differences of professional opinion as to diagnosis, prognosis, and appropriate treatment. The point was made in the Scottish case of *Hunter v Hanley*[25] in which it was said:

In the realm of diagnosis and treatment there is ample scope for genuine difference of opinion, and one man clearly is not negligent because his conclusion differs from that of other professional men, nor because he has displayed less skill or knowledge than others would have shown. The true test for establishing negligence in diagnosis or treatment on the part of a doctor is whether he has been proved to be guilty of such failure as no doctor of ordinary skill would be guilty of acting with ordinary care.

In England and Wales, the principle is known as the *Bolam* test of medical negligence, derived from the case of *Bolam v Friern Hospital Management Committee*.[26] The case concerned a patient receiving electro-convulsive treatment. The shock administered during the procedure was sufficient to make limbs flex violently and doctors had to decide on the best way of reducing the risk of patients being

---

[19] *AB v Leeds Teaching Hopsital NHS Trust* [2004] EWHC 644, para. 30, *per* Gage J.

[20] See *Edward Wong Finance Co Ltd v Johnstone, Stokes and Masters* [1984] AC 296 (PC).

[21] *Smith v Eric S Bush* [1990] 1 AC 831.

[22] *Greaves & Co v Baynham Meikle & Partners* [1974] 1 WLR 1261.

[23] See *Lloyds Bank v Savory & Co* [1933] AC 201.

[24] Bearing in mind, as we noted in Ch. 4, that these rights and responsibilities are not limited to doctors and are being extended to nurses, pharmacists, and others. See *Liberating the Talents—Helping Primary Care Trusts and Nurses to deliver the NHS Plan* (Department of Health, 2002) and *Supplementary Prescribing by Nurses and Pharmacists within the NHS in England* (Department of Health, 2003).   [25] 1955 SLT 213 at 217.

[26] [1957] 2 All ER 118.

damaged by such a convulsion. Some doctors administered relaxant drugs to patients, but others considered the risks of doing so unnecessary. Others simply tucked their patients up in bed to prevent them falling to the ground. The defendant doctor in this case preferred to do nothing and his patient suffered serious damage to his thighs and hips when the shock of the treatment caused a spasm which propelled him from the hospital bed on to the floor where he was injured. McNair J instructed the jury as follows:

A doctor is not guilty of negligence if he has acted in accordance with a practice accepted as proper by a responsible body of medical men skilled in that particular art . . . a doctor is not negligent if he is acting in accordance with such a practice merely because there is a body of opinion that takes a contrary view. At the same time, that does not mean that a medical man can obstinately and pig-headedly carry on with some old techniques if it has been proved to be contrary to what is really substantially the whole of informed medical opinion.[27]

This approach to medical malpractice has been adopted to questions of diagnosis[28] and prognosis[29] and may vary according to the degree of skill and expertise of the particular doctor concerned, so that more is expected of a consultant than a junior house officer.[30] It reflects the degree of skill and experience the doctor ought to possess.[31] It is designed to balance the disadvantage of having doctors constantly in fear of litigation with the need to provide patients with a fair and just system of compensation when things have gone wrong.[32] How do the courts strike the balance? Are they largely uncritical and deferential toward the professions, or do they conduct an independent and critical analysis of the circumstances leading to the claim?

B. Court's Role in Assessing Clinical Logic

How could courts assess standards of clinical logic? A spectrum of four broad responses has been suggested in which scrutiny becomes progressively more intense and critical[33] (bearing in mind that the reality of practice blurs the lines

[27] *Bolam v Friern Hospital Management Committee* [1957] 2 All ER 118, 122.
[28] *Maynard v West Midlands RHA* [1985] 1 All ER 635 and *Hinfey v Salford HA* [1993] 4 Med LR 143. But contrast *Sa'd v Robinson* [1989] 1 Med LR 41 (failure to diagnose burns to a child's throat and trachea, as opposed to her mouth, after sucking on the spout of a pot of tea) and *Bova v Spring* [1994] 5 Med LR 120 (failure to diagnose pneumonia).   [29] *Whitehouse v Jordan* [1981] 1 All ER 267.
[30] See *Sidaway v Bethlem Royal Hospital Governors* [1985] 1 All ER 643 at 660, *per* Lord Bridge. But if the individual specialist has greater knowledge of risks and dangers than the average, he may be held to his own, higher, standard. See *Stokes v Guest, Keen and Nettlefild (Bolts & Nuts) Ltd* [1968] 1 WLR 1776, 1783, *per* Swanwick J.
[31] The Royal College of Surgeons estimates that the European Working Time Directive reduces the number of hours hospital doctors will work before becoming consultants from 30,000 to 6,000. A reduction by 80% of time spent on duty will be reflected in their training and experience. Inevitably, this will reduce the standard of care to be expected of them. See J. Chikwe, A. de Souza and J. Pepper, "No Time to Train the Surgeons" (2004) 328 *British Medical Journal* 418.
[32] See the comments of Lord Denning in *Roe v Minister of Health* [1954] 2 QB 66 and *Hatcher v Black* The Times, 2 July 1954.
[33] See H. Davies and S. Harrison, "Trends in doctor-manager relationships" (2003) 326 *British Medical Journal* 646.

between these "idealised" types). First, the most passive and deferential approach to clinical practice respects *reflective practice* and emphasises the individual nature of the doctor's experience. Here, doctors should be accorded a very large measure of individual clinical freedom in deciding what is best for their patient because their practice is predominantly concerned with their own responses to problems rather than the extent to which they conform to external guidelines and protocols. Such a principle is most plausible when there is little settled clinical evidence available to guide the doctor, and often describes the approach of the law when medical knowledge is limited, as it was before (say) the 1930s, or in new areas of medical science which are being developed by a small number of clinical pioneers.[34]

However, as evidence of clinical outcomes accumulates and doctors begin to understand the best techniques, the complications, the most suitable patients, the rates of success and failure, a different approach emerges. This has been referred to as the *professional consensus* model which requires doctors to demonstrate that they are abreast of modern learning in their field and have adjusted their practice accordingly. It would be insufficient for a doctor to fail to keep up to date with clinical advances. The confidence which patients should have in their doctor requires not just that he has reflected carefully about treatment, but that his reflection is put in the context of modern understanding about the risks and benefits of the treatments available. Thus, the clinical guidelines published by the Royal Colleges and authoritative societies should be known to, and carefully considered by doctors. Note that within both of these first two models, the judgment of reasonableness remains largely within the authority of the medical profession itself. Both permit a wide spectrum of clinical differences of clinical opinion.

With the increasing availability of sophisticated data on clinical evidence, greater clinical authority can pass to managers. Hence, the third model of assessment, *critical appraisal*, explains that doctors may be asked to account for their decisions to health care managers. Managers may strongly recommend that certain procedures are conducted in a particular way and demand explanations if not. Why, for example, did the doctor depart from a well-respected guideline, especially if there was a cost attached to doing so, say in terms of the patient's clinical outcome, or the length of time the patient was required to stay in a hospital bed? As *institutions* become responsible for patient safety, so their managers will be entitled to ask why guidelines have not been adhered to. As evidence of clinical and cost effectiveness improves, so the balance of power swings to managerial authorities. But even in this model, doctors retain the right to depart from those guidelines and protocols for good reasons based on their reasonable clinical judgment. In this model, managerial authority may question doctors, but it does not displace the

---

[34] e.g. on the treatment of new variant Creutzfeld-Jacob disease, see *Simms v Simms* [2003] 1 All ER 669: "Where there is no alternative treatment available and the disease is progressive and fatal, it seems to me to be reasonable to consider experimental treatment with unknown benefits and risks, but without significant risks of increased suffering to the patient, in cases where there is some chance of benefit to the patient" (para. 57, *per* Buler-Sloss P).

Hippocratic ethic which commits the doctor to promote the best interests of each patient and this may require a departure from accepted practice in exceptional circumstances.

Lastly, consistent with this trend of shifting authority away from individuals and towards agencies, the *bureaucratic-scientific* (or managerial control) model emphasises robust and reliable clinical evidence as the principle for decision-making (referred to as "evidence-based medicine"). Here, clinical freedom is subject to external scrutiny and doctors are encouraged to adhere to managerial protocols unless there is convincing clinical and economic evidence to support their action. Clearly, this approach is much more severe and shifts the balance of authority to health service managers.

Which of these approaches to clinical "reasonableness" most closely resemble the law? As we discuss the cases, note the general trend of the courts is to become more critical of medical decision-making, but the trend is by no means consistent

1. Reflective Practice and Professional Consensus—the First Two Models

Both the reflective practice and professional consensus models of assessment emphasise the role of professionals as judges of themselves. In modern times, the *reflective practice* model of assessment has never played a significant role in judging the adequacy of medical practice. Both *Hunter v Hanley* and the *Bolam* case endorse the rule that doctors are not assessed according simply to whether they reflected carefully about their practice. They insist on the need for a *professional consensus* accepted as proper by a reasonable and responsible body of opinion. These cases were decided in the 1950s, but neither received significant recognition until later,[35] perhaps because they were thought to raise no new, or surprising issue. However, when they were brought into prominence by a number of authoritative cases in the 1980s, it was suggested that the role of the courts in assessing the reasonableness of clinical opinion would be essentially passive.

The first significant case to reconsider the *Bolam* case was *Whitehouse v Jordan*,[36] in which an obstetrician was alleged to have attempted to deliver a baby by forceps and to have pulled so long and so hard that the child suffered brain damage. The doctor was considered to have acted within the discretion conferred by a responsible body of medical opinion and was acquitted of negligence. He had not exposed the baby to unreasonable pressure by trying to force a forceps delivery. The House of Lords did not subject the accident to close scrutiny. It did not enquire how a doctor could exert so much pressure on baby's head during childbirth, why he would do so, how often would the risk normally materialise, and how it could be minimised? One senses that the court was not so much concerned with what

---

[35] "It is not possible to find [*Bolam*] cited (apart from *Chin Keow*) until after it was given the accolade in the House of Lords . . . in *Whitehouse v Jordan* (1981) and . . . *Sidaway* (1985) [after which] it became an icon of medical malpractice law." See Commentary [1994] 5 Med L Rep 239, 250.

[36] [1981] 1 All ER 267 (HL).

ought to have happened in the case, as much as with what doctors accepted as reasonable at the time. This "passive" approach to the assessment of reasonable care emphasises the professional consensus model of decision-making in which the court defers uncritically to professional experience and judgment without exercising significant independent judgment of its own.

A similarly deferential approach was adopted in *Maynard v West Midlands Regional Health Authority*.[37] The plaintiff had symptoms which suggested she was suffering from either Hodgkin's disease (a form of cancer) or tuberculosis. Given the additional risks of the former, two doctors advised her to undergo a test (a mediastinoscopy), the side-effects of which damaged her vocal chords. She was subsequently diagnosed as having tuberculosis so that the test had been unnecessary. She sued for her loss. At the trial, the plaintiff offered evidence showing that the likelihood of her symptoms being Hodgkins' disease were so small, and the diagnosis of her condition so improbable, that it could never justify exposing her to the risk of damage by the exploratory procedure. The more likely explanation was "almost certainly tuberculosis from the outset".[38] The trial judge found the defendants' explanation for their action unconvincing and that the tests had exposed her to an unreasonable risk. He upheld the plaintiff's claim. However, the health authority appealed to the House of Lords in which Lord Scarman said:

> . . . a judge's preference for one body of distinguished medical opinion to another also professionally distinguished is not sufficient to establish negligence in a practitioner whose actions have received the seal of approval of those whose opinions, truthfully expressed, honestly held, were not preferred . . . For in the realm of diagnosis and treatment negligence is not established by preferring one respectable body of professional opinion to another.[39]

Their Lordships reversed the decision of the judge and found for the defendant on the basis that the court was precluded from judging the matter for itself.[40]

2. Critical Appraisal

Under the critical appraisal model of assessment, external agencies may play a role in assessing clinical standards. The point was made as long ago as 1960 by Lord Goddard.[41] Criticising (what we have called) the *reflective practice* approach, he said it would not be sufficient for a doctor to present the court with two colleagues prepared to support his action, if there was evidence which suggested negligence. In such a case the judge would be entitled to find fault. And Lord Donaldson said

---

[37] [1985] 1 All ER 635.   [38] ibid., 638.
[39] *Maynard v West Midland RHA* [1985] 1 All ER 635, 639. And see, to the same effect, his opinion in *Sidaway v Royal Bethlem Hospital Governors* [1985] 1 All ER 643. *Hucks v Cole* was cited in neither case.
[40] Note, however, that even under a *critical appraisal* of the medical evidence, the plaintiff's case was difficult because "the defence had called a formidable number of distinguished experts . . . all of whom . . . approved the course of action taken in deferring diagnosis and performing the operation". See ibid., 639, *per* Lord Scarman.   [41] In *Chapman v Rix* [1994] 5 Med LR 239, 247.

in *Sidaway v Royal Bethlem Hospital*: "I think that, in an appropriate case, a judge would be entitled to reject a unanimous medical view if he were satisfied that it was manifestly wrong and that the doctors must have been misdirecting themselves as to their duty in law."[42] This suggests a more independent role sensitive to criticism voiced by others in which the court should be satisfied of the logical steps on which the decision was based. Clearly, this approach takes note of authoritative clinical guidelines. Say the National Institute for Clinical Excellence (NICE) recommends certain practices, or procedures. Under the critical appraisal approach, clinicians ought to bear them in mind. Within their *Bolam* discretion, they are not bound to follow them. But, if they depart from them, they should have sound and logical reasons why they are not appropriate.[43]

Recent cases have voiced support for this more critical approach. A good example of the process of appraisal is contained in *Hucks v Cole*.[44] The patient presented the doctor with an infected finger. The doctor prescribed tetracycline instead of penicillin. Penicillin is known to be bacteriocidal; tetracycline is not. The patient suffered puerperal septicaemia and brought proceedings in negligence. Sachs LJ was satisfied that if penicillin had been administered the infection would not have occurred and the patient would have avoided serious illness. Thus, he said, unless there was a good cause for not administering it:

> ... the onset was due to a lacuna between what could easily have been done and what was in fact done. According to the defence, that lacuna was consistent with and indeed accorded with the reasonable practice of others with obstetric experience. When the evidence shows that a lacuna in professional practice exists by which risks of grave danger are knowingly taken, then, however small the risks, the Courts must anxiously examine that lacuna—particularly if the risks can be easily and inexpensively avoided. If the Court finds, on analysis of the reasons given for not taking those precautions that, in the light of current professional knowledge, there is no proper basis for the lacuna, and that it is definitely not reasonable that those risks should have been taken, its function is to state the fact and where necessary to state that it constitutes negligence. In such a case the practice will no doubt thereafter be altered to the benefit of patients. On such occasions the fact that other practitioners would have done the same thing as the defendant practitioner is a very weighty matter to be put in the scales on his behalf; but it is not ... conclusive. The Court must be vigilant to see whether the reasons given for putting a patient at risk are valid ...

> ... this is not apparently the case of "two schools of thought"; it appears to be case of doctors who said in one form or another that they would have acted or might have acted in the same way as the defendant did for reasons which on examination do not really stand up to analysis.[45]

---

[42] [1984] 1 All ER 1018, 1028 (CA). See also the comments of Lord Bridge in the House of Lords, [1985] 1 All ER 643, 662. The same view was taken in the Canadian case of *Reibl v Hughes* (1980) 114 DLR (3d) 1, 13.

[43] The question might also extend to matters of hospital policy. Should a maternity unit routinely listen to the mother's womb to check if she is carrying twins? See *Dunne v National Maternity Hospital* [1989] IR 91.   [44] *Hucks v Cole* [1993] 4 Med LR 393 (decided in 1968).

[45] ibid., 397. See also *Helling v Carey* ((1974) 519 P.2d 981, Wash Sup Ct). An optician failed to test the plaintiff's eyes for glaucoma. She was 32 and the incidence of the disease in people of a similar

Exercising its own judgment as to the adequacy of the doctor's reasoning, the court said that the risk of failing to treat appropriately was septicaemia and, ultimately, death. Given that penicillin presented no serious danger and was readily available to the doctor, he ought to have administered it to his patient. Although other doctors might have proceeded in the same way, their reasoning did not withstand logical analysis. The duty under the critical appraisal approach requires the court to examine the substance and rationale of the decision, not merely the fact that others can be found to support it.[46]

Despite the relative clarity of this approach, the rhetoric of critical appraisal is not consistently reflected in the decisions themselves, which may have more in common with the professional consensus model of analysis. For example, in *Defreitas v O'Brien*,[47] although *Hucks* reasoning was discussed, it does not clearly determine the outcome of the case. Over many years, the claimant had suffered severe and disabling pain in her back. Despite being seen by a number of specialists, no firm diagnosis of the cause could be made. The defendant decided to undertake exploratory surgery of the plaintiff's spine. The operation carried unavoidable risk of infection which materialised in damage.[48] Her experts said that spinal surgery was always hazardous. Given the inescapable risk of serious harm, doctors should not undertake spinal surgery for exploratory reasons only. A clear diagnosis was always a prerequisite. By contrast, the defendants' experts said that they constituted a sub-group of "specialist" specialists, amounting to some eleven practitioners out of over 1,000 neurosurgeons in the UK, who dealt exclusively with the spine and that they had additional expertise in spinal surgery.[49] In the right hands, they said, the risks associated with an exploratory operation were acceptable, given the severity of the plaintiff's condition, at around 15 to 20 percent.[50] Despite having access to the clinical evidence which divided the parties, the court did not subject the defendants' reasoning to close logical scrutiny. Instead, it confirmed that the decision to operate was supported by a responsible body of medical opinion (albeit a minority) and accepted their judgment that exploratory spinal surgery was justified even in the absence of a firm diagnosis.

---

age is around one in 25,000. The professional standard did not offer routine testing for those under the age of 40 because it was not thought cost-effective to do so. The court held that the matter was not governed by the medical standard because, as a matter of law, the relevant test was so simple and inexpensive that it ought in all the circumstances to have been offered to the plaintiff.

[46] Notice that the case was decided in 1968, but (like *Hunter* and *Bolam*) left no impact on medical jurisprudence until its significance was re-emphasised in the late 1980s by I. Kennedy and A. Grubb, *Medical Law: Cases and Materials* (Butterworths, 1989).   [47] [1995] 6 Med LR 108.

[48] The plaintiff's spinal fluid became infected. She alleged that, although such a risk was an unavoidable part of the surgery in question, it was unreasonable to have exposed her to such a risk in the first place.   [49] See ibid., 114, col. 1.

[50] See the report at first instance [1993] 4 Med LR 281. Why a "15–20%" incidence of risk? The trial court judge accepted the statistic as a fact, but how can such a precise figure, from such a small sample of doctors, be reliable? In how many patients, with what cross-section of patients, over how many years, with what medical facilities and with what severity of injuries was the figure based? See D. Eddy, "Variations in Physician Practice: The Role of Uncertainty" (1984), 3 *Health Affairs* 74, who doubts the value of precise statistics in these matters.

Clearly, eminent and well-respected medical views in areas outside the court's own experience will continue to command considerable respect and authority. Indeed, many areas of clinical disagreement may be so unfamiliar to the court that it will never confidently master the logical basis for differing clinical opinions. In such cases, it is likely to assume they are reasonable provided they have the support of others and, to this extent, there is a logical limit to the courts' scrutiny in the critical appraisal approach. The difficulty is illuminated in another case concerning the propriety of brain surgery, which caused the plaintiff damage. The clinical experts differed as to need for surgery and offered different diagnoses of the patient's condition because they interpreted the physical signs of the brain lesion in different ways. As the judge said: "When experts of this distinction cannot agree upon the correct interpretation of what is under their noses, the task of a judge, almost wholly unversed in these matters, can hardly be described as easy."[51]

Bolitho v City and Hackney Health Authority expressed a similar commitment to the critical appraisal model of analysis, but ultimately failed to subject the clinical decision-making to close scrutiny.[52] The plaintiff, a two-year-old boy, was being treated in hospital for breathing difficulties caused by patent ductus arteriosus, a condition of the heart. The staff responsible for his care knew of his condition and the danger it presented. He suffered an episode of breathlessness but, in breach of their duty of care, the doctors responsible for his care failed to respond and attend to him. He suffered a cardiac arrest and severe brain damage. The defendants admitted negligence in failing to attend the patient. Their defence, however, was that even if they had attended him, they would probably not have assisted his breathing by intubation and, therefore, their negligence did not cause his damage which he would have suffered in any event. Their reason was that his condition in the past had improved spontaneously and that, since intubation involved the risk associated with the use of anaesthetic, they would have decided against it. The plaintiffs, on the other hand, said that no reasonable doctor could fail to have intubated the patient. Of course there was a risk in doing so but it was acceptably small. But the great benefit of doing so was to avoid precisely the tragedy which in fact occurred, i.e. a cardiac arrest and brain damage. As Simon Brown LJ put it: "It was . . . the defendants' case that it would have been positively wrong for an attending doctor to intubate. But that is surely an impossible contention having regard not least to the agreed fact that intubation alone would have averted this tragedy."[53]

Weighing together the risks and the benefits presented by intubation, the plaintiff alleged that "it was unreasonable and illogical not to anticipate the recurrence of a life-threatening event and take the step which it was acknowledged would probably have saved Patrick from harm".[54] Thus, it was argued, the principle

---

[51] *McAllister v Lewisham and N Southwark HA* [1994] 5 Med LR 343, 348 col. 1.
[52] [1997] 4 All ER 771.
[53] (1993) 13 BMLR 111, Simon Brown LJ, dissenting in the Court of Appeal at 128.
[54] ibid., 122. This was described by the judge as "a powerful argument—which I have to say, as a layman, appealed to me".

in *Hucks v Cole* permitted the court to examine and condemn a practice which exposed the patient to such an unreasonable and avoidable danger. The trial judge rejected the claim. He took an entirely passive view of his function in the case. He said:

It is not for me to make a choice between [the plaintiffs' and defendants' experts], one of whom is convinced that any competent doctor would, the other that she would not, have undertaken that procedure. Plainly, in my view, this is one of those areas in which there is a difference of opinion between two distinguished and convincing medical witnesses, as to what as a matter of clinical judgment proper treatment requires.[55]

Under this *professional consensus* approach, no question arose of requiring the defendant to satisfy the judge of the reasonableness of her opinion; it was reasonable by virtue of the support it attracted from another specialist. By contrast, on appeal, the House of Lords emphatically re-affirmed the responsibility of the court to scrutinise the reasonableness of clinical discretion. Lord Browne-Wilkinson said:

... the court is not bound to hold that a defendant doctor escapes liability for negligent treatment or diagnosis just because he leads evidence from a number of experts who are genuinely of the opinion that the defendant's treatment or diagnosis accorded with sound medical practice ... The use of these adjectives—responsible reasonable and respectable—all show that the court has to be satisfied that the exponents of the body of opinion relied upon can demonstrate that such opinion has a logical basis. In particular, in cases involving, as they often do, the weighing of risks against benefits, the judge before accepting a body of opinion as being responsible, reasonable or respectable, will need to be satisfied that, in forming their views, the experts have directed their minds to the question of comparative risks and benefits and have reached a defensible conclusion on the matter.

... In the vast majority of cases the fact that distinguished experts in the field are of a particular opinion will demonstrate the reasonableness of that opinion ... But, if, in a rare case, it can be demonstrated that the professional opinion is not capable of withstanding logical analysis, the judge is entitled to hold that the body of opinion is not reasonable or responsible.[56]

This clearly asserts the need for a *critical appraisal* of these cases. Yet, on the facts, their Lordships held that the claim should fail because it accepted the evidence of the doctor (contradicting Simon Brown LJ, above) that even if she had attended the patient, it would have been reasonable *not* to intubate him, given the risks of doing so. In many cases, therefore, notwithstanding the rhetoric of clinical appraisal, the threshold of logic on which the courts assess clinical reasonableness has remained relatively low.

On the other hand, in *Marriot v West Midlands Health Authority*[57] the claimant fell down stairs and suffered a serious blow to his head. After a number of days in which he had complained to his GP of serious and persistent headaches, he was not referred to hospital for a CT scan. He had suffered a lesion to his brain which bled

---

[55] Cited in *Bolitho* 13 BMLR 111, 122.   [56] [1997] 4 All ER 771, 778–9.
[57] [1999] Lloyd's Rep Med 23.

and caused brain-damage and which would probably have been avoided had the patient been treated in time. In the Court of Appeal, it was said:

Although the risk was described as small, the judge was correct in carrying out her assessment of the small likelihood that there was such a lesion, and of the serious consequences to the plaintiff if there was. The facilities available in modern hospitals for carrying out scans are readily available. It was open to the judge to hold that . . . it could not be a reasonable exercise of a general practitioner's discretion to leave a patient at home and not to refer him back to hospital.[58]

Thus, the cases are not wholly consistent. In some, the rhetoric of judicial "hard-look" is more apparent than real, whereas in others the review may appear to take a far from "passive" approach to clinical decision-making.[59] Of course, medicine permits a range of opinion. If there is substantial agreement about the choices available to doctors because there is "agreement about disagreement" (i.e. agreement about the various merits and demerits of different forms of treatment available for use), the court should naturally be inclined to accept the judgment of doctors that the differences of opinion are reasonable. But if the practice is both condemned as simply wrong and is supported only by an extremely small number of specialists, the court should be the more anxious to examine the reasons behind the decision in order to be satisfied that they are responsible.

3. Bureaucratic-Scientific Model

As we have seen, courts in medical negligence cases seldom defer to the opinions of a single doctor, unless it has the approval of "a body", a *reasonable* and logical opinion to support it. But the size of that body may be small, and the veracity of the opinion may remain largely beyond the competence of the court. This suggests that the *bureaucratic-scientific* model of clinical assessment, in which managerial influence becomes the dominant feature of clinical decision-making is not yet ready to have a significant impact in medical negligence. Of course, as we have seen under the critical appraisal model, authoritative agencies may seek to persuade clinicians as to the manner in which they should respond to patients, and clinicians are bound to incorporate their guidance in their assessment of patient need. No such agency, however, has sought to usurp completely the uniqueness of the relationship between doctor and patient which has an enduring and distinctive quality One should not under-estimate, however, the pressure that could be imposed on a doctor to comply with institutionally-endorsed guidelines. Take the example of a doctor whose further employment, or future promotion, is subject to managerial approval. Clearly, if conformity to accepted clinical standards is a component of the managerial decision concerning the doctor's advancement,

---

[58] *Per* Beldam LJ, 28, col. 2.
[59] For successful applications of the "hard-look" approach, *Townsend v Worcester DHA* (1995) 23 BMLR 31 and *Bouchta v Swindon HA* [1996] 7 Med LR 62.

there will be a strong inducement not to depart from those expectations. In this environment, clinical "outliers" (as they are sometimes called in the US) have every incentive to dilute their individual clinical discretion and comply with standard expectations. This pressure is subtle and difficult to measure. It has the potential to affect the whole concept of clinical freedom.

Today, therefore, the courts have reasserted their power to subject medical discretion to an independent and logical review. Within the spectrum of the four models discussed above, neither at the extremes are generally accepted. Only in exceptional circumstances will the law be satisfied with decision-making wholly based on *reflective practice*. Yet it is not so insensitive to the nuances of an individual patient's need that it adopts a *bureaucratic-scientific* approach to clinical assessment. Accordingly, the common law tolerates differing responses to guidelines provided they are based on a logical foundation of professional opinion (even if it is a minority opinion). Equally, if mere personal preference is no longer a sufficient basis for clinical judgment, nor is it for judicial decision-making either. If a judge finds a doctor's explanation unpersuasive and intends to criticise it, he is under a duty to explain why. The matter was put as follows in the Court of Appeal: "In resolving matters of expert evidence, the judge remains the judge; he is not obliged to accept evidence simply because it comes from an illustrious source; he can take account of demonstrated partisanship and lack of objectivity. But . . . a coherent reasoned opinion expressed by a suitably qualified expert should be the subject of a coherent reasoned rebuttal."[60] This cautions the courts to have robust and logical reasons for criticising clinical opinion.

III. Informed Consent to Care

Doctors are under a duty to obtain competent patients' informed consent to treatment. Breach of the duty exposes the doctor to the risk of liability in negligence. We discuss how this duty has evolved and the problems it presents today as follows by (A) balancing partnership and paternalism in medical care, (B) tracing the evolution of the law of informed consent, (C) discussing the duty to disclose that things have gone wrong, and (D) developing a concept of informed *denial* of care.

A. Balancing Partnership and Paternalism

For some time, the law of informed consent took an essentially *paternalistic* view of the doctor-patient relationship and it is only more recently that it has stressed the equality between them which, it is said, is more akin to a *partnership*. What is the balance of risks and advantages between the two? The danger of too paternalistic an

---

[60] (1998) *Knight v West Kent HA* 40 BMLR 61 *per* Kennedy LJ, 65; quoting Bingham LJ in *Eckersley v Binnie* (1998) 18 Con. LR 1, 77–78. See also *Parry v NW Surrey HA* [1994] 5 Med LR 259.

approach is that it may undermine patient autonomy. If it permits doctors to withhold information "in the patient's best interests", it will tend to disempower patients and generate an environment of inequality which may not promote trust and confidence between the parties. The problem was illustrated in 1954, when Lord Denning suggested it might be permissible to tell patients untruths about their condition if it was in their best interests to do so. The case concerned a broadcaster who had a toxic thyroid gland. She was concerned about the risk an operation presented to her voice and was assured that there was none. The reassurance was for the best of motives but the plaintiff's voice was damaged in the operation and she was no longer able to broadcast. Lord Denning said that though her doctor had told a lie, other doctors were not prepared to criticise him, and nor would the court.[61] This view must surely be wrong today.

Over the past two decades, we have developed a wider duty on clinicians to inform patients of the risks and benefits they might expect from treatment. The Department of Health, sensitive to this less deferential relationship between doctor and patient, put it as follows:

The idea of the patient as the passive recipient of care is changing and being replaced by a new emphasis on the relationship between the NHS and the people whom it serves—one in which health professionals are genuine partners seeking together the best solution to each patient's problem, one in which patients are empowered with information and can contribute ideas to help in the treatment of their case.[62]

This suggests that medical professionals should have much the same relationship with their patients as do accountants, surveyors, and lawyers with their clients. We would expect our non-medical advisers to be entirely candid about the risks and benefits of the course of action they proposed and to disclose that they had made a mistake and caused us loss. We would not expect significant information to be withheld from us because (say) our accountant considered it is too difficult for us to understand, or our lawyer thought it would not be in our best interests to know about it. This is appropriate to non-clinical professional relationships, but is it appropriate in the doctor-patient relationship?

We should not over-do the *partnership* model of informed consent for at least three reasons. First, many of us will never fully understand the choices available to us. If legal theory always matched medical practice, competent patients would have to understand and remember the information doctors presented to them be able to analyse the information and put it to practical use. Yet many of us will often be unable, or unwilling, to achieve these standards. A number of studies have demonstrated that many entirely independent and competent people have a limited understanding of the treatment to which they have given

---

[61] See *Hatcher v Black* The Times, 2 July 1954. Contrast his view in *Chapman v Rix* (1994) 5 Med LR 239, 248, in which he said that such an approach was understandable, but should never prejudice the right of a patient to receive proper treatment.

[62] *The Expert Patient* (Department of Health, 1999) 8.

their consent.[63] "[I]f full comprehension were the literal standard, much beneficial medical care could simply not be rendered . . . some people will never sufficiently comprehend the medical options they face regardless of how thorough the explanation."[64]

This is hardly surprising. Many of us misunderstand common medical terms so that doctor and patient may unwittingly speak at cross-purposes.[65] Clinical information is often unfamiliar, the evidence is often ambiguous, incomplete, tentative, and subject to differing interpretations. Both the diagnosis and prognosis may be uncertain. It may be offered to us over a period of time, not by a single doctor, but by a team of clinicians who emphasise different things so that it is difficult to focus on a single adviser. The problem is compounded when treatment stretches over many months and requires a series of decisions. It is compounded still further if we suffer more than one illness at the same time and are treated by different teams. Doctors have to *translate* complex information and, unless they have suffered from the particular condition themselves, may understand little of the patient's *personal* experience of illness. Some say, therefore, that the objective of informed patient consent may not be achieved "even when extraordinary efforts are made to provide complete information and to ensure their understanding. This appears to be true regardless of the amount of information delivered, the manner in which it is presented, or the type of medical procedure involved."[66]

The second reason for caution is that patients may simply reject the "partnership" model of decision-making. Of course, some patients (or their carers) know more about their condition than the doctors treating them, especially if they have lived with their illness over many years. Some may demand to see all the latest research papers in order to weigh and balance the benefits of various forms of treatment; their firm wish is to take complete control themselves and not to trust the experts.[67] Others, however, take the opposite view. They say the relationship between doctor and patient is very different from that of client and professional adviser because illness can undermine our autonomy and willingness to take difficult decisions alone.

When you are ill you are weary. When you are ill you are distracted by a regiment of unfamiliar problems, not least reconciling yourself to your disease, reconstructing your future, and coping with [every day]. You may want to avoid facing the dismal facts of your illness.

---

[63] See, e.g., A. Meisel and L. Roth, "Toward an Informed Discussion of Informed Consent: A Review and Critique of the Empirical Studies" (1983) 23 *Arizona Law Review* 267 and J. Merz and B. Fischoff, "Informed Consent Does not Mean Rational Consent: Cognitive Limitations on Decision-Making" (1990) 11 *Journal of Legal Medicine* 321.

[64] M. Hall, *Making Medical Spending Decisions—The Law, Ethics and Economics of Rationing Mechanisms* (Oxford University Press, New York, 1997) 208.

[65] Boyle, "Differences Between Patients' and Doctors' Interpretation of Common Medical Terms" [1970] 2 *British Medical Journal* 286.

[66] B. Cassileth *et al.*, "Informed Consent—Why Are Its Goals Imperfectly Realised?" (1980) 302 *New England Journal of Medicine* 896, 896.

[67] See R. Giulliani, *Leadership* (Little Brown, 2002) ch. 6 on taking control of the treatment decisions for his prostate cancer.

You may even want to "deny" your condition . . . And you may be so frightened that you cannot think lucidly and dispassionately.[68]

The point is made by an editor of the New England Journal of Medicine, himself an eminent doctor with expertise in the treatment of precisely the cancer he came to suffer himself. He spoke of his own experience with cancer of the oesophagus. His own doctors, respecting his own expertise, left the hard choices to him. With his own knowledge and understanding, who better to make the difficult decisions that lay ahead? He explains, however:

As a result, not only I, but my wife, my son and daughter-in-law (both doctors) and other family members became increasingly confused and emotionally distraught. Finally, when the pangs of indecision had become near intolerable, one wise physician friend said "What you need is a doctor" . . . When that excellent advice was followed, my family and I sensed immediate and immense relief.[69]

For some patients, a disproportionate focus on the need for autonomous decision-making will provide an additional, wholly unwanted burden and distraction from the main purpose of seeking medical help. We should be concerned to ensure that informed consent does not encourage doctors to focus simply on patient rights of choice if it deflects doctors from giving help and care to their patients. One study suggests that although most patients want to be informed of their medical circumstances, a substantial number do not want to make their own medical decisions. It does not explain fully which patients would prefer to decide matters entirely for themselves, but it reveals two interesting patterns. "First, the elderly are less likely than the young to want to make medical decisions. Second, the graver the patient's illness, the less likely the patient is to want to make medical decisions."[70] Informed consent, therefore, should seek to discover how much the patient wants to know and, within that framework, transfer sufficient information to enable the patient to make a well-informed and balanced decision about their treatment.[71]

Thirdly, "informed" consent often concerns the communication and assessment of "risk". But the subject of risk is notoriously difficult and abstract. By definition, risk refers to aggregates of people, rather than single individuals. If I smoke, are my health risks the same as for the population in general—after all, I may know an 80-year-old smoker who has never had a day's illness. There is often no "objective" or "neutral" way of communicating the relative risks and benefits of treatment. The question what to disclose and how is one of *perception*, based on incomplete

---

[68] A. Schneider and M. Farrell, "Information, Decisions and the Limits of Informed Consent" in M. Freeman and A. Lewis (eds) *Law and Medicine* (Oxford University Press, 2000) 109 analysing the uncertainties surrounding the treatment of prostate cancer.

[69] F. Ingelfinger, "Politics and Public Health" (1996) 334 *New England Journal of Medicine* 203–7, cited in M. Hall, *Making Medical Spending Decisions—the Law, Ethics, and Economics of Rationing Mechanisms* (Oxford University Press, New York, 1997) 37.

[70] See the fascinating study by C. Schneider, *The Practice of Autonomy—Patients, Doctors and Medical Decisions* (Oxford University Press, New York, 1998) 41.

[71] See O. O'Neill, *Autonomy and Trust in Bioethics* (Cambridge University Press, 2002), chs 2 and 7.

information, which is susceptible to unconscious bias.[72] How can information be conveyed to patients clearly and helpfully, without diluting the danger, or creating undue alarm? The difficulty is illuminated by the experience of the Department of Health and Committee on the Safety of Medicines (CSM) in connection with warnings about the increased risk of thromboembolism present in certain categories of oral contraceptives. Responding to new clinical evidence of a slightly increased risk of one type of contraceptive, the CSM sent a letter to doctors warning that "the chance of a thrombosis occurring in a vein increases around two-fold for some types of pill compared with others".[73] As a result, there was widespread and entirely unintended public concern at the apparent danger of some contraceptives as a result of which many women stopped taking the pill. There is a suspicion that the 11 per cent increase in abortions recorded between December 1995 and February 1996 must, at least in part, have been provoked by that announcement.[74] Yet, had the risk been expressed in *absolute* terms, it would have been less alarming. The increased risk was in the region of one death per 1.3 million users, or to put it another way, the percentage of those free of thrombosis would decline from 99.993 per cent to 99.985 per cent.[75]

What is the best way of communicating risks of this magnitude, perhaps to populations of patients?[76] Informed consent is not simply about conveying parcels of information. Decisions have to be made as to the manner in which the information is transferred. As the CSM case demonstrates, the process may cause misunderstanding and serve patients badly. In the mid-1990s, there was talk of the Department of Health publishing a comparative ranking of risk to assist a better public understanding of the subject and there is much to recommend such a "generic" approach to the subject.[77] But it was not pursued, and doctors and health authorities have been left to communicate "risks" to patients without assistance. In these circumstances, we should expect to find wide differences of practice amongst them.

Routinely, therefore, for many patients the extent of disclosure presupposed as necessary by the theory may be unhelpful and irrelevant. We may not comprehend the complexity of the information, we may be unable to detach ourselves from our condition of dependence, we may have mis-placed attachments to preconceived ideas, or may simply have insufficient personal experience of our situation on which to base a well-informed decision.[78] Yet it would be absurd if, under the informed consent rule,

---

[72] D. Kahneman, P. Slovic and A. Twersky (eds) *Judgment Under Uncertainty: Heuristics and Biases* (Cambridge University Press, 1982).

[73] *Combined oral contraceptives and thromboembolism* (CSM, October 1995).

[74] F. Furedi and A. Furedi, *The International Impact of Pill Panic in the UK* (Birth Control Trust, 1996) 3.   [75] ibid., at 24.

[76] The problem is discussed, though not resolved, in *Securing Good Health for the Whole Population* (The "Wanless Report", HM Treasury, 2004) ch. 7.

[77] *On the State of Public Health 1995: the annual report of the chief medical officer of the Department of Health for the year 1995* (HMSO, 1995).

[78] See J. Le Grand, "From Pawn to Queen" in A. Oliver (ed.) *Equity in Health and Healthcare* (The Nuffield Trust, 2004) and the commentary that follows. To some extent, doctors too may be subject

a doctor was required to *refuse* treatment to a patient considered competent because the patient had an incomplete understanding of the nature and consequences of the proposed treatment. Should the patient be required to demonstrate "fully informed" consent by means of a short written test of the essential information surrounding the treatment, its complications and alternatives? We should recognise, therefore, that patients are not a homogeneous group with identical requirements for medical information. Some of us may wish to become "expert patients" and want as much information as possible, others may prefer to transfer the burden of decision-making entirely to the doctor's judgment, and still others may choose to share decision-making with the doctor. For those who prefer not to have certain information forced upon them we should recognise their right to delegate decision-making authority, to such extent as the patient considers appropriate. All these factors suggest that the law should approach the balance between partnership and paternalism with caution.

There is a further impediment to the objective of informed consent, namely the time-constraints imposed on doctors and patients. Doctors do not have unlimited time to spend with each patient. In surgery, GPs often average between eight and ten minutes with each patient. More demanding requirements of disclosure put additional strain on consultations with patients. As the Bristol Inquiry observed, "pressures of time are a factor inhibiting good communication . . . We heard repeatedly that pressure of time means that patients often get a strictly limited amount of time to talk, particularly when seeing a consultant."[79] *Institutional* limitations will one day be blamed for limited dialogue between doctor and patient and the courts will be asked to consider whether resource constraints may modify the duty to obtain patients' informed consent.

B. Evolution of the Law of Informed Consent

The general law of consent to treatment focuses on the individual relationship between doctor and patient. It insists that patients cannot give *informed* consent unless they are given sufficient information of the risks, benefits, and alternatives to the proposed treatment to enable them to weigh and balance the options available. Patients have the right to accept, or reject, the advice of their doctors for good reason, bad reason, or no reason at all. Provided they are competent to make the decision, the choice is a matter for them.[80] Certainly, evidence of a signature on a form the patient has never read, or only signed on their way to the operating theatre, is entirely ineffective for this purpose. *Informed* consent requires the patient to have time to absorb and reflect on the information.[81]

---

to these limitations of comprehension. See also B. New, "Paternalism and Public Policy" (1999) 15 *Economics and Public Policy* 63.

[79] *Learning from Bristol* (Cm. 5207, 2001) 290, para. 28.

[80] *Re T* [1992] 4 All ER 649. The difficulty of communicating complicated information in a sometimes unequal relationship is well recognised.   [81] ibid., at 663.

The need for balance in this matter was considered in the *Sidaway* case, in which the court leaned heavily towards the *paternalistic* approach, but stopped short of conferring on doctors full discretion as to the disclosure of information. A patient agreed with her doctor that she should have a laminectomy to her spine to relieve pain caused by the oppression of nerve roots. She was not informed that the surgery carried an unavoidable risk, even when performed carefully, of interfering with blood vessels around the spine. The likelihood of such an event was less than 2 per cent and the damage to be expected was of temporary or permanent immobility. In the most serious case, the patient would suffer partial paralysis. In the event, this most serious risk materialised. The plaintiff's complaint was that she ought to have been informed about these risks and that, had she known about them, she would have chosen more conservative treatment (say) by analgesics which carried less risk. Their Lordships, though expressing differing views, agreed that the matter was largely, though not entirely, within the discretion of the medical profession. Lord Bridge said that:

> . . . the issue whether non-disclosure in a particular case should be condemned as a breach of the doctor's duty of care is an issue to be decided primarily on the basis of expert medical evidence, applying the *Bolam* test . . . But even in a case where . . . no expert in the relevant medical field condemns the non-disclosure as being in conflict with accepted and responsible medical practice, I am of opinion that the judge might in certain circumstances come to the conclusion that disclosure of a particular risk was so obviously necessary to an informed choice on the part of the patient that no reasonably prudent medical man would fail to make it.[82]

Similarly, Lord Templeman said that, notwithstanding medical discretion, there was no doubt that a doctor ought to draw the attention of the patient to dangers which may be special in kind or magnitude or special to the patient.[83] More cautiously, Lord Diplock inclined to the view that "the *Bolam* test of medical negligence should be applied"[84] since the issues of disclosure of risks and the standard of care in treatment concerned the same exercise of professional skill and should be governed by the same test. But he too, stopped short of declaring the matter to be wholly within the discretion of doctors because some patients would be entitled to information sufficient to enable them to decide for themselves whether or not to go ahead with the treatment. He said:

> When it comes to warning about risks, the kind of training and experience that a judge will have undergone at the Bar makes it natural for him to say (correctly) *it is my right to decide* whether any particular thing is done to my body, and I want to be *fully* informed of any risks there may be involved of which I am not already aware from my general knowledge as a highly educated man of experience, so that *I may form my own judgment* as to whether to refuse the advised treatment or not.[85]

---

[82] *Sidaway v Royal Bethlem Hospital Governors* [1985] 1 All ER 643, 662. Lord Keith agreed.
[83] ibid., at 665.   [84] ibid., at 659.   [85] ibid., at 659, emphasis added.

So the matter does not lie within the absolute discretion of the doctor. His Lordship used the example of judges, but it must also be true of other educated and experienced people. It must be true of doctors, nurses, and a host of professional, and other people. This is the more so when a patient asks the doctor for specific information. Lord Diplock continued: "No doubt, if the patient in fact manifested this attitude by means of questioning, the doctor would tell him whatever it was the patient wanted to know."[86]

The *Sidaway* case, therefore, left unresolved the question of the precise extent of disclosure necessary for informed consent. Perhaps, for this reason, two subsequent cases adopted a strongly deferential view of the duty which demonstrates the danger of uncritical paternalism. The first was *Blyth v Bloomsbury Health Authority*,[87] in which the plaintiff was a nurse. She was prescribed the long-acting contraceptive drug, Depo-Provera. Having previously reacted very badly to a contraceptive drug, she had good reason to ask specific questions of her doctor about Depo-Provera; and her training enabled her to understand the information she sought. She alleged that she was not given an adequate warning of the side-effects of the drug and would have chosen other means of contraception had her questions been answered properly. Rejecting her claim, the Court of Appeal said that *Bolam* permitted doctors to determine how much information should be disclosed, even to the extent of deciding how, and if, specific questions should be answered.[88] Is this satisfactory? Especially when there is no urgent medical "need" for treatment, why should the doctor be presumed to know what is best? A similar case arose in connection with a failed sterilisation in *Gold v Haringey Health Authority*.[89] The claimant argued that, given the non-therapeutic nature of the operation, she should have been given sufficient information to choose for herself what was best. Her claim was dismissed on the ground that disclosure was a matter for professional discretion.

Such an uncritically passive application of the duty of disclosure is now subject to doubt.[90] First in North America, then Australia and later in the UK, individual patient rights have come to dominate the relationship. In doing so, the courts have imposed more demanding standards on doctors. The reason this is no longer appropriate has been explained in an Australian case as follows:[91]

. . . there is a fundamental difference between, on the one hand, diagnosis and treatment and, on the other hand, the provision of advice or information to a patient. In diagnosis and

---

[86] ibid. Lord Bridge agreed saying, at 661: "when questioned specifically by a patient of apparently sound mind about risks involved in a particular treatment proposed, the doctors duty must . . . be to answer both truthfully and as fully as the questioner requires."   [87] [1993] 4 Med LR 151.

[88] ibid., at 157. Kerr LJ said "I am not convinced that the *Bolam* test is irrelevant even in relation to the question of what answers are properly to be given to specific enquiries." Neill LJ agreed at 160.

[89] *Gold v Haringey HA* [1987] 2 All ER 888.

[90] These approaches have been described as "a conflict between the old Hippocratic paternalism and the non-consequentialist principles of veracity, fidelity, and especially autonomy". See R. Veatch, *The Patient-Physician Relation: The Patient as Partner, Part 2* (Indiana University Press, 1991) 157.

[91] *Rogers v Whitaker* (1992) 109 ALR 625, 632, (1994) 16 BMLR 148, 156. So too in Canada. See *Reibl v Hughes* (1980) 114 DLR (3d) 1. In *Sidaway*, at 63 Lord Bridge entirely supported the duty in

treatment, the patient's contribution is limited to the narration of symptoms and relevant history; the medical practitioner provides diagnosis and treatment according to his or her level of skill. However, except in cases of emergency or necessity, all medical treatment is preceded by the patient's choice to undergo it . . . the choice is meaningless unless it is made on the basis of relevant information and advice . . . it would be illogical to hold that the amount of information to be provided by the medical practitioner can be determined from the perspective of the practitioner . . . or the medical profession.[92]

This more demanding approach seems to have influenced a number of subsequent cases in England. For example, *Smith v Tunbridge Wells Health Authority* concerned a patient suffering from a rectal prolapse. The doctor failed to warn him that the operation to remedy the condition could cause erectile and bladder dysfunction. The operation was not essential because the patient managed the problems the condition presented. The plaintiff consented to surgery and the damage occurred. The patient said that, had he been told of those risks, he would have refused the operation. The doctor was able to find other colleagues who would not have made such a disclosure in these circumstances. This support notwithstanding, the judge said "although some surgeons may still not have been warning patients similar in situation to the plaintiff of the risk of impotence, that omission was neither reasonable nor responsible".[93] More recently, the duty to disclose was explained in *Pearce v United Bristol NHS Healthcare Trust*[94] by Lord Woolf MR who said:

In a case where it is being alleged that a plaintiff has been deprived of the opportunity to make a proper decision as to what course he or she should take in relation to treatment, it seems to me that the law [is] that if there is a significant risk which would affect the judgment of a reasonable patient, then in the normal course it is the responsibility of a doctor to inform the patient of that significant risk, if the information is needed so that the patient can determine for him or herself what course he or she should adopt.

This appears to be more patient-centred, but what is a "significant risk" and who is a "reasonable patient"?[95] Who is the judge; doctor, patient, or court? Note that in the *Pearce* case, the risk of which the patient was unaware was 0.1 to 0.2 per cent of losing her baby in the final days of her pregnancy. Lord Woolf said that "the doctors . . . did not regard that risk as significant; nor do I . . . one cannot criticise [the doctor's] decision not to inform Mrs Pearce of that very, very

Reibl v Hughes to disclose a 10% risk of a stroke. "[Sometimes] disclosure of a risk [is] so obviously necessary to an informed choice on the part of the patient that no reasonably prudent medical man would fail to make it . . . for example the 10% risk of stroke."

[92] Indeed, in Australia, the duty has been extended to include disclosure of doctors' positions in clinical league tables. See *Chappel v Hart* [1999] Lloyd's Rep Med 223. However, when statistics are created from relatively small numbers of patients, the position of each doctor in the table is likely to fluctuate so that the information may be misleading. Also, those at the very top of their professions, and acknowledged to be amongst the best in their field, may also be poorly represented by league tables because they consistently have referred to them the most difficult cases.

[93] *Smith v Tunbridge Wells HA* [1994] 5 Med LR 334 at 339.	[94] (1999) 48 BMLR 118, 124.

[95] The more serious the risk, the more urgent the need for a warning. See also *Joyce v Merton, Sutton and Wandsworth HA* (1996) 27 BMLR 124.

small additional risk."[96] This suggests that patients do not have a right to know of *every* risk, no matter how unlikely. The alternative would surely be unworkable. If a clinical trial in mice had raised the possibility of liver dysfunction never yet seen in humans, would that count? Every procedure carries a wide range of risks (not all of which will be known to the doctor). How would the weight of information be accumulated? How much time would be spent explaining it, bearing in mind the needs of the doctor's other patients. Bear in mind too the difficulty encountered by the Committee on the Safety of Medicines. How should the risks be communicated without creating needless anxiety amongst those who are already sick? Such a principle of *absolute* disclosure (whatever that means) could do more harm than good.

Inescapably, therefore, the court recognised that, even within this more patient-centred approach, judgment and discretion are endemic. Clearly, the matter is not wholly for the medical profession to decide. It will be subject to final scrutiny by the court. But the precise point at which disclosure of risks becomes unnecessary will depend on the facts of each case and, in particular, the patient's illness and their ability, or wish, to absorb the information. Perhaps the case marks a shift of legal value: "respect for the patient's right to choose and decide what is to be done to his, or her body. Reasoning based on 'the need not to trouble the patient', the 'desire to avoid worrying the patient unduly', or 'the fear of refusal' will simply not stand up to analysis because they embody the wrong values."[97] This is especially significant when there is real choice whether to embark on treatment, or not (as in *Smith v Tunbridge Wells Health Authority*). The point was endorsed in *Chester v Afshar*, in circumstances similar to those of *Sidaway*, in which there was a failure to warn of the unavoidable risk of paralysis of around 1 per cent following surgery to the spine. The risk is present even when surgery is performed perfectly competently (as it was in *Chester*). Holding the doctor responsible, the Court of Appeal said that:

The purpose of the rule requiring doctors to give appropriate information to their patients is to enable the patient to exercise her right to chose whether or not to have the particular operation to which she is asked to give her consent . . . If the doctor's failure to take that care results in her consenting to an operation to which she would not otherwise have given her consent, the purpose of the rule would be thwarted if he were not held to be responsible when the very risk about which he failed to warn her materialises and causes an injury which she would not have suffered there and then.[98]

Disclosure of "appropriate information" is especially important for patients who have a genuine choice whether or not to proceed because the treatment is elective and may be postponed, or refused. Here, patients need adequate information on

---

[96] (1999) 48 BMLR 118, 125. The court also considered that, even if that information had been communicated, the patient would have reluctantly followed her doctor's advice and that, therefore, the failure to disclose was not the cause of her loss.

[97] I. Kennedy and A. Grubb, *Medical Law* (3rd edn, Butterworths, 2000) 710.

[98] (2002) 67 BMLR 66, para. 47.

which to exercise that choice. For example, the question has arisen in relation to treatment with a risk of 1:14,000 that the patient would go blind when she had been living with her condition for many years,[99] the risk of impotence from non-essential surgery,[100] the risk of regaining fertility after sterilisation,[101] and the risk that mastectomy might be performed during surgery.[102] Patients are entitled to choose even if the procedure will probably have to be performed at a later date because the matter of timing is also for them. Thus, even for cases of serious and persistent back-pain, the patient should be encouraged to reflect on the pros and cons of treatment,[103] including alternative forms of treatment. For example, in a Canadian case,[104] in circumstances very similar to those of the *Sidaway* case, the plaintiff was not warned of risks of a laminectomy to fuse some of the vertebrae in her back and she suffered disability following the operation. The court held that there was a duty "to advise the appellant of the consequences of leaving the ailment untreated *and the duty to advise of alternate means of treatment*".[105] This emphasis on a more extensive duty of disclosure is especially significant in relation to *elective* care.

On the other hand, it may be less appropriate for severely ill patients, or more dependent patients, who may prefer more support and guidance from their doctors. Their primary concern may be for care and, if possible, cure, rather than to express rights to autonomy. Common law must respect these patients too and encourage trust and candour between doctor and patient which permits some of the decision-making surrounding treatment to be "delegated" to the doctor if the patient wishes to do so. Judicial sympathy has been expressed for those who do not wish to become experts in their condition; indeed, their right to self-determination has been upheld even when their doctors believe it would be in their best interests to accumulate greater knowledge of their condition before reaching an irreversible decision.[106] In *Re B* a woman suffered a serious hemorrhage in her spinal column

---

[99] Australian law has answered in the affirmative, see *Rogers v Whittaker* (1994) 16 BMLR 148.

[100] *Smith v Tunbridge Wells HA* [1994] Med LR 334.

[101] *Newell and Newell v Goldenberg* [1995] 6 Med LR 371.

[102] *Williamson v East London and City HA* (1998) 41 BMLR 85.

[103] See *Chester v Afshar* (2002) 67 BMLR 66. In such a case, the quantum of damages might be limited to the period between the time that informed consent was not obtained and the time when the patient would otherwise have chosen to have the procedure (see ibid., para. 42), though the matter will be difficult to determine.   [104] (1987) *Haughian v Paine* 37 DLR (4th) 624.

[105] ibid., at 639, my emphasis. A still more onerous duty was imposed by the Supreme Court of California in *Truman v Thomas* (1980) 611 P.2d 902 to inform patients of the dangers of *not* consenting to treatment. The patient could not afford the costs of a cervical smear and her cancer of the cervix was undiagnosed until it became inoperable and from which she died. Given the patient's symptoms, the doctor "has the additional duty of advising of all the material risks of which a reasonable person would want to be informed before deciding not to undergo the procedure" (at 906). Note, however, the powerful dissent of Clarke J who said such an onerous duty "will result in reduced care for others. Requiring physicians to spend a large portion of their time teaching medical science before practising it will greatly increase the cost of medical diagnosis" (at 910). US courts have been reluctant to follow the majority approach. See M. Hall, note 64 above, at 202–4.

[106] A right confirmed in *St George's Healthcare NHS Trust v S* [1998] 3 All ER 673 in which an expectant mother suffering severe pre-eclampsia was said to be entitled to refuse a caesarian section even though the decision would expose both her and her unborn child to risk of death.

and neck which rendered her tetraplegic and entirely dependent on life-support machinery. Her intellect was unimpaired. She decided that she did not want to continue living in such a condition and instructed her doctors to withdraw the life-preserving treatment, knowing that it would lead to her death. However, her doctors resisted her request on the ground that many patients in similar circumstances, who initially withdrew their consent to further life-saving treatment, adjusted to their disabilities over a period of time. Over time, they were able to lead a fulfilling life on life-support machinery and were glad they had done so. In other words, they said, at the time of her original decision, the decision was not *fully* informed of the advantages of the decision to remain alive. Thus, her doctors suggested, until such understanding had been achieved over a longer period of time, the patient was not competent and treatment should be continued in her best interests.

The Court of Appeal rejected the doctors' argument. The view of the doctors that "not to have experienced rehabilitation means that the patient lacks informed consent cannot be the basis for the legal concept of mental capacity. If [this] were correct, the absence of experience in the spinal rehabilitation unit clinic would deny Ms B, or any other similar patient, the right to choose whether or not to go on . . . This is not the state of the law."[107] Once the patient had demonstrated that she could understand and weigh in the balance the consequences of her decision, she was presumed to be competent and to have full capacity. The fact that the doctors believed that such a decision was not in her "best interests" did not affect her right to choose. The Court of Appeal said that "we have to try inadequately to put ourselves into the position of the gravely disabled person and respect the patient's *subjective character of experience*".[108] Here, therefore, the competent patient's right to *reject* medical advice was affirmed irrespective of her doctor's opinion of the limits of her understanding.

C. Disclosure when Things have Gone Wrong

Should clinicians disclose when treatment has gone wrong? Should doctors in effect encourage the taking of legal advice against themselves? In principle, the doctor's Hippocratic commitment to patients' best interests suggests such a duty should not be in question. The General Medical Council insists that, as a matter of professional ethics:

If a patient under your care has suffered serious harm . . . you should explain fully to the patient what has happened and the likely long, and short-term effects. Where appropriate you should offer an apology. If the patient is under 16 and lacks maturity to consent to treatment, you should explain the situation honestly to those with parental responsibility for the child.[109]

---

[107] *Re B (adult: refusal of medical treatment)* [2002] 2 All ER 449, para. 93.
[108] ibid., para. 94, my emphasis.
[109] *Good Medical Practice* (General Medical Council, 1999) para. 17.

Does the law take the same view? We examine the common law and the Human
Rights Act 1998.

1. The Common Law

A common law duty may exist to disclose medical errors so that the patient can
take further action if he or she so chooses. The Court of Appeal has supported the
logic of such a claim on the grounds that, if the principle of informed consent provides a right to information *before* the carrying out of medical procedures, there is
no reason why it not should also extend to a right to an explanation *after* things
have gone wrong. Accepting the principle of informed consent, Lord Donaldson
MR speculated on the position of the law governing a patient who was wrongly
transfused with air during a blood transfusion:

> Why, we ask ourselves, is the position any different if the patient asks what treatment he has
> in fact had? . . . Is he not entitled to ask what treatment he in fact received, and is the doc-
> tor and hospital authority not obliged to tell him, "in the event you did not only get a blood
> transfusion. You also got an air transfusion"? Why is the duty different before the treatment
> from what it is afterwards?[110]

In the Canadian case of *Stamos v Davies*[111] the defendant doctor negligently damaged the plaintiff's spleen in his attempt to take a biopsy from his lung, as a result of
which the spleen had to be removed. The plaintiff recovered damages for the negligence but claimed an additional sum for the doctor's failure to inform him that he
had injured him. The court accepted that doctors do indeed have such a duty in
Canada and that the defendant was in breach of the duty. However, this second head
of damages was denied. The error was discovered and dealt with within a week and
the patient could not prove that the doctor's breach was the cause of any additional
pain and suffering or other loss. Similarly, in England, in *Gerber v Pines*,[112] the doctor failed to tell his patient that a hypodermic needle had snapped during a procedure and remained lodged inside her body. The error became quickly apparent and
the needle was removed within a few days. However, the judge said that: "A patient
in whose body a doctor had found that he had left a foreign substance was entitled
to be told at once. [In this case] there was a breach of duty and negligence on the
doctor's part in not at once informing either the patient or her husband on the day
of the accident." However, given the duration of the discomfort suffered by the
patient, damages of just over £5 were awarded (*without* the plaintiff's costs).

---

[110] [1987] 2 All ER 385, 389–90. See similar views expressed in *Naylor v Preston AHA* [1987] 2 All
ER 353. In *AB v Tameside & Glossop HA* [1997] 8 Med LR 91, the authority conceded that it had a
duty to take reasonable steps to contact and inform obstetric patients that they had been treated by a
doctor subsequently diagnosed to be suffering HIV. See also N. Mullany, "Liability for Careless
Communication of Traumatic Information" (1998) 114 LQR 380.
[111] 21 DLR (4th) 507 (1985). See generally, G. Robertson, "Fraudulent Concealment and the
Duty to Disclose Medical Mistakes" (1987) 25 *Alberta Law Review* 215.
[112] (1934) 79 *Solicitors Journal* 13.

On the other hand, if the failure to disclose the accident causes the patient to suffer additional, avoidable harm, substantial damages may be available. In *Pitman v Bain*,[113] in 1984, the Canadian Red Cross transfused the plaintiff with blood contaminated with HIV, before the virus could have been detected. The following year, a test for identifying infected blood was developed and it became possible to trace the recipients of the infected transfusions in previous years by a process of "look-back". However, it was only in 1989 that the plaintiff's doctor was informed that his patient was at serious risk of having been contaminated with HIV, by which time his wife had also become HIV positive. The Supreme Court of Canada was satisfied by analogy with the product liability cases that the blood transfusion service was in a proximate relationship with those to whom it transfused blood and was under a duty to advise the recipient of the risk and to do so expeditiously. Similarly once the hospital had been informed of the danger, it had a duty to examine its own records to determine which of its patients may have been exposed to danger and to inform the responsible GPs accordingly. Both the Canadian Red Cross and the hospitals were held to have failed in their duty to establish effective systems by which such accidents could be examined, and for failing to act with proper haste once the systems had been put in place. The claims by both the patient and his wife were successful.[114]

2. The Human Rights Act 1998

The law in this area has also been heavily influenced by the Human Rights Act 1998. The point arose in *R (on the application of Khan) v Secretary of State for Health*,[115] in which the applicant's daughter, aged three, died in hospital of a heart attack in circumstances strongly suggestive of gross negligence. Internal investigations were carried out into the cause of death, but none involved the applicant, or his family and none were wholly independent. Further, although a date for a coroner's inquest was arranged, the applicant could play no active part in the hearing because he could not afford the cost of legal representation. The applicant claimed that there should be some independent investigation of the circumstances of his daughter's death with a view to understanding what had gone wrong and how to reduce the risk in the future, and that he should be entitled to participate in the inquest without incurring costs.[116]

The Court of Appeal acceded to both claims for the following reasons. Article 2 of the European Convention on Human Rights protects the "right to life". It imposes

---

[113] 112 DLR(4th) 257 (1994).

[114] In addition, the GP was held responsible for failing to notify the plaintiff with proper haste. The award of damages to the patient reflected the years of life lost through not having had proper care. The wife's claim was for the loss to her life, which could have been avoided.

[115] [2003] 4 All ER 1239.

[116] The need for independent investigation in these circumstances was recognised by Professor Sir Ian Kennedy in *Learning from Bristol* (Cm. 5207) ch. 2 for its capacity to enhance learning, improve discipline, aid catharsis, and provide reassurance to the public.

on the state a *substantive* duty to protect the right itself, and a *procedural* duty to seek to discover why breaches of Article 2 have occurred and the responses needed to minimise the danger in the future. This explanation of Article 2 originated in *Osman v United Kingdom*, in which the applicant was given inadequate protection from the police against a man known to be dangerous and who had made clear his intention to harm the applicant and his family. In the event, the applicant was seriously injured and his father killed by the man. The question arose as to the state's obligation to provide adequate protection to the applicant and his family. The European Court said that:

Art 2(1) enjoins the state not only to refrain from the intentional and unlawful taking of life, but also to take appropriate steps to safeguard the lives of those within its jurisdiction . . . [T]he state's obligation in this respect extends beyond its primary duty to secure the right to life by putting in place effective criminal law provisions to deter the commission of offences . . . art 2 of the convention may also imply in certain well-defined circumstances a positive obligation on the authorities to take preventive operational measures to protect an individual whose life is at risk from the criminal acts of another individual.[117]

Medical accidents in hospital are far removed from the criminal intentions of a highly dangerous individual. Never the less, if a dangerous practice is implicated in the death of a patient, the principle may impose a duty to discover how the accident occurred and how it should be avoided in the future. In the hospital context the point arose in *Powell v United Kingdom*.[118] A boy died in hospital as a result of the failure of doctors to diagnose his condition. His parents alleged that there had been an attempt to cover up the true circumstances of their son's death and sought full disclosure of all the circumstances.[119] Although the claim was declared inadmissible for procedural reasons, the European Court of Human Rights accepted that the acts and omissions of health authorities (acting as agents of the state) could give rise to claims under Article 2. The nature and extent of the scrutiny required will vary from case to case depending on the circumstances. Provided the state has made adequate provision for securing high professional standards among health professionals, not every death in hospital arising from an error of judgment, or operational negligence, could trigger the duty to account under Article 2. Thus "matters such as error of professional judgment . . . on the part of a health professional are not of themselves sufficient to call that State to account".[120] On the other hand, where there was evidence of a *systematic failure* by the public authority, suggesting that the risk was deep-seated and likely to recur, further independent and public investigation may be required. It said:

The events leading to the tragic death of the applicant's son and the responsibility of the health professionals involved are matters which must be addressed from the angle of the

---

[117] (1998) 5 BHRC 293, 321, para. 115.   [118] 45305/99 (4 May 2000).
[119] The action was rejected by the Court of Appeal in *Powell v Boldaz* (1997) 39 BMLR 35.
[120] *Glass v UK* [2004] Lloyds Rep Med 76, 85, col. 1, in which there was a complaint under Art 2 concerning the exercise of clinical discretion. The application was declared inadmissible on the grounds that there had been a proper response to the complaint.

adequacy of the mechanisms in place for shedding light on the course of those events allowing the facts of the case to be exposed to public scrutiny—not least for the benefit of the applicant . . . the obligation at issue extends to the need for an effective independent system for establishing the cause of death of an individual under the care and responsibility of health professionals and any liability on the part of the latter.[121]

Thus, in the *Khan* case, applying human rights law, the Court of Appeal said that the circumstances of the case required much more than internal investigations carried out privately. The hospital's blanket admission of liability did not affect the need for a proper public investigation in which the events leading to the accident could be uncovered and assessed. Further, it was for the state to initiate inquiries to discover the truth in the matter, not the deceased's family.[122] No such inquiry could be effective unless the deceased's family could play an effective part. Given that the hospital and its doctors would all have the benefit of legal advice and representation, the applicant was entitled to his own legal assistance without personal cost.[123] Clearly, these cases put an extensive obligation on the state to both investigate publicly the circumstances of some deaths arising from medical accidents and to assist the families of the bereaved to contribute to that investigation without incurring financial cost.

This approach concerned a patient who had died in hospital and the right to life enshrined in Article 2 of the European Convention. What about those who survive their injuries? Should the same general approach apply? A number of reasons suggest that it should. First, Article 8 of the Convention protects the right to "private and family life" and those who are merely injured may argue that their private rights to claim compensation and an explanation will be frustrated unless they have the benefit of a proper investigation into their complaint. Given that, even under Article 2, the right is limited to cases in which there appears to have been a systematic or persistent failure (rather than an isolated event), it would not be unreasonable to extend similar rights to those who have been injured in these circumstances.

D. Informed *Denial* of Care

We discussed, in Chapter 3, how rationing may occur covertly, without the patient's knowledge. The pressure to ration treatment is contained in the statutory duty on health authorities not to exceed their budgets. Sometimes it is contained

---

[121] (2000) 6 EHRLR 650 (Case No. 9301/81). See also for similar reasoning *Sieminska v Poland* (37602/97, 29 March 2001) and *Calvelli v Italy* [2002] ECHR 32967/96.

[122] [2003] 4 All ER 1239, 1257, para. 71. For a similar duty to investigate the circumstances leading to the death of an inmate in a young offenders institution, see *R (on the application of Amin) v Secretary of State for the Home Department* [2003] 4 All ER 1264 (HL).

[123] ibid., paras 74–75. The court questioned whether procedures under a coroner's inquest would satisfy these requirements. It suggested an independent inquiry established by the Secretary of State under s. 84 of the National Health Service Act 1977. See similar misgivings as to coroner's inquests expressed by Pill LJ in *Sacker v West Yorkshire Coroner* [2003] 2 All ER 278, paras 24–25.

in an explicit priorities framework created by PCTs, but the pressure may equally be imposed randomly in response to cost pressures when they arise. Take the following example. A patient suffers from a debilitating chronic condition (say, multiple sclerosis, Alzheimer's disease, or motor neurone disease). There is only one treatment available to treat it. It is effective in 10 per cent of the patients with the disease and it is impossible to identify the group that will benefit before treatment. Amongst the 10 per cent, the benefit may be significant for some and prolong their mobility and independence. For others, the benefit may be entirely marginal and short-lived. The treatment is only capable of delaying the progress of the disease, it cannot cure it, so that the prognosis for all is ultimately the same. If these were the only considerations, such treatment would always be offered to patients. However, the treatment costs £10,000 per patient per year and the group for whom it is potentially suitable numbers (say) 1,000 people. The health authority (or doctor) decides that it cannot afford to purchase such an expensive treatment which will deliver such a relatively small benefit to the patient population. Instead, the money should be spent on the same group to provide improved support services because this is a better "investment" for the group of patients as a whole. The treatment will not, therefore, be made generally available. Should the patients (or their carers) be made aware of this decision? How should law and ethics respond?

A strong pragmatic case can be made that there should be a duty to disclose the reasons for rationing treatment. Patients refused access to care on economic grounds for whom treatment could provide valuable medical benefit, ought to be able to consider arranging their finances so that it could be provided privately. They may be denied that opportunity unless the reasons for the decision not to treat are made clear. The patient might wish to modify the way in which the system of priorities has been set, organise a petition, or raise the money through charity, or write to his or her MP.

> Some patients may have their own resources for obtaining medical care . . . Others may choose to invest their energies in trying to change rationing policies rather than passively accepting [them]. In any event, many patients may have personal or professional priorities and commitments that would change in the light of full, truthful information about their medical conditions and treatment options. To deny such patients such information is to compromise the exercise of personal autonomy, the *raison d'etre* of the informed consent doctrine.[124]

Also, as a matter of principle, the law of disclosure is intended to promote the relationship of trust and confidence between doctor and patient, based on a collaboration where "decisions are made through frank discussion, in which the doctor's clinical expertise and the patient's individual needs and preferences are shared, to select the best option".[125] There is a risk that, unless medical decisions based

---

[124] F. Miller, "Denial of Health Care and Informed Consent in English and American Law" 18 *American Journal of Law and Medicine* 38, 71 (1992).

[125] *Medical Ethics Today—Its Practice and Philosophy* (BMA, 1993) 1.

on economic considerations are also disclosed to the patient, the relationship will be eroded. We consider (1) whether a duty to disclose should exist and (2) the justification for a modified Hippocratic commitment to patients.

1. A Duty to Disclose?

The idea of promoting trust and confidence is an attractive way of explaining a duty to disclose decisions of this nature. However, the law presents two obstacles in the way of doing so. The first is that the law of informed consent has developed out of the law of battery concerning the unlawful touching of another's body.[126] Is there a right to information as to the *denial* of care when there is no question of any touching, or battery? The point has not arisen clearly in English law. One response is to say that this traditional explanation of the right of the doctor to treat a patient based on the law of battery is too limited because it fails to capture the nature and quality of the relationship which is based on trust and confidence. One of the purposes of this trust and confidence is to enable patients, so far as possible, to understand the choices available and to make informed decisions for themselves. The law should respect the principle that we are masters over our bodies with the right to determine what will happen to us.[127] Such a right is not properly recognised if we are denied access to information we would wish to know to protect our health. To recognise this right, we might say that the right of true self-determination is incomplete in the law of negligence unless "non-treatment" decisions are disclosed.

Alternatively, such a right may be said to arise out of a fiduciary duty owed by the doctor to his patient. Fiduciary duties arise in circumstances appropriate to the doctor-patient relationship in the sense that the patient is vulnerable, almost entirely dependent on the doctor for advice, will disclose confidential information to the doctor, and may suffer exploitation if that trust is abused.[128] Never the less, *breach* of fiduciary duties normally occurs where there has been culpable abuse, or lack of good faith. These are not entirely apt descriptions of a doctor's duty to disclose information about treatment that cannot be made available, particularly where the doctor has no direct financial stake in the decision in any event. Would such a duty extend to cases in which the treatment offered was *modified* (but not denied altogether) as a result of clinical guidelines issued by the health authority, or hospital? Say a CAT scan is not routinely offered to those suffering headaches, or diagnostic tests, or post-operative days spent in hospital are restricted. If the patient belongs to a low-priority category for reasons of their own life-style (e.g. smokers and drinkers) ought he to be told? Should the patient be entitled to know

---

[126] See the discussion by Lord Donaldson MR in *Re R (a minor)* [1991] 4 All ER 177 and *Re W (a minor)* [1992] 4 All ER 627.

[127] *Schloendorf v Society of New York Hospital* 105 N.E. 92 (NY, 1914).

[128] See A. Grubb, "The Doctor as Fiduciary" (1994) *Current Legal Problems* 311; I. Kennedy, "The Fiduciary Relationship and its Application to Doctors and Patients" in P. Birks (ed.) *Wrongs and Remedies in the Twenty First Century* (Oxford University Press, 1996); and P. Bartlett "Doctors as Fiduciaries: Equitable Regulation of the Doctor-Patient Relationship" (1997) 5 *Medical Law Review* 193.

that a decision has been made to use a less expensive, or less effective, method of treatment? Clearly a fiduciary duty has the advantage of flexibility, but the disadvantage of providing uncertain answers to these questions.[129]

The question has been addressed in the US in connection with the doctor's duty to disclose financial incentives in relation to treatment. In *Shea v Esensten*[130] the patient was a member of a health maintenance organization (HMO) which undertook to provide all medically necessary care. Unknown to the patient, the contract between the doctor and the HMO "created financial incentives that were designed to minimise referrals. Specifically, the primary care doctors were rewarded for not making covered referrals to specialists, and were docked a portion of their fees if they made too many."[131] The patient's family had a history of heart disease. The patient visited his doctor on a number of occasions with chest pains but the doctor advised that referral to a cardiologist was unnecessary. The pains continued, the patient offered to pay for the referral himself, but the doctor offered the same reassurance. A few months later the patient died of heart failure. The plaintiff's widow alleged that, had her husband known of these incentives, he would have disregarded the doctor's advice and sought the advice of a specialist at his own expense and would have been more likely to avoid his heart attack. The court reasoned as follows:

> . . . a financial incentive scheme put in place to influence a treating doctor's referral practices when the patient needs specialized care is certainly a material piece of information. This kind of patient necessarily relies on the doctor's advice about treatment options, and the patient must know whether the advice is influenced by self-serving financial considerations created by the health insurance provider . . . We conclude Mr Shea had the right to know [the HMO] was offering financial incentives that could have colored his doctor's medical judgment about the urgency for a cardiac referral[then] he could have made a fully informed decision about whether to trust his doctor's recommendation that a cardiologist examination was unnecessary.[132]

No such argument has been considered in the English courts, but it has an appealing logic if the duty of trust and confidence is to be preserved. Certainly, incentives are controversial and have the capacity to work against the trust that should form the basis of the doctor-patient relationship. Sensibly used, however, as a means of discouraging needless or wholly marginal treatment, they may be justified if they generate legitimate savings by encouraging doctors to be prudent in their clinical decision-making. If we have to live with incentives, it is their capacity to distort clinical judgment which must be addressed. To minimise the danger to professional trust, patients should

---

[129] The House of Lords has doubted the existence of such a duty, although the matter was not subjected to scrutiny. See *Sidaway v Bethlem Royal Hospital Governors* [1985] 1 All ER 643, 650–1, *per* Lord Scarman.

[130] *Shea v Esensten* 107 F.3d 625 (8th Cir, 1997). A similar point is made by the Supreme Court of California in *Moore v Regents of the University of California* 793 P.2d 479 (Cal. 1990), "a physician must disclose personal interests unrelated to the patient's health, whether research or economic, that may affect the physician's professional judgment", at 483.   [131] ibid., at 627.

[132] ibid., 628–9.

understand the system of incentive payments and the manner in which they are controlled.[133] Such systems should be designed to reassure patients that standards of care will be maintained and that they will be reviewed by the regulatory authorities to ensure that they are used for legitimate purposes only.[134] Clearly, such systems of reassurance are not identical to the traditional notion of the Hippocratic ethic in which doctors promise to treat their patients solely on the basis of clinical need and, to this extent, the traditional notion of trust may have to be modified. As the doctor becomes more closely associated with public institutions which impose their own restraints, and the limitations of the system become more widely discussed and understood, there is a danger that the relationship will become less personal. The challenge in this new environment is to acknowledge the reality of the service in which patients and doctors exist and preserve a sense of personal commitment and professional trust within that framework. It is to this question we now turn.

2. A Modified Hippocratic Commitment

Perhaps we should re-assess the doctor's role within the system as a whole and, in particular, as to decisions around health care resources. Should doctors act as "gatekeepers," both serving patients, but also guarding the NHS resources? Or should they detach themselves entirely from matters economic and managerial and commit themselves whole-heartedly to the interests of each of their patients? And if they co-operate with cost-containment mechanisms, should they tell the patient, or keep the matter secret? If hard decisions between deserving cases become more common, doctors will need to consider whether their first loyalty is to the patient, or whether they act primarily for a public authority—is their first duty to the patient, or to the Treasury?[135]

We discussed (in Chapter 5) the duty of PCTs to have a procedural framework within which rationing decisions should be made. If doctors refuse to have regard to the policies and priorities such a policy recommends, there is a danger that finite budgets will simply be exhausted before the end of the financial year and needy patients who present after that time will be denied adequate care and put on waiting lists. Decisions of this nature, therefore, are unavoidable. What is the doctor's role in this process? Doctors and other clinicians must be involved in the difficult

---

[133] See David Orentlicher, "Paying Physicians More to do Less: Financial Incentives to Limit Care" (1996) 30 *University of Richmond Law Review* 155, 162–4, favouring the use of modest incentives for doctors. The American Medical Association considers that "[r]easonable limits should be placed on the extent to which a physician's ordering of services can affect his or her income. For example, quantitative financial incentives should be calculated on groups of physicians rather than individual physicians." See "Ethical Issues in Managed Care" (1995) 273 *Journal of the American Medical Association* 330, 334.

[134] D. Mechanic, "The Functions and Limitations of Trust in the Provision of Medical Care" (1998) 23 *Journal of Health Policy, Politics and Law* 661.

[135] M. Angel, "The Doctor as Double Agent" (1993) 3 *Kennedy Institute of Medical Ethics Journal* 279 and S. Woolf, "Conflict Between Doctor and Patient" (1988) 16 *Law, Medicine and Health Care* 197.

"macro" decisions surrounding the allocation of scarce resources and play an active role on priorities committees. Clinicians understand both the clinical merits of the treatments in question and the needs of their patients. Equally, these macro-decisions are not for doctors alone. They are heavily influenced by policy, politics, and economics. They should be governed by a broad cross-section of decision-makers including clinicians from other specialties, NHS managers and, increasingly, those representing the public.

Conversely, trust will never thrive if patients suspect there is a hidden rationing agenda dominating the doctor's decision-making process. So far as possible, decisions of this nature should not be taken covertly, at the bedside, by the doctor who happens to be on duty at the time, depending on his or her own perceptions and prejudices. They should be taken within a clear, consistent, and cogent priorities framework to which patients have free access. Thus, doctors' responsible clinical freedom should remain intact unless the proposed treatment is subject to guidance within the ethical framework. In this way, doctors can retain the trust of the patient and be open about the funding constraints imposed upon them. Such an approach is surely desirable in principle for supporting the doctor patient-relationship.

Doctors obliged to make resource-sensitive decisions should be able to say to the patient:

(1) I will always act in your best interests.
(2) Sometimes, for reasons of NHS policy, treatment may be available only in limited circumstances. I will inform you of that policy.
(3) If you have exceptional need for treatment which is not generally available I will inform you about it.
(4) In such a case I will, if you wish, advise the health authority of your special need and request that you be treated as an exceptional case.[136]

In this way, in an environment which recognises the need for hard choices, patients could be reassured of the doctor's commitment to their best interests and of his or her willingness to act as their advocate in favour of exceptional care. Given the institutional constraints that may be imposed upon them, the commitment may fall short of a guarantee of treatment. Instead, it is to promote patients' best interests within the confines imposed by the system as a whole. A failure to commit to this principle and, instead, to encourage the mistaken belief that care will always be available on the basis of patient need alone will surely hasten the erosion of patients' trust in doctors and the NHS.

---

[136] Compare this with the following:

Asking the clinician to be cost-conscious in order to eliminate marginally beneficial care would require a major shift in traditional professional ethics. Physicians would be required to abandon traditional patient-centredness. They would be asked to remove the Hippocratic Oath from their waiting room wall and replace it with a sign that read, ". . . I will generally work for your rights and welfare, but if the benefits to you are marginal and costs are great, I will abandon you in order to protect society". R. Veatch, *The Patient-Physician Relation: The Patient as Partner, Part 2* (Indiana University Press, 1991) 173.

7

Liability of Health Authorities
and Government

Negligence may be the responsibility of a single individual. On the other hand, it may also arise by virtue of the *system* within which the clinician works. This chapter considers the institutional dimension of negligence in which hospitals, health authorities, and government itself may bear responsibility. The idea of a "systems failure" is illustrated by *Learning from Bristol*,[1] which inquired into the standards of care achieved in the treatment of young children in the Bristol Royal Infirmary. The Bristol Inquiry found that many of the shortcomings in Bristol existed throughout the NHS. Paediatric care was provided on a split-site, there was no *systematic* way of monitoring clinical standards, there were staff shortages, children were often treated together with adults despite their differing clinical needs, and there was poor teamwork so that problems were not addressed in the hospital, nor were there systems in the NHS as a whole to provide outside assistance.[2] In Bristol, this combination of circumstances is estimated to have caused the deaths of between thirty and thirty-five more children under one year of age than might have been expected in other paediatric care units in the NHS.

Exactly why the Bristol Inquiry had such a dramatic impact both in public perception and government has more to do with our changing expectations of the NHS than the uniqueness of the circumstances themselves. Recall the case of *Ex p Collier*, discussed in Chapter 5. The patient was a four-year-old boy who required urgent surgery to repair a hole in the heart in 1987 and he was listed as a priority case by his responsible doctor. Yet the authority failed to treat him, or transfer him to another specialist centre in time to save his life.[3] This should have been sufficient to alert hospitals and purchasers to the need for a system of intensive care that does not abandon cases of this nature. Yet in 1993, in *The Care of Critically Ill Children*, the British Paediatric Association (BAP) noted that "the lack of qualified nurses in children's wards may have direct implications for the prompt recognition

[1] *Learning from Bristol: the Report of the Public Inquiry into Children's Heart Surgery at the Bristol Royal Infirmary 1984–1995*, (Cm. 5207, 2001).
[2] Similar concerns was expressed when a consultant whose performance was known to be poor was permitted to continue in practice in *Inquiry into Quality and Practice within the NHS Arising from the Actions of Rodney Ledward* (Department of Health, 2001).
[3] The political consequences of the case are discussed in Webster, *The National Health Service—A Political History* (2nd edn, Oxford University Press, 2002) 184.

and referral of children requiring intensive care".[4] It reported that every children's intensive care unit in the UK had refused admission to critically ill children in 1991–92 because of a shortage of both beds and nursing staff.[5] Indeed, "many units informed us that one or more of their beds are in effect permanently closed because of lack of staff. Even those beds which were open were often grossly understaffed."[6]

Similarly, the Clinical Standards Advisory Group[7] said in the same year: "Not enough attention has been paid to planning neonatal services . . . As a result, in many areas, cot numbers and their location are not appropriate for the population." In *Which Way Forward for the Care of Critically Ill Children?* the NHS Centre for Reviews and Dissemination, published a report analysing the BAP report and found "unequivocal evidence of extremely fragmented care for critically ill children in the UK . . . Because there are so many units providing intensive care to children, an average of only 47 children were admitted to each unit in 1991. This fragmentation means that many of the units are likely to be delivering a sub-optimal standard of care."[8] These examples illustrate that the problems in Bristol were not unique. On the contrary, difficulties of various kinds persisted in paediatric and neonatal care throughout the NHS.

Concern of a different nature was expressed in the inquiry into the circumstances surrounding the death of Nicholas Geldorf who was ten years old when he suffered a fit at home in Manchester.[9] He was taken by ambulance to his local hospital, Stepping Hill, where it was recognised that he needed a CT scan. However, CT scanning was not available at Stepping Hill out of hours. The doctors had no mechanism for locating a suitable alternative unit, and Nicholas was transferred to three further hospitals before proper facilities became available and much time was wasted in doing so, by which time he had died. As the Report into the incident commented:

. . . the absurd nature of this arrangement became apparent when patients at Stepping Hill Hospital—like Nicholas—needed a scan and had to travel ten miles for it when there was a scanner down the corridor . . . the failure of the Trust to provide for an out-of-hours scanning service—if only by having a computer-based link with another fully staffed centre [was] censorious.[10]

The incident highlighted a lack of clear lines of responsibility and communication between hospital consultants when dealing with acute neurosurgical or neurological problems. In the circumstances of this case, the delay in providing adequate care was not responsible for causing his death, which was caused by an aneurysm in his brain. Therefore no action in negligence was available against the hospital. As the Report noted, however, it was only by chance that Nicholas's death was not caused by organisational problems in obtaining appropriate CT scanning services. "Had he died from

[4] British Paediatric Association, 7.   [5] ibid., 8.   [6] ibid., 13.
[7] *Neonatal Intensive Care* (HMSO, 1993) 25.
[8] Centre for Reviews and Dissemination, University of York, 1995, at 20.
[9] See *Inquiry into the Care and Treatment of Nicholas Geldorf* (North West Regional Health Authortity, 1996).   [10] ibid., para. 99.

progressive cerebral compression due to the original clot, rather than from a massive re-bleed, then his death could clearly have been attributed to these shortcomings."[11]

These reports emphasise the difficulty of apportioning blame in the circumstances; is it the fault of the doctors, the managers, government, or all three? How does the law identify those responsible for systems failures in the NHS? This chapter traces the recent evolution of the law relating to public services generally in order to assess the exposure of NHS institutions to liability in negligence. It considers (I) the "policy/operational" distinction, (II) the movement to protect public authorities from liability, (III) operational, or "system", negligence in the NHS, (IV) liability for resource allocation policy, and (V) corporate manslaughter.

I. The Distinction Between "Policy" and "Operations"

The common law recognises that public authorities often have to make difficult choices with scarce resources. There is always more that could be done to improve a public service than there is money available to pay for it, whether it is in respect of maintaining standards in hospitals, schools, law and order, or the quality of roads and public transport. It is mistaken to think in terms of right and wrong solutions to the problem. Reasonable people may identify differing priorities. In the end, however, a decision has to be made about a suitable course of action, based on a democratic expression of feeling, or some other means of arriving at a decision. This is a problem faced by health authorities.

Understandably, the courts are reluctant to interfere with decisions of this kind, since their own opinions could not be expected to be superior to those who have been appointed to do so. On the other hand, the courts recognise equally well that public authorities are not solely concerned with the difficult problems of making policy and assessing priorities. They also undertake day-to-day responsibilities about which it is possible to expect minimum standards of care. With respect to these, the courts can apply the same principles of negligence as they would to an individual, since the matter is within the competence of reasonable people. This distinction is often referred to as the "policy" and "operational" spheres of decision-making, but it is crucial to understand that the two elements cannot be separated as if they were black and white. The issue is better considered on a spectrum in which decisions will usually involve aspects of both. The matter was considered in 1978 in the *Anns* case by Lord Wilberforce who said:

Most, indeed probably all, statutes relating to public authorities or public bodies, contain in them a large area of policy. The courts call this "discretion" meaning that the decision is one for the authority or body to make, and not for the courts. Many statutes also prescribe or at least presuppose the practical execution of policy decisions: a convenient description of this is to say that in addition to the area of policy or discretion, there is an operational area.

[11] ibid., para.149.

Although this distinction between the policy area and the operational area is convenient, and illuminating, it is probably a distinction of degree; many "operational" powers or duties have in them some element of "discretion". It can safely be said that the more "operational" a power or duty may be, the easier it is to superimpose upon it a common law duty of care.[12]

At each end of the spectrum, the decision of the court to intervene or not may be relatively straightforward. But as the decision under review approaches the centre, it becomes increasingly one of judicial instinct, about which reasonable judges may differ.[13] In one case, for example, the courts accepted a Home Office *policy* designed to rehabilitate juvenile offenders by allowing them to live in relatively open conditions of detention in Borstal. Of course, such a policy inevitably carries the risk that boys will escape and cause damage. But it also has the benefit of giving them the opportunity for initiative and to develop a better relationship of trust with those who supervise them. On one occasion, a number of boys escaped and damaged neighbouring property because their supervisors had fallen asleep. The House of Lords held the Home Office responsible, not for the policy of having open conditions, but for the negligence with which it *operated* its policy.[14]

II. Insulating Public Authorities from Liability

Recently, however, there has been concern to insulate public authorities from claims in negligence, driven by the fear that such actions create a "defensive" and inappropriate attitude to decision-making and divert substantial sums of money (in damages and costs) from the very services the authority is supposed to provide. Note, for example, the comment of the Public Accounts Committee of the House of Commons in respect of the NHS. It said: "We are appalled that there are at least 15,000 cases of clinical negligence on the NHS books, and that there may be far more. These cases represent a tragedy for the people involved. And the level of outstanding liabilities, which may be as high as £2.8 billion, is a significant drain on stretched health care resources."[15] Bear in mind too that public authorities are not like private companies. Unlike private companies bound by the law of contract, they do not choose to go into business; they may not be free to withdraw, or vary a service if it becomes uneconomic, or increase the price at which it is sold. They operate within fixed budgets and may be subject to inflexible public duties.[16]

---

[12] *Anns v Merton LBC* [1978] AC 728, 753. This part of the *ratio* of the case, based on *Dorset Yacht Co v Home Office* [1970] AC 1004, survived the reappraisal of the law of negligence made in *Murphy v Brentwood DC* [1991] 1 AC 398 (HL). See Bingham LJ in *Re HIV Haemophiliac Litigation* (1990) 41 BMLR 171.

[13] Compare the differing conclusions in *Jost v British Columbia* [1997] 3 SCR 624 with *Brown v British Columbia* 112 DLR (4th) on similar facts concerning the negligence of government departments for failing the clear the highways.   [14] See *Dorset Yacht Co v Home Office* [1970] AC 1004.

[15] HC Public Accounts Committee, 5th Report, Session 1999–00, 15 December 1999, para. 68.

[16] See S.H. Bailey and M.J. Brown, "Public Authority Negligence Revisited" (2000) 59 *Cambridge Law Journal* 85.

For similar reasons, therefore, during the 1990s the reasoning in the *Anns* case was doubted and a number of cases sought to develop greater protection for public authorities. Thus, Lord Keith said in 1988 that *Anns* "does not provide a touchstone of liability [because] classification of the relevant decision as a policy or planning decision . . . may exclude liability; but a conclusion that it does not fall within this category does not . . . mean that a duty of care will necessarily exist".[17] And in 1996 Lord Hoffmann considered that the distinction was "an inadequate tool with which to discover whether it is appropriate to impose a duty of care or not".[18] As a result, two legal techniques were employed to promote a change of judicial attitude and to provide broader protection to public authorities, i.e.: (A) principles of statutory interpretation, and (B) the distinction between statutory duties and mere "targets". Ultimately, as we shall see, neither is entirely persuasive.

A. Principles of Statutory Interpretation

The question whether damages are recoverable against a public authority for breach of statutory duty depends on the construction of the statute from which it derives its powers. Very often, however, statutes offer no express statement on the matter. In the absence of clear guidance from the statute, what presumption should the courts make as to the intention of the statute? Two approaches have been taken to this matter. The first seeks a specific statutory intention which permits the public authority to be held liable in negligence, in the absence of which liability will be denied. Lord Hoffmann has said that one should find a statutory presumption in favour of liability as a pre-condition to considering an action in negligence.

Whether a statutory duty gives rise to a private cause of action is a question of construction . . . It requires an examination of the statute to decide whether it was intended to confer a right to compensation for breach . . . The same is true of omission to perform a statutory duty . . . If the policy of the act is not to create a statutory liability to pay compensation, the same policy should ordinarily exclude the existence of a common law duty of care.[19]

This appears to require a positive intention within the statute to create a right of private action in negligence and has led to a number of cases being struck out for having no reasonable prospects of success. Put another way, "when one is considering whether a duty of care at common law exists, one would expect that it is to be found, if at all, in the statute, so that if the statute on its true interpretation provides none, then none should be owed by the local authority".[20] In the *Capital and*

---

[17] *Rowling v Takaro Properties* [1988] 1 All ER 163, 172. See generally, P. Craig, "The Courts, Human Rights and Judicial Review" (2001) 117 LQR 589.
[18] *Stovin v Wise* [1996] 3 All ER 801, 827.   [19] ibid.
[20] *Danns v Department of Health* (1995) 25 BMLR 121, 133, *per* Wright J. His Lordship continued: "to put it the other way round, if no action for breach of statutory duty lies in respect of what the council did or failed to do in the exercise of its functions, it is not immediately obvious why a common law claim in negligence . . . should lie."

Counties case, for example, action was commenced against the fire services for failing to respond reasonably to emergency calls, as a result of which property was destroyed. The Court of Appeal refused to hear claims for damages against fire authorities for failing to attend, or failing to respond competently to, properties on fire. It said that the Fire Services Act 1947 was not intended to confer a right of private action in negligence.[21] This has led to the extraordinary situation in which the common law imposed no duty on firemen to attend fires and, indeed, no sanction against their going to a party instead of rescuing defined individuals in need of assistance. Similarly, a coastguard was held to be under no private law duty to respond reasonably, or at all, to an emergency call to rescue school children being blown out to sea in canoes,[22] nor was a health authority under a private law duty to prevent a seriously mentally disturbed man from killing an innocent bystander.[23]

Statutes often fail to express exactly what their intentions are as regards rights of private individuals to bring actions in negligence. As a consequence, the process of discovering statutory intention has been said to be "a patent fiction, which serves only to conceal the policies or intuitions which lie behind the decision to impose or deny liability".[24] An alternative, more persuasive view considers that the presumption should normally be to the contrary. Indeed, it is axiomatic that "unless the statute manifests a contrary intention, a public authority which enters upon an exercise of statutory power may place itself in a relationship to members of the public which imports a common law duty to take care".[25] The latter view accords with the principle of statutory interpretation that statutes do not remove existing common law rights unless they say so expressly or by necessary implication.[26] As Lord Hoffmann himself said subsequently:

. . . the principle of legality means that Parliament must squarely confront what it is doing and accept the political cost. Fundamental rights cannot be overridden by general or

---

[21] [1997] 2 All ER 865, 896.

[22] *OLL v Secretary of State* [1997] 3 All ER 897, 905: "there is no obvious distinction between the fire-brigade responding to a fire where lives are at risk and the coastguard responding to an emergency at sea . . . the coastguard would be under no enforceable private law duty to respond to an emergency call, nor, if they do respond, would they be liable if their response was negligent, unless their negligence amounted to a positive act which directly caused greater injury than would have occurred if they had not intervened at all."

[23] *Clunis v Camden and Islington HA* (1997) 40 BMLR 181, 192. "Is it, in the circumstances, just and reasonable to superimpose . . . a common law duty of care on an authority in relation to the performance of its statutory duties to provide after-care? We do not think so. We find it difficult to suppose that Parliament intended to create such an extensive and wide-ranging liability for breaches of responsibility under s.117 [of the Mental Health Act 1983]."

[24] R.A. Buckley, "Negligence in the Public Sphere: Is Clarity Possible?" (2000) 51 NILQ 25, 28. As Lord Denning MR said: "in many of these statutes the legislature has left the point open . . . you might as well toss a coin to decide it" in *Ex p Island Records* [1978] Ch 122, 135. See also D. Fairgrieve, *State Liability in Tort* (Oxford University Press, 2003) 37–41.

[25] *Sutherland Shire Council v Heyman* (1985) 157 CLR 424, 459, emphasis added. See also the view of the ECHR in *Osman v UK* [2002] HRLR 7, para. 147–51.

[26] See *Pierson v Secretary of State for the Home Department* [1997] 3 All ER 577, 590 (HL) and *Raymond v Honey* [1982] 1 All ER 756 (HL).

ambiguous words . . . In the absence of express language or necessary implication to the contrary, the courts therefore presume that even the most general words were intended to be subject to the rights of the individual.[27]

This is surely correct. The courts should require firm persuasion before striking out actions on grounds of statutory intention; and there should certainly be no general statutory presumption against individual rights to litigate, unless a contrary intention is manifest. Of course, when statutes confer a broad discretion upon the Secretary of State, actions in negligence which challenge the exercise of such discretion will face considerable difficulty because ministers are entitled to work within a broad range of *policy* options.[28] On the other hand, as we discuss below, such actions are not impossible and should remain amenable to assessment by the law of negligence on the "policy/operational" distinction.

B. Statutory Duties, or Mere Targets?

A second way of limiting public authority liability for damages is to describe the statutory duty imposed as a mere "target," breach of which carries no common law consequences. On this approach, if the public authority misses such a target, the failure will not translate into a cause of action in negligence. The purpose of targets is to impose desirable administrative standards on the public authority, not to confer private rights of action on individuals. Judicial review is the appropriate way of assessing whether the authority has complied with the statutory obligations imposed upon it. For example, the following duty upon the fire services is worded in a way which is similar to the duties under the National Health Service Act 1977 and is instructive by comparison. Section 1 of the Fire Services Act 1947 provides that: "It shall be the duty of every fire authority . . . to make provision for fire-fighting purposes, and in particular every fire authority shall secure [the specific services listed in paras (a)–(f)]." And section 13 provides that: "A fire authority shall take all reasonable measures for ensuring the provision of an adequate supply of water, and for securing that it will be available for use, in case of fire." In the *Capital and Counties* case, the Court of Appeal considered the objective of the fire brigade to attend a fire and react reasonably to it. It said this statutory duty was not limited and specific. Rather, it was a general administrative function of procurement placed on the fire authority to supply water for firefighting generally. No right of action was conferred on any class of person short of the public as a whole. The court continued "it seems to us that the duties . . . are collectively in the nature of statutory provisions establishing a regulatory system or scheme of social welfare for the benefit of the public at large".[29]

---

[27] *R v Secretary of State for the Home Department, ex p Simms* [1999] 3 All ER 400, 412.

[28] See, e.g., the minister's discretion in *Danns v Department of Health* (1995) 25 BMLR 121, 133, not to disseminate public warnings of the small risk that sterilsation operations might leave men fertile.

[29] As adumbrated by Lord Browne-Wilkinson in *X v Bedfordshire CC* [1995] 3 All ER 353, see *Capital and Counties plc v Hampshire CC* [1997] 2 All ER 865, 896.

Much of the regulation of the NHS could be described in terms of "targets". Referring to the duty imposed on the Secretary of State by the National Health Service Act 1977 to "continue to promote a comprehensive health service", Lord Woolf MR has said "this duty is an exhortatory or target duty which does not create a statutory right, the breach of which can give rise to a private law right to damages".[30] But this approach fails to resolve the issue of liability in negligence for two reasons. First, breach of a statutory "duty" by itself creates no automatic right to damages in any case[31] because the issue of negligence must be determined within the common law.[32] Thus, even if the statute does impose a clear *duty*, rather than a target, its breach can have no automatic consequences in damages. Secondly, there may be circumstances in which a failure to achieve a "target" may be so outrageous that it creates a common law duty. In *Kent v London Ambulance Service*,[33] for example, the statutory duty to provide adequate ambulance services and respond to emergency calls may be described as a target. But once the identity of the patient and the urgency of her need for care were known a common law duty arose to attend the call with reasonable speed.[34] Thus, whether a responsibility is a "duty" or a mere "target" is not crucial to the issue of public authority liability. Of course, this does not lead to the conclusion that such cases should generally succeed.[35] It suggests, however, that the merits of such cases deserve proper consideration by the courts and should not be automatically struck out.

Thus, neither argument against public authority liability is decisive and there remains "some validity in the [policy/operational] distinction".[36] How have these developments been applied to the NHS in particular? Curiously, despite the attempt to protect public authorities in general from negligence, a number of cases have assumed that no such exemption from liability should extend to the NHS. Lord Jauncey in *X v Bedfordshire County Council* said that "the owners of a National Health Service hospital owe precisely the same duty of care to their patients as do the owners of a private hospital and they owe it because of the common law of negligence and not because they happen to be operating under statutory provisions".[37] And in *Capital and Counties* the Court of Appeal said: "There is no doubt that once the relationship of doctor and patient or hospital authority and admitted patient exists, the doctor or the hospital authority owe a duty to take reasonable care to effect a cure, not merely to prevent further harm."[38] Perhaps this is

---

[30] *Griffiths v London Ambulance Service* [2000] Lloyds Law Rep Med 109, 116, col.1. Similarly, His Lordship has said: "The [NHS] Act does not impose an absolute duty to provide the specified services. The Secretary of State is entitled to have regard to the resources made available to him under current government economic policy." *R v North East Devon HA, ex p Coughlan* (1999) 51 BMLR 1, 11.

[31] *X v Bedfordshire CC* [1995] 3 All ER 353,365.

[32] Under the guidelines laid down in under *Caparo Industries plc v Dickman* [1990] 1 All ER 568, i.e. foresight, proximity, fairness, justice and reasonableness.

[33] *Kent v Griffiths, Roberts and the LAS* [2000] Lloyds Law Rep 109, discussed below.

[34] [1999] Lloyd's Rep Med 58, 62, *per* Kennedy LJ.

[35] See Lord Woolf, "The Human Rights Act 1998 and Remedies" in Andenas and D. Fairgrieve (eds), *Judicial Review in International Perspective, Vol II* (Kluwer Law International, 2000).

[36] *Phelps v Hillingdon BC* [2000] 4 All ER 504, 522, *per* Lord Slynn.

[37] *X v Bedfordshire CC* [1995] 3 All ER 353, 362.

[38] See also *Capital and Counties plc v Hampshire CC* [1997] 2 All ER 865, 883.

because much of their work arises within the "operational" area of activity. But, as we will see, liability may also arise in the "policy" area of the spectrum.[39] With this in mind, we now consider "systems negligence" in the NHS.

III. Systems Negligence in the NHS

In the introduction to this chapter, we mentioned systems failures specifically in relation to children. Now we look more broadly at cases concerning inadequate supervision and training of clinical staff and the distinction between operational and policy decisions.

A. Inadequate Supervision and Training

Consider the following case in which junior doctors were left unsupervised in charge of *vincristine* which was administered in error and the patient died. Given their inexperience, the doctors were acquitted of *criminal* negligence. The drug was known to have fatal consequences if injected into the wrong site in the body, yet the drug was administered in precisely that way. The circumstances were described as follows:

Dr Prentice was required to give treatment without the consultant who prescribed it giving any instruction or thought as to who should do so. This, despite the fact that Dr Prentice was inexperienced, reluctant to give the treatment and wholly unaware . . . of the likely consequences. Dr Prentice did not have the data chart on the cytotoxic trolley because the trolley was not in use. The senior nurse was not present, leaving only two students at the scene. Moreover, having asked for supervision and believing that Dr Sullivan was supervising the whole treatment, he was actually handed each of the two syringes in turn by Dr Sullivan . . . So far as Dr Sullivan was concerned, he believed he was simply required to supervise the insertion of the lumbar puncture needle by an inexperienced houseman . . . He did not have special experience or knowledge of cytotoxic drugs.[40]

Clearly, there was fault in the system surrounding junior doctors' training with *vincristine*. In *By Accident or Design—Improving A&E Services in England and Wales*, similar misgivings are expressed by the Audit Commission in respect of the training and supervision of newly qualified doctors in Accident and Emergency units. It said

Most A&E patients are treated by SHOs [senior house officers], many of whom are relatively inexperienced. Senior doctors in hard-pressed departments seldom have sufficient time for effective supervision, informal teaching and management . . . Even some quite busy departments are staffed outside the normal working week by SHOs alone, despite the fact that almost 60% of new attenders (and 70% of "999" calls) arrive at these times.[41]

---

[39] ". . . the fact that the defendant's relationship with the plaintiff arose from the exercise a statutory power [rather than a duty] does not prevent the plaintiff from claiming that the defendant owed him a common law duty of care, unless the defendant is entitled to contend that the claim is barred because it alleges negligence in the exercise of a discretion given by statute." *Barrett v Enfield LBC* [1999] 3 All ER 193, 217, *per* Lord Hutton.   [40] *R v Prentice and Sullivan* [1993] 4 All ER 935, 949.
[41] Audit Commission (HMSO, 1996) para. 52.

Complaints of this nature are limited to junior doctors. *The Inquiry into Quality &*
Practice within the NHS Arising from the Actions of Rodney Ledward considered the
failure of hospital managers to deal with the poor standards of a consultant gynae-
cologist, as a result of which a number of women were damaged. It said:

Some members of the Management Team were aware of concerns about his practice and
indeed some had concerns of their own. We accept that certain individuals tried to take steps
to deal with a number of problems but our strong impression is that there was no concerted
effort, no one took charge of the problem and each concern was dealt with on an ad hoc basis.
[The District General Manager] told us that he was unaware of any concerns about Rodney
Ledward's clinical practice. If that is so then he should have been. [He] told us that in his view
there was no system in place to identify and deal with problems involving a consultant.[42]

A number of cases suggest that the courts will be unsympathetic to hospitals which
admit patients to units which cannot guarantee minimum standards of reasonable
care. In *Wilsher v Essex Area Health Authority*[43] a premature baby received improper
treatment due, in part, to the failure to supervise an inexperienced doctor who
shared responsibility for his care. In the Court of Appeal, Sir Nicolas Browne-
Wilkinson exonerated the junior doctor from responsibility for the damage
caused, on the ground that he was simply not to blame for it. But he criticised the
Health Authority for failing to provide hospital staff with sufficient skill to undertake the duties assigned to them. He said: "In my judgment, a hospital authority
which so conducts its hospital that it fails to provide doctors of sufficient skill and
experience to give the treatment offered at the hospital may be directly liable in
negligence to the patient."[44]

Similarly, in *Bull v Devon Health Authority*,[45] the defendants operated a split-site
hospital. The plaintiff was in one of its hospitals expecting twins. The first twin was
born without complication, but the second could not be delivered and expert assistance was required. The responsible obstetrician was on duty in the other hospital site
but was unable to attend the plaintiff and deliver the second twin for over an hour, by
which time the child had suffered asphyxia and brain damage. The system intended to
provide the assistance of a consultant within twenty minutes of his being summoned.
The defendant explained the failure by saying that the hospital operated on two sites
and that there would inevitably be occasions when senior staff would be required in
both places at once; the system for summoning consultants from one site to another
was "par for the course" by comparison with other NHS hospitals. Therefore, the
Health Authority said, it had not fallen below the standard of care that could reasonably be expected in the NHS. Mustill LJ rejected this defence. He said:

I see nothing ideal about a system which would have given the mother and child the protection against emergencies when it was needed . . . the system should have been set up so

---

[42] Department of Health, 2001, paras 25.1–25.2.   [43] [1986] 3 All ER 801.
[44] ibid., at 833. Glidewell agreed at 831. The judgment was subsequently reversed by the House of
Lords on the question of causation, but not on this point. See *Wilsher v Essex AHA* [1988] 1 All ER 871.
[45] (1989) 4 Med LR 117.

as to produce a registrar or consultant on the spot within twenty minutes, subject to some unforeseeable contingency. In the present case there was an interval of about an hour during which the mother and child were at risk, with nobody present who could do anything if an emergency were to develop. The trend of the evidence seems to me manifestly that this interval was too long. Either there was a failure in the operation of the system, or it was too sensitive to hitches which fell short of the kind of major breakdown against which no system is invulnerable.[46]

The defendants were held liable for failing to implement a system capable of providing the plaintiff with an acceptable standard of care. In *Robertson v Nottingham Health Authority* the complaint arose from a failure to have a reliable system of medical notes by which doctors and nurses could communicate with one another. As a result, a baby suffering pre-natal distress was not delivered until some six hours after the time at which delivery ought to have been arranged. The Court of Appeal confirmed that a hospital:

. . . has a non-delegable duty to establish a proper system of care just as much as it has a duty to engage competent staff and a duty to provide proper and safe equipment . . . if a patient is injured by reason of a negligent breakdown in the systems for communicating material information to the clinicians responsible for her care, she is not to be denied redress merely because no identifiable person or persons are to blame for the deficiencies in setting up and monitoring the effectiveness of the relevant communications systems.[47]

System errors were also blamed in *Penny, Palmer and Cannon v East Kent Health Authority*[48] for the failure of a hospital cytology department to conduct proper screening of cervical smears. As a result the claimants lost the chance of obtaining treatment which could have prevented the onset of cervical cancer. An independent report concluded that the cytology department was isolated, under-staffed, and badly managed, working relations between staff were poor and the performance of the laboratory was sub-standard. The court considered that the system in the cytology department enabled cytoscreeners to make significant errors of judgment without supervision or review. The defendants were held responsible for its failures.

This demanding approach to standards of care in the NHS extends to the ambulance services. Although, as we have seen, the fire services and air-sea rescue services have been held to owe no duty to those who need their help, ambulance services are subject to a different approach. In *Kent v Griffiths* a doctor made a "999" emergency call for his patient, the claimant, who was suffering a very severe asthma attack. The call was accepted by the London Ambulance Service (LAS) and an ambulance was despatched. However, instead, of the expected twenty minutes, it took forty-three minutes to arrive and the additional delay caused the claimant irreversible brain-damage. The ambulance crew falsified the record of their time of arrival and the

[46] ibid., at 141.
[47] [1997] 8 Med LR 1, cols 1–2. On the facts of the case liability was denied because it could not be shown that the negligence caused the baby's damage, which would most probably have occurred in any event.   [48] [1999] Lloyd's Rep Med 123.

system could provide no explanation of why they took so long. In the Court of Appeal, Lord Woolf MR confirmed that common law duties may arise in the performance of statutory functions both in the manner in which discretion is exercised and in the practical implementation of policy. The LAS was held liable in damages for the practical implementation of the the the duty. The court imposed a duty on the ambulance on the following reasoning:

> In the case of health services under the [1977] Act the conventional situation is that there is a duty of care. Why should the situation of the ambulance staff be any different from that of a doctor or nurse? . . . In addition the arguments based on public policy are much weaker in the case of the ambulance service than they are in the case of the police or the fire service . . . Its care function includes transporting patients to and from hospital when the use of an ambulance for this purpose is desirable. It is therefore appropriate to regard the LAS as providing services in the category provided by hospitals and not as those rendered by the police or fire services.[49]

Had the circumstances been different and hard choices had been needed to allocate resources (say) to victims of a motorway accident, very different considerations could apply and such a duty might not have arisen. Here, however, no such conflict of priorities existed. There were no circumstances which made it unfair or unreasonable or unjust that liability should exist. The grounds for distinguishing the fire-services case of *Capital and Counties* were that personal safety was involved and that, once the call had been accepted, the claimant was owed a personal duty of care that the service would respond to her need reasonably.[50] Equally, precisely such emergency circumstances may apply to an individual stranded on a canoe at sea, or in a burning block of flats. The reasons for treating the other emergency services so differently are not persuasive and will need to be reconsidered.

B. Operational Negligence or Deliberate Policy?

As we have seen, the case for negligence is more difficult when the complaint arises from a policy decision, and more straightforward when there has been "operational" error or inadvertence. Let us examine cases where the distinction has arisen in the NHS. In *Department of Health and Social Security v Kinnear*[51] the claimants alleged that they had suffered brain-damage following the administration to them of pertussis vaccine when they were babies. They made a number of allegations against the

---

[49] *Kent v Griffiths, Roberts and the LAS* [2000] Lloyd's Rep Med 109, para. 45.

[50] In the High Court, Turner J said: "it is possible to distinguish *Capital & Counties* from the present case . . . First, . . . there must be the initiating call to the ambulance service which has provided sufficient information to enable it to understand the nature of the call upon its services. The service must thereafter have accepted it by allocating an ambulance to meet the request. The ambulance service must have been informed that time was of the essence of the call. Next the ambulance must have failed to arrive at the casualty within a reasonable time, having regard to the traffic conditions or other avoidable factors inducing delay." *Kent v Griffiths and the LAS* [1999] Lloyd's Rep Med 424, 453, col. 1.

[51] 134 NLJ 886 (QBD, 1984). The case was ultimately abandoned for lack of evidence.

Secretary of State and the relevant health authorities. They said, for example, that given that the risk of suffering a severe form of whooping cough was very small, the whole policy of mass immunisation of babies was misconceived because the dangers presented by the vaccine were so high. This allegation was struck out on the ground that the matter was within the policy discretion of the Secretary of State and beyond the jurisdiction of the court. On the other hand, a separate allegation was allowed to go forward. This was that doctors and parents ought to have been warned that some children (for example, those with asthma) were at much higher risk than others and their damage was easily avoidable. Stuart Smith J said the foundation of the plaintiff's case against the defendants was that:

> . . . they advised how and in what circumstances the treatment should be administered, but this advice was misleading and negligent because it did not indicate that a respiratory disease was a contra-indication for vaccination. [Counsel for the plaintiff] submits that, in giving advice on these matters, the [Department of Health] were acting in the operational sphere and were no longer protected by the limits of discretion . . . To my mind it is at least arguable, in giving such advice, that the [Department of Health] has entered the operational area.[52]

Presumably, the case was only "arguable" because the Secretary of State might have said that the matter was still within his discretion. The inclusion of too many warnings and notices of contra-indications could have alarmed parents and doctors so much that the entire public policy of vaccination could have been undermined and rendered ineffective. Concern for the public interest might have brought such a decision within the ambit of ministerial "policy".

A similar point arose in *Smith v Department of Health*[53] concerning damage caused to a child by taking aspirin. In April 1968, Secretary of State was advised by the Committee on the Safety of Medicines that aspirin was probably one of the causes of Reyes syndrome in children. In less than 1 in 100,000 children, the illness can cause devastating physical and intellectual disability. Given the popularity of aspirin, the number of children at risk was significant and, of course, equally effective alternative analgesics present no such danger. Responding to this advice, in June 1986 and with the co-operation of the pharmaceutical industry, the Secretary of State gave warnings to doctors, dentists, and pharmacists not to prescribe aspirin to children under 12. The claimant, a girl of six, was given aspirin in May 1986 *after* the Department of Health had been warned of the danger, but *before* it issued its general warning to the public. She was severely disabled by Reyes syndrome. In an action in negligence, it was alleged that Secretary of State's failure to exercise his powers promptly to modify the licence for aspirin in children was responsible for causing her disability.[54] Dismissing her claim, however, the High Court held that the decision as to the

---

[52] See *Bonthrone v Secretary of State for Scotland* (1987) SLT 34 and *Ross v Secretary of State for Scotland* [1990] Med LR 235. This aspect of the Scottish law may not be identical to that in England and Wales.   [53] [2002] Lloyd's Rep Med 333.

[54] The power to suspend, revoke, or vary licences for the sale of medicines is contained in Medicine Act 1968, s. 28.

warnings to be given, in what terms, and how to implement the process were all matters of policy within the discretion of the Secretary of State.

The court reasoned as follows. On the one hand, there was a "real risk of grave or fatal injury to two or three children as a result of a month's delay".[55] On the other, there was a public interest in presenting an unambiguous and unanimous message from the Department of Health and the pharmaceutical industry. Yet the logistics of arranging suitable meetings between the parties would necessarily take some weeks. The matter was one of balance within the legitimate discretion of the Secretary of State for Health. A similar response was given in a case under the Food Act 1990 in which the Secretary of State ordered that food should be destroyed because there was a *suspicion* that a manufacturer's premises had become contaminated with *E. coli*. When, and how, should such powers be exercised in circumstances of uncertainty when the evidence is incomplete? On the one hand, people may be at risk of serious food poisoning. On the other, the unnecessary use of such powers will cause considerable damage to business interests. The Court of Appeal said:

> The department faced the classic dilemma of any regulator: if strong action is taken and the apprehended harm to the general public does not ensue, the authority is criticised for taking unnecessarily draconian action and causing damage which would otherwise have been avoided; if on the other hand the authority holds its hand and harm does follow, the authority is castigated for abdicating its responsibility to exercise powers which Parliament has conferred for dealing with such a situation. The danger of hindsight is obvious.[56]

Matters of judgment and balance are unlikely to be regarded as *operational* matters. Rather, they fall within the policy, or discretion of the decision-makers and are, as a result, more difficult to attack in negligence.

Never the less, to say that negligence is more difficult to establish in "policy" cases is not to say that it is impossible to do so. In the following section, we consider the role of negligence specifically in respect of NHS resource-allocation policies.

IV. Resource Allocation—Negligence, or Reasonable Discretion?

In an environment of scarce resources, hard choices between competing demands are unavoidable. What does the law of negligence have to say when resource policies inevitably lead to damage? The National Health Service Act 1977 confers on decision-makers a statutory discretion to make decisions between deserving patients. The lawfulness of that discretion in negligence must be assessed with reference to the principles of judicial review, i.e. illegality, irrationality, and procedural propriety.[57] The following explains this uncertain area of law by

---

[55] *Smith v Secretary of State for Health* [2002] Lloyd's Rep Med 333, para. 106.

[56] *R v Secretary of State for Health, ex p Cheapside Cheese Co* (2000) 55 BMLR 38, 54 *per* Lord Bingham LCJ.

[57] Discussed in Ch. 5. The cases are divided as to the relevance of judicial review to public authority negligence. In *X v Bedfordshire CC* [1995] 3 All ER 353, 369–70 Lord Browne-Wilkinson said

considering the prospects of actions in negligence where the decision complained of is (A) within the ambit of statutory discretion, (B) outside the ambit of statutory discretion, or procedurally defective. In each case, if the complainant can bring himself within one of the grounds of judicial review, negligence requires that he also satisfies the tri-partite test laid down in the *Caparo* case,[58] namely that the damage was foreseeable, that the claimant was in a *proximate* relationship to the defendant, and it is fair just and reasonable to impose liability in the circumstances.[59] Lastly, we consider (C) whether the standard of care demanded in negligence is sensitive to the resources available to the public authority.

A. Decisions within the Ambit of Statutory Discretion

Lawful decisions (i.e. made *within* the ambit of statutory discretion) may be (1) rational, or (2) irrational and it is important to distinguish the two to understand the response of the law of negligence. The logic of the different grounds of complaint may be drawn as follows, where lawful discretion exists above the horizontal line:

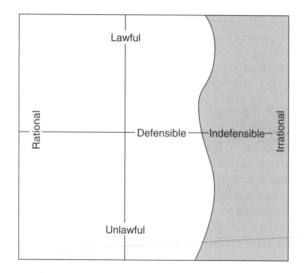

Figure 7.1. Logic of grounds of complaint

that "I do not believe it is either helpful or necessary to introduce public law concepts as to the validity of a decision into the question of liability at common law for negligence", yet continued that "the first requirement is to show that the decision was outside the ambit of the discretion altogether". But in *Stovin v Wise* [1996] 3 All ER 801, 828 Lord Hoffmann considered "the minimum pre-conditions for basing a duty of care upon the existence of a statutory power[is] that it would in the circumstances have been irrational not to have exercised the power, so that there was in effect a public law duty to act". See D. Fairgrieve, *State Liability in Tort* (Oxford University Press, 2003) 41–51.

[58] *Caparo Industries plc v Dickman* [1990] 1 All ER 568.
[59] *X v Bedfordshire CC* [1995] 3 All ER 353, 371, *per* Lord Browne-Wilkinson.

1. Rational Decisions made within the Ambit of Statutory Discretion

Rational decisions made lawfully, i.e. *within* the ambit of statutory discretion must be immune from action in negligence. This is the case even when the decision causes harm. The principle is illustrated by the case of the Borstal boys discussed above. The policy of conferring greater freedom and independence upon them was a reasonable policy intended to encourage their reform and rehabilitation. Inevitably, such a policy increased the risk of their absconding from detention and damaging those living in the neighbourhood. Never the less, such a policy, reasonably adopted and within the ambit of the discretion conferred, would not be amenable to action in judicial review or in negligence. Although the policy gave rise to foreseeable damage, the risk had impliedly been permitted by the statute and, in such circumstances, the common law adapts itself to the will of Parliament.[60]

Similarly, as the Court of Appeal has said, the National Health Service Act 1977 imposes a duty to "promote" a comprehensive health service, but not to *provide* all the care which patients need. Accordingly, within their finite allocations, health authorities must necessarily allocate resources according to a system of priorities and, to this extent, rationing in the NHS is lawful.[61] Hard choices between deserving patients will inevitably arise from time to time. Provided health authorities act reasonably and remain within the ambit of the discretion conferred upon them, they will be immune from action in negligence.[62]

2. Irrational Decisions made within the Ambit of Statutory Discretion

The position with respect to *irrational* decisions made within the ambit of statutory discretion is entirely different. Conclusions may be reached which are *within* the range of decisions conferred on the decision-maker, yet the decision may be so defective, or illogical as to be irrational.[63] Do cases in this category generate better prospects of success in negligence? Mere "irrationality" alone is insufficient to found an action in negligence. In addition, there must be a duty to act and exceptional circumstances for thinking that liability should be imposed.[64] The following distinguishes the circumstances in which irrational decisions will, and will not, give rise to a right of action in negligence by suggesting two forms of irrationality.

---

[60] See *Home Office v Dorset Yacht Co Ltd* [1970] 2 All ER 294.

[61] See, e.g., *R v N and E Devon HA, ex p Coughlan* [1999] Lloyd's Rep Med 306, 314 and *R v NW Lancashire HA, ex p A, D and G* (2000) 53 BMLR 148.

[62] The ambit of PCT discretion is explained in Ch. 5 above.

[63] This approach to judicial review has probably developed since the end of the 1980s, before which the courts would only examine the reasonableness of the *conclusions* reached by public authorities. Today, however, especially in cases involving individual rights, the courts will scrutinise the reasons and logic on which conclusions are based. See, e.g., *R v NW Lancashire HA, ex p A, D and G* (2000) 53 BMLR 148 and pp. 100–3 above.

[64] See Lord Hoffmann, in *Stovin v Wise* [1996] 3 All ER 801, 828.

Before doing so, note that my analysis presumes the existence of a claim for personal injury damages. It is appropriate when claims to individual rights are in issue, but less so when the dispute is between institutions where (as we saw in Chapter 5) the court's scrutiny may be less intense. With this caveat, we consider cases where the decision-makers' conclusion is (a) *defensible*, in the sense that it remains available to the decision-maker, but the considerations on which it is based must be reconsidered, and (b) *indefensible*, in the sense that, although it remains within the ambit prescribed by the statute, it is so unreasonable that no sensible person could have reached it.[65]

(a) *Irrational*, but defensible

Ex p Fisher[66] is an example of a case in which the decision-making *process* was irrational, but the conclusion reached was plausible and available to the health authority. The patient suffered multiple sclerosis. The health authority refused to pay for an expensive treatment, beta interferon, to treat his condition because it considered the cost of the drug was disproportionate relative to its modest benefits. By itself, this was not irrational (the decision being theirs to make). However, the health authority entirely failed to give proper consideration to a relevant factor in reaching its conclusion, i.e. a circular published by the Secretary of State encouraging health authorities to accommodate the costs of the drug in their spending plans. Their failure to do so was irrational for failing to take into account a relevant consideration. Now let us consider whether the patient would be entitled to pursue an action in negligence (say) because his condition deteriorated in a way that would have been avoided had he been permitted beta interferon.

His prospects of success in these circumstances would be poor. Although the decision was unlawful in judicial review, the health authority could have re-affirmed its original refusal to fund the treatment. To succeed in negligence, the claim must satisfy the tri-partite test in the *Caparo* case. Clearly, in litigation, each of these factors would receive more extensive argument than can be attempted here, but we can outline the salient issues. First, was the patient in a *proximate* relationship with the health authority sufficient to trigger a duty to act? Even if the authority could reasonably foresee that his health would suffer without access to the treatment, does this impose a duty to fund it? The answer must be No. Given the therapeutic profile of the drug and the other pressing demands made upon its resources, a reasonable health authority would be entitled to allocate a low priority to the treatment (provided, of course, that it admitted the possibility of exceptional cases). Arguably, no automatic duty to fund would exist and, accordingly, no proximity between health authority and patient. Much the same argument is available in respect of *fairness justice and public*

---

[65] Sometimes referred to as irrationality in the (a) broad and (b) narrow sense. See *Associated Provincial Picture Houses v Wednesbury Corporation* [1948] 1 KB 223 and *R v N and E Devon HA, ex p Coughlan* [1999] Lloyd's Rep Med 306, 323 col. 2, explaining that rationality has two faces: one, a decision which has proceeded by flawed logic, the other, "the barely known decision which simply defies comprehension" and pp. 97–107, above.
[66] [1997] 8 Med LR 327, discussed in Ch. 5 above.

policy. Given the opportunity costs of diverting limited resources from one category of patients to another, it would not be fair, just, or reasonable in public policy to impose a duty of care in these circumstances. Since there is no automatic duty to provide the treatment concerned, it is unlikely that the common law would endorse a right of action in negligence for failure to do so.

Exactly the same arguments would be available in respect of the "transsexuals" case of *Ex p A, D and G* [67] in which it would be equally difficult for the complainants to bring an action in negligence. Although these decisions fail the test of *rationality* in judicial review, the authority remains free to reach the same conclusion provided it takes full account of the court's observations as to the manner in which the decision should be taken.

(b) *Irrational* and indefensible

What, however, if the public authority adopts a policy which is within the range of decisions available to it, yet neither its conclusion, nor the manner in which it has been reached are defensible? The policy is within a theoretical range available to the authority, but the conclusion is so unreasonable that no sensible person could have come to it—it is outrageous. Although it has been said that "nothing which the authority does within the ambit of this discretion can be actionable at common law", [68] and this might be thought to insulate from negligence all "policy" decisions, this surely refers to the *reasonable* exercise of discretion. "There must come a stage when the discretion is exercised so carelessly or unreasonably that there has been no real exercise of the discretion which Parliament conferred. The person purporting to exercise his discretion has acted in an abuse or in excess of his statutory power. Parliament cannot be supposed to have granted immunity to persons to do that." [69]

Clearly, policies which are both irrational and indefensible will be exceptional. However, recall the case of *Smith* above, in which the court held that the delay in banning the use of aspirin in children had been reasonable. The court also said that if the delay had been brought about by wholly improper reasons, for example, a cynical attempt to win a by-election in "a marginal constituency with a large aspirin factory", or because the medical advisers preferred to attend the Epsom Derby meeting, then liability in negligence for such a flagrant exercise of discretion could have arisen. [70] This suggests that irrationality characterised by bad faith would be sufficient to found an action in negligence. Is it possible to create more plausible examples of such failures sufficient to give rise to action in negligence?

[67] See 101–2 above.
[68] *X v Bedfordshire CC* [1995] 3 All ER 353, 371, *per* Lord Browne-Wilkinson.
[69] *Home Office v Dorset Yacht Co Ltd* [1970] 2 All ER 294, 132. See also Lord Jauncey in *X v Bedfordshire CC*, at 362 and Lord Hutton in *Barrett v Enfield LBC* [1999] 3 All ER 193, 222: "the fact that the decision . . . was made within the ambit of a statutory discretion and is capable of being described as a policy decision is not in itself a reason why it should be held that no claim in negligence can be brought in respect of it . . . It is only where the decision involves the weighing of competing public interests or is dictated by the considerations which the courts are not fitted to assess that the courts will hold that the issue is non-justiciable on the ground that the decision was made in the exercise of a statutory discretion." [70] [2002] Lloyd's Rep Med 333, para. 95.

Let us test this question by inventing a case, adapted from the facts of *Ex p Collier*. Say a boy needs a routine operation to repair a hole in the heart and is top of his consultant's list of priority cases. The hospital authorities cancel his appointment for operating space, but the reason is because the case is creating adverse publicity for the government and the authority is using the case as way of bargaining with the Department of Health for additional NHS resources. Say the operation is delayed so long that the boy dies. Would his estate have grounds to bring an action in negligence on his behalf? There is no absolute obligation to provide treatment and the matter is for the authority to decide. Yet such a reason to refuse treatment would surely be condemned in judicial review as irrational for taking into account irrelevant considerations both as to its conclusion and with respect to the manner in which it was taken. How could an action proceed in negligence?

Assuming such a decision would be indefensible in judicial review, the complainants will be required to overcome the three hurdles imposed by the *Caparo* case. Presumably *foresight* exists in this case. The boy's condition would be described as "acute-fatal" in the sense that he will die unless he is treated and the prospects following surgery are good. Does *proximity* exist between the parties? Here too, a strong argument is available. The boy is well-known to the authority because he is top of his consultant's list. By analogy with *Kent v Griffiths*,[71] the authority had accepted responsibility for his care by scheduling (but then cancelling) operating space within which the surgery could be performed. Finally, would it be *fair, just and reasonable in public policy* for the authority to be held liable in these circumstances? Unlike the cases discussed above, there must be a strong presumption that appropriate treatment will be given, unless very persuasive reasons exist to the contrary.[72] Of course, some such persuasive reasons may exist from time to time, for example, an overwhelming emergency has enveloped the hospital and staff are simply not available. But the authority would be required to explain what those circumstances were and why they prevented routine treatment from being made available (or the patient being transferred to another hospital). In the absence of such persuasive reasons, the *conclusion*—the refusal to treat—would be difficult to justify. The decision exposed the patient to a foreseeable, proximate, serious, and avoidable risk of death. Particularly if it had been made in bad faith, it be would fair, just and reasonable to impose a duty of care under *Caparo*.

Challenges to policy decisions in negligence will be unusual, but such an example was considered in *Re HIV Haemophiliac Litigation*, in which there was no allegation of bad faith.[73] Here, the question arose in the context of a group action taken on behalf of 962 haemophiliac patients (many of whom died) and their

---

[71] [2000] Lloyd's Rep Med 109, discussed above at 172.

[72] ". . . the court's respect for the sanctity of human life must impose a strong obligation in favour of taking all steps capable of preserving life, save in exceptional circumstances" *per* Cazalet J in *A NHS Trust v D* [2000] Lloyd's Rep Med 411, 417.

[73] (1990) 41 BMLR 171. In France, the scandal attracted criminal prosecutions against the Ministers of State responsible. See J.P. Soulier, *Transfusion at SIDA—Le droit à la vérité* (Editions Frison-Roche, 1992) arguing that more rapid protection from HIV-infected blood was not practicable.

relatives after patients had been transfused with Factor VIII (a blood product) which was contaminated with HIV. The plaintiffs alleged negligence against the Secretary of State, the health authorities of England and Wales and the Committee on the Safety of Medicines on the basis of their purchasing policy for blood products. Salient amongst the plaintiffs' complaints were the allegations that (1) given the knowledge about the human immuno-deficiency virus, the defendants ought to have become self-sufficient with respect to blood and blood products in preference to purchasing those products from the US, where donors are paid for giving blood and the system tends to rely more heavily on categories of donor whose blood is more likely to be contaminated; and (2) if the blood transfusion service was not to be made self-sufficient, more ought to have been done to warn and inform patients of the dangers presented by HIV, to screen donors in this country and to introduce a system of heat-treatment of blood to minimise the risks of contamination.[74]

In reply, the defendants argued that matters, such as these, concerning the allocation of health service resources, were exclusively for the discretion of Secretary of State and that the claim was not justiciable by individual patients. Accordingly, they said, no duty of care was owed to the defendants in negligence because there was no sufficient relationship of proximity between the plaintiffs and defendants, and it would not be fair and reasonable to impose a duty of care between the parties.[75] In preliminary proceedings the Court of Appeal allowed the case to proceed to trial. The plaintiffs had presented an arguable case that the defendants' policy of importing blood and failing to use heat-treatment was unreasonable and amenable to an action in negligence. The court was influenced by the fact that the dangers threatened patients' lives and that the catastrophe could largely have been avoided had measures been introduced at an earlier date. Bingham LJ appeared to agree with the submission of counsel for the plaintiffs that "the fact that the decision attacked is a matter of discretion or policy-making does not make the decision immune in law. If it is *ultra vires* or wholly unreasonable the authority will be liable in negligence if the decision is shown to be negligent by reference to proximity and foreseeability."[76] This is surely correct. His Lordship continued:

. . . where, as here, foreseeability by a defendant of severe personal injury to a person such as the plaintiff is shown and the existence of a proximate relationship between plaintiff and defendant is accepted, the plaintiff is well on his way to establishing the existence of a duty of care . . . While the court cannot review the merits of a decision taken by a public authority if it fell within the area of discretion conferred by Parliament, it may do so even in a common law action for damages for negligence if satisfied that the decision in question for any of the recognised reasons fell outside the area of such discretion.[77]

[74] The matter was made the subject of Health Service Guidelines. See *Provision of haemophilia treatment and care* (HSG(93)30, NHSME, 1993).
[75] These arguments were based on *Rowling v Takarro Properties Ltd* [1988] AC 473 and *Hill v Chief Constable of West Yorkshire* [1989] 1 AC 53.   [76] (1990) 41 BMLR 171, 190.
[77] (1990) 41 BMLR 171, 200.

And Ralph Gibson LJ said: "if it is proved that the information as to the nature and gravity of the risk, and of the steps available to eliminate or reduce it, was supplied to those who were required to make the decisions, then, in my judgment, the plaintiffs would have a *prima facie* case for asserting that the decisions were such that no reasonable or responsible person could properly make them."[78] Allowing the case to proceed to trial, the court observed that its prospects of success were not guaranteed. Ultimately, the government settled the case which never proceeded to trial. Never the less it well illuminates the potential for negligence in matters of deliberate policy-making. Clearly, the distinction between defensible and *in*defensible decisions will be difficult. It will tend to exclude from negligence many complaints of technical "judi-cial review error" made in good faith. On the other hand, as *Re HIV Haemophiliac Litigation* demonstrates, it is not limited to cases of bad faith and may extend to decisions in which obvious precautions were not taken, especially if the costs of doing so were modest. Putting it another way, the decision was such that no reasonable person addressing themselves to the question could have arrived at it.

B. Unlawful or Procedurally Improper Decisions

How does this analysis accommodate decisions made unlawfully, i.e. *ultra vires*, outside the ambit of statutory discretion, or in circumstances of procedural impro-priety? Note first that such decisions may also be *irrational*—they may be both out-side the ambit of discretion or procedurally defective *and* irrational. In this case, the analysis of irrationality suggested above, and the distinction made between defensible and indefensible reasons, would apply. On the other hand, decisions may be reasonable as a response to the management of scarce resources, but illegal for being in breach of the statute under which the power is conferred. This does not provide a good complaint in negligence. Take the legal duties imposed by the National Institute for Clinical Excellence (NICE), in which Primary Care Trusts are duty-bound by directions "to ensure that a health care intervention that is recommended by [NICE] is, from a date not later than three months from the date of the Technology Appraisal Guidance, normally available" to be prescribed for patients.[79] What if a PCT sets insufficient funds aside to do so, patients are denied access to treatment and their condition deteriorates in a way that would not have happened had the treatment been available? Would action against the PCT be available in negligence?

Let us first consider illegal decisions taken outside the ambit of statutory discre-tion. The PCT may say that its decision not to fund NICE guidance is driven by the competing demands on its resources, that its decision is fair and reasonable between

---

[78] On the facts, however, Ralph Gibson LJ considered it more probable that "such an error [of] failing to act appropriately upon available information, was the result of failure at some level within the Department to pass that available information to those who were required to make decisions" (at 193).
[79] As discussed in Ch. 4 above, "directions" have statutory force and are binding on those to who they are directed. We discuss NICE in more detail in Ch. 8 below.

patients and that the decision is not, therefore, irrational. Whether or not this is true, however, such a decision must surely be *illegal* in the sense that it contradicts the statutory instruction contained in the direction. Once the threshold of judicial review is crossed, the next obstacle for the claimant is *Caparo's* three-part test. As we noted in the case of *Ex p Fisher*, even if foresight of damage is present, it is necessary to show *proximity* in the relationship between the complainant and the PCT. This requirement presents a serious hurdle. The PCT may be able to persuade the court that, notwithstanding its *illegal* conduct in failing to fund the treatment in question, it is not in a relationship of proximity to patients awaiting treatment. On the contrary, it has duties to entire communities of people and, as the courts recognise, it has to make difficult choices between them and to prioritise their competing demands. Accordingly, there will always be the danger that, within current resourcing policy, some patients will wait longer for treatment, receive "second-best" treatment or, indeed, no treatment at all. Arguably, the purpose of the NICE directions is not to confer individual rights of action in negligence or to create new "proximity" between PCTs and patients. On the contrary, it is an administrative measure intended to establish reasonable standards upon PCTs alone.[80]

So too with *fairness, justice and public policy*. Would it be fair, just, or reasonable to confer special rights solely on those fortunate enough to benefit from NICE guidance? Bear in mind that the capacity of NICE to issue guidance is limited. Very many treatments, both old and new, will never be considered by NICE. What is the position of those whose treatments have not been considered by NICE? They remain subject to the general rule that the NHS does not provide guarantees of treatment. Yet, to introduce a "two-speed" NHS is this way, in which those with NICE-approved treatment have higher rights to care than those without, supported by rights to damages, would surely be unacceptable and contradict the intention of the statute. It would do nothing to promote the principles of fairness, justice, or reasonable public policy. For these reasons, I suggest that, notwithstanding the illegal conduct of the PCT in judicial review, the requirements of the *Caparo* case would present a very serious obstacle in the way of an action in negligence. The only exception to this approach would be a decision which was not simply *illegal*, but also *indefensible* (in the sense discussed above) both as to the manner of its reasoning and its conclusion.

This approach applies equally to complaints which establish *procedural impropriety* in judicial review. The prospects of an action in negligence are subject to similar hurdles. Here too, therefore, unless the complaint is based on unreasonableness of an indefensible kind, an action in negligence is also likely to fail.[81]

---

[80]   See by analogy *Danns v Department of Health* (1995) 25 BMLR 121 concerning the duty to provide contraceptive services. Wright J said "this is an excellent example of a statutory 'duty' in respect of which the minister is answerable to the public at large through Parliament, and not by way of private litigation" (at 130).
[81]   e.g., a patient is damaged because the merits of her case are not properly considered in a PCT committee motivated by malice. (Such a case may also give rise to the separate, but uncommon, action of misfeasance in a public office.)

C. Are Negligence Standards Resource-Dependent?

We now turn to a related matter. Suppose that the claimant has surmounted the hurdle of judicial review. Further, suppose he has gone on to satisfy the tri-partite test of *Caparo* and established the existence a duty of care. He now has a further hurdle, i.e. to establish that the defendants are in *breach* of their duty of care. This is also likely to present a substantial hurdle because "the claimant must be able to demonstrate that the standard of care fell short of that set by *Bolam* . . . That is deliberately and properly a high standard in recognition of the difficult nature of some decisions . . . and of the room for genuine differences of view on the propriety of one course of action against another."[82]

Such differences of view will be the more likely in relation to decisions made under financial constraint. This provokes the question: are resource considerations relevant to identifying the appropriate standard of performance to be expected of the defendants? In other words, in circumstances of resource shortages, should a more modest standard be required so that the ambit of liability is reduced?

The difficult balance between deference to public authority discretion and private rights to compensation in circumstances of scarce resources is demonstrated in *Knight v Home Office*.[83] An inmate was held in the hospital wing of Brixton Prison. He suffered serious mental illness and was a recognised suicide risk. Owing to lack of staff and facilities, he was treated in a way that would not have been considered adequate by a mental hospital outside prison. He was not provided with counselling and interactive support, or given continuous observation, treatments which would have been expected in a non-prison setting. Instead he was confined alone for long periods of time and succeeded in hanging himself from the bars of his cell. On behalf of the deceased, it was said that his management had fallen below the standard required of reasonable doctors under the *Bolam* test. It was no defence that the standard was as good as in other prisons because that was not the relevant test. The hospital facilities in the prison were inadequate with reference to what ought reasonably to have been available to patients suffering this form of mental illness in an appropriate hospital.

The court rejected the defendant's contention that, since prison funding depended on the Home Office and, ultimately, the Treasury, the plaintiff had no claim in negligence and that his only remedy was a political one. Pill J said:

It is for the court to consider what standard of care is appropriate to the particular relationship and in the particular situation. It is not a complete defence for a government department . . . to say that funds are not available for additional safety measures . . . To take an extreme example, if the evidence was that no funds were available to provide any medical facilities in a large prison there would be a failure to achieve the standard of care appropriate to prisoners.[84]

---

[82] *Phelps v Hillingdon BC* [2000] 4 All ER 504, 534, *per* Lord Clyde. The reference to *Bolam* includes professionals generally and is not restricted to doctors alone.   [83] [1990] 3 All ER 237.
[84] *Knight v Home Office* [1990] 3 All ER 237, 243.

On the other hand, his Lordship gave no indication of the means by which the courts could provide remedies to those who had suffered injury from decisions of this nature. Rejecting the plaintiff's claim, he said simply:

> In making the decision as to the standard to be demanded the court must . . . bear in mind as one factor that resources available for the public service are limited and that the allocation of resources is a matter for Parliament . . . I am unable to accept . . . that the law requires the standard of care in a prison hospital to be as high as the standard of care for all purposes in a psychiatric hospital outside prison. There may be circumstances in which the standard of care in a prison falls below that which would be expected in a psychiatric hospital without the prison authority being negligent.[85]

On this analysis, resources are relevant to the standard of care to be expected of public authorities. Perhaps the medical standard is measured by a sliding scale, depending on what ought to be expected from reasonable doctors, or reasonable hospitals, in the circumstances, given the limited available funds, but subject to a minimum obligation.[86] If this is correct, standards demanded in negligence could diminish dramatically in circumstances of scarce resources. Regrettably, on this crucial point, no principle on which such a rule depended was discussed, nor were the reasons to justify such diminished standards in this case explained.[87] One is left wondering precisely on what basis was the court satisfied that a reasonable standard of care had been achieved and that no breach of duty had occurred. By contrast, in *Brooks v Home Office* Garland J considered the standard of care owed to an expectant mother detained in prison. His Lordship took the contrary view: "I cannot regard *Knight* as authority for the proposition that the plaintiff should not, while detained in Holloway, be entitled to expect the same level of ante-natal care, both for herself and her unborn infants, as if she were at liberty, subject of course to the constraints of having to be escorted and, to some extent, her movement being retarded by those requirements."[88] Clearly, this is a matter for the Court of Appeal to resolve. Intuitively, however, one senses a danger in the courts permitting standards to fall (and fall) in response to financial pressures.

---

[85] *Knight v Home Office* [1990] 3 All ER 237, 243. Agreeing with the "variable standard" approach, see J. Siliciano, "Wealth, Equity and the Unitary Medical Standard" (1991) 77 *Virginia Law Review* 439, 466.

[86] The general rule is to the contrary. Negligence does not consider the idiosyncrasies of the particular defendant (*Glasgow Corpn. v Muir* [1943] AC 448, 457; *Nettleship v Weston* [1971] 2 QB 691). But a small number of cases have enabled the standard of care to vary. See, e.g., *Goldman v Hargrave* [1967] 1 AC 645; *Watt v Hertfordshire CC* [1954] 1 WLR 835 (duty of emergency authorities hurrying to site of accident) and R. Kidner, "The variable standard of care, contributory negligence and *volenti*" (1991) 11 *Legal Studies* 1.

[87] His lordship said, at 243: "Even in a medical context outside prison, the standard of care will vary with the context. The facilities available to deal with an emergency in a general practitioners surgery cannot be expected to be as ample as those available in the casualty department of a general hospital." With respect, however, this precisely misses the point. Of course the facilities differ, but the GP has a continuing duty to his patient to take reasonable steps to safeguard his welfare (e.g. by transferring him to hospital) which is not affected by the issue of resources. Why should a similar duty not also apply for the benefit of prisoners?   [88] (1999) 48 BMLR 109, 114.

Some indication of the Court of Appeal's response to this question is indicated by a case concerning the resourcing of medical posts in NHS hospitals. For many years, doctors were engaged on contracts which required them to work an average of 88 hours per week. The policy reason for this approach was clear. This relatively inexpensive labour meant that the system could engage more doctors and have them on call during longer hours of the week. In *Johnstone v Bloomsbury Health Authority*[89] a doctor had been regularly on duty without proper rest for 90 hours, as required by his contract of employment. He claimed damages on the ground that the burden of the work had affected his health. The Court of Appeal was sympathetic to the claim that the stress and over-work was making him ill. His action for damages was allowed to proceed. This suggests that the *institutional* limitations imposed on managers as to the manner in which they should engage junior doctors does not constitute a blanket ban on actions in negligence by junior doctors, or entitle employers to impose unreasonable demands on their employees. This too is consistent with the framework of analysis we have discussed in which policy decisions should not, by definition, be sufficient to exclude action in negligence.

V. Corporate Manslaughter

Having discussed the ways in which corporate bodies may be liable for negligence in *civil* law, we now consider the *criminal* liability of NHS bodies for corporate manslaughter. A number of cases have provoked calls for this area of law to be reformed, notably, the case of the *Herald of Free Enterprise*, in which a cross-channel ferry capsized in 1987, killing 187 of its crew and passengers as a result of sailing with its bow doors open in rough seas; the King's Cross fire of the same year, which claimed 31 lives; the Clapham rail crash from which 35 people died; and the Southall rail crash which resulted in 7 deaths and 151 injuries.[90] How does the law of corporate manslaughter apply to corporate bodies, including the NHS?[91]

Manslaughter is the unintentional, but unlawful killing of another. Manslaughter may arise from negligence so gross that the risk should have been obvious to any reasonably prudent person in the defendant's position and that to have failed to have taken precautions against the danger was reckless.[92] In addition, *corporate* manslaughter requires further elements to be satisfied which severely

---

[89] [1991] 2 All ER 293. Doctors' hours on call are now subject to the European Working Time Directive in which working hours have been reduced to 56 hours per week (Council Directives 89/391/EEC and 93/104/EEC). See also *Sindicato de Medicos de Assistencia Publica v Consellara de Sanidad Consumo de la Generalidad Valencia* (Case C–303/98), confirming that the directives apply to doctors.

[90] See *Reforming the Law on Involuntary Manslaughter: The Government's Proposals* (Home Office, 2000).

[91] See M. Childs, "Medical Manslaughter and Corporate Liability" (1999) *Legal Studies* 316.

[92] Or in the medical context, something was done which no reasonably skilled doctor would have done. See *R v Bateman* (1925) 19 Cr App R 8 and *R v Prentice and Sullivan* [1993] 4 All ER 935.

limit its application. The obstacles facing a charge of this nature have been explained by the government as follows:

Before a company can be convicted of manslaughter, an individual who can be "identified as the embodiment of the company itself" must first be shown himself to have been guilty of manslaughter. Only if the individual who is the embodiment of the company is found guilty can the company be convicted. Where there is insufficient evidence to convict the individual, any prosecution of the company must fail. This principle is often referred to as the "identification" principle. [93]

Unsurprisingly, as the government observes, especially in larger companies, it will be impossible to identify a single individual responsible for gross negligence in the management of the company. More probably, the company will be operated by separate directorates in which responsibility is diffused so that it is the "systems" throughout the company, rather than a single individual, who is to blame. The difficulty was explained in the *Herald of Free Enterprise* case. As with many cases in which proceedings for corporate manslaughter have begun, the prosecution in this case was terminated because it was impossible to prove manslaughter against the "controlling mind of one of its agents . . . which fulfills the prerequisites of the crime of manslaughter". [94] Clearly, this requirement severely limits the application of the law of corporate manslaughter to the NHS.

The Law Commission has recommended reform of this area of law in a way that is likely to widen the impact of criminal liability for corporate manslaughter and the government has accepted the need for "radical reform". [95] What is proposed? The Law Commission criticises the fiction that the corporation ought to have known of a risk. [96] The "corporation" has no "mind" of its own; it is composed of individuals. Thus, the focus on the fault of particular individuals, it says, should be removed. Instead, the focus should be on the management and organisation of the body and, in particular, the duty to provide a safe place of work, to engage competent staff, to provide and maintain safe appliances, and to provide a safe system of work. With this new focus, "there would be no need to identify the controlling officers of the company. The question would be whether there had been a management failure, rather than, at present, whether there was blameworthy conduct on the part of any individual." [97] Such a test would not impose liability on the corporate body for the "operational" negligence limited to the conduct of individuals, although the body would continue to be vicariously liable in civil law for their work-related negligence.

---

[93] See *Reforming the Law,* note 90 above, at para. 3.1.3.

[94] See *P & O European Ferries (Dover) Ltd* (1991) 93 Cr App R 72, 83–4 (Central Criminal Division). For a similar result in relation to the Southall rail accident, see *A-G's Reference (No. 2 of 1999)* [2000] 3 All ER 182.

[95] See *Reforming the Law,* note 90 above, Foreword by the Home Secretary, Rt Hon Jack Straw.

[96] *Involuntary Manslaughter* (1996, HC 171, Law Commission, No. 237) para. 8.3.

[97] ibid., para. 8.20.

How would such a principle apply to some of the cases we have examined in this chapter? Were they to cause death, such an approach could embrace many of the examples of "systems" negligence we have discussed above, for example, the management of split-site hospitals,[98] the supervision of junior doctors,[99] the circumstances discussed by the Bristol Inquiry, and the Anthony Ledward Inquiry. In each, senior NHS managers failed to introduce systems to manage risks about which they ought to have known. Of course, there will be also be the difficulty of making the distinction between "systems" negligence for which corporate manslaughter might be available, and "operational" negligence which remains the responsibility of the individual clinician, or manager; a difficulty which will be the more difficult if resource shortages are partly responsible for the error. Never the less, assisted by the various regulatory bodies which have been created to improve safety in the NHS, any reform in this area will encourage NHS directors to be astute as to the adequacy of the systems of safety in their hospitals.

There remains the problem of the appropriate sanction. Assuming no individual can be identified as bearing personal responsibility for the accident, action will be taken against the corporate body itself. With respect to a private company, the sanction is usually a fine. Although such a penalty tends to hit shareholders first, rather than individual directors, the shareholders are free to replace members of the board. Public bodies, on the other hand, are in a different position. The imposition of a significant fine upon them would simply serve to reduce the funds available to perform their statutory functions to the public. A public body is not free to put up prices, or reconfigure its business so as not to provide services—it is under a statutory duty to do so. There is a danger of straining scarce resources still further and making future accidents still more likely than before. Bearing this in mind, the solution is for the court to impose a modest fine on public authorities which recognises the inflexibility of their responsibilities. Such a response to public authority damages has been adopted to claimants under the Human Rights Act 1998 and it would seem appropriate to successful prosecutions for corporate manslaughter too.[100] Further remedial action would also be expected by the various statutory bodies which have been established to superintend safety in the NHS and to comply with the Article 2 requirement of the Convention, that public authorities are subject to proper investigation as to the circumstances in which people die whilst in their responsibility.[101]

---

[98] *Bull v Devon HA* [1993] 4 Med LR 117.
[99] *R v Prentice and Sullivan* [1993] 4 All ER 935.
[100] See f. 229 above.
[101] See the discussion of *R (Khan) v Secretary of State for Health*, pp. 157–9, above.

8

NHS Governance and Accountability

Chapters 5 to 7 considered accountability in the context of judicial review and the law of negligence. Now we move to the new procedures created within the NHS designed to regulate its governance. Until the mid-1990s, NHS governance had developed piecemeal in response to specific issues and problems as they arose from time to time. Indeed, in the 1980s, the talk was of "de-regulation", of easing the burden imposed by "red-tape" and bureaucracy.[1] But this was short-lived. Introducing the *Citizen's Charter*, the Prime Minister of the time, John Major, deplored the absence of proper accountability in many areas of public service. As he saw it: "Telephones answered grudgingly or not at all. Booths closed while customers were waiting. Time pointlessly lost when appointments were not made or kept. Unacceptably long waiting times . . . People left in the dark about why something was happening—or more often not happening. Anonymous voices and faces who refused to give you a contact name . . . This was the weekly reality for millions of people in Britain up to the end of the 1980s."[2]

The real catalyst for greater NHS governance, however, was *Learning from Bristol* and the conviction for murder of Harold Shipman, both of which profoundly changed attitudes to the manner in which the NHS is managed and organised. Before the introduction of the "internal market" for health care in 1992, managerial power in the NHS was dominated by the medical profession. Supervision of clinical standards was undertaken by the General Medical Council (GMC)[3] and clinical audits undertaken in hospitals, but the system tended to be reactive, in the sense that it was motivated by concerns as to the performance of individuals after the event. There was no supervision of standards in the system as a whole, and no means by which performance in one place could be reliably compared with that of another. *Learning from Bristol* says: "We cannot say that the

---

[1] Although much of the talk was empty rhetoric because regulation proliferated during this time. See K. Walshe, *Regulating Healthcare—A Prescription for Improvement* (Open University Press, 2003) 12–15.

[2] John Major, *The Autobiography* (Harper Collins, 1999) 247.

[3] J. Allsop and L. Mulcahy, *Regulating Medical Work, Formal and Informal Controls* (Open University Press, 1996). The Medical (Professional Performance) Act 1995 amends the Medical Act 1983 to provide for the retraining of doctors.

external system for assuring and monitoring the quality of care was inadequate. There was, in truth, no such system."[4] The report remarks:

> In the decades after the establishment of the NHS (in fact right up until the late 1980s) central government, through the Department of Health . . . interpreted its responsibility for the NHS largely in terms of planning and allocating resources. It did not see itself as being responsible for, and thus accountable for, the quality of clinical care, either in terms of setting standards or of monitoring clinical performance. Quality was regarded by government as a matter for individual healthcare professionals. For their part, healthcare professionals, particularly hospital doctors, had deeply embedded in their culture the notion of professional autonomy, often expressed in the form of "clinical freedom".[5]

As the Bristol Inquiry demonstrates, such a state of affairs exposes government to risk. Government carries ultimate responsibility for the stewardship of the NHS. If waiting lists rise, or vulnerable patients are denied effective treatment; if accident and emergency departments leave patients stranded on trolleys; or hospital wards are closed for lack of nurses; it is the Minister who must explain why and what is being done about it. One response is simply to promise greater investment in the NHS—to increase *inputs* in terms of additional investment. On the other hand, unless inputs result in improved *outputs* in terms of improved standards and quality of care, the political risk remains. With the benefit of hindsight, such managerial passivity throughout the NHS is striking. *Learning from Bristol* and the conviction of Harold Shipman created an environment in which government was constrained to respond to the absence of any effective *systems* for identifying, quantifying and responding to failure. Thus, governance has become the trademark of the government's "third way" in health care,[6] both in respect of the clinical care given to patients and the corporate regulation of the NHS as an institution. Even today, however, the system of regulating the NHS has been described as "a distinctly Gothic machinery of accountability, as successive generations of politicians have added new buttresses and spires to the building".[7] This is the background against which the discussion in this chapter should be understood and it explains the creation of large number of new regulatory bodies with powers to audit and supervise doctors and NHS managers.

---

[4] *Learning from Bristol: The Report of the Public Inquiry into Children's Heart Surgery at the Bristol Royal Infirmary, 1984–95* (Cm. 5207, 2001) 6, para. 30 and 192, para. 21. The Department of Health had a role in which "the factors which were set out and monitored were focused on finance and the volume of patients treated. The quality and performance of clinical services were regarded as matter for the local hospital or health service, not the DoH." (186–7).

[5] *Learning from Bristol* 303, para. 2. The same practice was common throughout the world, see E. Docteur and H. Oxley, *Health-Care Systems: Lessons from the Reform Experience* (OECD, 2003).

[6] K. Walshe, "The Rise of Regulation in the NHS" (2002) 324 *British Medical Journal* 967.

[7] P. Day and R. Klein, *Auditing the Auditors—Audit in the National Health Service* (Nuffield Trust, 2001) 19, although it is also described as a more temporary "organisational shantytown in which structures and systems are cobbled together or thrown up hastily in the knowledge that they will be torn down again in due course", K. Walshe, "Foundation Hospitals—a new direction for NHS reform?" (2003) 96 *J Royal Society of Medicine* 106.

This chapter considers (I) the risks and benefits of governance, (II) accountability through NHS contracts, (III) governance of priority setting, (IV) accountability to the public, and (V) oversight of NHS performance.

I. The Risks and Benefits of Governance

We should note at the outset that audit is not an entirely passive activity. "Far from being passive, audit actively constructs the contexts in which it operates."[8] In doing so, it presents risks, as well as benefits. How does governance impact upon the systems it regulates? Let us discuss two aspects of governance to illustrate the point, namely the *purpose* of governance and the *means* of governance, identifying the problems and difficulties which arise as we go.

A. The Purpose of Governance

What is the objective of governance? Is it clinical, economic, social, or political?[9] In reality, governance pursues a number of different objectives at the same time, not all of which are compatible, but each may affect the system it inspects. For example, as we discuss below, one of the purposes of the National Institute for Clinical Excellence (NICE) is to enable patients throughout the NHS to have equal access to new and effective medicines. Its rationale is fundamentally clinical. Similarly, the Commission for Health Audit and Inspection (CHAI), the National Patient Safety Agency (NPSA) and the National Clinical Assessment Authority (NCAA) are designed to improve the quality of clinical care to patients. Unsurprisingly, by focusing on *clinical excellence*, their tendency is to raise NHS costs.

By contrast, the reforms introduced by the Conservatives in 1990 and continued in modified form by Labour after 1997 address an *economic* question—how can incentives be used to make the NHS more conscious of value for money? Prior to 1990, in the absence of "purchasers" and "providers", overall spending decisions were made by large health authorities. Unlike many other areas of consumer spending, there are huge information asymmetries in health care; patients and their GPs do not always know which hospitals provide the best care, nor, in a publicly funded system, how one hospital's costs compare with another. A "market" for health care attempts to increase the power of choice by making differences in cost and quality more transparent. Within this economic framework, clinical excellence is not the only objective; *value for money* is also relevant and it may argue in favour of compromising some aspects of care in favour of benefits available elsewhere.

Equally, governance may pursue what may be called "social" objectives. Health, after all, is largely perceived as a public good to society as a whole and health policy

---

[8] M. Power, *The Audit Explosion* (Demos, London, 1994) 8.
[9] See generally, K. Walshe, note 1 above, ch. 2.

can be used to promote social goals. Modern health care policy, for example, has attempted to reduce inequalities in standards of health between different parts of the community by concentrating resources on those in most need of care.[10] Similarly, the wider social objective of providing a publicly-funded service which responds to its citizens on the basis of need is central to the sense of social solidarity in the NHS. Yet these objectives may not be identical to the clinical, or economic principles discussed above. After all, a fair and consistent system available to everyone on the basis of need may require some expensive treatments to be rationed. And social policies may not be consistent with the dictates of a market.

Lastly, one of the purposes of governance may be "political": to distance central government from responsibility for local decision-making. We discussed in Chapter 3 the eternal conflict between the "command-economy" model of health care management and the need to empower local communities to respond to the needs of local people. The modern trend across many of the developed nations is to encourage diversity in the provision of health care, including the use of private providers. But as direct state control diminishes, and especially given the large sums of public money involved, it becomes necessary to devise alternative mechanisms for managing and regulating health care.

When power is diverted to separate "regulators", it becomes crucial to understand how independent the regulator is from government itself. Who appoints those who serve on the regulatory body and to whom are they themselves accountable? The argument for truly independent regulators was made in *Learning from Bristol*:

The regulation of the NHS in this broad sense must not, in our view, be in the day-to-day control of the Department of Health. While it is the proper role of government to establish the regulatory framework, to ensure safety and promote quality, that framework must be as independent as possible of the Department of Health. That is quite simply because it is not in the interests of the public or of patients that the monopoly provider should also set and monitor the standards of care. Instead, those functions should be carried out by independent bodies within a statutory regulatory framework.[11]

Thus, we should be sensitive to the various, and sometimes inconsistent, objectives of governance. We now consider some of the means by which those purposes may be achieved.

B. The Means of Governance

Governance is unlikely to be an entirely neutral observer over that which it assesses because the manner in which it is performed is likely to influence the result of the process. The more external and quantitative the audit, the more an institution may have to adapt its own procedures to suit its auditors. In doing so, it may also modify its own perception of quality and performance. Meeting targets may become the

---

[10] See *Tackling Health Inequalities* (Department of Health, 2002).
[11] (Cm. 5207, 2001) 261, para. 27.

most urgent managerial imperative, even if it means that more important matters take second place. Indeed, this "gaming" of the system may lead managers to falsify records (such as waiting times) in an attempt to manage the process of audit.[12] In this case, insensitive systems of governance may report high standards in institutions that have simply learned how to play the system and there will be "a risk of relying too heavily on an industry of empty comfort certificates [and] shallow rituals of verification at the expense of other forms of organisational intelligence".[13] Let us look at the side-effects of governance in respect of both managers and clinicians.

1. Managers

In her 2002 BBC Reith lecture, Baroness O'Neill made similar comments on the impact of accountability and "governance" on the public interest and its potential to distort the objectives of public service and to damage the trust that should exist between professionals and those they serve. She expressed concern that a culture which treats professional groups as if they all have something to hide will damage the public interest:

> The pursuit of ever more perfect accountability provides citizens and consumers, patients and parents with more information, more comparisons and more complaints systems; but it also builds a culture of suspicion, [and] low morale and may ultimately lead to professional cynicism; and then we would have grounds for public mistrust.[14]

Aggressive, unsympathetic audit may tend to de-personalise and distance the parties from each other and deflect the parties from the core purpose of their relationship. The danger of the erosion of professionalism under systems driven by performance management and patients' rights has been described as follows. "Trust wanes as relationships become more formal and bureaucratic and less personal. This creates a call for rights. The rights solution further alienates doctor and patient because it distances them and because the doctor resents the distrust that motivated the solution."[15] Concern about excessive "governance" is not restricted to hospitals and doctors. The Chief Inspector of Schools expresses similar misgivings in relation to the distorting impact of too many targets on schools and emphasises the need for balance in the concern for quality. He said:

> . . . an excessive or myopic focus on targets can actually narrow and reduce achievement by crowding out some of the essentials of effective and broadly-based teaching. The innovation

---

[12] *Inappropriate Adjustments to NHS Waiting Lists* (House of Commons Public Accounts Committee, 46th Report, Session 2001–02). See also *Waiting List Accuracy: Assessing the Accuracy of Waiting List Information in NHS Hospitals* (Audit Commission, 2003) reporting that three trusts had misreported data.

[13] M. Power, *The Audit Society—Rituals of Verification* (Oxford University Press, 1999) 123.

[14] Baroness O. O'Neill, *Called to Account* (www.bbc.co.uk/radio4/reith2002/3).

[15] C. Schneider, *The Practice of Autonomy—Patients, Doctors and Medical Decisions* (Oxford University Press, New York, 1998) 201. Making a similar point, see also S. Sitkin and N. Roth, "Explaining the Limited Effectiveness of Legalistic 'Remedies' for Trust/Distrust" (1993) 4 *Organization Science* 367.

and reform that we need to see in our schools may be inhibited by an over-concentration on targets . . . there is a crucial balance to be struck between governmental initiative and legitimate powers of intervention on the on the one hand, and the professional responsibility of individuals making decisions in the best interests of their pupils.[16]

These observations are equally applicable to doctors and their patients.

An alternative, more sympathetic approach to governance is to set fewer "hard" targets and permit those subject to audit a measure of discretion over "soft" *aspirations*. Here, regulator and regulated deal with one another as equals with a high degree of trust between them. Of course, the disadvantage of such latitude is that with fewer targets and greater discretion, government is exposed to risk if its promises to improve standards are not kept. What will be the balance of governance in the NHS? The government has introduced a range of new systems of NHS governance. This suggests that the "soft" approach to governance, in which targets become negotiable and may not always be achieved, will not commend itself. Indeed, government may take an entirely unsympathetic view and threaten "failing" managers with sanctions. As a result, however, complaints of unreasonable interference from the centre are likely to increase. "Managers have complained that they have been promised the freedom to run their organisations, but that it has been rendered largely nugatory by a stream of informal guidance often driven by political imperatives rather than by the best interests of the organisation."[17] An ex-Minister of Health expressed sympathy for this view shortly after resigning from the government: "I am sorry that we never got to grips with 'targetitis'. Some targets are essential . . . unless you set targets, [the NHS] will go its own anarchic way at the expense of the taxpayer. But we set far too many, and the beleagured NHS is still suffering under the weight of it all."[18]

2. *Clinicians*

It is not only managers who may be affected in this way. Doctors too may be rated according to league-tables of clinical success and failure. And, of course, hospital managers will be keen to demonstrate to the public the excellent standards of quality that those tables disclose. But will the focus of too much attention on doctors distort their sense of clinical judgment? Will it tend to divert attention away from the needs of patients and toward the doctor's (or hospital's) position on the league table? The concern is illuminated by research conducted by the National Bureau of Economic Research into cardiac surgery in New York and Pennsylvania. It considers whether the disclosure of each cardiologist's performance record (known in the

---

[16] David Bell, Chief Inspector of Schools, 2003, speech to City of York annual education conference, 28 February 2003, www.education.guardian.co.uk/ofsted/story/0,7348,904453

[17] A. Davies, *Accountability—A Public Law Analysis of Government by Contract* (Oxford University Press, 2001) 117–18.

[18] Lord Hunt of Kings North, in the wake of his resignation prompted by the allied invasion of Iraq, see "Goodbye to all that" *Health Service Journal*, 3 April 2003, 18.

US as "report cards") produces incentives not to treat more difficult, severely ill, patients for fear of damaging the doctor's position in the league. It made two key findings. First, performance data led to substantial patient selection by hospitals and, in particular, a decline in the severity of the illness of patients receiving coronary artery bypass graft (CABG) by comparison with hospitals where such data was not published: "the increase in the quantity of CABG for the healthy was accompanied by a significant decrease in the quantity of CABG for the sick."[19]

Secondly, the system discouraged the admission of very sick patients: "more severely ill [heart] patients experienced dramatically worsened health outcomes. Among more severely ill patients, report cards led to substantial increases in the rate of heart failure and recurrent [heart attacks]"[20] In summary, report cards tended to encourage doctors to select less sick patients for treatment, but, more strikingly: "For sicker patients, doctors and hospitals avoided performing cardiac surgical treatments of all types. These changes were particularly harmful, leading to sicker patients to have substantially higher frequencies of heart failure and repeated [heart attacks], and ultimately higher costs of care."[21]

Perhaps unwittingly, their impact was to distort patient selection in a way that would benefit the doctor's clinical performance record. A related risk of "targets" arises if the target becomes more important than the patient. For example, targets on waiting times encourage doctors to treat patients within a specific time-period. There is a danger that *non-urgent* patients waiting near the end of the time-period may be treated with greater urgency than those with the most urgent clinical needs. In this way, the time target is achieved, but the net result is that some urgent patients suffer avoidable loss as a consequence. For example, one doctor has observed that:

The waiting time targets for new outpatient appointments at the Bristol Eye Hospital have been achieved at the expense of cancellation and delay of follow-up appointments. At present we cancel over 1,000 appointments per month. Some patients have waited 20 months longer than the planned date for their appointment. We have kept clinical incident forms for all patients, mostly those with glaucoma or diabetes, who have lost vision as a result of delayed follow-up; there have been 25 in the past 2 years . . . One particularly sad case was that of an elderly lady who was completely deaf and relied upon signing and lip-reading for communication . . . Her follow-up appointment for glaucoma was delayed several times and during this time her glaucoma deteriorated and she became totally blind.[22]

Clearly, therefore, clinical performance management has the capacity to bring both advantages and disadvantages.[23] The challenge to find a proper balance is made

---

[19] D. Dranove, D. Kressler, M. McClennan and M.Satterthwaite, "Is More Information Better? The Effects of 'Report Cards' on Health Care Providers" (National Bureau of Economic Research, Paper 8697, 2002) 18.   [20] ibid.

[21] ibid. "Health Care Report Cards May Fail Patients"—Executive Summary.

[22] Dr Richard Harrad, Clinical Director of the Bristol Eye Hospital, in evidence to the House of Commons Public Administration Committee. See *On Target?—Government by Measurement* (HC 62–1, 2003) paras 52–3.

[23] See A. Maynard, "A double-edged sword" *Health Service Journal*, 25 March 2002, 20.

difficult by the sensitivity of the subject and the challenge of presenting ambiguous and provocative information in a meaningful and non-sensational manner.[24] We need a robust method of identifying and ranking patient need so as to make a more sensitive assessment of clinical performance. If we fail to do so, those in most urgent need of care may find themselves least likely to receive treatment.

In the light of these comments and misgivings, we now consider the new mechanisms of governance in the NHS.

II. Accountability Through NHS Contracts

Following the model of the internal market introduced in 1991, primary care trusts (PCTs) arrange for appropriate care to be provided to patients by entering into "NHS contracts" with NHS Trust hospitals and GPs.[25] (Foundation hospitals enter ordinary private contracts enforceable through the courts.) In theory, this arrangement permits PCTs to promote public health policies by contracting with providers that best serve the public interest. In practice, however, "purchasers [have] very little discretion to pursue local concerns in their contracts, because their actions [are] so heavily influenced by central priorities".[26] Also, within the NHS, there is a limited market for health care. Neither purchaser nor provider can abandon a contract and move their business elsewhere because NHS services have to be provided to patients locally and PCT purchasers often have a small number of local NHS trust hospitals with whom to contract. In other words, there is often insufficient competition in the market to provide meaningful incentives. As a result, few of the benefits of delegation, such as greater responsiveness to local needs, have been achieved. Bearing these limitations in mind, we discuss the nature of NHS contracts, and how disputes between the parties are resolved.

A. The Nature of NHS Contracts

"The phrase 'NHS contract' means an agreement under which one health service body ('the acquirer') arranges for the provision to it by another health service body ('the provider') of goods and services which it reasonably requires for the purposes of its functions."[27] And 'health service body' means any of the following, *inter alia*:

(az) a Strategic Health Authority;
(a) a Health Authority;

---

[24] See, e.g., "Heart surgeons' death figures to be published", *The Times*, 18 January 2002, 8, on rates of clinical success amongst cardiologists.

[25] GPs may choose to enter NHS contracts, or ordinary private contracts with PCTs, see the National Health Service (General Medical Services Contracts) Regulations 2004 (SI 2004 No. 291), reg. 10 (equivalent provisions exist for PMS providers).

[26] A. Davies, note 17 above, at 116–17.

[27] National Health Service and Community Care Act 1990, s. 4(1).

(aa) a Special Health Authority
 (b) a health board . . . ;
(bb) a Primary Care Trust
 (c) the Common Services Agency for the Scottish Health Service;
 (e) an NHS trust;
 (ff) the Commission for Health Improvement;
 (g) the Dental Practice Board or the Scottish Dental Practice Board;
 (h) the Public Health Laboratory Service Board; and
 (i) the Secretary of State . . .[28]

NHS contracts are intended to enable the parties to agree matters of quality, quantity, and cost. Parties to NHS contracts may undertake such obligations as they see fit. Since 1997, NHS contracts are generally expected to last for "at least three years, but could extend in some circumstances for five to ten years".[29] Guidance published during the Conservative administration of the NHS suggested three basic models of NHS contracting, i.e. "block contracts", "cost and volume contracts" and "cost per case contracts".[30] *Block contracts* are agreements in which hospital units undertake to provide an unlimited number of facilities, or a maximum number, expressed, for example, in terms of beds, over a specified period of time. Under these arrangements PCTs may commit resources to a hospital provider irrespective of the actual usage of the facilities and, in so doing, will have difficulty being precise with respect to quality.[31]

This model of contracting for services, however, will become less common. In Chapter 3, we discussed the introduction of health related groups (HRGs) as a mechanism for paying hospitals for the services they provide. These resemble the old *cost and volume contracts* which offer the opportunity to agree a particular service, or range of services, for a specific price. Their emphasis is on output in the sense that the parties agree specific requirements for an exact price. With HRGs, however, prices will be set according to a central tariff, adjusted to accommodate local cost differentials. This has the advantage of reducing the transaction costs which arose previously during the making of each contract and it will reward those who can perform their procedures at levels below their cost as set by the tariff. In this case, more revenue will be available to treat more patients and generate more income. By contrast, severe pressure will be imposed on hospitals which cannot achieve similar levels of efficiency, who will lose patients to the more cost-effective

---

[28] 1990 Act, s. 4(2), as amended by the National Health Service Reform and Health Care Professions Act 2002, Sched. 5, para. 31. Subpara. (d) referred to Family Health Service Authorities and is deleted.
 [29] *The New NHS—Modern, Dependable* (Cm. 3807, 1997) paras 9.19 and 19.20.
 [30] See J. Appleby, *Developing Contracting: A National Survey of District Health Authorities, Boards and NHS Trusts* (NAHAT, 1995) 8. Non-NHS and private work made up the majority of the remainder.
 [31] See J. Appleby, P. Smith *et al.*, 'Monitoring Managed Competition', in R. Robinson and J Le Grand (eds) *Evaluating the NHS Reforms* (King's Fund Institute, 1994) ch. 2.

hospitals. In this way a new form of internal market for NHS services has been introduced with less time and money spent on the contracting process, but more vigorous competition between hospitals.

Lastly, *cost per case contracts*, or individually agreed contracts, inevitably carry larger transaction costs. They may be most appropriate where existing agreements fail to accommodate the special needs of a particular patient, say because they have an uncommon condition. In this event, an out of area transfer (OAT) may be suitable on a one-off basis. Purchasers may be reluctant to enter cost per case contracts based on a cost per day basis, for fear of losing control over their resources. The alternative is to use the contract as a means of negotiating entire episodes of care, with the emphasis on the provider to assess the average cost of each episode, allowing for occasional complications, or to refine cost and volume contracts after specified threshold targets have been achieved.

These processes give the parties discretion as to how strictly, or liberally, to observe their rights and obligations. A "hard" approach to contracting would be characterised by low levels of trust between the parties in which negotiations were conducted in a competitive environment. The contract would be framed in a way that sought to achieve minimum levels of flexibility, it would be monitored closely and regularly and there would be the threat of withdrawal by dissatisfied parties and a claim for compensation. By contrast, a "soft" approach would be based on trust and confidence between the parties in which matters could be developed *during* performance of the contract on the basis of collaboration. Matters could be left undefined in the contract in the knowledge that they would be resolved by negotiation, without the need for conflict, because the parties have a shared purpose. Labour's emphasis on "service level agreements" may be intended to foster a co-operative, "soft" approach to the process between parties to NHS contracts. On the other, the speed of NHS reform means that its "organisational memory" is very short and, in reality, individuals seldom develop sufficiently stable contacts with colleagues to permit such a mature relationship to arise.

B. Disputes Resolution

PCTs will monitor the performance of the hospitals to which patients have been sent with a view to encouraging improvements in standards, or a change of hospital if performance is unsatisfactory. And hospitals themselves may make "tertiary referrals" of patients who need specialist treatment to other hospitals with particular expertise. They too will want to safeguard quality. Each will want to know that it has received the goods and services paid for in the right quantity, quality, and at the right time. In cases of dispute what action may be taken where an amicable settlement between the parties is impossible? The National Health Service and Community Care Act 1990 removes the possibility of disputes over

NHS contracts being heard in the courts on grounds of breach of contract. It provides:

> Whether or not an arrangement which constitutes an NHS contract would, apart from this subsection, be a contract in law, it shall not be regarded for any purposes as giving rise to contractual rights and liabilities, but if any dispute arises with respect to such an arrangement, either party may refer the matter to the Secretary of State for determination.[32]

An adjudication may: "contain such directions (including directions as to payment) as the Secretary of State or, as the case may be, the person appointed under subsection (5) . . . considers appropriate to resolve the matter in dispute; and it shall be the duty of the parties to the NHS contract in question to comply with any such directions."[33]

The adjudicator also has authority to vary the terms of an NHS contract, or bring it to an end.[34] In addition to these rules which assume the existence of an NHS contract, a procedure is available to negotiators who consider that:

(a) the terms proposed by another health service body are unfair by reason that the other party is seeking to take advantage of its position as the only, or the only practicable, provider of the goods and services concerned or by reason of any other unequal bargaining position as between the prospective parties to the proposed arrangement, or

(b) that for any other reason arising out of the relative bargaining position of the prospective parties any of the terms of the proposed arrangement cannot be agreed . . .[35]

The procedure by which such disputes should be resolved is set down in regulations,[36] but no substantive guidelines have been suggested as a means of settlement. The explanatory notes state, rather ambiguously, that the adjudicator's decisions "will not constitute precedents for the determination of other disputes, but they will be useful learning tools for all parties in reaching a shared understanding of the ways contracts might develop".[37] Generally, statutes do not exclude the right to natural justice and judicial review would be available to parties who considered they had been dealt with unfairly by an informal adjudicatory body. Both parties must be heard in order for the adjudicator to have a balanced view of the dispute;[38] and the adjudication must be fair, in the sense that it must be truly independent of the parties.[39] There is a "presumption . . . that the outcome will give effect to the agreement which was originally reached, rather than a new agreement which the parties should have reached".[40] Some measure of consistency

---

[32] National Health Service and Community Care Act 1990, s. 4(3). The matter may be determined either by the Secretary of State, or by his appointee. See 1990 Act, s. 4(5).

[33] See 1990 Act, s. 4(7).   [34] See ibid., s. 4(8).   [35] See ibid., s. 4(4).

[36] See the National Health Service Contracts (Dispute Resolution) Regulations 1996 (SI 1996 No. 623).

[37] See NHS Contracts: Arrangements for Resolving Disputes, HO 302/6 and EL(91)11 (NHSME, 1991).

[38] *Ridge v Baldwin* [1964] AC 40; *Schmidt v Secretary of State for Home Affairs* [1969] 2 Ch 149.

[39] *R v Kent Police Authority, ex p Gooden* [1971] 2 QB 662; *Metropolitan Properties Co (FGC) Ltd v Lannon and others* [1969] 1 QB 577.

[40] NHS Contracts: Arrangements for Resolving Disputes, H.O. 302/4 (NHSME, 1991).

ought to exist between adjudications so that if similar cases were to be treated inconsistently, the matter could be amenable to judicial review.[41]

This adjudication machinery has been little used. Occasionally, an informal conciliation and arbitration system has been employed to avoid the statutory mechanisms. But, "contracting parties were firmly discouraged even from using this informal system. Health authorities and providers were told that invoking it would be a sign of management failure."[42] Within the "NHS family", therefore, agreements between purchasers and providers are both legally and (often) practically unenforceable. In the absence of market incentives to encourage competition, an informal adjudicatory procedure might have provided an alternative means of encouraging parties to adhere to their contracts. "But the absence of such a procedure created problems for purchasers seeking to set standards of their choice . . . it seemed to render the contractual accountability process *less* effective."[43] As in the area of resource allocation and clinical governance, the government prefers to leave matters of this nature to the discretion of local parties. The ostensible reason is to permit local forces to shape the service in the light of their own needs. Yet, in reality, government retains a firm grip over the choices that are available to local decision-makers and much of the benefit that flows from the devolution of power is not realised.

With respect to the process of NHS contracting, as with the other matters, the government could make much clearer the framework within which contracting should occur. Under current arrangements, in our *national* health service, there is no generally agreed template within which such agreements should be made, or procedures by which disputes should be resolved, or remedies agreed. Instead, hundreds of PCTs are obliged to contract with hundreds of NHS hospitals without guidance. This wastes time and energy and produces variations throughout the NHS which diminish the authority of NHS contracts as a whole. There is no need for an Act of Parliament to resolve this matter. The Department of Health is equipped to produce guidance on "model contracts" (as it has for Foundation Trust hospitals) which would be available to contracting parties. They would not bind PCTs which could vary or depart from them as they saw fit. They could, however, generate greater uniformity of expectation and an informal stock of "cases" illustrating how disputes would expect to be resolved.

III. Governance of NHS Resource Allocation—NICE

The National Institute for Clinical Excellence (NICE) has responsibility for reviewing health technologies and recommending whether they should be provided

---

[41] See *Metropolitan Properties Ltd v Lannon* [1969] 1 QB 577, which concerned consistency between levels of rent established by rent assessment committees.

[42] A. Davies, note 1 above, at 33. See also R. Flynn and G. Williams (eds), *Contracting for Health: Quasi-Markets and the National Health Service* (Oxford University Press, 1997).

[43] A. Davies, note 1 above, at 169.

within the NHS. NICE was created in response to concern surrounding "post-code prescribing" in which there is tendency for patients in different parts of the country to have different access to care depending on the commissioning policies of each local health authority. Clearly, within a system that delegates discretion to over 300 PCTs, different priorities are inevitable. NICE is intended to provide a "more uniform uptake of treatments which work best for patients" by creating a limited number of "ambitious but achievable national targets".[44] Its duty is to advise PCTs whether to fund a particular technology having regard to "the promotion of clinical excellence *and of the effective use of available resources* in the health service".[45]

A. Selection and Appraisal[46]

NICE provides significant commercial advantage to those companies whose health technologies are approved. For this reason, the selection and appraisal of new health technologies is sensitive and NICE has introduced procedures to make both more transparent. Selection is made by the Secretary of State[47] on the advice of the Advisory Committee on Topic Selection (ACTS), a body of around 30 members representing the Department of Health, NHS bodies, patient groups, and the pharmaceutical industry.[48] A number of broad criteria have been developed to guide ACTS in recommendations. First, is the technology likely to result in significant health benefit taken across the NHS as a whole (for example, would it address a condition which is associated with significant disability, morbidity, or mortality; would it tend to improve existing clinical practice; or improve the efficiency with which health resources were used)? Secondly, is the technology likely to result in a significant impact on other health-related Government policies such as the reduction of health inequalities? Thirdly, is the technology likely to have a significant impact on NHS resources (financial or other) if given to those for whom it is indicated? Fourthly, is NICE likely to be able to add value by issuing national guidance (for example, is there sufficient clinical evidence on which to develop robust guidance, or such divergent practice amongst clinicians as to make further guidance desirable)? ACTS may also advise whether NICE should issue a firm and mandatory technology appraisal guidance or rather a broader discretionary *guideline*; the time at which an appraisal should be undertaken; and, if

---

[44] *The NHS Plan—A plan for investment. A plan for reform* (Cm. 4818–I, 2000) para. 6.10. See the National Institute for Clinical Excellence (Establishment and Constitution) Order 1999 (SI 1999 No. 220), reg. 3, as amended by SI 1999 No. 2219.

[45] National Institute for Clinical Excellence (Establishment and Constitution) Order 1999 (SI 1999 No. 220), the italicised words were added by SI 1999 No. 2219.

[46] See generally, C. Newdick, "Evaluating Health Technology Appraisal in the UK" in T. Jost (ed.), *Health Care Coverage Determinations: An International Comparative Study* (Open University Press, 2004).

[47] National Institute for Clinical Excellence Regulations 1999 (SI 1999 No. 260), reg. 13.

[48] See *Topic Selection and Timing of Guidance on New Technology* (NICE, 2002) Annex B.

clinical evidence is still developing, whether the balance of advantage favours delaying an appraisal until further data become available.[49]

Once selected for review, technologies pass through stages of appraisal. In particular, NICE nominates "consultees" to submit written evidence (including clinicians, pressure groups and the manufacturer of the technology in question) and a broad cross-section of "commentators" to comment on evidence submitted during the appraisal. The process culminates with a final appraisal document (FAD) prepared by authoritative, independent assessors considering the best clinical and economic evidence available. If NICE accepts the FAD, it will form the basis of its recommendations to the Secretary of State.

NICE considers the full hierarchy of clinical evidence from authoritative, large-scale, randomised trials, to the anecdotal experience of carers, but greater weight is given to evidence from high-quality studies with methodology designed to minimise bias.[50] With respect to NICE's duty to promote cost-effectiveness, NICE takes account of:

The overall resources available to the NHS when determining cost effectiveness. Therefore, decisions on the cost effectiveness of a new technology must include judgments on the implications for healthcare programmes for other patient groups that may be displaced by the adoption of the new technology. [It] does not consider the affordability of the new technology but does take account of how its advice may enable the more efficient use of healthcare resources.[51]

But it is not clear how this principle enables NICE to assess the impact of its decisions on PCT resources, or which local programmes should be withdrawn as a result. Sympathising with the "opportunity costs" of NICE guidance on fixed PCT budgets, the World Health Organziation (WHO) says "it is important to develop methods for budget modeling that would enable NICE to provide more detailed information on the implementation costs to the local [health] authorities".[52] It has been suggested that NICE has adopted a quality adjusted life year (QALY) threshold of around £30,000 per patient as a guide to the limit at which approval will usually be given,[53] but the WHO review of NICE considered the cost thresholds used to be unclear. It recommended "NICE must resolve the confusion related to the use of a value-for-money threshold. If a threshold is to be used as the basis for recommendations, it needs to be specified and justified for reasons of transparency."[54] NICE explains that it does

---

[49] See *Guide to the Technology Appraisal Process* (NICE, 2004) para. 2.2, and *National Arrangements for Clinical Excellence Arrangements for Topic Selection—Overview of the New System* (NICE, 2002) Annex B.   [50] See Guide to Methods of Technology Appraisal (NICE, 2004) para. 6.2.5.

[51] See *Guide to the Technology Appraisal Process* (NICE, 2004) paras 6.2.6.1 and 6.2.6.2.

[52] See *Technology Appraisal Programme of the National Institute for Clinical Excellence* (WHO, 2003) 6, see also 33.

[53] See J. Raftery, "NICE: Faster access to modern treatments? Analysis of guidance on health technologies" (2002) 323 *British Medical Journal* 1300.

[54] See *Technology Appraisal Programme of the National Institute for Clinical Excellence* (WHO, 2003) 32.

not use a fixed incremental cost-effectiveness threshold, above which a technology would automatically be rejected. Instead, it takes a more flexible approach, so that:

... below a most plausible ICER [incremental cost effectiveness ratio] of £20,000/QALY, judgments about the acceptability of a technology as an effective use of NHS resources are based primarily on the cost-effectiveness estimate. Above [that figure] judgments ... are more likely to make more explicit reference to factors including the degree of uncertainty surrounding the calculation of ICERs, the innovative use of the technology, the particular features of the condition and population receiving the intervention [and] appropriate wider societal costs and benefits. Above an ICER of £30,000/QALY, the case for supporting the technology on these factors has to be increasingly strong.[55]

NICE guidance may take a number of different forms. It may recommend the use of the technology for all patients for whom it is intended, recommend its use for a limited category of patients only, indicate that further clinical trials should be undertaken, or where evidence of clinical and cost effectiveness is not persuasive, recommend that the technology is not adopted in the NHS.[56] The latter option presents the greatest challenge. Hard-pressed PCTs will soon request NICE to appraise technologies with a view to their being de-commissioned from the NHS. Clearly, guidance which supports the *withdrawal* of treatment from the NHS is likely to present more controversy than that which mandates that new technologies be adopted. Bearing in mind that matters are referred to NICE by the Secretary of State, will government be prepared to submit such delicate matters to NICE for appraisal? The criteria on which ACTS currently advises the Secretary of State on selection for NICE review do not comfortably accommodate the question of reducing expenditure on particular treatments. If government is serious about promoting "treatments which work best for patients",[57] they should be revised to do so.

B. Impact of NICE

Before 2002, NICE had limited impact on health authorities because they were not bound to adopt its recommendations. Of course, such guidance had to be considered in the decision-making process,[58] but PCTs were free to depart from it in their own reasonable discretion. However, as part of the policy to reduce post-code differentials in access to NHS care, from 2002, NICE guidance has assumed the status of *Directions*. Today, therefore,

... a Primary Care Trust shall, unless directed otherwise by the Secretary of State ... apply such amounts of the sums paid to it ... as may be required to ensure that a health

[55] See *Guide to Methods of Technology Appraisal* (NICE, 2004) paras 6.2.6.10 and 6.2.6.11.

[56] C. Ham and G. Robert, *Reasonable Rationing—International Experience of Priority Setting in Health Care* (Open University Press, 2003) 73.

[57] *The NHS Plan— A plan for investment. A plan for reform* (Cm. 4818–I, 2000) para. 6.10. A new NICE "guideline" on caesarian sections has recommended more cautious use of the procedure, see *Ceasarian Section* (NICE, Clinical Guideline 13, 2004). This is welcome.

[58] See *R v N Derbyshire HA, ex p Fisher* (1997) 8 Med LR discussed in Ch. 5 above.

intervention that is recommended by [NICE] in a Technology Appraisal Guidance is, from a date not later than three months from the date of the Technology Appraisal Guidance, normally available (a) to be prescribed for a patient on a prescription form for the purposes of his NHS treatment, or (b) to be prescribed or administered to any patient for the purposes of his NHS treatment.[59]

Thus, there is a clear presumption that funding will be set aside to accommodate the costs of NICE guidance. In making its recommendations, however, to what extent is NICE sensitive to the resource constraints imposed upon PCTs? In other words, should NICE regard itself as operating within NHS cash-constraints and so have regard to issues of "*cost*-effectiveness", or should its guidance focus simply on "*clinical*-effectiveness", irrespective of its cost? A Secretary of State said in response to this question:

There are two quite separate distinctions . . . which is about assessing clinical and cost effectiveness and a quite separate set of decisions which are around affordability issues. In the end you would want . . . affordability decisions to be located with an accountable politician who has to answer to the House of Commons and to Parliament.[60]

This suggests, quite rightly, that NICE's expertise is in matters *clinical* and that the more sensitive, "political" issues of affordability belong to the Secretary of State. So if there is good clinical evidence that a health technology is effective, NICE will recommend it. It is then for the Secretary of State to preserve the balance of NHS spending by making affordability decisions. However, decisions to refuse funding on affordability grounds are almost never made by the Secretary of State because successive governments have refused to enter the resource allocation debate.[61] This means that the economic agenda is ignored and that every NICE recommendation becomes binding on PCTs.

The funding implications are considerable and NICE is a significant factor driving growth in prescription costs.[62] Since the cost of its recommendations has to be provided within existing budgets, PCTs have to *disinvest* from some areas in order to accommodate NICE guidance. This "blanket" duty to pay for NICE guidance is questionable. NICE makes recommendations as to clinical *effectiveness*. But evidence of efficacy is entirely different to the question whether it should take automatic priority over everything else. Should a recommendation automatically command access to NHS irrespective of the demands made for other

---

[59] Secretary of State's Directions (undated) of 2003. NICE guidance remains *discretionary* in Wales.

[60] Mr Alan Milburn, Evidence to HC Health Committee, 8 November 2000, para. 336. The same distinction is made by NICE: "The Board draws a distinction ... between advising on cost effectiveness within the resources available for health care, and affordability. The latter is properly the responsibility of government and subject to scrutiny by Parliament." *Response to the Bristol Royal Infirmary Inquiry* (NICE, 2001) 3.

[61] For a single exception, see the discussion of the "Viagra" case, discussed at pp. 111–12, above.

[62] See *Growth in Prescription Volume and Cost Report* (NHS Prescription Pricing Authority, 2002, www.ppa.org/uk/pdfs/publications) 19.

treatment? I put this point to the the House of Commons Health Committee who responded:

> . . . in establishing NICE and making its guidance mandatory, the Government has provided a centralised valuation system for one area of service provision, namely new and/or controversial drug treatments and health interventions, without balancing this against guidelines for any other elements of service provision. This was illustrated very clearly by Mr Newdick . . . who argued that NICE's recommendations of a treatment for reducing the symptoms of *influenza* by one day commands the same access to resources as recommended *cancer* treatments.[63]

This is the impact of the mandatory status of NICE guidance on PCTs. Yet the government provides no assistance on the manner in which such *disinvestment* should take place. Unsurprisingly, therefore, PCTs have not been able to divert sufficient resources to provide uniform adoption of NICE guidance in the manner directed. Figure 8.1, from the National Audit Office,[64] demonstrates the variations in the uptake of treatment recommended by NICE to treat cancer.

As for the remainder of new and established treatments which have not received NICE review, the strain on scarce resources has intensified. In the absence of central guidance of any sort, local responses are likely to be even more varied and inconsistent than before.[65] The preferable approach is not to single out certain relatively new and sometimes very marginal treatments in the NHS for special "prized" status. It is to encourage PCTs with guidance of the type that existed before 2002. PCTs should adopt such guidance because it is well reasoned and persuasive, but would retain authority not to follow it, having given the matter serious consideration, if it would seriously impede the provision of other local services and objectives.

Notice, however, that the NICE directions insist that NICE guidance should be "*normally*" available". If the guidance is intended to be mandatory, why qualify the duty with the word "normally"? Does this provide PCTs with some latitude in decision which guidance to implement? In what abnormal circumstances would the Guidance not be mandatory? The question was raised by the House of Commons Health Committee and the Government responded that:

> The word "normally" was included . . . to cover unusual circumstances outside the control of PCTs such as disruption to the supply of a medicine . . . Scarce resources is not a good reason for failure to implement NICE guidance . . . PCTs are expected to manage their budgets so that patients can be *guaranteed* that if a treatment recommended by NICE is appropriate for them, they will receive it.[66]

---

[63] *National Institute for Clinical Excellence*, Second Report of Session 2001–02, HC 515–I, para. 132.

[64] See *Tackling Cancer in England—Saving More Lives* (HC 364, Session 2003–04) 44. The legal implications of this failure for patients' rights of access are discussed at pp. 185–6, above.

[65] See R. Cookson, D. McDaid and A. Maynard, "Wrong SIGN, NICE mess: is national guidance distorting allocation of resources?" (2001) 323 *British Medical Journal* 743.

[66] *Government's Response to the Health Committee's Second Report of Session 2002–02 on the National Institute for Clinical Excellence* (Cm. 5611, 2002) 8. My emphasis.

Proportion of eligible women receiving the treatment has increased, on average 500 per cent—but the increase is not uniform across England.

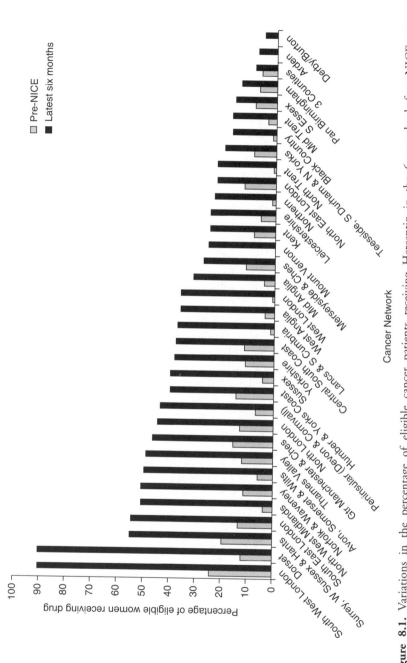

Figure 8.1. Variations in the percentage of eligible cancer patients receiving Herceptin in the 6 months before NICE approval (October 2001– March 2002) and 12 to 18 months afterwards (April–September 2003)

Source: National Audit Office: Tackling Cancer in England—Saving More Lives (HC 364, Session 2003-4), 44.

But this is a very narrow view of the meaning of "normally" which suggests that implementation is not mandatory when it is practically *impossible* to do so. With respect, the word is capable of a wider interpretation and may extend to circumstances where it is practically *possible*, but very difficult to do so without distorting existing arrangements. For example, NICE may recommend treatment which requires further investment in additional specialist staff. Despite the reasonable efforts of the PCT to recruit suitable staff, it may be very difficult to do so within existing salary scales because of shortages of available expertise. Surely, in these circumstances, the treatment could not "normally" be made available. It might also extend to cases where the cost of the guidance is so high that it would dislocate important existing services and put vulnerable patients at risk. Arguably, in such a case the three-month time limit could be legitimately extended to allow greater time for arrangements to be put in place. Similarly, NICE guidance might be discreditied by subsequent clinical evidence so that it was no longer appropriate. Here, too, PCTs could be justified in departing from it. Never the less, the NICE Direction does not permit PCTs the same breadth of discretion as existed before 2002. Very good reason would be required to demonstrate why the guidance could not be implemented.

What happens while we await publication of NICE guidance? Could a PCT refuse to fund treatment until NICE has spoken (colloquially known as "NICE blight")? Recall that PCTs are entitled to have policies which promote some treatments over others. However, such a process of priority setting must be fair, consistent, and transparent. It cannot introduce "blanket bans" on treatment because it must recognise that exceptional patients may have exceptional needs which are entitled to special consideration.[67] This applies equally to treatments awaiting NICE guidance. As a matter of legal principle, unless the guidance is expected imminently, PCTs should allocate resources according to the best information available to them in the present—and accept that if that information changes, policies may have to be adjusted in the future.

NICE may also publish more generic *guidelines* (as opposed to technology appraisal guidance). NICE guidelines do not have mandatory force and remain at the discretion of PCTs. Do not, however, under-estimate the political pressure to implement these guidelines. Recent guidelines concern providing in vitro fertilisation (IVF) to couples having difficulty conceiving a child.[68] This discretionary guideline came with significant political weight attached. Pressure was immediately imposed by the Secretary of State on PCTs to implement this "voluntary" guideline. He said:

Our immediate priority must be to ensure a national level of provision of IVF is available wherever people live. As a first step, by April next year I want all PCTs, including those who at present provide no IVF treatment, to offer at least one full cycle of treatment to all those

---

[67] We elaborate on this principle in Ch. 5 above.
[68] *Fertility: Assessment and Treatment for People with Fertility Problems* (NICE Clinical Guideline, 11 February 2004).

eligible. In the longer term I would expect the NHS to make progress towards full implementation of the NICE guidance.[69]

PCTs may feel constrained to adopt it, notwithstanding its discretionary status. Given the financial pressures upon them and the demands for resources elsewhere, many have set aside little resource to provide IVF treatment. NICE guidelines on the subject will now exert considerable pressure on PCTs to change that approach and to divert resources from other areas of care which they consider to be in greater need of support. PCTs should be careful to distinguish between NICE "guidance" and "guidelines". A decision to treat NICE *guidelines* as binding would be open to challenge in judicial review for failure to exercise the discretion conferred upon it. Such a failure would demonstrate that the PCT had misunderstood its rights and duties and excluded from consideration options that ought to have been available for discussion—in the language of the cases, it "fettered its discretion".[70]

In addition, NICE guidance is binding on NHS *institutions*. But it is not binding on individual doctors. The decision whether to use the treatment remains entirely a matter for their reasonable clinical discretion. As NICE says, its guidance will be good for a large proportion of patients. But there will always be a significant minority for whom the treatment is inappropriate. Doctors must consider the impact of the guidance and bear it in mind in deciding what treatment is best for individual patients.[71] It could be negligent to use it inappropriately just because it emanates from NICE.

IV. Accountability to the Public

Under the "Westminster" model, ministers of health are held accountable to Parliament for their decisions and MPs must submit themselves for re-election every five years. They will be held to account for their success and failures and may seek re-election by offering a broad platform of promises and pledges, some of which will never be fulfilled. Routinely, a minority of voters under the "first-past-the-post" system secure a majority for the party elected. And the new government will remain in power until the next election. Not surprisingly, perhaps, this model

---

[69] Department of Health Press Release, 25 February, doh.gov.uk. Priority should be given to couples "who do not have any children living with them". Does this exclude couples who have re-married and who look after children born to their spouse's *previous* partner? No guidance is offered as to whether it includes unmarried, or lesbian couples.

[70] See generally, K. Syrett, "NICE Work? Rationing, Review and the Legitimacy Problem" (2002) 10 *Medical Law Review* 1.

[71] "The Institute has always indicated that health professionals, when exercising their clinical judgement, should take its guidance fully into account; but that it does not override their responsibility for making appropriate decisions in the circumstances of the individual patient. This principle is important because even the best clinical guideline is unlikely to be able to accommodate more than around 80% of patients for whom it has been developed." *Response to the Report of the Bristol Royal Infirmary Inquiry* (NICE, 2001) 8.

of accountability is sometimes considered too detached, insensitive, and infrequent to provide proper public reassurance.[72] Accordingly, a range of alternative mechanisms for increasing public accountability have been introduced (since the early 1990s) to accommodate local voices.[73] But what exactly does this seek to achieve and how does it affect accountability? Does it confer executory power to make decisions, or is it merely a consultative process intended to *influence* them? If it is executory, how is the body itself accountable and what responsibility remains with government for its decisions? And if it is advisory, is the body truly representative of public opinion, or is it a vehicle carrying single-agenda pressure-groups?

Also, one of the assumptions underlying public involvement is that we understand the need for hard choices in the NHS and wish to contribute local solutions. But is that true? For example, at the level of *national* policy, should priority be given to maximising overall levels of public health, or reducing health inequalities? Should individual *choice* take priority over *social equity* in the system as a whole? Should funding be diverted to some patients rather than others—paediatric, geriatric, obstetric, orthopaedic—or to public health, community care, or primary care? And at *local* strategic level, should a local hospital be closed, or merged with another? Should additional funding be invested in hospital care, or GP services? These are political questions, yet many citizens may not see "health" as a political issue involving "opportunity costs". Encouraged by government, we may simply want access to care on the basis of clinical need; where is the politics in that? Although patients may demand greater *patient* involvement with their own care, their *public* involvement in health care may not excite significant interest. Unless a significant number of people choose to involve themselves in this process, decision-making will not properly represent the public view and the *raison d'etre* of the policy will not be achieved.[74] We should also bear in mind that if the policy implies the devolution of power to local decision-makers, this too has its limits because the Secretary of State and other NHS bodies remain bound by their statutory obligations (including the Human Rights Act 1998) regardless of expressions of local opinion.

With these issues in mind, we consider (A) the duty to consult, (B) patients' forums and independent advocacy services and (C) local authority overview and scrutiny committees.[75]

A. Duty to Consult

With the abolition of community health councils,[76] a variety of alternative mechanisms have been introduced for monitoring the NHS, increasing public involvement

---

[72] See A. Weale, "Democratic Values, Public Consultation and Health Priorities: A Political Science Perspective", in A. Oliver (ed.), *Equity in Health and Healthcare* (The Nuffield Trust, 2003).

[73] *Local Voices: Views of Local People in Purchasing for Health* (NHS Management Executive, 1992).

[74] See D. Florin and J. Dixon, "Public Involvement in Health Care" (2003) 328 *British Medical Journal* 159.

[75] Note also the governance of Foundation Trust Hospitals which must include a public constituency, see Ch. 4 above.

[76] See National Health Service Reform and Health Care Professions Act 2002, s. 22.

and assisting patients to bring complaints. The Health Act 2001 imposes a duty on strategic health authorities, PCTs, and NHS Trusts:

To make arrangements . . . that persons to whom . . . services are provided are directly or through representatives involved and consulted on—

(a) the planning of the provision of those services,

(b) the development and consideration of proposals for changes in the way those services are provided, and

(c) decisions to be made by that body affecting the operation of those services.[77]

Whether or not consultation of interested parties and the public is a statutory requirement, if it is embarked upon it must be carried out properly:

To be proper, consultation [1] must be undertaken at a time when proposals are still at a formative stage; [2] must include sufficient reasons for particular proposals to allow those consulted to give intelligent consideration and an intelligent response; [3] adequate time must be given for this purpose; [4] the product of consultation must be conscientiously taken into account when the ultimate decision is taken.[78]

Exactly how the health service body should respond to the product of the consultation is a matter for local discretion. A decision to close an old and well-liked hospital is likely to generate hostility, yet the need to do so may be irrefutable, for example, because standards of safety can no longer be maintained given the limited numbers and cross-section of patients admitted for care. Nevertheless, the decision must remain open for reconsideration or modification.

A number of mechanisms have been developed for consulting the public, including health forums, citizens' (or patient/carer) panels, focus groups, and newsletters.[79] A project of this sort at national level has been undertaken by NICE where a "Citizen's Council" of 30 individuals has been established to consider "what should NICE take into account when making decisions about clinical need?" Clearly, the Council is not equipped to advise on the clinical and scientific merit of the matters brought before NICE. Its function is to consider "the hopes, values and priorities of people generally".[80] Such a body gives NICE some added legitimacy, but it is difficult for a body of non-elected individuals to have significant authority over policy. It has recommended, for example, that "the response to clinical need should be to provide without prejudice or political, geographical, economic, or social preference, the best care or treatment that can be provided within the resources available, to make the most improvement to a patients' well-being".[81] It also recommends that NICE should consider "factors such as the individual's value system and their cultural and religious views should be taken into account",

---

[77] Health and Social Care Act 2001, s. 11.
[78] *R v North and East Devon HA, ex p Coughlan* [1999] Lloyd's Rep Med 306, 332 col. 1.
[79] For many of the difficulties associated with extending democracy in the NHS, see R. Klein and B. New, *Two Cheers?—Reflections on the Health of NHS Democracy* (King's Fund, 1998).
[80] *Report of the First Meeting of the NICE Citizens' Council* (NICE, 2002) 8.   [81] ibid., 14.

but "clinical need should not be determined by only listening to the voices of more powerful, better known, or more popular groups in the population".[82] These sentiments would surely attract general support but they provide limited guidance (perhaps wisely) on many of the policy choices dictated by scarce resources.

Obtaining a fair and representative cross-section of public views will not be simple. Whilst well-represented pressure groups will be assisted by the duty to consult, less articulate, or popular groups may find it more difficult to be heard. Special steps will be required to hear from, for example, children, elderly and disabled patients.[83] Since the process is likely to reveal as much disagreement as harmony of opinion between differing groups, decision-makers will need to be the more transparent as to the procedures by which contradictory recommendations have been resolved. Unsatisfactory processes risk provoking further complaint and resort to judicial review.

There is a similar risk of including lay representatives on committees with insufficient experience to influence decision-making. Will they be capable of providing more than a "token" of public involvement?[84] These observations highlight the difficulty of involving the public in the NHS. Who should be consulted? How should they be consulted? How can inarticulate groups be reassured that their views are not over-whelmed by well-organised pressure groups? And how should the product of consultation be incorporated into the decision-making process? Unfortunately, although government has introduced the duty to consult, it has offered no guidance on these most difficult and delicate questions. It stresses that "it is important that involvement and consultation is adequate in terms of time and appropriate to the scale of the issue being discussed",[85] but the manner in which this task is fulfilled has been left to the discretion of the 300-odd PCTs throughout the country. As with a number of other areas, PCTs ought to collaborate closely and regularly with one another in order to share best and most effective practice. Until their collective experience matures, we ought to expect considerable variations in practice. Ultimately, however, the duty is to consider and balance the views of the public in developing local policy. The health body, and not democratic expressions of opinion, must make, and be responsible for, the final decision.

B. Patients' Forums and Independent Advocacy Services

Each NHS trust hospital and each PCT shall have "a body to be known as a Patients' Forum" whose members will be appointed by the Commission for Public

---

[82] *Report of the First Meeting of the NICE Citizens' Council* (NICE, 2002) 19 and 22.

[83] See *Consultation and Public Involvement in Service Change—Draft Interim Guidance* (HDL (2002) 42, Scottish Executive, 2002) Annex C, para. 9.

[84] *The Role of the Lay Member in Primary Care Groups: Do they enhance public accountability?* (Bristol School for Policy Studies, 2002).

[85] *Strengthening Accountability—Involving Patients and the Public* (Department of Health, 2002) 1.

and Patient Involvement in Health.[86] Its duty is to:

(a) monitor and review the range and operation of services provided by, or under arrangements made by, the trust for which it is established;

(b) obtain the views of patients and their carers about those matters and report on those views to the trust;

(c) provide advice, and make reports and recommendations about matters relating to the range and operation of those services to the trust;

(d) make available to patients and their carers advice and information about those services; and

(e) in prescribed circumstances, perform any prescribed function of the trust with respect to the provision of a service affording assistance to patients and their families and carers.[87]

Private providers are also subject to review by patients' forums. PCTs which contract with private providers are duty-bound to include a term in the contract that "the Patients' Forum established for that trust [may] enter and inspect premises where such services are provided."[88] Similarly, patients' forums may request information from, enter, and inspect the premises of primary care contractors.[89]

Patients' forums may make such representations, to such bodies as they think fit arising from the exercise of their functions. In particular, they may refer a matter to an Overview and Scrutiny Committee, or the Commission for Patient and Public Involvement in Health.[90] In addition, patients' forums are responsible for performing the Secretary of State's duty to arrange for independent advocacy services to assist and, if needs be, represent, individuals intending to make a complaint to an NHS body, an independent provider of NHS services, or the Health Service Ombudsman.[91] The duty is to provide independent advocacy services for persons in the Trust's area, or who have been provided with services within the Trust. Patients' forums provide advice and information about the making of complaints. They may make representations to those who exercise functions (including overview and scrutiny committees) concerning the views of members of the public about matters affecting their health. Patients' forums also promote public involvement in consultation processes and advise public health bodies on how to encourage further public involvement in their activities.[92]

---

[86] National Health Service Reform and Health Care Professions Act 2002, s. 15 (1). The CPPIH refers to patients' forums as "Patient and Public Involvement Forums", see Minutes of the CPPIH Board Meeting of 27th march 2003, para. 2.3.

[87] National Health Service Reform and Health Care Professions Act 2002, s. 15 (1)–(3).

[88] See *Directions to Primary Care Trusts on Patients' Forums Rights of Entry and Access to Information in Respect of Independent Providers of Health Services* (Department of Health, 27 November 2003) para. 2.

[89] National Health Service (General Medical Services Contracts) Regulations 2004 (SI 2004 No. 291), Sched. 6, paras 78 and 90.

[90] National Health Service Reform and Health Care Professions Act 2002, s. 15(5)–(6).

[91] See Health and Social Care Act 2001, s. 12, inserting s. 19A of National Health Service Act 1977.

[92] National Health Service Reform and Health Care Professions Act 2002, s. 16.

These arrangements are complemented by Patient Advocacy Liaison Services (PALS) which are non-statutory bodies designed to assist and support the process. Misleadingly, PALS are not limited to patients, nor do they provide advocacy services. Guidance says: "PALS . . . are not advocates. Advocates are wholly on the side of the person they represent . . . As well as representing the interests of users, staff will also be clients of the PALS team. As employees of the Trust, PALS will be in a better position . . . to represent the interests of staff."[93] PALS, then, are more in the nature of a conciliation service, enabling parties to settle complaints without the need for more lengthy, formal internal procedures, or litigation. Their purpose is to provide complainants with an identifiable person to turn to if they have a problem, or if they need information. "Patient advocates will act as an independent facilitator to handle patient and family concerns, with direct access to the chief executive and the power to negotiate immediate solutions."[94] There is no prescribed model on which PALS should operate because the Department of Health considers that each should respond to the particular needs of its own locality. However, direct access to senior staff would, presumably, be a central function of PALS.[95] The service is managed through strategic health authorities.[96] The purpose of the service is primarily to provide an effective, speedy, and informal mechanism for resolving specific problems, if needs be by taking pro-active steps on behalf of patients.

Guidance insists that there should be no requirement that patients should use PALS before engaging a formal NHS complaint. On the other hand, it advises that it is not appropriate to use both PALS and the formal procedure at the same time.[97] Equally, if the formal route is chosen, PALS should be available to advise and guide the complainant through the process. Internal governance of PALS is at local discretion. PALS may have very clear insights into clinical and managerial failings in trusts and will play an important role in the governance of the NHS as a whole. Sometimes contact with other regulatory bodies within the NHS may be required (such as the National Patient Safety Agency). Given the diversity of problems that will be dealt with informally by PALS, it is essential that NHS bodies share experience and co-operate in developing a reasonably coherent and consistent system for responding to complaints.

Since PALS have no formal status, Trusts might consider limiting the time and resources committed to the scheme. However, each Trust will be subject to review and assessment by, for example, the strategic health authority (StHA), CHAI, or the Commission for Public and Patient Involvement in Health, and patients' forums. There will, therefore, be an imperative at managerial level to introduce and manage PALS effectively.

---

[93] *Supporting the Implementation of Patient Advice and Liaison Services* (Department of Health, 2002) para 11.6.
[94] See *The NHS Plan—A Plan for Investment, A Plan for Reform* (Cm. 4818–I, 2000) para. 10.18.
[95] *Supporting the Implementation of Patient Advice and Liaison Services* (Department of Health, 2002) paras 1.7 and 1.8.   [96] ibid., at para. 1.13.
[97] ibid., at paras 4.1 and 4.5.

C. Local Authority Overview and Scrutiny Committees

Further "public" oversight of the NHS is exercised by local authority overview and scrutiny committees (OSCs).[98] The logic of OSCs may be to encourage greater understanding by NHS bodies of the views and concerns of local people. For example, local authorities may have constructive advice and information about a local community affected by industrial decline and redundancy. The role of OSCs is comparable to that of parliamentary select committees which do not have executive functions and may be more detached from party political issues. Scrutiny may take place before decisions have been made, or after the event. They may concern generic matters such as expenditure plans and performance statistics, or specific issues such as the care of a particular category of patient, including matters raised by patients themselves.[99] They may consider, for example, the substantive impact of decisions, the procedures by which they have been reached, or the location in which consultation took place. To foster a constructive relationship between them, NHS bodies should routinely disclose reports of critical incidents, performance management reports, inspection findings, and the results of consultations with patients. In response, OSCs will need to plan how their responsibilities should be organised and discharged, being careful not to duplicate the "review" functions performed by other regulatory agencies.

Local NHS bodies must provide such information about the planning, provision, and operation of health services in their area as an OCS may reasonably require.[100] This duty is imposed on StHAs, PCTs, NHS Trusts and Foundation Trusts which provide services to people living in the area of the OSC's local authority.[101] The OSC has the right to require "an officer" of a local NHS body to appear before it to answer "such questions as appear to the committee to be necessary for the discharge of its functions"[102] relating to the planning, provision, and operation of health services in the area of its local authority. The procedure is for the committee to determine, having regard to any guidance issued by the Secretary of State, the views of interested parties, and any relevant information provided to

---

[98] Created under Local Government Act 2000, s. 21, as amended by s. 7 of Health and Social Care Act 2001.

[99] P. Corrigan, *Overview and Scrutiny: a practitioner's guide* (Improvement and Development Agency, 2000).

[100] The Local Authority (Overview and Scrutiny Committees Health Scrutiny Functions) Regulations 2002 (SI 2002 No. 3048), reg. 5(1), subject to exceptions created for confidential and other sensitive information, unless the information can be "anonymised" by the NHS body. The regulations are made under the authority of the Health and Social Care Act 2002, s. 7.

[101] ibid., reg. 1(3). Foundation Trust hospitals are included by the Health and Social Care (Community Health and Standards) Act 2003 (Supplementary and Consequential Provisions) (Foundation Trusts) Order 2004 (SI 2004 No. 696), reg. 46. Hospitals often provide services to people living in a number of surrounding local authorities. For this reason, joint committees may be appointed by two or more authorities to perform functions on behalf of each local authority on such terms as they agree. See reg. 7. Similarly, a local authority may agree to delegate its powers to another OSC if the other is better able to perform its functions. See reg. 8.

[102] ibid., reg. 6, again there is no duty to answer questions of a confidential nature.

it by a patients' forum.[103] OSC recommendations to local NHS bodies shall explain the matters reviewed and summarise the evidence considered. Where the OSC requests a response to its recommendations, the NHS body shall do so in writing within 28 days of the request.[104]

OSCs assume some of the responsibilities previously carried out by community health councils (CHCs). Thus "where a local NHS body has under consideration any proposal for a substantial development of the heath service in the area of the local authority, or for a substantial variation in the provision of such a service, it shall consult the overview and scrutiny committee of that authority".[105] Complaints have arisen that proper consultation was not carried out under comparable provisions governing CHCs. In *R v NW Thames Regional Health Authority, ex p Daniels*[106] the authority was responsible for a bone marrow transplant unit at Westminster Children's Hospital, in which Rhys Daniels, aged two, was a patient. Without consultation, the authority closed the unit and Rhys was offered treatment in Bristol instead. The Court of Appeal accepted without hesitation that, notwithstanding the small size of the unit concerned, its closure without the required consultation with the CHC was unlawful for failing to comply with the Community Health Council Regulations.

The need for prior consultation is waived if "a decision has to be taken without allowing time for consultation because of a risk to safety or welfare of patients or staff" but in such a case, the NHS body must notify the OSC immediately of the decision and the reason why no consultation has taken place.[107] A comparable matter arose in *R v North and East Devon Health Authority, ex p Pow*.[108] The Health Authority, conscious of its duty to balance its books under section 97A of the National Health Service Act 1977, published a Health Action Plan as a response to a proposed shortfall in resources. From around September 1996 a number of proposals to make savings were canvassed, including the closure of (or rather the cessation of the purchase of services from) the Lynton Community Hospital, but no final decision was arrived at. Eventually, on 28 May 1997, the decision to close the hospital was taken without consultation, on the ground that there was insufficient time to consult "in the interests of the health service". The failure contradicted the regulations. Consultation should have taken place at an earlier stage. Moses J said:

> . . . the process envisaged by the regulation is a process whereby the community health council and the health authority jointly seek to reach a solution to the problem with which the health authority is presented. The health authorities are under a duty, once they are considering a proposal, to consult the community health council before that proposal has evolved into a definite decision . . . it would seriously undermine the purpose of the

---

[103] Local Authority (Overview and Scrutiny Committees Health Scrutiny Functions) Regulations 2002 (SI 2002 No. 3048), reg. 2.   [104] ibid., reg. 3.
[105] ibid., reg. 4(1).   [106] (1994) 19 BMLR 67.
[107] See SI 2002 No. 3048, above, reg. 4(2).   [108] (1998) 39 BMLR 77.

regulation if a health authority could allow time to pass to the point where matters were so urgent that there was no time left for consultation.[109]

I well understand the frustration that the respondent must feel, faced as it is with its duty to make savings which are bound to disappoint . . . A period of consultation of six weeks may only confirm the authority in its original view, although it may reveal the opportunity for savings from other sources. [Never the less] such a process will have inspired the confidence in its decision which that regulation is designed to achieve.[110]

Clearly, the very process of consultation may suggest alternative solutions to a problem. During, or following consultation, the NHS body may be attracted by a proposal which was not included in the consultation process. Is it bound to enter into another period of consultation in respect of the new proposal? The question arose in *R (on the application of Smith) v East Kent Hospital NHS Trust*,[111] in which the consultation proposed four models for re-organising local health services. Ultimately, however, the model finally adopted contained elements of a number of the proposals without being identical to any one of them. The court considered that there was a need for balance. If the trigger for further consultation became too sensitive, the system would become very resistant to change, either because health authorities are disinclined to consider reform, or decision-making is impossible because consultation never comes to an end.[112] It said:

[The authority] had a strong obligation to consult with all parts of the local community. The concept of fairness should determine whether there is a need to re-consult if the decision-maker wishes to accept a fresh proposal but the court should not be too liberal in the use of its power of judicial review to compel further consultation on any change . . . a proper balance has to be struck between the strong obligation to consult on the part of the health authority and the need for decisions to be taken that affect the running of the Health Service. This means that there should only be re-consultation if there is a fundamental difference between the proposals consulted on and those which the consulting party subsequently wishes to adopt.[113]

Thus if the decision-maker arrives at a conclusion which emerges from the consultation in the sense that it reflects the process, further consultation is not required. This question whether there is a "fundamental difference" is ultimately a matter for the court to determine. It is not within the *Wednesbury* reasonable discretion of the public authority.[114] In any event, where an OSC is not satisfied with the reasons for a decision, or the process of consultation has been inadequate, it may report the matter to the Secretary of State who may require the NHS body to carry out such further consultation with the OSC as he considers appropriate. Ultimately, the Secretary of State "may make a final decision on the proposal and require the local NHS body to take such action, or desist from taking such action, as he may direct" by issuing Directions.[115]

---

[109] ibid., 87–8.   [110] ibid., 90.   [111] Unreported, Divisional Court, December 2002.
[112] See also *R v Shropshire HA and Secretary of State, ex p Duffus* [1990] 1 Med LR 119.
[113] Unreported, Divisional Court, December 2002, para. 45.
[114] ibid., para. 51.   [115] See SI 2002 No. 3048, above, regs 4(5)–(7) and 10.

Clearly, these powers give local authorities the opportunity to both help and hinder NHS bodies. For example, a proposal to close a hospital may attract local opposition and elected councilors may be under pressure to represent local opinion in objecting to it. On the other hand, the decision may be supported within the NHS on grounds of safety. For example, if the number of patients being referred to the hospital is insufficient to maintain minimum standards of clinical competence, the NHS may prefer to sell the hospital and divert the resources to expanding another hospital where larger numbers of patients can be treated to a higher standard of care. Co-operation and understanding will be required. The NHS body is not bound by the recommendations of the OSC; on the contrary, it is duty-bound to decide matters for itself in the light of those recommendations. NHS and local authority officers will need to invest considerable time and resources understanding one another's views and aspirations. A failure to do so is unlikely to lead to a constructive relationship. In something of an under-statement, the Audit Commission remark:

OSCs may . . . recognise that the most difficult problems facing the NHS have no simple, or universally popular solution. Local NHS bodies have to make complex trade-offs between competing service demands, and have only limited room for manoeuvre within a national framework of policies and standards. And there will sometimes be tensions between the wishes of local people and what is affordable and/or clinically effective.[116]

V. Oversight of NHS Performance

A number of new bodies have been created with responsibility for oversight of NHS performance. We consider (A) CHAI, (B) the National Patient Safety Agency, (C) the National Clinical Standards Authority, and (D) the Council for Regulation of Health Care Professions.

A. The Commission for Healthcare Audit and Inspection (CHAI, or the Healthcare Commission)

Although CHAI is its statutory name, it prefers to be known as the "Healthcare Commission". The Healthcare Commission commenced work in April 2004. One of its purposes is to reduce the burdens imposed by regulatory bodies. There is a risk of different inspectors having different, perhaps contradictory, methods of assessment, or requiring the same information in different formats. As the Commission said in its first Corporate Plan: "organisations have to cope with

---

[116] *A Healthy Outlook—Local Authority Overview and Scrutiny of Health* (Audit Commission, 2002) para. 25.

multiple inspections or assessments and potentially conflicting recommendations. This can impose an unnecessary and disproportionate burden on providers of healthcare and is something that we are determined to change."[117] Accordingly, it published a Concordat of agreement with other health service and regulatory bodies designed to co-ordinate the process of inspection. For example, inspecting bodies should harmonize existing data sets so inspectors rely on the same information, they should share information with one another and rely on the findings of other inspectors. The agreement also undertakes to conduct proportionate inspections which evaluate their costs and benefits, to share good practice and remain transparent and accountable.[118] Given the risks of too much governance, this is a welcome aspiration.

The Healthcare Commission absorbs the responsibilities of the previous Commission for Healthcare Improvement and the value for money functions of the Audit Commission. It is also the independent health care regulator (a function previously exercised by the former National Care Standards Commission). The Commission will encourage improvement in the provision of health care by and for NHS bodies, and is concerned in particular with the availability of and access to health care, quality, and effectiveness, economy and efficiency, the availability of information to the public, and the rights and welfare of children.[119] Its Corporate Plan emphasises the need to give patients better information about health, both its provision and clinical outcomes, and better complaints systems. It must conduct reviews and inspections and has a right of entry to NHS premises and those used to provide NHS services, to examine and take documents and records,[120] and to require an explanation of documents or information supplied.[121] Its responsibilities extend to "any person who provides, or is to provide, health care for [an NHS body]" and it may inspect private bodies which provide services for the NHS[122] and the premises of general practitioners.[123] Its remit covers clinical and managerial aspects of the NHS as regards both quality and value for money.[124] It will conduct its own reviews and investigations in order to ensure NHS bodies comply with their duty of quality to continually monitor and imorive the quality of health care it provides.[125] In doing so, it may examine services generally or a specific service (such as cancer services) and will look into the reasons for failures in the service

---

[117] *Inspecting, Informing, Improving* (Healthcare Commission's Corporate Plan 2005/08) 7.

[118] *Concordat Between Bodies Inspecting, Regulating and Auditing Healthcare* (Healthcare Commission, 2004).

[119] Health and Social Care (Community Health and Standards) Act 2003, s. 48. CHAI's constitution is set down in Sched. 6.

[120] 2003 Act, ss. 66 and 67 and to have co-operation doing so (s. 66(4)).   [121] 2003 Act, s. 69.

[122] 2003 Act, s. 52(6)(b). CHAI is also responsible for functions under the Care Standards Act 2000 of inspecting and registering private hospitals, clinics and agencies, see s. 102 and 103 (inserting s. 5A to the Care Standards Act 2000) imposing on CHAI the duty to advise and report generally on the provision of independent health services.

[123] National Health Service (General Medical Services Contracts) Regulations 2004, SI 2004 No. 291, Sched. 6, para. 91.   [124] 2003 Act, s. 57.

[125] 2003 Act, s. 45.

and recommend the lessons that can be learned from them. It must report significant clinical or managerial failings in the system (including the practices of an individual) to the Secretary of State, or, in the case of NHS Foundation Trust hospitals, the independent regulator.[126]

The Commission also awards annual "star" ratings to NHS bodies according to criteria established by the Secretary of State (or, in Wales, the Welsh Assembly)[127] taking into account national standards, such as those published in National Service Frameworks and NICE. Previously, this function was undertaken by the Department of Health and some suspected that it had allowed politics to disort the assessment exercise.[128] The Healthcare Commission will add objectivity to the star ratings system. Its Corporate Plan 2004/05 states that it will conduct views on progress with the National Service Framworks on service for older people and coronary heart disease and, more generally, the safeguards surrounding children, especially those receiving long-term care, and value for money in acute care. It will collaborate closely with the Commission for Social Care Inspection to ensure joint approaches and integrated services.[129] The science of measuring and assessing performance in health care is relatively undeveloped and the Healthcare Commission is likely to make a significant contribution to understanding in this area. Significantly, it has insisted that is should be independent of government and it is accountable to Parliament, rather than the Secretary of State. Accordingly, it is to Parliament to whome it must take its annual report.[130]

B. National Patient Safety Agency

An Organisation with a Memory[131] observed how much can be learned from the trends and patterns in which accidents and adverse events occur and how the NHS as a single health care system, should take advantage of its experience and knowledge. Yet the circumstances in which they occur are not well understood and the costs are estimated to be in the region of "£2 billion a year as a result of hospital stays alone".[132] The National Patient Safety Agency (NPSA) has been created:

. . . to learn more from adverse incidents occurring in the NHS. As well as making sure that incidents are reported in the first place, the NPSA is aiming to promote an open and fair

---

[126] 2003 Act, s. 53. For foundation trusts, a report may also be made to the independent regulator, see s. 53(6).

[127] See *NHS Performance Ratings 2003/04* (Healthcare Commission, 2004). The "star ratings" system is discussed at folio 133, above.

[128] See "Milburn secured three stars for PM's trust", *Health Service Journal* 18 December 2003, 3.

[129] 2003 Act, s. 120.

[130] Which must be copied to the Secretary of State. See 2003 Act, s. 128, although CHAI must have regard to government policy, see s. 130. See its first *State of Healthcare Report* (Healthcare Commission, 2004). The Secretary retains the right to issue "directions" to CHAI in the event of it failing to fulfil its functions, see s. 132.   [131] Department of Health, 2000.

[132] *Building a Safer NHS for Patients—Implementing An Organisation with a Memory* (Department of Health, 2001) 10.

culture in hospitals and across the health service encouraging doctors and other staff to report incidents and "near misses" when things go wrong . . . We will collect reports from across the country and initiate preventive measures, so that the whole country can learn from each case . . . [133]

The Agency's functions are:

(a) to devise, implement and monitor a reporting system based on relevant national standards issued by the Department regarding the promotion of patient safety, (b) to collect and appraise information on reported adverse incidents and other material useful for any purpose connected with the promotion of patient safety, (c) to provide advice and guidance in the maintenance and promotion of patient safety and to monitor the effectiveness of such advice and guidance, (d) to promote research which the Agency considers will contribute to improvements in patient safety, (e) to report to and advise Ministers on matters affecting patient safety.[134]

The NPSA's approach to safety emphasises the "systemic" nature of many incidents and a culture which is sensitive to near-misses as well as accidents and the need to manage "risk".[135] It requires an open and candid system of reporting in which staff are trained to identify the root causes of problems rather than an individual to blame. In this way, principles of best practice may be identified and disseminated. Local systems of reporting will ultimately lead to a national database in which patterns of activity may reveal risks hitherto unrecognised. Patients themselves should be informed of adverse incidents affecting their care, especially if they have been harmed as a result. Following the practice of air-safety reporting, the NPSA expects that, as the habit of reporting develops and risks are better managed, the number of accidents will fall. As an early example of a national response to risk, the NPSA has issued a "patient safety alert" on administering *vincristine*, a chemotherapy drug, the dangers of which are well understood, but which continues to be misused to and to kill patients.

The NPSA recommends a number of specific local duties in relation to the management of the risk of accidents. Thus:

(1) individuals involved directly or indirectly in patient care should be aware of what constitutes an adverse patient incident.

(2) Incidents should be managed and reported to a designated authority in accordance with local arrangements.

(3) All serious incidents should be reported immediately and the information "fast-tracked" to relevant external stakeholders.

(4) All reported incidents should be assessed and graded according to their severity in terms of their actual and potential impact on patients.

---

[133] See the National Patient Safety Agency www.npsa.org.uk and the National Patient Safety Agency (Establishment and Constitution) Order 2001 (SI 2001 No. 1743).
[134] *Directions to the National Patient Safety Agency* (Department of Health, July 2001).
[135] *Seven Steps to Safety* (NPSA, 2003).

(5) Adverse patient incidents should be investigated at an appropriate level, subjected to a causal analysis and, where relevant, an improvement strategy prepared.

(6) Incidents graded as red (i.e. where serious actual harm has resulted) should be reported to the NPSA and the Department of Health within three working days of the date of occurrence.

(7) For all category red incidents, a causal analysis should be undertaken by the local organisation and reported to the NPSA and the Department of Health within forty-five working days of the incident.

(8) Where appropriate, there should be co-operation between the health body and the Department of Health (and other stakeholders) to establish an independent investigation or inquiry into the circumstances surrounding an adverse patient incident.

(9) Reviews of local incident data/information should be carried out on an ongoing basis by the organisation and significant results communicated to local stakeholders and sent to the NPSA on a quarterly basis.

(10) Lessons should be learned from individual adverse patient incidents, aggregate reviews and wider experiences, including feedback from the NPSA and other agencies.

In this way, improvement strategies may be developed and implemented to reduce risk to future patients.[136]

In *Making Amends*,[137] the Chief Medical Officer proposes a broad-ranging duty to report medical accidents on NHS staff in return for greater insulation from claims for medical negligence. Such a duty would illuminate many of the shortcomings inherent in the NHS, many of which may not be widely recognised or clearly visible. It would contribute to the work of the NPSA and enhance our understanding of the systemic and institutional risks inherent within the NHS.

C. National Clinical Assessment Authority

The National Clinical Assessment Authority (NCAA) has been created to enhance the ability of the NHS to address concerns about the performance of individual doctors. Its functions are described as follows:

(a) to develop and disseminate . . . good practice guidance for the handling of poor performance cases by trusts, health authorities and [PCTs]; (b) to identify, designate, oversee and set out the responsibilities of local performance assessment service provision and to invite proposals from potential providers; (c) to identify and agree methodologies for assessment and reporting, seeking advice from those with expertise in this field; (d) to work closely with the Royal Colleges, specialist societies, those with general practice interests and

---

[136] www.npsa.nhs.uk/static/reporting.asp.   [137] Department of Health 2003.

lay members representatives of the general public, to establish and maintain a list of lay assessors and medically qualified assessors in each specialty; (e) to undertake and approve the appointment of key staff to organise the assessment of performance at local level; (f) to quality control activities at local level to ensure consistency of advice and approach to performance assessment; (g) to quality assure assessment activity and reporting at local level, ensuring compliance with EC requirements, employment law and natural justice; (h) to work in partnership with and to liaise with the GMC and CHAI in developing policies to ensure that activity overlap is kept to a minimum and that effective channels of communication exist at both national and local levels . . . to look into and consider possible improvements in the assessment of clinical performance and the effective use of available resources, and such other matters as may be notified by the Secretary of State.[138]

NCAA assessment may consider doctors' occupational and psychological health, their basic clinical knowledge, their practice equipment, and medical records. It may also consider the views of patients and other colleagues.[139] The Authority is not primarily concerned with the issue of a doctor's fitness to practice, which is the concern of the GMC. Instead, it provides expert advice to PCTs and hospital managers about concerns raised relating to clinical performance. The NCAA will not take over the disciplinary role of the employer, nor will it function as a regulator. Rather, it will help the employer or health authority by carrying out an objective assessment, following which it will advise referring organisations on appropriate action. Exactly what form will such an "objective assessment" take? What criteria would be used and how? Would frequent staff turnover or the fact that patients were leaving the practice in above average numbers be relevant? Would excessive, or irregular prescribing be considered in the same way as a failure to meet immunisation targets, or poor clinical record-keeping? As independent contractors, doctors may organise themselves in very different ways and it is difficult to see how all can be assessed against the same standard. The particular standards chosen are likely to be the subject of disagreement and complaint. In any event, the NCAA has no direct power to regulate doctors. Its role is advisory only and does not affect the rights and responsibilities of NHS Trusts, health authorities and doctors.

Rather, it will help the employer or health authority by carrying out an objective assessment. Following such an assessment, it will advise referring organisations on appropriate action . . . The Authority's recommendations will be advisory and the creation of the NCAA does not in any way affect the rights and responsibilities of trusts, health authorities and doctors. [140]

Whenever a doctor is being assessed in this way, natural justice and NCAA guidance require that a distinction be made between the *investigation* and *adjudication* of the merits of the case. No central guidance has been offered to PCTs as to how

---

[138] Directions to the National Clinical Assessments Authority (undated) Annex A, para. 2(1).

[139] *NCAA Handbook—General Practice in England* (NCAA, 2002) para. 5.11. See also *NCAA Handbook—Hospital and Community Health Services* (NHS, 2002).

[140] *About the Authority* (NCAA 2002).

this process should work. Clearly, in the absence of such guidance it is absurd for over 300 PCTs to re-invent separate processes individually and collaboration between regions is sensible. The NCAA recommends:

> . . . a structure that separates [a] decision-making about the seriousness of concerns and the need for onward referral from [b] performance assessment and educational support. This can be achieved by means of . . . *Performance Decision-making Group* and a *Performance Advisory Group*. Local groups will want to find their own names, but distinguishing their functions is likely to be important. The Performance Advisory Group . . . will usually be external to the contracting organisation. [141]

The NCAA expects that in the majority of cases, concerns should be resolved satisfactorily by means of local procedures, if needs be, with the assistance of its advice but without the need for formal NCAA assessment. When such an assessment is required, however, it will undertake a formal assessment of the doctor in question and propose solutions. The GMS Contract Regulations require that practitioners co-operate with an assessment by the NCAA when requested to do so by the PCT. [142]

Although the NCAA has no direct power to regulate doctors, it will have an indirect influence by advising organisations of the responses available if a doctor's performance causes concern. Also, the duty of quality[143] imposed on the NHS will create a strong presumption that appropriate action will follow the NCAA's recommendations, and strategic health authorities and CHAI will want to see evidence of implementation of NCAA action plans within their review.[144] NHS trust employers have power to deal with the doctors within the terms of the contract of employment. PCTs have new powers to suspend, or disqualify doctors on grounds of "inefficiency", "fraud", and "unsuitability".[145] Suspension is available only if the authority is satisfied "that it is necessary to do so for the protection of members of the public or is otherwise in the public interests".[146] The nature of the procedures used to adjudicate in matters of this nature are at the discretion of health authorities, but it would be sensible for authorities to cooperate with one another in creating them. Those responsible for examining and reporting on the matters about which concerns have been raised should not be on the panel which assesses the doctor. The NCAA recommends that the doctor who is the subject of the assessment has the help and support of a "friend" of their own choice prior to the assessment.[147]

---

[141] *NCAA Handbook*, note 140 above, at paras 6.50 and 6.52.

[142] National Health Service (General Medical Services Contracts) Regulations 2004 (SI 2004 No. 291), Sched. 6, para. 68(1)(b).

[143] Health and Social Care (Community Health and Standards) Act 2003, s. 45.

[144] *NCAA Handbook*, note 140 above, at para. 5.27.

[145] See National Health Service Act 1977, s. 49F, inserted by s. 25 of Health and Social Care Act 2001. These provisions also apply to dentists and opticians.

[146] 1977, Act, s. 491(1). Advice on the meaning of these words is imprecise. See *Delivering Quality in Primary Care* (Primary Care Division, Department of Health, 2001) paras 6.2.5–6.2.8.

[147] *NCAA Handbook*, note 140 above, at paras 5.06 and 5.07.

D. The Council for the Regulation of Health Care Professionals

The Bristol Inquiry pointed to the need to align and co-ordinate the activities of regulatory bodies.[148] There was a concern that the interests of professionals were sometimes put above the public interest. Accordingly, the Council for the Regulation of Health Care Professionals (CRHCP) was created to regulate the professional bodies supervising health care professionals, namely, the GMC and the other regulatory councils governing dentists, opticians, osteopaths, pharmacists, nurses, and midwives. Membership of the Council is at the discretion of the Secretary of State and, to promote its independence, the government intends the power to be exercised by the NHS Appointments Commission. It is proposed that a small number will be appointed who will speak for the interests of health care providers, and a larger number who will speak for the interests of patients and the wider public.[149]

The function of the CRHCP is "to promote the interests of patients and other members of the public" in relation to those bodies, to promote "best practice", co-operation between the bodies and to formulate principles of good professional self-regulation.[150] The CRHCP has extensive powers to do "anything which appears to it to be necessary or expedient for the purpose of, or in connection with, the performance of its functions". It may investigate and report on each of the regulatory bodies and recommend changes, but it may not interfere with the case of any individual.[151] Each of the regulatory bodies must co-operate with the CRHCP which has powers to give directions requiring the body to introduce new rules to amend its procedures.[152]

The CRHCP may also investigate the way in which a regulatory body has exercised its functions. It has the power to refer to the High Court any adjudication by a regulatory body which it considers "unduly lenient, whether as to a finding of professional misconduct or fitness to practice on the part of the practitioner concerned (or lack of such a finding), or as to any penalty imposed, or both", or a decision to take no action at all, when it would be desirable for the protection of members of the public. In such a case, the High Court shall hear the matter as if it is an appeal by the CRHCP against the regulatory body. The court may dismiss the appeal, allow it and quash the relevant decision, substitute the decision with one of its own which was available to the regulatory body, or remit the case to the regulatory body in accordance with the directions of the court.[153]

---

[148] *Learning from Bristol* (Cm. 5207, 2002) 25, para. 75.

[149] National Health Service Reform and Health Care Professions Act 2002, Sched. 7, paras 4 and 5 and *Explanatory Notes to National Health Reform and Health Care Professions Act 2002*, para 134 *et seq.*

[150] National Health Service Reform and Health Care Professions Act 2002, s. 25.

[151] ibid, s. 26.

[152] ibid, s. 27. Such directions must be approved by the Privy Council and Parliament. The manner in which such directions are made may itself be subject to Secretary of State's directions, see s. 29.

[153] See generally ibid, s. 29.

In one of the first cases to test these powers, the Professional Conduct Committee of the GMC heard a charge of serious professional misconduct against a doctor who admitted that he had engaged in an inappropriate emotional and sexual relationship with a patient. The Committee had no evidence of the circumstances or context of the relationship and, in the absence of further facts, decided to acquit the doctor of the charge. The CRHCP "appealed" against the decision to the High Court. For the doctor, it was argued that the CRHCP did not have jurisdiction to re-open cases in which a doctor has been acquitted of disciplinary charges. Rather, its role was to consider any unduly lenient penalties imposed on those found guilty. Rejecting this argument, the court said:

The intention of Parliament is to provide the Council with the widest possible powers to oversee the activities of each of the regulatory bodies brought under its umbrella. With one exception, no aspect of the work of these bodies is exempt from investigation, recommendation or report . . . The exception is the case of an individual . . . during the course of any disciplinary investigation or while proceedings are on foot, the relevant self regulatory body is free from any interference and, to that extent, self regulation is preserved. After the investigation and any proceedings are over, however, the exception ceases to bite and not only can the council investigate, recommend and report but, in certain circumstances, it can intervene in the disciplinary process that has been undertaken and refer the matter to the Court.[154]

Thus, all such decisions including acquittals, are within the Council's jurisdiction.

On the other hand, the court will be astute to ensure that the power to appeal is not abused. It will consider the stress and hardship such cases may impose on individuals and "will not intervene unless there has been some error of principle so that public confidence would be damaged if the sentence were not altered".[155] In particular, it is not sufficient that the CRHCP considers the sanction "lenient"; the court must regard it to be "*unduly* lenient". This recognises that:

Different people might, perfectly legitimately, take a different view about the same conduct; provided that it is not outside the range of appropriate sanctions, it cannot be said to be "wrong". The fact that I might impose a graver sanction (or, conversely, a more lenient sanction) does not mean that the sanction originally imposed is . . . necessarily wrong.[156]

In one case, for example, a GP engaged in a sexual relationship with one of his patients. He had also falsified his curriculum vitae to suggest he was six years younger than he was. The GMC found him guilty of serious professional misconduct and suspended him for three months. The CRHCP argued that the penalty was too lenient, but the court said that, although it was at the lenient end of the spectrum, it was within the range of reasonable responses available to the GMC

---

[154] *Council for the Regulation of Health Care Professionals v The General Medical Council and Dr G. Ruscillo* [2004] EWHC 527 (Admin), para. 15.   [155] ibid, para. 38.
[156] *Council for the Regulation of Health Care Professionals v General Medical Council and Dr Solanke* [2004] EWHC 944 (Admin), para. 15.

and refused to interfere with it.[157] Another case concerned a paediatric nurse who had downloaded pornographic material from a website while on duty. None of his patients was at risk of seeing it and the police did not prosecute for any offences relating to paedophilia. The Nursing and Midwifery Council made his registration subject to a caution which would be on his record for five years. The CRHCP argued that, in the circumstances, nothing short of removal from the register was appropriate. Bearing in mind that the nurse had been dismissed by his employer, the court said that "the adverb 'unduly' must be given its proper weight. Accessing adult pornography is not criminal and the circumstances in which Mr Truscott accessed it demonstrates poor judgment but is more material to whether he could remain in employment. It fully justified his dismissal."[158]

The creation of this new body reflects the extent to which self-regulation alone is no longer considered a sufficient mechanism for regulating the health care professions. Nevertheless, the early responses of the courts suggest that the traditional deference to professional disciplinary tribunals will not be wholly disturbed.

VI. Conclusion

Governance has become a fact of life in the NHS. It is necessitated first by the Bristol Inquiry and Harold Shipman, and secondly by the paradox that, as central control relaxes, so there is a greater need for regulation, without which national standards and strategies could be undermined. The speed with which new regulatory agencies have been created since 1997 suggests that "governance" is perceived as a complete solution to the problems of the NHS, whereas, in reality, regulation often generates problems of its own. We have observed both how governance pursues different and sometimes inconsistent objectives and how it can distort proper standards of performance and damage patient care. With so many new bodies, there is also the danger that their responsibilities will overlap, that different bodies will impose different standards of inspection and this will serve to distract clinicians from their primary objective. Many suspect that, at present, the balance is wrong. Whilst we can never return to the unplanned and unco-ordinated systems that existed before 1997, some of our current arrangements are excessive and counter-productive. Conscious of the imposition of audit and governance, the Health Care Commission says:

. . . the system of regulating and inspecting health care has been seen as fragmented and burdensome . . . organisations have to cope with multiple inspections or assessments and potentially conflicting recommendations. This can impose an unnecessary and disproportionate burden and it is something we are determined to change.[159]

---

[157] ibid.
[158] *Council for the Regulation of Health Care Professionals v Nursing and Midwifery Council and Truscott* [2004] EWHC 585 (Admin), para. 27.
[159] *Inspecting, Informing, Improving* (CHAI, 2004) 7.

But change may not be simple. Once the regulatory bandwagon gains momentum, it is often difficult to slow it down. When regulation is shown not to work "the solution turned to by politicians and policy-makers is often more regulation, not less".[160] Governance is an imperfect tool, with the potential to hinder as well as help. There is an urgent need to evaluate the risks and benefits of governance, bearing in mind its costs and the need for trust between regulators and those they regulate.[161]

---

[160] K. Walshe, *Regulating Healthcare—A Prescription for Improvement* (Open University Press, 2003) 222. [161] See the helpful discussion, ibid. ch. 6.

9

NHS Care Outside the NHS

Perhaps there is an "ideal" view of the NHS in which all the hospitals and staff that provide care, and the health authorities that purchase it, are public authorities each uniquely committed to the public interest. Certainly, Aneurin Bevan, the architect of the NHS, favoured a system in which NHS care was both purchased and provided by the public purse. He said: "A free health service is a triumphant example of the superiority of collective action and public initiative applied to a segment of society where commercial principles are seen at their worst."[1] He considered that commercial motives were incompatible with the social values on which the NHS was based. Since the introduction of market principles in 1990, however, this view has not been influential.[2] In truth, even in 1948, it was not wholly accurate. The NHS has long made use of non-NHS providers. From the time of its commencement, primary care has been provided by GPs engaged as private contractors. Many mental health hospitals and long-term nursing homes are owned and run privately. And, of course, manufacturers of medicines are all in business as commercial companies. Does this contribution undermine the integrity, or effectiveness of the NHS? After all, social welfare systems exist elsewhere in Europe in which private hospitals play a significant role and where the idea of "social solidarity" is fully developed.[3]

Whatever one's instincts, successive governments in the UK have signaled their intention to expand the private sector's contribution to the NHS. For Conservatives the reason may be more ideological, whereas for Labour it is pragmatic. As the previous Labour Secretary of State for Health has said:

the NHS is short of capacity . . . right now we have what is an under-doctored, under-nursed and arguably under-bedded system. Certainly in the short-term we have very clear capacity constraints. Clearly, it takes time to put these right, it takes three or four years to train a nurse, it takes double that to train a hospital doctor or a GP . . . It seems slightly anomalous to me that, if there is spare capacity that is available within private sector hospitals, for example, that we should not be taking advantage of that for the benefit of NHS patients.[4]

---

[1] *In Place of Fear* (Quartet, 1978) 109.
[2] In its favour, see D. Marquand, *Decline of the Public* (Polity Press, Cambridge, 2004).
[3] Richard Freeman *The Politics of Health in Europe* (Manchester University Press, 2000).
[4] Evidence to the House of Commons Health Committee, 8 November 2000, para. 190. See also B. Finlanson, J. Dixon *et al.*, "Mind the Gap: the Extent of the NHS Nursing Shortage" (2002) 325 *British Medical Journal* 538.

After some hesitation, the Labour government committed itself to a long-term "concordat" with the private sector because "there should be no organisational, or ideological barriers to the delivery of high quality healthcare free at the point of delivery to those who need it".[5] The precise nature of such partnership agreements is subject to local discretion, but the concordat suggests a number of models on which agreement might be based. For elective care, a primary care trust (PCT) could pay for and use private sector operating and nursing wards while using NHS personnel; or the provision of a specific service could be contracted-out to a private hospital; or the NHS provider could commission the whole service from the private sector over a longer period of time.[6] This policy is intended to reduce waiting times for NHS treatment: "By 2005, the maximum wait for in patients will be six months, and for out patients 3 months."[7] This means that NHS patients may be admitted for NHS care in private hospitals in the UK, or be admitted to hospitals overseas.

There is another reason for engaging private interests in the NHS. Fiscal limitations set by the Treasury impose severe spending limits on government departments. These make it difficult for the Department of Health to commit to building large hospitals costing hundreds of millions of pounds. One solution is to hand responsibility to private enterprise to design, build, own, and operate new "private finance initiative" hospitals which treat NHS patients in return for annual fees paid by local health authorities.[8] Some will say it would be better to increase taxes and return to a publicly-funded building programme. However, in a fiscal climate which encourages countries to compete for inward investment by international companies, government seeks to increase the attractiveness of "UK plc" by maintaining a relatively low tax threshold. Nation states are no longer free to decide entirely for themselves appropriate levels of taxation, or public spending policies, for fear of creating an unattractive commercial environment in which investment declines with inevitable economic and social consequences to national prosperity.[9] This trend is common all over the Western world. As the Organization for Economic Co-operation and Development (OECD) warns: "Capital resources and key groups of highly skilled labour have become very mobile. Multinational businesses have flourished and seek attractive, well-educated, healthy, low tax-environments in which to re-locate."[10]

---

[5] See *For the Benefit of Patients* (Department of Health and Independent Healthcare Association, 2001) para. 1.1.   [6] ibid., para. 2.6.
[7] *Treating More Patients and Extending Choice—Overseas Treatment for NHS Patients* (Department of Health, 2002) para. 1.1.
[8] For a pessimistic view of the advantages offered by the PFI, see D. Gaffney and A. Pollock, *Can the NHS Afford the Private Finance Initiative?* (BMA Publications, 1997) and J. Shaoul, "Charging for Capital in the NHS trusts: to improve efficiency?" (1998) 9 *Management Accounting Research* 95.
[9] See the discussion in *Governance in Transition* (OECD, 1995) 10. To a limited extent governments have always depended on private finance for the provision of public services. "It has at no time been possible for the civil government or the foreign and domestic wars of the United Kingdom to be conducted without recourse to private individuals and firms for the supply of goods and services." See C. Turpin, *Government Procurement and Contracts* (Pitman, 1989) 257.
[10] *Governance in Transition* (OECD, 1995) 26. See also D. Andrews, "Capital Mobility and State Autonomy" (1994) 38 *International Studies Quarterly* 193 and A. Marr, *Ruling Britannia—The*

This chapter considers the implications of these developments for the NHS. We consider: (I) treatment in private hospitals and health centres, (II) negligence of non-NHS providers, (III) treatment abroad, (IV) the private finance initiative, (V) judicial review of non-NHS providers, and (VI) private providers and the Human Rights Act.

I. Treatment in Private Hospitals and Treatment Centres

In evidence to the House of Commons Health Committee, the Secretary of State suggested that "currently somewhere between 50–60,000 operations a year are funded by the NHS in private sector facilities. The Independent Healthcare Association maintained that it was reasonable to expect . . . a possible annual total of 200,000 [patients per year]."[11] Arrangements of this nature to use private sector capacity are possible under the National Health Service Act 1977 as follows: "The Secretary of State may, where he considers it appropriate, arrange with any person or body (including a voluntary organisation) for that person or body to provide, or assist in providing, any service under [the 1977] Act."[12] In this way, therefore, contracts may be made for staff, facilities, goods, materials, plant, apparatus, and premises on such terms as may be agreed.[13]

Private hospitals are not "health service bodies",[14] and cannot, therefore, enter into NHS contracts. As a result, the agreements they enter are enforceable in the courts under the law of contract. The contents of such contracts are never the less subject to the minimum standards required by statutory regulations. Private providers of services to the public (be they NHS, or private) are regulated by the Commission for Social Care Inspection and the Commission for Healthcare Audit and Inspection (CHAI).[15] Regulations provide a detailed code of conduct for private hospitals. They include a duty to provide a patient's guide setting out the basis on which the patient will be treated, to offer complaints procedures, provide proper premises and standards of care, devise clinical governance policies designed to monitor and improve standards of care, identify suitable people as registered providers and managers, and introduce and review resuscitation policies.[16] In addition, CHAI has access to private hospitals in respect of NHS patients.[17]

Failure and Future of British Democracy (Penguin Books, 1996) ch. 4. The emphasis of these explanations is economic. For a more political perspective see D. Oliver and G. Drewry, *Public Service Reforms—Issues of Accountability and Public Law* (Pinter, 1996).

[11] *Role of the Private Sector in the NHS*, House of Commons Health Committee (HC 308–I, Session 2002–03) para. 13.   [12] See National Health Service Act 1977, s. 23(1).

[13] ibid., s. 23(2) and (3).

[14] Under National Health Service and Community Care Act 1990, s. 4.

[15] Created by the Health and Social Care (Community Health and Standards) Act 2003, Part 2.

[16] See the Private and Voluntary Health Care (England) Regulations 2002 (SI 2001 No. 3968). Infringement of some, but not all of these duties carries criminal sanctions, see reg. 51.

[17] Health and Social Care (Community Health and Standards) Act 2003, s. 52(6)(b).

Also, Treatment Centres have been encouraged, which may be provided by private providers[18] to contribute to the government's target of reducing hospital waiting lists to six months. The private sector is expected to play a significant role in the provision of opthalmology, orthopaedics, and day-case work. Agreement is by contract for, say, five years in which the "assumption is that the NHS would have exclusive use of such facilities, however, we are also inviting variant bids, including bids for non-exclusive use." Payment will be dependent on results, i.e. the clinical output as regulated by CHAI.[19] With these incentives, Treatment Centres will provide faster treatment for relatively straightforward cases. However, in so doing, concern is expressed that they will deprive major hospitals of the critical mass of patients required to sustain large centres of excellence. In this case, there is a risk that more serious cases might find it more difficult to obtain proper treatment.[20]

If the NHS is short of clinical staff, is it prudent to encourage growth in the private sector which will tend to absorb still more NHS staff? The Health Committee expressed concern at the capacity of the private sector to expand at the expense of the NHS and pressed for further studies to balance the danger of doing so.[21] There is a risk that "NHS capacity" could be damaged by an expansion in the numbers of NHS patients treated in the private sector. If the private sector could offer improved waiting times to patients and better terms and conditions to staff, these arrangements could lead to further shortages of staff in NHS hospitals and the traditional split between public and private providers would become indistinct. The NHS might then begin to resemble the systems that exist elsewhere in Europe in which little distinction is made between public and private hospitals.

II. Non-NHS Providers of NHS Services—Whose Liability?

Care in private hospitals and clinics may present different issues and risks to that provided in NHS hospitals. For example, doctors more commonly operate alone and not in a "firm" and may be less amenable to the help and guidance of their colleagues if their performance gives cause for concern. Also, the general facilities available in a private hospital will often not include emergency equipment, nor experienced "crash" teams available to respond to an unexpected crisis. In addition, doctors may not be employees of a private hospital, but rather private *licensees* of staff and facilities. Against whom should action be taken in cases giving rise to complaint? When NHS patients are treated outside the NHS, do they retain rights

---

[18] *Growing Capacity—Independent Sector Diagnosis and Treatment Centres* (Department of Health, 2002).   [19] ibid., 5.
[20] See O. Dyer, "Eye Surgeon claims new Treatment Centres is a threat to NHS" (2003) 327 *British Medical Journal* 580.   [21] *Role of the Private Sector in the NHS*, note 11 above, at para. 17.

against the NHS if things go wrong? As a general rule, negligence is slow to impose liability on one party for damage caused by another[22] unless there is an especially close relationship between the parties,[23] or the first is under a duty to exercise control over the second.[24]

It may be anomalous if those treated outside the NHS have different, and perhaps less favourable, rights of redress than those treated within it. The Department of Health appears to sympathise with this view and has stated:

> . . . should a patient sent abroad for treatment wish to raise an issue of medical negligence, the courts may regard NHS bodies as having a non-delegable duty of care despite the fact that the treatment was being provided by a non-UK provider. Patients would then be able to sue in the English courts rather than have to take the case through the foreign courts. This approach is in line with the Government's policy preferences that patients travelling abroad for treatment should have the same rights and remedies as patients being treated in the UK.[25]

Accordingly, contracts governing the provision of care abroad should contain indemnities covering rights of recovery by NHS bodies. If an NHS body is responsible for paying damages to a patient injured outside the NHS, it should retain the contractual right to recover its liability from the hospital responsible for inflicting the damage.[26] When, therefore, will an NHS body be liable for damage suffered by a patient in a non-NHS hospital, or unit?

There are two ways in which a claim might arise against a non-NHS provider in these circumstances. The first is where the NHS provider has made arrangements for their NHS patients to be dealt with by non-NHS units, but has done so carelessly by using services that it should have known would be sub-standard. Perhaps, the hospital, or laboratory, had a poor safety record, or had received poor reviews from safety inspectors. In this case, an action would be available against the non-NHS provider itself in negligence. In addition, action could lie against the NHS provider for negligence for failing to take proper care to ensure that the private provider was competent to provide a reasonably safe service.

What happens, however, if the referral from the NHS has been undertaken competently in the sense that reasonable steps were taken to ensure that the provider was well-equipped and competent to perform the procedures? Yet, the patient is damaged through the private provider's negligence. Exactly the same question could arise in connection with a private caterer which failed to maintain proper standards of hygiene in its kitchens so that patients were poisoned, or a private clinical screening service failed to alert a hospital that a blood sample had tested positive for a disease, or a privately run hospital unit was so badly managed that patients were given inadequate care. Would a patient who suffered damage by

---

[22] See, e.g., *Perl Exporters Ltd v Camden LBC* [1984] QB 342; *Lamb v Camden LBC* [1981] QB 625.
[23] See *Smith v Littlewoods Organisation* [1988] AC 241, 272, *per* Lord Goff.
[24] *Home Office v Dorset Yacht Co* [1970] AC 1004; *Vicar of Writtle v Essex CC* (1979) 77 LGR 656.
[25] *Treating More Patients and Extending Choice*, note 7 above, at para. 6.1.
[26] ibid., para. 6.3.

the negligence of a private contractor retain a right of action against the NHS hospital by whom it was engaged? Or would the action be limited to the private contractor responsible for providing the service? Such a situation is also common *within* the NHS in relation to "tertiary referrals". Say a baby is transferred from a general hospital to a special care baby unit (SCBU) in another hospital. The "tertiary" hospital fail to take proper care of the baby who suffers damage. Which of the two hospitals should be held responsible? Ought the referring hospital to be held directly liable to the patient for the negligence of the tertiary provider? The same problem arises for GPs. If they engage a consultant from a local hospital on a private basis to take out-patient clinics in the surgery, who is liable if the consultant is negligent through no fault of the GPs?

The common law puts the question as follows: Do hospitals and GPs bear a non-delegable responsibility for independent contractors engaged to perform functions on their behalf, so that they will be held liable for the negligence of the contractor even without negligence on their part? Or is the duty limited to taking reasonable care in appointing and retaining them to ensure that they are competent to perform their duties, in which case liability lies against the contractor alone? In general, the rule as between employer and employee does not apply to those who engage independent contractors.[27] Is the position between NHS Trust (or health authority) and patient governed by the same rule? A number of influential cases have said that hospitals do owe a non-delegable duty to those treated in the hospital and it is irrelevant whether the consultant is the hospital's employee or not. In 1951, Lord Denning said that:

> . . . the hospital authorities accepted the plaintiff as a patient for treatment, and it was their duty to treat him with reasonable care. They selected, employed and paid all the surgeons and nurses who looked after him. He had no say in their selection at all. If those surgeons and nurses did not treat him with proper care and skill, then the hospital authorities must answer for it, for it means that they themselves did not perform their duty to him. I decline to enter into the question whether any of the surgeons were employed only under a contract for services [i.e. independent consultants], as distinct from a contract of service [i.e. employees] the liability of the hospital authorities should not, and does not, depend on nice considerations of that sort. The plaintiff knew nothing of the terms on which they employed staff: all he knew was that he was treated in the hospital by people whom the hospital had appointed; and that the hospital must be answerable for the way in which he was treated.[28]

Although his Lordship repeated this view,[29] in each case, all the doctors concerned appear to have been employees for whom the defendants were vicariously

---

[27] *Rivers v Cutting* [1982] 1 WLR 1146. Liability may be imposed in exceptional circumstances, e.g., if the contractor was authorised or condoned the tort, see *Ellis v Sheffield Gas Consumers Co* (1853) 2 E & E 767; *D & F Estates Ltd v Church Commissioners for England* [1988] 2 All ER 992.

[28] *Cassidy v Ministry of Health* [1951] 2 KB 343, 365. His lordship excluded from this rule cases in which the patient had chosen and engaged his own private doctor, at 362. See also *Gold v Essex CC* [1942] 2 KB 293, 394, *per* Lord Greene MR.

[29] In *Jones v Manchester Corporation* [1952] 2 All ER 125, 132 and *Roe v Ministry of Health* [1954] 2 QB 66, 82.

liable.[30] In addition, the issue today may be more complicated because the patient may be treated in another hospital or clinic not owned by the NHS. This is likely to become more pressing as the NHS enters agreements with non-NHS providers to provide services for NHS patients. In *M v Calderdale and Kirklees Health Authority*[31] it was suggested that the "non-delegable" duty theory applied even when the NHS body had referred the patient to a separate private hospital over which it had no control. A 17-year-old girl was referred as an NHS patient to have an abortion in a private clinic. The arrangement was made between the health authority and the clinic under a private contract. The procedure was unsuccessful and she gave birth to a boy. She obtained judgment against both the private clinic and the doctor responsible for the procedure. Neither, however, had obtained insurance cover and the action was recommenced against the NHS hospital from which the referral had been made. The health authority conceded that the clinic had behaved negligently. However, it said that there had been no negligence in the choice of the clinic, which was accredited by the appropriate authorities. Therefore, in the absence of any fault on its part, it should not be held directly liable for the negligence of the private clinic over which it had no control as regards training, supervising, or monitoring staff. Rejecting these arguments in the county court, His Honour Judge Garner found for the claimant on the ground that the patient was the responsibility of the health authority who owed her a non-delegable duty to provide her with reasonable care. His Honour observed that if this were not the case, those treated outside NHS institutions could lose rights of action in negligence and be in a less favourable position by comparison to those treated within the NHS, which would not be acceptable.

This approach was disapproved, however, in *A v Ministry of Defence and Guys and St Thomas's Hospital*.[32] The claimant and his mother were the family of a British serviceman living in Germany. Agreement had been made between the Ministry of Defence and Guys and St Thomas's Hospital under which the latter arranged hospital services for service personnel and their families to be provided by German hospitals. Under these arrangements, the claimant was admitted to Gilead Hospital. Her pregnancy was mis-managed (as the English and German parties accepted) and her child suffered serious brain-damage. The question arose as to her right of action against the defendants in the English courts. Following Lord Denning, Bell J considered that there is a special relationship between an NHS hospital and patients treated in the hospital under which it has a personal, non-delegable duty to use reasonable care and skill. This is so regardless of whether it uses its own employees or engages private contractors to administer care. However, the "wider personal, non-delegable duty still depends upon the hospital's

---

[30] Authorities abroad are divided on the point. Compare *Yepremian v Scarborough General Hospital* (1980) 110 DLR (3d) 513 (Canada) and *Ellis v Wallsend District Hospital* [1990] Med LR 567 (Australia).
[31] [1998] Lloyd's Rep Med 157 in Huddersfield County Court. The case has no binding authority, therefore, on other courts.   [32] [2003] Lloyd's Rep Med 339, [2003] EWHC 849.

acceptance of the patient for treatment, or advice".[33] In this case, however, neither defendant had clinical responsibility for the claimant because the treatment had been performed in a hospital outside their control. The defendants were under a duty to select appropriate hospital providers in Germany but there was no evidence that the choice of German hospital had been made negligently (its record of obstetric safety was comparable to that in the UK). As a result, it was held that negligence could not be shown against the defendants, that no right of action existed in the UK and that action should be pursued against the German hospital in the German courts.

This approach distinguishes between the location at which patients are treated and may make the government's policy of extending patient choice to non-NHS providers less attractive to patients, especially if they have to contemplate litigating abroad to enforce their rights. If the government wishes to encourage patients to take advantage of the policy, it may have to direct that NHS bodies retain legal responsibility for those treated outside the NHS even in the absence of clinical responsibility for the patient's care. The liability to pay damages in the absence of fault can be accommodated by including an indemnity in favour of the NHS body within the terms of its contract with the non-NHS provider.

III. Treatment in Overseas Hospitals

How may patients obtain treatment abroad? We consider the practical arrangements for doing so and the right to treatment abroad under EU law.

A. Practical Arrangements for Treatment Abroad

Treatment elsewhere in Europe for *individual* patients with special health needs has long been available within the NHS under reciprocal arrangements with the member states of the EU. However, longer-term contracts with overseas hospitals are entirely new. Of course, the patients most likely to take advantage of such arrangements will tend to be reasonably fit, able to withstand the strain of travelling, and will tend to live close to convenient air and sea-ports.[34] Contracts are arranged with overseas providers by Guy's and St Thomas's hospital (which is responsible for arrangements with northern European hospitals) and Kent Strategic Health Authority (for contracts with southern European hospitals). The arrangements have the status of ordinary contracts in law (and not "NHS contracts", which have no legal status) and are entered between the relevant PCT and the overseas hospital. They are often governed by the law of the overseas provider. The additional costs of such treatment, including the costs of travel, have to be met from existing PCT

---

[33] [2003] Lloyd's Rep Med 339, [2003] EWHC 849, para. 68.
[34] *Evaluation of Treating Patients Overseas* (Department of Health and York Health Economics Consortium, 2002). Cataract and orthopaedic care abroad is common.

resources.[35] Of course, patients are free to decline the option to travel abroad for treatment if they wish.

Commissioning of overseas care requires assessments of the quality of hospitals and the standard of care they provide. This is achieved through analysis of the hospital's own record of clinical standards, as well as any further review from national inspectorates, from visits by UK commissioning teams, and within the terms of the contract itself in which specific standards can be identified. The Department of Health recommends that all such contracts specify a number of minimum requirements, namely:

(1) the professional expertise required of responsible doctors;
(2) standards of infection control;
(3) standards of clinical governance and adherence to evidence-based practice;
(4) availability of bi-lingual staff;
(5) medical notes to be translated into English;
(6) the availability of complaints procedures and adverse incidents protocols;
(7) patients to be discharged with sufficient medication for the journey home, and
(8) the provision of procedures for NHS commissioners to review compliance with these terms, including visits by CHAI.[36]

Special care will also be required to ensure that the flow of care is not disturbed when the patient is returned to the supervision of the UK doctor.

Travel costs are subject to regulations which permit reimbursement of the costs of travel on an income-related sliding-scale. Travelling companions will not generally have their travelling costs met unless it is medically necessary. Clearly, if a patient is to spend a number of weeks abroad, a travelling companion might be necessary. In this case, the companion's costs are to be assessed as if they were those of the patient.[37]

B. Rights to Treatment under EU Law

What is the nature and extent of the right to treatment in the EU? Put another way, can government restrict patients' access to treatment as NHS patients in the EU? We consider (1) European health care rights, (2) rights of member states to control national health care policy, and (3) the position in the NHS.

1. *European Health Care Rights*

The essential principle of the European Community is to promote freedom of trade between the member states and, in particular, freedom of movement of

---

[35] *Treating More Patients and Extending Choice*, note 7 above, at para. 2.18.
[36] ibid., para. 3.5 and *Evaluation of Treating Patients Overseas*, note 34 above, ch. 4.
[37] National Health Service (Travelling Expenses and Remission of Charges) Regulations 1988 (SI 1988 No. 551).

goods, services, labour, and capital. Are *health* services included within this freedom so that patients have the right to obtain public health services in a member state of their choice? Until relatively recently, the jurisprudence of the European Court of Justice (ECJ) suggested that public services were not "services" within the provisions concerning free movement under Article 49 of the EU Treaty. Thus, in the *Humbel* case, national education services were not provided as part of a private, commercial activity for profit, but as public services for which no payment was made. As a consequence, the principle of the free movement of services did not enable a resident of one member state to have his children educated in another.[38] Such an approach clearly defers to member states in matters of social planning and welfare.

Does the same principle apply to public *health* services? The question arose in the *Gereats-Smits and Peerbooms* case,[39] in connection with the Dutch system of health insurance in which Dutch health providers are reimbursed by social insurance schemes. Consistent with previous cases, the ECJ was urged by its Advocate-General to follow its approach in the *Humble* case for two reasons:

(1) that publicly provided *medical* care is not a "service" and that, in any case,

(2) the financial and organisational stability of the health care systems of member states could be seriously undermined if they were not permitted to regulate the outflow, and inflow, of patients.

However, without explaining why, the ECJ rejected this advice. It affirmed the right of patients to obtain health care services under the terms of the EU Treaty. It reasoned that the element of remuneration, which is necessary for the provision of health services, was present because hospital providers were always remunerated by a health fund, albeit at a fixed rate and that payment does not have to be made by patients themselves.[40] The Court added that no distinction could be drawn between (a) health care systems in which patients paid for services under a private contract and re-claimed their expenses from an insurance fund, and (b) those which provided health care without direct charges to patients by supplying benefits in kind; a view it confirmed in the *Muller-Faure and Van Riet* case.[41] In England, the Court of Appeal has expressed surprise at this unreasoned judicial creativity. It comments that, in developing this area of law, the ECJ has put on the foundations of Article 49 "a substantial edifice not immediately apparent from its literal terms . . . There has been much judicial policy-making, and the policy goes well beyond the words of the Article."[42] It also observes that Article 49 was created to protect *commercial* interests from unfair trade barriers and "it is not immediately clear why a state-funded national health service should be required to fund those who provide medical services in other member states . . . Nor is it comfortable to

---

[38] C–263/86 *Belgium v Rene Humbel and Marie-Therese Edel* [1988] ECR 5365, paras 16–18.
[39] C–157/99.   [40] See paras 56–8.   [41] C–385/99, para. 39.
[42] *Secretary of State for Health v R (on the application of Watts)* [2004] EWCA Civ 166, para. 31.

derive a potential obligation on a member state to provide larger resources to a publicly funded national health service from a principle designed to protect commercial service providers in other member states."[43]

Exactly what has motivated this policy is not clear. Never the less, the ECJ acknowledges that an unrestricted right to treatment anywhere in the EU could affect financial, and organisational stability within member states' health care systems. In particular, long-term planning would be difficult. Consequently, the ECJ says (1) that it is for each member state to decide upon the *extent* of its health care coverage and each is free to exclude certain treatments from the public health care menu, or to charge for services. However, subject to this limitation, (2) any restriction on a patient's right to obtain treatment elsewhere in the EU will be presumed to be an unlawful barrier to the free movement of services unless it is justified. Such a justification requires the member state to show that it can provide the patient with "normal" treatment at home without "undue delay".

What do each of these propositions mean and to what extent will they secure the financial and organisational stability of health care in member states?

2. Member States' Control over National Health Policy

Unrestricted access to care in the EU has the potential to destabilise the central, financial, and operational planning of governments, and health insurers. Should health systems expect a net inflow, or *outflow* of patients? In either case error is likely to lead to inefficiency together with its implications for other patients. Surely such a policy would increase costs and, within a finite budget, divert resources from others on whom it would otherwise have been spent. And apart from the organisational issue, if waiting lists are common within a system as a result of funding decisions made at national (and electoral) level, is it fair that some patients should jump the queue by getting treatment abroad? Should European law interfere with health policies introduced at national level? It is crucial, therefore, to know when a member state can insist on prior authorisation as a pre-condition to patients obtaining treatment abroad.

Any such obstacle should be justified within the recognised exceptions to Article 49. One such exception to the right to free movement is the stability of national health care systems. Thus, the ECJ acknowledged in the *Muller Faure and Van Riet* case the right of Member States to circumscribe the benefits available under their health care systems: "it is for the Member States alone to determine the extent of the sickness cover available to insured persons, so that . . . they can claim reimbursement of the costs of the treatment given to them only within the limits of the cover provided by the sickness insurance scheme."[44] It said: "Treaty provision permits Member States to restrict the freedom to provide medical and hospital

---

[43] [2004] EWCA Civ 166, para. 103. We discuss the case below.
[44] *Muller-Faure*, at para. 98.

services in so far as the maintenance of treatment capacity . . . is essential for public health . . . However . . . it is necessary . . . to ensure that the measures taken . . . do not exceed what is objectively necessary for that purpose and that the same cannot be achieved by less restrictive rules."[45] Thus, in the UK, the General Medical Services Contracts Regulations include a "black" and "grey" list of drugs and treatments which are excluded from the NHS, or are restricted.[46] And health care systems may require patients to pay a contribution towards the costs of their care. Reasonable, proportionate, and transparent restrictions of this nature are acceptable. Although purely economic aims cannot justify a barrier to the fundamental principle of freedom to provide services, "the risk of seriously undermining the financial balance of the social security system may . . . constitute *per se* an overriding general interest reason capable of justifying a barrier of that kind".[47]

What does this mean? There is no objective yardstick by which health care entitlements can be measured. Patients' rights of access are determined by a mixture of clinical, social, political, economic, and legal factors. Each may influence practice. There is no reliable measure which determines what is "objectively necessary" to promote a public health service. The difficulty of imposing an "objective" measure was discussed in relation to treatment for erectile dysfunction. In *Ex p Pfizer*[48] the pharmaceutical company argued that the Secretary of State's reasons for placing its drug ("Viagra") on the restrictive GMS "grey" list were irrational and unsupported by objective evidence and therefore should be declared unlawful. The court rejected the complaint. It said that the decision to restrict access to treatment for erectile dysfunction was political; it was not amenable to more "objective" detailed economic, or ethical analysis. As such, it was within the Secretary of State's discretion. In the context of treatment for erectile dysfunction this is surely correct. The ECJ's suggestion that decisions of this nature can be taken on "objective" grounds is impossible to apply consistently between differing treatments.

These difficulties notwithstanding, the Court sought to develop a principle governing the right to obtain treatment in the EU which distinguished between hospital, and non-hospital care. With respect to hospital care, the Court said that the right to obtain treatment abroad requires two conditions to be satisfied:

(1) the treatment is regarded as "*normal* in the professional circles concerned", in the sense that it is "sufficiently tried and tested by international medical science"; and

(2) it cannot be obtained at home "without *undue delay*".[49]

---

[45] See ibid., paras 67–8.

[46] National Health Service (General Medical Services Contracts) Regulations 2004 (SI 2004 No. 291), Sched. 6, paras 42 and 43, see pp. 113–14 above.

[47] *Muller-Faure and Van Riet*, paras 72–3 and *Kohll* (1996) C–158/06, para. 41. Note, however, that it is notoriously difficult to exclude, or restrict health services in this way and most health systems simply promise a "comprehensive" package, or one based on "medical necessity". To this extent, the Court's concession is likely to have limited impact.

[48] *R (Pfizer) v Secretary of State for Health* [2002] EWCA Civ 1566, [2003] 1 CMLR 19. Such restrictions must be transparent and not discriminate against other member states.

[49] *Smits and Peerbooms*, para. 108.

Neither criterion is helpful. The first condition, that the treatment be "normal" is impossible to define because there are many areas of care in which we do not possess a common understanding of illness and treatment. For example, thalassotherapy (spa treatment) is a common treatment in France, but largely unknown within the NHS. The National Institute for Clinical Excellence (NICE) did not recommend the use of beta interferon for the treatment of multiple sclerosis, but it is more widely used elsewhere in Europe. The word "normal" appears to assume that there is a generally recognised "international medical science" throughout Europe, whereas, in truth, there is such a diversity of medical opinion that exists locally, nationally, and internationally, that the word is unhelpful.

Secondly, the phrase "undue delay" is problematic. The Court insists that "the national authorities are required to have regard to all the circumstances of each specific case and to take account not only of the patient's medical condition at the time when authorisation is sought and, where appropriate, of the degree of pain or the nature of the patient's disability . . . but also his medical history".[50] This emphasises the need to consider "delay" from the perspective of the individual patient and not the customary length of waiting lists. When, however, will delay be "undue" and who is to judge? Doctors will disagree, as will patients. Orthopaedic doctors will have a very good understanding of their patients' suffering and needs. Is a nine-month wait an "undue delay" for an artificial hip when the patient is otherwise strong, healthy, and fit? And how should such needs be compared to those of patients suffering cancer, heart disease, multiple sclerosis, dementia, or schizophrenia? And what if waiting times in France and Germany are generally shorter than those in the UK? There is no objective yardstick on which the measurements of "undue delay" can be made.

With respect to *non-hospital* care, as we have observed, member states may exclude, or restrict some services from the health care menu, or require co-payments from patients. However, within these limitations, patients have unrestricted access to non-hospital services in other member states and are able to recover the costs of their care from the health care "system" of the member state in which they are insured.

3. The Position in the NHS

How do these principles affect NHS patients? The matter arose in *Secretary of State v Watts*[51] in which the applicant, Mrs Watts, aged seventy-two, required bi-lateral hip replacement. The maximum waiting time for NHS treatment was twelve months and, since her responsible doctor did not consider her case to be urgent, she was promised treatment within that time. Mrs Watts was not prepared to wait and obtained the same treatment in France three months later. She paid the bill of £3,900 and claimed reimbursement from Bedfordshire PCT, her responsible health authority. It refused to reimburse her, saying that, so long as she

---

[50] ibid., para. 103, *Muller-Faure and Van Riet*, paras 90 and 92.   [51] [2004] EWCA Civ 166.

was treated within standard NHS waiting times, she had not suffered an undue delay.

Following the *Gareats-Smits* and *Muller-Faure* cases, the High Court considered that national waiting times had very little relevance to the central issue, namely, Mrs Watts' clinical need for treatment. Accordingly, Mrs Watts succeeded in her argument that the treatment was "normal" and that a twelve-month delay was "undue".[52] The case was taken to the Court of Appeal which was more sympathetic to the *institutional* constraints that exist within the NHS. In particular, it was uneasy with a law that would enable some NHS patients to by-pass others by virtue of European law. It said:

> We consider that the court should proceed on the assumption that, if the NHS were required to pay the cost of some of its patients having treatment abroad at a time earlier than they would receive it in the United Kingdom, this would require additional resources. In theory, these could only be avoided if those who did not have treatment abroad received their treatment at a later time than they otherwise would or if the NHS ceased to provide some treatments that it currently does provide.[53]

The Court of Appeal was sufficiently troubled by the implications of the case to refer a number of specific questions to the ECJ for clarification, for example, given its separate system of funding, is the NHS subject to the principles in the *Gareats-Smith* and *Muller-Faure* cases? Is the UK obliged to ignore the fact that in the UK the same approach may require increased NHS funding? May the NHS refuse to authorise treatment abroad in the interests of fair waiting lists? Does European law permit NHS patients to jump the queue of NHS waiting lists? And by what criteria should "undue delay" be judged?[54]

This is welcome. Neither the ECJ, nor the High Court seem to have understood the "opportunity costs", of diverting finite resources from one patient to another.[55] For example, in the *Watts* case, Munby J in the High Court assumed that, in a service suffering *under-capacity* if large numbers of patients chose to go abroad for treatment, pressure on the service would decline. From this, his Lordship deduced that, over time "any medical incentive to travel abroad for treatment will simply evaporate, for there will no longer be the delays which at present induce patients . . . to go abroad for treatment".[56] However, unless the point of equilibrium is measured with immense accuracy, the truth may be very different. Money lost from the "NHS loop" is no longer available for the NHS to invest. If patients prefer to go abroad, there is a risk that NHS hospitals will fail to generate revenue from providing

---

[52] Note, however, that shortly before leaving for France, her doctor became concerned that her condition had deteriorated and the PCT promised to provide treatment within three to four months. This, the High Court said, was not an undue delay. Therefore, although Mrs Watts won the principle, she lost her claim for reimbursement.   [53] [2004] EWCA Civ 166, para. 105.

[54] ibid., para. 112.

[55] National Health Service Act 1977, s. 97 imposes a duty on PCTs not to exceed their annual financial allocations.   [56] *Watts v Bedford PCT* (High Court), para. 148.

services to purchasers. Their loss of revenue may mean they are forced to contract, or close altogether. It may not be true to say that pressure on resources will "evaporate"; on the contrary, it may escalate. If NHS funds are diverted to European hospitals, NHS wards and specialist units may contract with the result that waiting lists will not decline.

It is not simply a question of economics. There is also the *politics* of the proper ambit of discretion accorded to the duly elected governments of the member states. Take, for example, NICE and National Service Frameworks. Both have been created by government to assist local resource allocators develop a more effective and consistent health service. In doing so, they recommend that certain treatments and patients should receive special attention in the NHS, say coronary heart disease, cancer, diabetes, or elderly patients. This enables the NHS to identify its own national priorities. This means that "low-priority" treatment may be subject to longer waiting lists (although not wholly *excluded* from coverage in the manner discussed by the ECJ). Should EU law seek to undermine national policy by encouraging "low-priority" patients to obtain treatment abroad? Given the need to make difficult choices, surely national governments are best placed to determine national health priorities. In such a delicate area, EU law should defer to national discretion in matters of social welfare in exactly the way identified by the ECJ in the *Humble* case with respect to public education.

And there is an *organisational* problem. If we promote a *micro*-perspective of health care rights, government will find it increasingly difficult to manage and direct health priorities. Ad hoc responses to individual claims as they arise will benefit the articulate and powerful. For the rest, however, they are more likely to produce an unpredictable, unco-ordinated, and chaotic health service. If "long-waiters" are given an automatic entitlement to seek treatment abroad, monies set aside to promote national policy (for example, the speedy diagnosis and treatment of cancer) may have to be diverted to pay for other care in another member state. An individualistic approach to rights, dictated by judges with limited knowledge of national circumstances, aspirations, and limitations is not a proper way to manage the NHS. In matters concerning the entitlements of groups to societal benefits (the very "stuff" of politics), judges should tread warily.

This elevation of the role of the courts and individual rights may have a superficial attraction, but it has serious financial, political, and organisational consequences. Social justice requires individual claims to be considered in the light of all the demands made upon the health service. A focus on individual claims as and when they arise will achieve less in aggregate for the community and will detach government from its responsibility for health care policy. When it considers the questions raised by the Court of Appeal's reference in the *Watts* case, the ECJ will again hear from a cross-section of member states urging it to reconsider its adventure into cross-border health rights. The gravity of the questions raised are plain to see. Let us hope that it balances the arguments more evenly when it delivers its judgment in the case.

IV. The Private Finance Initiative

We have noted the way in which international economic forces inhibit governments from raising revenue from taxation without regard to the impact of their policies on inward investment. For this reason, the Department of Health has adopted the private finance initiative (PFI) as a way of raising money for NHS Trusts, which have power "to enter into such contracts as seem to the trust to be appropriate".[57] PFI uses capital from the private sector to design, build, own, and operate new hospitals, in return for periodic repayments from the local health authorities and PCTs over a period of (say) twenty or more years. PFI has become the main source of capital funding for major NHS projects. Between 1997 and 2001, 85 per cent of the funds for major NHS capital projects came from PFI sources.[58] Given that public funds will repay the commercial costs of the agreement, the term "*private* finance initiative" may be misleading. Rather than invest a single sum in a capital project, the government commits itself to repaying the debt in the future in the same way that borrowers repay a mortgage.[59] Major PFI projects have concerned the construction of hospitals with values of, perhaps, £100 million (and in the case of University College London Hospital, £422 million).[60]

PFI is not limited to large hospital projects. Under Local Improvement Finance Trust (LIFT) arrangements, the scheme has been extended to primary care and the development of the infrastructure in which patients visit their GPs. The Secretary of State explained the need for this support as follows: "Primary care in many parts of the country, particularly the poorest parts of the country, is appalling. 40% of GPs surgeries are purpose built, virtually the remainder are adapted houses, residential buildings, adapted shops ... 80% of the accommodation is too cramped to meet modern requirements now."[61]

In response, the government committed itself to entering public-private partnerships to invest up to £1 billion in primary care facilities, and to refurbish or replace up to 3,000 family doctors' premises. It also proposes to build 500 "one-stop" primary care centres in which medical, dental, optical, pharmaceutical, social, and community services can all be provided under one roof.[62] Unlike the PFI, however, government has also invested in LIFT and will be a partner in the enterprise through Partnerships for Health. This element of partnership is reflected in the powers which enable the scheme to operate. Thus, "the Secretary of State may

---

[57] National Health Service and Community Care Act 1990, Sched. 2, para. 16(1)(b).

[58] J. Sussex, *The Economics of the Private Finance Initiative* (Office of Health Economics, 2000) 12.

[59] See also National Health Service (Private Finance) Act 1997, passed in response to *Credit Suisse v Allerdale BC* [1996] 4 All ER 129 in which the Court of Appeal considered similar arrangements in relation to a local authority to be *ultra vires*.   [60] J. Sussex, note 58 above, at 32.

[61] *Role of the Private Sector in the NHS*, House of Commons Health Committee (HC 308–I, Session 2002–02), para. 125.   [62] *The NHS Plan* (Cm. 4818–I, 2000) paras 4.11–4.12.

form, or participate in forming, companies to provide facilities for (a) persons or bodies exercising functions, or otherwise providing services, under this Act; or (b) NHS trusts."[63]

How are PFI contracts regulated and how do they affect patients' access to judicial review? We consider (A) the terms of the contract, (B) access to judicial review, and (C) the intensity of review.

A. Terms of the Contract

PFI arrangements are negotiated within the private law of contract. The contracts are intended to run over many years and will certainly include measures by which performance may be assessed and damages awarded if promises are not kept. Given the duration of the contract, there will inevitably arise many unforeseen problems not expressly provided for which will have to be resolved by negotiation and good faith, or litigation. Note, however, that private contractors generally have a "right" to breach their contracts and to withdraw from further performance. Of course, they may incur liability in damages (assuming they remain solvent), but there may be circumstances in which the "cost-efficient" breach is commercially attractive. Indeed, with duties owed primarily to shareholders rather than the public interest, such a course of action may be inevitable. If this happened in connection with a PFI hospital, the pressure on government to resume responsibility for its management would be irresistible. To this extent, the policy underlying the PFI is always subject to government re-insurance.

As a mechanism for regulating contracts, this may be satisfactory as between the parties, but how does it benefit the patient? Those not parties to a contract (third parties) have no right to enforce it.[64] Actions in negligence, of course, are available against any party, including a PFI hospital, which has caused damage in breach of their duty of care. But patients will not be entitled to take an action in contract. Unless the matter is resolved by the NHS body, patients will require an alternative remedy to require a private provider to comply with the terms of their contract.

B. Access to Judicial Review

Private contractors are normally regulated according to their terms of contract with the other party. What difference does it make that they are providing a public service and will judicial review offer a solution?[65] We are becoming accustomed to

---

[63] Health and Social Care Act 2001 ss. 4 and 5 (amending s. 96C of National Health Service Act 1977).

[64] Except within narrow exceptions under the Contracts (Rights of Third Parties) Act 1999.

[65] This question is far from simple. For a fuller discussion, see generally C. Newdick, "The NHS in Private Hands—Regulating Private Providers of NHS Care" in M. Freeman and A. Lewis (eds) *Law and Medicine—Current Legal Issues, vol. 3* (Oxford University Press, 2000).

a "mixed-economy" of public services in which:

> . . . the legal relationships that arise out of these new forms of service provision are neither wholly "public" nor "private". They involve a complex mixture of regulatory activity on the traditional "command and control" model, intertwined with regulation based on contractual-type arrangements between the direct provider of services and the ultimate purchaser, consumer or customer.[66]

Judicial review is often unsuitable against private bodies because it is designed to regulate *public* authorities as to the manner in which they perform their *statutory* duties. Private companies clearly fall outside this framework. And it is not just a question of legal definitions. Compare, for example, the acquisitive and profit-driven motivations of private companies with the values recommended by the *Nolan Committee on Standards in Public Life*, namely: selflessness, integrity, objectivity, accountability, openness, honesty, and leadership.[67] Should private providers of public services be expected to modify their approach to business?

Exceptionally, therefore, private bodies may be subject to public law review when they perform a public function. They may be treated as if they were public bodies and have public law standards applied to their conduct. The first case to establish this principle arose in an area well removed from the NHS in a dispute concerning a private regulator. The imprecise nature of the test to determine whether a private body should be subject to judicial review was explained by Lloyd LJ in *Ex p Datafin*:

> . . . if the source of power is a statute, or subordinate legislation under statute, then clearly the body in question will be subject to judicial review. If, at the other end of the scale, the source of power is contractual, as in the case of private arbitration, then clearly the arbitrator is not subject to judicial review . . . But in between these extremes there is an area in which it is helpful to look not just at the source of the power but at the nature of the power. If the body in question is exercising public law functions, or if the exercise of its functions have [sic] public law consequences, then that may . . . be sufficient to bring the body within the reach of judicial review. It may be said that to refer to "public law" in this context is to beg the question. But I do not think it does. The essential distinction, which runs through all the cases . . . is between the domestic or private tribunal on the one hand and a body of persons who are under some public duty on the other.[68]

What is the nature of this "public duty"[69] and, crucially, how do these observations apply, not to private regulators, but to bodies providing substantive services to NHS patients? Recall the case of *Ex parte Collier*,[70] in which a four-year-old boy

---

[66] De Smith, Lord Woolf and J. Jowell, *Judicial Review of Administrative Action* (5th edn, Sweet and Maxwell, 1995) para. 3–019. See also, I. Harden, *The Contracting State* (Open University Press, 1992); and C. Harlow and R. Rawlings, *Law and Administration* (Butterworths, 1997) 328–52.

[67] 1995, Cm. 2850.

[68] *R v Panel on Take-overs and Mergers, ex p Datafin plc* [1987] 1 All ER 564, 583.

[69] See P. Craig, "Public Law and Control over Private Power" in M. Taggart (ed.), *The Province of Administrative Law* (Hart Press, 1997).

[70] *R v Central Birmingham HA, ex p Collier* (Court of Appeal, unreported, 1988).

was denied the surgery to his heart that he "desperately needed" because sufficient nurses could not be made available. He was not treated, or referred elsewhere in time to save his life. The issue in the case was substantive, not procedural—was the boy entitled to care? Similarly, *Ex parte Fisher*[71] concerned a right of access to expensive medicine. How would these matters have been dealt with had they arisen in the context of a *privately* owned hospital providing NHS services? Similar questions arise in relation to GPs allocating resources within their practice, or striking patients from their list. Is judicial review of private providers available and, if so, what level of intensity will be appropriate?

There has been a suggestion that judicial review should be extended to the activities of private bodies which provide substantive public services. In two education cases Dyson J reviewed the decisions of private schools to admit or exclude their local authority assisted students. His Lordship accepted that in principle "such decisions, if made by private schools, are not subject to judicial review. This is because the source of power of such schools is not statute but consensual, and the decisions are not made in the exercise of public law duties or functions."[72] However, as the interest of the state in the enterprise increases, together with the degree of statutory supervision which it imposes upon the private provider, judicial review becomes more likely. And in a case concerning the power of a private school to dismiss a pupil who had been admitted under the assisted places scheme (in which local authorities could pay for students to attend fee-paying schools)[73] his Lordship said:

In relation to the 15 assisted pupils, the school was performing functions very similar to those of a publicly maintained school. I accept the analogy is not exact ... But it seems to me that in relation to pupils who have been selected, the analogy is close. The state has an interest in the education of the assisted pupils at public expense. Parliament has reflected that interest by imposing significant controls over the way in which assisted pupils are educated by an independent school. Those controls take two forms. First, the controls imposed directly by the regulations by which the schools are bound. Secondly, by giving the Secretary of State considerable powers of control ... All these factors lead me to conclude that the respondent exercises public functions in relation to its assisted pupils.[74]

His Lordship concluded that the court did have jurisdiction to reinstate the pupil on a non-paying basis. One of his concerns was the absence of any alternative remedy. In *Ex p Tyrell*, he said: "If CTCs [City Technology Colleges] are not susceptible to judicial review, pupils ... will be left without a remedy if they are victims of a wrong ... unless they have private law rights ... There is no contractual relationship between parents and CTCs. That is not, of course, determinative of

---

[71] *R v North Derbyshire HA, ex p Fisher* [1997] 8 Med LR 327.
[72] See *R v The Governors of Haberdashers Aske's Hatcham College Trust, ex p Tyrell* The Times, 19 October 1994.
[73] Under the Education (Schools) Act 1997. The powers have since been repealed.
[74] *R v Cobham Hall School, ex p S* The Times, 13 December 1997.

the issue that I have to decide. It does, however, reinforce the conclusion that I have reached."[75]

A similar issue also arose in respect of the refusal of a private water company to act on the recommendations of its local health authority to fluoridate its water supply. Section 87 of the Water Industry Act 1991 permitted water authorities wide discretion on whether to fluoridate water supplies. In *R v Northumbrian Water Ltd, ex p Newcastle and North Tyneside Health Authority*[76] there was no dispute as to the scientific and medical evidence that fluoridation was of substantial public benefit, particularly in the prevention of childhood tooth decay. Following a request by the local health authority that it do so, was the company's refusal amenable to judicial review? Without elaborating on the difficulties in the law, Collins J said that:

> ... the decision of the respondent water company is amenable to judicial review. That, of course, is because it carries out functions which can be described as public ... It may be that 50 years ago the Respondent would not so readily have been considered to be within the scope of the judicial review and it might have been considered that it was analogous to, for example, a nationalised industry which the courts in those days did not regard in the same way. But we have moved on since then and the scope of a judicial review is very much wider ...

These cases provide a basis on which analogous arguments could be used against private providers of NHS care. In particular that, unless some from of judicial scrutiny is made available, patients treated in private hospitals would be excluded from an effective supervisory remedy in the courts. If these arguments can be used to support *public law* claims in these circumstances, the crucial question then concerns the *intensity* of the review in question.

C. Intensity of Review

Assuming a private body is performing a public function, how should the courts ensure that it performs its duties properly and responsibly? The question of the appropriate level and intensity of review in these cases is illustrated in the *Northumbrian Water* case. Collins J sought to balance the company's *public*, statutory duties to the community as a whole, with its *private* obligations to promote the interests of its shareholders. The following extract from the judgment illuminates the limited scrutiny thought appropriate to these cases. He said:

> It is perfectly clear that as a commercial organisation the respondent company cannot be said to possess powers solely in order to use them for the public good. It has its commercial obligations to its shareholders. It must exercise its powers in accordance with those obligations. Equally it must comply with any statutory duties imposed upon it by Parliament. It must also exercise any discretion that it may be given within the scope of the statute which confirms it. Thus if it is clear that the discretion given by the statute is to be confined

---

[75] *R v The Governors of Haberdashers' Askes Hatcham College Trust, ex p Tyrell* The Times, 19 October 1994.			[76] LEXIS, Unreported, 1998.

because of the particular wording of the statute, then it would be wrong to exercise it outside those confines . . .[77]

Thus a water authority is entitled to say no [to fluoridation], even though it has no reason to doubt that it would be in the interests of the health of its customers, that its customers want it, that the health authority wants it and that it is in accordance with the policy of the government. It is entitled to say to itself "it would involve us in expense. It will involve us in a potential liability if things go wrong, and it is quite impossible to be sure that there will not be a mistake made by an employee which creates a liability in those circumstances. We are very sorry but we do not think that we wish to take the risk."

. . . that would be a perfectly proper approach for a water company to take and that is because it does not have the same duty that a public body, which is not a commercial undertaking, has. It is entitled to look to the interests of its shareholders and that is something which is inevitable, as it seems to me, when privatised bodies are given control of matters such as the provision of water, and something which no doubt Parliament has recognised. If Parliament wishes to ensure that a discretion is exercised on particular principles, then it must set out those principles in the statutory provisions.

Strikingly, therefore, although the company was exercising a public function, its obligations were owed only to its shareholders and not to the public. Although it was subject to the procedural supervision of judicial review, the substantive principles regulating it were entirely private in origin because the "public" duties owed by the company were contained only in its contractual arrangement with the health authority. Minimalist reasoning of this nature would clearly have the most profound implications for those providing public services to the NHS. The logic of construing the nature and extent of the obligation in accordance with the empowering statute is impeccable and is consistent with the rule of statutory interpretation that private law rights remain intact unless they are expressly and unambiguously taken away by statute.[78] On the other hand, the case suggests that even if private providers are amenable to judicial review, the nature and extent of the review may be so limited that patients will derive very little benefit from its use.

If NHS patients have unequal access to judicial review, depending on whether they are treated within a "public" or "private" institution, this presents a significant problem. Equally, it has no easy solution. Although, in principle, contracts with private providers could include clauses guaranteeing patients equivalent rights, government may be in no position to insist they are included. Private companies need to be offered a reasonably attractive commercial proposition. In a free market,

---

[77] To the same effect see *Mercury Energy Ltd v Electricity Corporation of New Zealand Ltd* [1994] 1 WLR 521, 528, *per* Lord Templeman:

"The express statutory duty of the defendant is to pursue its principal objective of operating as a successful business, by becoming profitable and efficient, by being a good employer and by exhibiting a sense of social responsibility. It was for the defendant to determine whether its principal objective would best be served by allowing the contractual arrangement to continue or by terminating the contractual arrangements."

[78] See *Pierson v Secretary of State for the Home Department* [1997] 3 All ER 577, 592 *per* Lord Browne-Wilkinson. See also *Raymond v Honey* [1982] 1 All ER 756.

government cannot force private contractors to agree to terms they consider unacceptable. If it requires new hospitals to be built, it may have to enter PFI contracts. The problem of variable rights of redress is difficult and, other than mandatory regulatory standards (which may not be feasible), has no immediate solution.

V. Private Providers and the Human Rights Act

Are private providers subject to the Human Rights Act 1998? The question becomes increasingly important as public services are provided by private providers. The Act provides: "It is unlawful for a public authority to act in a way which is incompatible with a Convention right." And a "public authority" is described as "any person certain of whose functions are functions of a public nature."[79] Clearly, the Act applies to all the purely statutory authorities performing functions within the NHS. Can it also apply to the various private providers of NHS services? The line that separates public from private functions is far from clear. It has been suggested that the tests to determine whether a party is a "public body" under the Human Rights Act is the same as for amenability to judicial review—if a private body is amenable to judicial review, it must be a "public body" under the Human Rights Act.[80] But, as we noticed in examining the cases that have followed *Ex p Datafin*, this provides a far from certain test. Also, the House of Lords has observed that our domestic approach to the law of judicial review should not necessarily determine the different regime introduced by the European Convention on Human Rights.[81] On the other hand, it must surely be influential since (similar to *Ex p Datafin*) the factors to be considered include "the extent to which in carrying out the relevant function the body is publicly funded, or is exercising statutory powers, or is taking the place of central government or local authorities, or is providing a public service".[82]

One of the first cases to consider the matter arose in the context of compulsory detention under the Mental Health Act 1983. In *R (A) v Partnerships in Care Ltd*[83] the claimant had a severe personality disorder and was detained as an NHS patient in a private psychiatric hospital. The hospital managers had to change the organisation of the hospital wards in order to focus on other areas of psychiatric care. They intended to move patients for whom the new regime was not suitable to other units more appropriate to their needs. However, over a year later, no such appropriate alternative had been found for the claimant and the defendants admitted that "the claimant has not received such care and treatment as it would wish".[84] An application was made by way of judicial review to challenge the company under

---

[79] Human Rights Act 1998, s. 6(1) and (3).
[80] *Hampshire County Council v Graham Beer t/a Hammer Trout Farm* [2003] EWCA Civ 1056, paras 7 and 9.
[81] See *Aston Cantlow PCC v Wallbank* [2003] 3 All ER 1213, para. 52, *per* Lord Nicholls.
[82] ibid., para 12.   [83] [2002] 1 WLR 2610.   [84] ibid., para. 6.

Articles 3 (freedom from degrading treatment) and 8 (right to respect for private and family life) of the European Convention. The court permitted the application to proceed on the ground that the company was "a public authority". Although the company had entered a voluntary, private contract to provide NHS services, it had undertaken crucial statutory responsibilities on behalf of the health authority. The nature of their responsibilities brought them within the control of the Human Rights Act. The need for the company's patients to receive care and treatment was a matter of public concern. More importantly, many had been admitted under the *compulsory* powers of detention of the Mental Health Act 1983.[85] Thus, the company was acting as a public authority and amenable to judicial review in the same way as an NHS hospital.

A similar issue arose in connection with residents of a residential home in *R (Heather) v the Leonard Cheshire Foundation*[86] concerning the status of a long-term nursing home. The home provided care and accommodation for disabled people. Thirty-eight of its forty-three residents had been placed there and paid for by local authorities. The placements were made under the authorities' statutory duty to provide residential accommodation to people in need of care and attention under the National Assistance Act 1948. Local authorities are at liberty to commission such care from private providers.[87] In doing so the local authorities were performing a public function. The Leonard Cheshire Foundation (LCF) proposed to close the home and to re-locate the residents. The question arose whether LCF was itself performing a "public function" subject to the Human Rights Act 1998 and amenable to the claim that to close the home would be in breach of private and family life provisions of Article 8 of the European Convention. For the residents, it was argued that the home, like all residential and nursing homes, was closely regulated by statute (the Registered Homes Act 1984). If the home had been unable to accept the residents, then the function would have been performed by a public authority subject to the Human Rights Act 1998. It would be unfair, therefore, if the residents were to lose their human rights protection simply because the functions had been contracted to a private provider.

The Court of Appeal decided that LCF was not a public authority for the purposes of the 1998 Act. Lord Woolf CJ said: "The fact that LCF is a large and flourishing organisation does not change the nature of its activities from private to public." He continued:

While the degree of public funding of the activities of an otherwise private body is certainly relevant as to the nature of the functions performed, by itself it is not determinative of whether the functions are public functions ... There is no other evidence of there being a public flavour to the functions of LCF or LCF itself. LCF is not standing in the shoes of the local authorities ... LCF is not exercising statutory powers in performing functions for the appellants.[88]

---

85 ibid., para. 25.   86 [2002] 2 All ER 936.
87 Under National Assistance Act 1948, s. 21.   88 ibid., para. 35.

What would have been the position if all the LCF residents were placed by the public authority (as they had been in *Partnerships in Care Ltd*) so that their responsibilities were largely indistinguishable from those owed by local authority nursing homes? Would this fact bring them any closer to performing a "public function"? The Court of Appeal's judgment suggests not, because the test appears to require the private provider to "stand in the shoes" of the public authority. This appears to take a different approach to *Partnerships in Care Ltd*, and to put special emphasis on the *legal authority* under which a function is exercised, rather than on the *nature* of the function; the question is not one of fact, but of law.[89] The same view was taken by the trial judge, Stanley Burnton J, who said:

> Bodies such as fringe theatres often benefit from State funding by way of grants. This does not mean that they are public authorities. Where funding is by payment pursuant to contract, the inference of a public function is even weaker. Contracting by public authorities cannot make public authorities of the otherwise private provider of services or goods. It is only if there is a true delegation or sharing of functions that this may occur.[90]

On this test the phrase: "functions of a public nature" does not ask about the *factual* content of the function, or whether the private body was performing a statutory function under contract with a public authority. It requires, perhaps, that the public authority has delegated its public functions to a private provider under the authority of an Act of Parliament.

The Court of Appeal in the *Leonard Cheshire* case was sensitive to the argument that beneficiaries of public services provided by private bodies could lose the protection of the Human Rights Act—that there was a "protection gap" into which fell many needy people by the accident of the circumstances by which their care was arranged. It had two responses. First, the rights of the residents to Human Rights Act protection was not lost. "The local authority is under an obligation under s 21 of the 1948 Act and remains under an obligation under art 8 to the appellants."[91] For example, in *Costello-Roberts v United Kingdom*[92] a school boy was sent by his local education authority to a private school. The boy was subject to corporal punishment which the European Court of Human Rights held to be in breach of Convention rights, yet the action was successful against the government, not the private school. To this extent, therefore, the residents retained rights against their referring local authorities. This is true, but the authority had no power in relation to the resident's rights to remain in the Leonard Cheshire home. The right against the local authority was only to apply for alternative accommodation (which is precisely what the residents sought to reject).

Secondly, the court said that if the arrangements which the local authorities made with Leonard Cheshire had been made after the 1998 Act came into force, it

---

[89] For a critical analysis of the decision, see P. Craig, "Contracting Out, the Human Rights Act and the Scope of Judicial Review" (2002) 118 LQR 551.

[90] *Heather v the Leonard Cheshire Foundation* [2001] EWHC (Admin) 429, para. 48.

[91] *Heather* [2002] note 86 above, at para. 33.   [92] (1995) 19 EHRR 112.

would have been possible to require the local authority to enter into a contract with its provider on terms which protected residents' Article 8 rights. In this way, Human Rights Act protection would exist within the terms of the contract and "not only could the local authority rely on the contract, but possibly the resident could also as a person for whose benefit the contract was made".[93] But this too may not be a complete solution. There is no power to force local authorities to insert particular clauses into the contracts they enter with private providers. Unless specific directions of this nature were issued by the Secretary of State, such a course would be voluntary. But even if such a clause was enforceable between local authority and private provider, it could remain unenforceable by the resident unless it was also included in each resident's contract of residence.[94]

This more restrictive test in the *Leonard Cheshire* case will exclude many private providers of NHS services from Human Rights Act regulation. Private hospitals, treatment centres, caterers, and providers of diagnostic services do not "stand in the shoes" of the public authority. They are private companies that sell their services to NHS bodies under commercial agreements. However, this approach may be reconsidered in the light of the House of Lords decision in the *Aston Cantlow* case. Although the circumstances were unrelated to the NHS, Lord Hope emphasised that it is "the *function* that the person is performing that is determinative of the question whether it is . . . a 'hybrid' public authority".[95] This suggests the matter is not dependent on the legal/institutional relationship between the parties, but the facts surrounding the service provided. The Joint Committee on Human Rights also supports a more inclusive definition based on the nature of the function, rather than its legal provenance. It explained:

Discharge of duties necessary for provision of the government programme of healthcare is a public function. Discharge of healthcare services, in itself, is not. It is the doing of this work as part of a government programme which denotes a public function, rather than the provision of healthcare in itself. In performing duties as part of the State programme of healthcare, a private organisation is assisting in performing what the State itself has identified as the State's responsibilities.[96]

On this reasoning, direct statutory authority is not necessary to create a "hybrid" public authority. It is sufficient for the state's public functions to be performed by a private organisation. Such an approach would bring the *Leonard Cheshire* case within the ambit of the Human Rights Act. But it would also embrace a whole range of other private service providers. Is it intended to include the taxi company engaged to take patients to hospital from time to time, the cleaning company that

---

[93] *Heather* [2002] note 86 above, at para. 34.
[94] Or, perhaps, under the Contracts (Rights of Third Parties) Act 1999 by which certain third parties who are not party to a contract may enforce the contract for their own benefit.
[95] *Aston Cantlow PCC v Wallbank* [2003] 3 All ER 1213, para. 41.
[96] *The Meaning of Public Authority under the Human Rights Act* (House of Lords, House of Commons Joint Committee on Human Rights, Seventh Report of Session 2003–04, HL 39, HC 382), para. 141.

cleans the hospital wards, and hospital caterers? If so, the Human Rights Act will provoke much litigation, not just against the state, but between *private* litigants; it will have *horizontal*, as well as vertical effect. This carries the risk of encouraging litigation against parties ill-equipped to bear the costs, and of discouraging private providers from co-operating with the policy of contributing to the public services.

There is another risk. In the *Leonard Cheshire* case, the trial judge acknowledged the danger of opening up a "protection gap" that could exclude private bodies from the Human Rights Act jurisdiction.[97] Although the matter has yet to be settled, it is argued that public authorities have no Convention rights because the Convention confers citizen-rights against public authorities, rather than in their support. As his Lordship commented,[98] too broad a test would have the disadvantage that such bodies would themselves *lose* the protection of the Human Rights Act 1998 against the government. Should a publicly subsidised theatre lose its Article 10 protection of freedom of expression against government?[99] What would be the position of charities, legal aid funded solicitors, building contractors of municipal roads, schools and hospitals, and private hospitals admitting NHS patients? To some extent, this concern may have been addressed by the House of Lords in the *Aston Cantlow* case, in which their Lordships distinguished "core" public authorities, from "hybrid" authorities which exercise both public and private functions. Hybrid authorities do retain Human Rights Act protection in respect of their *private* functions. But this is good only so long as they are not performing public functions.

The question will inevitably be asked of GPs. They normally contract to provide NHS services. Do they perform functions of "a public nature" for the purposes of the 1998 Act? Can their patients bring judicial review proceedings against them? The previous Lord Chancellor, speaking in the Parliamentary Debates on the 1998 Act, assumed that GPs would be performing functions of a public nature.[100] Most (but not all) of their work is provided within a statutory framework and designed to promote the public interest. GPs are heavily regulated by statute, which governs their rates of remuneration, standards of performance, and disciplinary matters and considerations of this nature may be said to confer "functions of a public nature" on GPs. On the other hand, GPs may be said to be no different to high street solicitors who derive most of their income from Legal Aid practice. Their income too is substantially derived from public funds. Never the less, they are engaged as private contractors in business on their own accounts. They choose to contract with statutory authorities, but this is not sufficient to be regarded as public authorities. If a GP's *NHS work* is considered to be a "public function" under the Human Rights Act, this may exclude GPs themselves from Human Rights Act protection. Given the sensitive political and personal environment in which they work, and the intense scrutiny of their conduct by public regulatory

---

[97] *Heather* [2001] note 90 above, at para. 106.
[98] Agreeing with Professor Dawn Oliver [2000] *Public Law* 476.
[99] *Heather* [2001] note 90 above, at para. 105.
[100] 683 House of Lords Official Report (5th Series) col. 811, 24 November 1997.

bodies, many will say such a rule would be unfair and unreasonable. Indeed, GPs may feel especially in need of human rights protection. How can their human rights be recognised too?

Let us assume for a moment that the wider view of "public functions" is adopted and private providers of public services are controlled by the Human Rights Act. This will not guarantee improved access to public services for two reasons. First, as the *Northumbrian Water* case demonstrates, private providers, even when performing public functions, have different rights and duties to public authorities. Unlike public authorities, their *raison d'etre* is not wholly to serve the public interest. Companies retain duties to their shareholders and may pursue self-interested policies which are not always consistent with the public interest. Making a private company subject to the Human Rights Act will make it amenable to judicial review, but it will not generate the same matrix of obligations as if it were a public authority. It must be entitled to pursue its own, commercial ambitions. Secondly, many of the rights contained in the European Convention on Human Rights are subject to exceptions. Take the rights of the LCF residents to remain in the home. The individual's right to "private and family life" in Article 8(1) is balanced with "the protection of the rights and freedoms of others" under Article 8(2). Say it was proposed to close the home in question because it was an elderly building which was unduly expensive to maintain and was absorbing monies the organisation could divert to the more productive benefit of residents in other homes. The rights of others also need to be put in the balance; they cannot be excluded from consideration. To put it another way, assuming finite resources, the right to remain a resident in one home would not automatically override the rights and interests of other residents elsewhere. This balance of this argument would still remain to be resolved under the Human Rights Act. Given the private (albeit charitable) nature of the enterprise, is this best performed by the private body concerned, or the courts?

We should think carefully about the risks and benefits of extending Human Rights Act regulation to all those that provide public functions for public authorities. Consistent with the *Leonard Cheshire* case, it is suggested that "only those activities which involve the exercise by private bodies of specifically legally authorised coercion or authority which it would normally be unlawful for a private body to exercise" should be considered as "functions of a public nature".[101] With this more restrictive approach, the onus would be on public authorities to enter appropriate agreements with private providers that provided comparable human rights protection for those to whom they provide services. As we have noted, however, it may not always be possible for public authorities to insist that such protection is included in their contracts. Private companies may simply refuse to enter contracts they consider present unreasonable commercial risks.

---

[101] D. Oliver, "Functions of a Public Nature under the Human Rights Act" [2004] *Public Law* 329, 330.

10

Conclusion

Some may be surprised that a book which poses such an apparently simple question cannot provide a league-table of the order in which deserving patients should be treated. This is because the hard choices we make are based on so many variables—clinical, personal, social, economic, political, and legal—there will always be room for disagreement. In the absence of a universal slide-rule to answer the question, it is more important to understand the ways in which decisions can be made, the ingredients of the decision, who makes them, and according to what process. In this concluding chapter we bring together some of the major problems facing health care resource allocators by re-considering the debate as to the proper *locus* of decision-making in the NHS, the issue of trust in the NHS, and the potential for conflict between private rights and public interests.

Until the election of the Thatcher government in 1979, the organisation of the NHS did not give rise to serious political, or ideological, differences. The objective was to reduce levels of ill-health in society and this was a practical, rather than ideological objective. Accordingly, matters of resource allocation were managed by the consensus between clinicians and NHS managers from place to place, always subject, of course, to the resources made available by central government. By the end of the 1970s, however, this model of "consensus management" was being doubted by the political right, which favoured market forces as a mechanism for organising health care, including the competition provided by private hospitals.[1] For the first time, health policy became dominated by an ideological agenda. Clearly, part of the logic of the market is to distribute power and influence to purchasers and this inclination to shift power towards local people has continued through the creation of many new NHS institutions since 1997.

In an area so dominated by disagreement and uncertainty, it may be astute for central government to seek to distance itself from the heat of the debate and create alternative bodies to manage and regulate the service. But it does not remove health from politics; nor, in the NHS, does it remove the responsibilities of the Secretary of State to fulfil the statutory duty to promote a "comprehensive health service". Although he may delegate specific functions to local decision-makers, such as PCTs and Foundation Trust hospitals, it is right that he remains answerable to Parliament for the performance of the system as a whole.

---

[1] C. Webster, *The National Health Service—A Political History* (Oxford University Press, 2002) ch. 3.

When decision-making is subject to such a variety of differences of opinion, government ought to play a more prominent role in explaining how NHS resources should be allocated. A *national* health service ought to work to a minimum set of basic principles to reassure patients that the system is fair and reasonable. With the creation of so many intermediate commissioners, regulators, and inspectors, it is notable that none has been set up to assist in the process of NHS resource allocation. If government is unable to contribute to this process, local decision-makers should co-operate with one another to develop an ethical framework capable of demonstrating basic standards of consistency, equality, and transparency in the service. Without it, we will never properly understand how decisions have been made, or what the NHS ought to achieve.

This brings us to the question of trust. What is it to "trust" the NHS? Was there once a golden age when patients had confidence that their doctors and the system as a whole would provide them with the treatment they needed, when they needed it and to a reasonable standard? Perhaps. But the basis of any such belief may equally have been an absence of reliable information on which to question doctors. Medicine too could provide less security, especially before the discovery of many modern treatments. And at a time when there was a greater sense of inevitability surrounding illness (and, indeed, death), both our expectations and our willingness to challenge and criticise may have been more limited.

Today, things are very different. We are less deferential to professional authority and more inclined to speak up when things seem wrong and we have more effective means of measuring and comparing medical standards. The courts too are willing to subject doctors and health authorities to closer scrutiny by insisting they have good reasons for their decisions. At the same time, medical and pharmaceutical advances present us with an increasing range of interventions that promise much therapeutic benefit, but their cost will impose further strain on finite health care budgets and more hard choices between deserving patients.

Can we do more to enhance trust in an institution such as the NHS? Trust is difficult to define and often impossible to quantify. It may be described in three forms, *deterrence-based* trust, *professional* trust, and *intimate* trust.[2] Deterrence-based trust is based wholly on self-interest either in terms of an advantage to be obtained, or a penalty to be avoided for failure. In commerce, I may have the scantest regard for another party, yet I may trust him to perform his obligations for no better reason than the penalty clause to which he will be subject if he fails to do so. Clearly, such a fragile, utilitarian relationship needs the support of regular inspections, audits, verifications and "governance" precisely to reflect the lack of trust between the parties. But this is surely too fragile a basis on which to build trust in the NHS. By contrast, *professional* trust depends on the confidence that the other will achieve certain minimum levels of conduct. It may depend on the

[2] Based on R. Lewicki and B. Bunker, "Developing and Maintaining Trust in Work Relationships" in R. Kramer and T. Tyler (eds), *Trust in Organisations—Frontiers of Theory and Research* (Sage Publications, 1996).

reliable behaviour of the other in the past, perhaps by being a member of an honourable institution governed by professional ethics, or previous personal dealings. The trust depends on the ability to predict how the other will behave and, most of all, to be able to rely on the benefit that has been promised.

This more accurately describes the trust we should seek to preserve in the NHS. It is not dominated by targets and the threat of reaction in case of failure. Instead, it is based on credible expectations of performance in which unreasonable demands are less likely to be made. It should be founded on a confidence that the system operates openly and fairly between patients and provides access to common levels of service to all. To this extent, professional trust is more enduring than that based on a crude calculation of personal benefit. It may withstand occasional disappointment, perhaps because the failure was predictable and the actors' other strengths justify the continued relationship. This model better describes the relationship we should seek to develop between patients and the NHS as an institution. In an open and candid system of NHS funding, patients would understand the limitations inherent in such a system. On the other hand, if promises are made of the performance to be expected of the NHS which cannot reasonably be fulfilled, trust and confidence will not develop. Far from encouraging the public to believe that the NHS can achieve the impossible, government must contribute to the debate as to its limitations. In this way, patients will develop credible expectations of the service they can expect and be more inclined to contribute to the choices dictated by NHS resources. Perhaps government is taking its first steps in the debate about health care priorities. As it now acknowledges: "Patients realise . . . that there are limits to choice. Over 80% of the people who replied to the Choice Consultation Survey agree that their personal choices should be limited in whole or part by the need to be fair to other NHS users and the wider community."[3]

Intimate trust is founded on a real empathy with the other's hopes and aspirations. Such an approach is inherent in the best personal relationships and depends on a knowledge of the other person's standards of conduct, hopes, and aspirations. There may also be a mutual understanding which permits a party discretion to make decisions on another's behalf in the knowledge that it will promote the other's best interests. This describes the "ideal" relationship between doctor and patient, especially when illness erodes our confidence and vitality. But it surely asks too much of the trust that can be expected between a patient and the NHS as an institution. The trust central to the NHS, therefore, should be based less on the expectations of a *personal* relationship, and more on a *professional*, knowledge-based understanding built on reasonable and achievable expectations.

If trust in the NHS wanes because the benefits of our investment are thought too unpredictable or inconsistent to offer reasonable security, patients will seek the relative certainty of private health care. This may possess the limited "deterrence-based" advantage of offering benefits enforceable under a contract, but it also

---

[3] *Building on the Best—Choice, Responsiveness and Equity in the NHS* (Cm. 6079, 2003) 19.

carries the disadvantage of cost and the danger of introducing more aggressive and commercial relationships in health care. On the other hand, nor can modern health care systems promise nothing. Recall the case of *Ex p Collier* in which the court refused to inquire why life-saving treatment could not be provided to a young boy who was top of his consultant's list of clinical priorities. The case was decided in 1988 at a time when individual rights played an insufficient role in disputes over access to health care. How should health care rights be assessed and enforced today?

The modern solution to this problem in judicial review is to subject resource allocators to close scrutiny, to require convincing explanations for the difficult decisions required, but to leave the final decision-making responsibility firmly in the hands of those appointed to do so within a fair and consistent framework. In turn, those subject to review will learn to refine their processes and weigh and balance competing factors with greater sensitivity, keeping in mind their duties to the entire community. This is the preferable way to balance the potentially competing demands of the individual and the community. It offers few guarantees of *substantive* access to health care. Instead, it creates *procedural* rights designed to give reassurance that the system is responding to patient need equally and fairly. Such a system will be most successful if the public are involved in developing and applying the framework. Judicial review defers to reasonable assessments of the public interests assessed elsewhere.

On the other hand, this balanced approach will increasingly come under pressure as the "rights revolution" gathers pace and the courts are invited to adjudicate over matters of dispute. The trend started with the *Patient's Charter* of the mid-1990s in respect of waiting-time targets, but it has gone a step further in European law which gives patients rights to obtain elsewhere in the EU services that cannot be obtained at home. This promotion of *substantive* rights is a very different approach to resource allocation. The tendency to promote individual rights to health care resources will benefit those who shout loudest. But it will not protect less articulate groups and, without additional investment in the NHS, will distort health care policy. There is an urgent need to rediscover the notion of "public interest", which is so obscured by party politics and the effects of competitive markets.[4] No doubt the excessive deference that surrounded the notion until the 1990s is now inappropriate and much greater involvement must be given to patients and the public generally. The first step in developing a fair and consistent approach to health care resource allocation is for government to make a more candid contribution to the limitations inherent in the way we choose to fund the NHS. Until government can discuss the subject more openly, local decision-makers will find it hard to convince patients that rationing is really necessary.[5]

[4] See the persuasive case in D. Marquand, *Decline of the Public* (Polity Press, Cambridge, 2004).

[5] See D. Mechanic, "The Functions and Limitations of Trust in the Provision of Medical Care" (1998) 23 *Journal of Health Policy, Politics and Law* 661.

Index